THE BEST OF CAMERON

'A fine showing of the old master's talent in his times, from BBC scripts in early wartime, via travels and wars, to the Indian summer of his last seven years with the Guardian.'

Guardian

'Entertaining and moving. The collection has been assembled so well that it reads coherently as an expression of what a very sentimental man has felt and has seen during the last forty years. And that is a lot.'

Woodrow Wyatt, *Sunday Times*

'James Cameron, a man of sensitivity and conscience, uses the English language like a true craftsman. A humane man whose views are worth listening to.'

Manchester Evening News

D0619119

By the same author:

TOUCH OF THE SUN
MANDARIN RED
1914
THE AFRICAN REVOLUTION
1916
WITNESS
HERE IS YOUR ENEMY
WHAT A WAY TO RUN THE TRIBE
POINT OF DEPARTURE

THE BEST OF CAMERON

James Cameron

NEW ENGLISH LIBRARY

First published in Great Britain in 1981 by New English
Library

Copyright © 1981 by James Cameron

All rights reserved. No part of this publication may be
reproduced or transmitted, in any form or by any means,
without permission of the publishers.

First NEL Paperback Edition December 1983

Conditions of sale: This book is sold subject to the
condition that it shall not, by way of trade or otherwise,
be lent, re-sold, hired out, or otherwise circulated without
the publisher's prior consent in any form of binding or
cover other than that in which it is published and without
a similar condition including this condition being imposed
on the subsequent purchaser.

NEL Books are published by
New English Library,
Mill Road, Dunton Green,
Sevenoaks, Kent.
Editorial office: 47 Bedford Square, London WC1B 3DP

Printed and bound in Great Britain by
Cox & Wyman Ltd, Reading

0 450 05646 5

About the only tribe or society this book does not describe is my own.

My family is a living testimony to the truth that humans of different backgrounds, races, colours and cultures can be a real and living entity, not just in peace but in love.

So this book is for my children, Elma, Sabita, Fergus, Kiron, Nicholas and Margaret. And above all for the focus of us all, my wife Moni.

CONTENTS

Acknowledgements   xi
Foreword   xiii

B.B.C. RADIO, 1941–2
    Footnote to an old friendship   1
    To my envoy extraordinary in the U.S.A.   6

DAILY EXPRESS, 1948–9
    Power without the sword   12
    The new 'idiot's delight'   15
    I've never seen people so eager to be shackled   19
    Operation Crossroads   22

PICTURE POST, 1950–52
    Inchon   28
    A voice above the battle   32
    Tibet dissolves   35

THE ILLUSTRATED LONDON NEWS, 1952
    The King is dead   41

NEWS CHRONICLE, 1953–60
    Thumbprint among the mulga trees   50
    Hunger is the big persuader   54
    Who is to blame for Mau Mau?   57
    How long can they walk the tightrope?   59
    At noon Nye Bevan heard the jeers of the left   61
    The God Incarnate reaches Happy Valley – but where next?   64
    Bats in my baggage *or* why I can't do the cha-cha-cha   67
    The smile on the face of that Laotian wizard   69
    This man Verwoerd   71
    Years ago I lost a job for exposing this monster   74

DAILY MAIL, 1961–2
    Darkness at noon – and yet I see some hope   78
    Watch this space shot . . . and I hope that's all we do   80
    How could the world come to such a loose end?   82
    This strange paradox that is Paris at peace   84

Shqiperi! I was fleetingly your man in Tirana   86
Up there the glory, down here the shame   89
The trap!   91

HARPER'S BAZAAR, 1963
Britain's grand illusion   95

DAILY HERALD, 1962–4
This is the year we make our choice   102
To what shall a man be true?   103
But the plague is in the air again   106
What an exciting assembly-line!   108
The political obituary of Harold Macmillan   111
Don't rejoice at the Moscow row   113
The great march for freedom   116
The American tragedy   119
Nelson's desperate message   122
An empire – and a trail of lost causes   124
Frontline Harlem   126

EVENING STANDARD, 1965–6
On the way   132
Victory if it takes forever   136
A North-Vietnamese Colonel talking   141
And behind every drawing, such anguish   145
Something important, possibly dramatic, is in the air   146
Lord Moran and Churchill: what a storm in a teacup!   149
The six day war   151
Catastrophe unlimited   152

NEW STATESMAN, 1965–7
A question of identity   156
Confessions of an addict   159
Don Quixote answers back   163

B.B.C. RADIO AND TELEVISION, 1968–72
Ho Chi Minh   168
Arab–Israeli peace talks   170
The boat people   172
Nixon's visit to China   174
Martin Bormann   176
Cameron Country – 'Point of departure'   178
Cameron Country – 'Nobody ever asks why'   198

Cameron Country – 'The guns of Aphrodite'   221
Cameron Country – 'Prejudice on the face of it'   242
Cameron Country – 'Why patriotism?'   270

OBSERVER, 1978
  Brittany remembered   299

GUARDIAN, 1974–
  Ward perfect   303
  It isn't Allahabad   308
  Oily waters   311
  Dr Norman stands accused . . .   314
  Empire gains   316
  Afghan roulette   318
  I could do no less than go on strike . . . but whom to go on
    strike against?   320
  The edge of reason   322
  Heaven raiser   325
  Bertie's booster   327
  Riotous gentiles   329

SUNDAY TIMES
  A life in the day of   333

SUNDAY TELEGRAPH MAGAZINE
  The Royal Wedding   337

JOURNALIST
  The foreign beat   339

  Index   343

ACKNOWLEDGEMENTS

The publishers thank the B.B.C. and all the newspapers, periodicals and magazines who have been so generous in allowing the use of material for this anthology. In particular the editors of *The Illustrated London News*, the *New Statesman*, the *Daily Mail*, the *Observer*, the *Telegraph Sunday Magazine*, the *Daily Express*, the *Sunday Times*, the *Evening Standard*, the *Guardian*, *Harpers & Queen Magazine* and Challice Reed of the B.B.C. Script Library.

FOREWORD

Anyone who has spent his whole working life as a newspaper correspondent – or journalist, or columnist, or editorialist, or any of the fancy euphemisms with which we try to dignify our simple reporters' trade – knows the mortal hazards of Looking Back. It is a risky business for anyone, but a special hazard for those of us who have the past forever looking back at *us* from the obstinate and imperishable Files – sardonically, mockingly, sometimes unexpectedly with a brief reward, but for good or ill on the record, for the Files will last longer than we shall.

Everyone knows that we write our stuff for the day, the hour, occasionally even the minute, sometimes under a stress when information is so much more important than elegance. We are not, after all – we say – in the business of literature. Kidding ourselves that we are is the secret consolation of the journalist. It sometimes works, though I doubt if we would admit it.

Foreign Correspondents pretend to be persecuted, bullied, over-worked and underpaid, but they are a pretty pampered lot in the sense that they have no need, let alone energy, to keep Diaries. The Files are the Diaries. There they sit in meaningless immortality, yellowing away on dusty shelves, immutable and now uncorrectable, growing, like the correspondents themselves, older and older and more and more irrelevant, more and more symbolic of the times that then were than of the times that are, and for us fading gladiators a constant source of wonder and regret. Did *I* do this? Could it have been I who had this or that preposterous notion of history, could it have been this brash young reporter who stumbled on the fortunate phrase that somehow or other turned into prophecy? It could, and was. Thus we differ from the fortunate and flexible politicians. Nothing can be done about us now; we are on the record.

Any journalist, if he has been on the road as long as I, has gestated and delivered a fair amount of writing of which he is not wholly ashamed. Sometimes out of the oblivion of the Files things emerge that give the reporter the illusion we all long for: that this was done not too badly, considering; if I can read it without flinching after all these years I could not necessarily have been such a fool as I felt at the time, with the editor pressing and the telegraph-office about to close.

These are the pieces that we have revived here. They are the essence of what Wordsworth called emotion recollected in tranquillity. I could not possibly have been trusted to choose them myself. My indomitable friends and editors Simon Scott and Romey Fullerton undertook the daunting task of resurrecting the necessary fraction of what must have seemed to them like ancient history. I remain forever grateful for their patience, and for the help of the libraries who disinterred words of mine that for me now belong to another life.

The process of exhumation began modestly, gathered in alarming momentum. Out of these famous Files emerged more and more ghosts, some benign and some embarrassing, but all rather terribly revealing of their period, and I am obliged to say of me. It was difficult to believe that one had written so many hundreds of thousands of words from so many places, and indeed for so many masters. They, the masters, were of curiously little importance for me; I was mostly so far away from them that I hardly knew them, nor indeed could see their – and my – newspapers. I covered the negotiations for Indian independence, for instance, for the *Express*, in my innocence wholly unaware that Lord Beaverbrook loathed Lord Mountbatten and Gandhi and deplored the whole Independence idea of which I was fanatically in favour; it did not prevent him from printing my stuff, so that his editorials could contradict it. I can fairly say that I have never been oppressed by proprietors, though they may often have been oppressed by me.

I happily haven't had a boss for twenty years. It makes for quite serious economic uneasiness, and it plays hell with the bank account, but you can breathe.

So we go on, not exactly merrily but with the willing acknowledgement that it was fun. Not always, but often enough.

I once wrote in a passing moment of honesty that all my life I never once sat down before that sheet of empty paper without feeling in my heart: this time they'll find me out.

Again I am taking the awful chance that this time I may be right.

Not every reporter has the good fortune to be given that chance.

*   *   *

B.B.C. RADIO, 1941–2

These scripts are almost my very first association with the B.B.C. – for that matter the radio medium at all. It is not really fair to call them scripts; they were more or less improvisations, and it shows. They were done in the London wartime, directed wholly at the North American Service. I doubt if anyone heard them in Britain.

They were made under some stress. At the time I was working as a night sub-editor in Fleet Street. I knocked off about midnight, and then had to walk to the studio in Oxford Street, simultaneously dodging the air-raids and scribbling notes about what the hell I was going to talk about. Reading these scripts after forty years is rather like blundering on the Dead Sea Scrolls, so far removed are they in time and memory.

The essay 'To My Envoy Extraordinary' strikes me, looking back, as pretty adventurous for a broadcast that was overtly and unashamedly propaganda. It took the accepted cliché that we were fighting for our freedom and turned it upside down, admitting that at that dangerous wartime moment the British had virtually no freedom at all. The theme was rather crafty, if I may say so after all this time: that we were fighting for the freedom to surrender freedom, and that we bloody well had the liberty to exist in bondage. It was a dotty argument, of course, but it made a nice change from Rule Britannia.

It is a measure of the B.B.C.'s forbearance that in the years to come I did hundreds more such solo jobs, and plays and documentaries. At one time, after a major disenchantment with Fleet Street, I fell earnestly for the television medium, and I still feel that its crossbred culture is probably more potent than any other. But that, as the late Mr Kipling used to say, is another story.

*　　*　　*

FOOTNOTE TO AN OLD
FRIENDSHIP

I saw it first in a little news item – one of those inconsiderable little paragraphs they use in newspapers when the lead story is a bit short of the column. I daresay hundreds of people saw it, but I can't imagine very many of them felt particularly deeply about it one way or the other. It merely mentioned – as part of some other story, I forget what – that the Hotel du Cerf Blanc, in a place called Armege, in Normandy, had gone out of business.

It has gone out of business because it no longer exists.

It used to stand among some chestnut trees opposite the Mairie, on the road south, and where it stood there is now, I understand, a pile of old stones and some broken wood. Someone dropped a bomb on it some little time ago, and so the Hotel du Cerf Blanc has gone the way of plenty other hotels between Brittany and the Rhine.

Well, that casual little par was rather like an obituary notice to me, because the Cerf Blanc and the township around it meant about as much home to me as Leicester Square, or the Chiltern Hills, or Sauchiehall Street, Glasgow. When I was a little boy at school not many kilometres from Armege I used to be very friendly with it. I knew Marcel Dubocq, who owned it – his father had owned it before him, and I remember the old man too, as a vague great fellow with sabots painted green. I remember that because he was the only person I ever knew with green sabots. I lived in France all my life as a boy, and that appealed to me.

I know that road so very well. Not as the soldiers must have known it, as one short and nondescript halt on the long passage to somewhere else of much greater importance, but as a place where I used to go to pick nuts, and get new leathers on my trousers, and talk to Elie who kept – of all combinations – a garage and a horse-butcher's. And then, later, I used to go back – all roads from the Channel ports seemed to me to go through Armege automatically – and as I grew up the Hotel du Cerf Blanc went into the category of old friends. My people used to take me there for Mi-Carême lunch, just after the last war, when money – real money – was so scarce that our department was using little cardboard discs bound with tin with stamps stuck on them as two-sou pieces, and when you could buy a great deal, indeed, with an English penny, if you ever got one, and when the steam-trams gave you your change in 'tram-money', which you could spend only on having more tram-rides . . .

That was long before I came back here, and it doesn't matter much nowadays anyhow. However, I kept up my friendship with the Cerf, though as I grew older it seemed to shrink – until I finally knew it was really not much more than a nice little auberge with a bit of a name locally for cooking river-fish. And with very lovely seventeenth-century walls. They must look so pathetic and futile now.

And then, the year before this war began, we went there on my honeymoon. That was about the best compliment I could pay it . . .

Well – that part of life is finished now. But I think a lot about these things nowadays, as typifying something we ought to value a bit more than perhaps we do. It is all very well to be nostalgic and reminiscent and romanticise things – we can't really afford to do that now. You might say that the restitution of these things is one of my private War Aims – not that that matters much. But I am terribly curious to know what is going on there now. I'm glad we are doing something for these people – more than just fighting for them, I mean. I'm glad we are telling them what is going on here. I like to think that Marcel Dubocq and Elie and the rest of them can turn on their radios – if they still have them – and hear a decent friendly non-German voice telling them – in their own thick Norman voice, maybe – that we over here are still for them. They won't be able to gather round the applewood fire in the Cerf Blanc any more, but somehow they'll manage, I'm pretty sure. They are almost certainly a great deal more courageous than I am. I know I don't like even thinking of Calais and Dieppe and St Malo now, whereas they can hardly avoid it.

That is the thing that has troubled me most ever since last June. I remember that when the war first came on to us one of its most worrying aspects – maybe it seems trivial enough now . . . but it was that I wouldn't be able to go to France; for the first time since the last war I should have to miss what was always the happiest part of any year. However, I thought, that is only a very temporary thing; after the war I shall go back and things will be more or less as they always were, and meanwhile if this war is doing any good at all it is at least reaffirming and tightening up that friendship and liaison between our countries.

There must have been a great many people feeling like that – the school teachers who used to go to Dinard, the art-students with their travelling scholarships, the ordinary people who had days at Boulogne and the extraordinary people who had six weeks at Antibes . . . but I liked to think that nobody's regrets were quite so personal as mine – and after all, all this is only one man's view. But all through that deadening, boring winter I knew that, after all was said and done, France was still there – we still got the French papers, you knew the service to Paris was still running even though you couldn't use it.

Then, of course, there came June, 1940, and that gloomy business of the Bulge – and the Gap – and Sudan, and the Meuse, and the Somme, and Paris – when I got as scared as most people did. . . . And finally Vichy, and all that desperately miserable bleak, dreary thing that seemed – quite honestly, it seemed incredible. To me, anyway. Now I have had time to think about it I think I realise how inevitable it was, and hate it for that reason, but I think I know just enough about it to keep my mudslinging quiet in the meantime.

But it altered everything. You didn't have to wait very long before you heard people talking – in buses, and pubs, and so on – saying these painful things . . . about being 'let down', and forcing up all those queer little national prejudices and misunderstandings that used to be funny, and aren't any more. It didn't help to know that on the other side of that little bit of water my friends Marcel and Elie and the others were saying much the same things, and with a deeper and more poignant bitterness which must, I suppose, come when you are defeated, and betrayed, and bewildered, and unhappy.

Hitler has done one of his worst jobs, I thought, when he started that.

So when I heard people over here discussing these things I have always wanted to say: 'I know, I know – it looks so wretched, but don't condemn too hastily. There's only *one* way to look at this beastly affair. You've got a friend, and he's ill. He's very badly ill, and in his – delirium, let's say – he's saying things and doing things that have absolutely no relation to his honest feelings. He's a sick man, and he's on his back, with a dreadful wasting at his soul, and a malign little ambulance-chaser masquerading as a doctor at his bedside. It's up to you to be – not charitable, because you owe more to an old friend than charity – but reasonable. He is suffering more than you, remember that. Give him that much understanding and he'll cooperate with all his heart, when he gets his wind back. . . . The French are above all things no fools. It may not be much fun to know that your colleagues are smashing up parts of your country every day, but give him a chance and he'll realise that if you've got to knock·the shackles from a man's limbs with a heavy hammer, it is bound to hurt. But in the end, of course, it means freedom.'

And I don't think anyone will deny that freedom is a word with a bigger meaning – a more definite, concrete, personal meaning – to a Frenchman than to almost anyone else.

I think that's pretty generally appreciated, in a way. I know the British press, for instance, has been very, very fair and objective in its treatment of France just now. I say that because I know jolly well what the French papers would have said about the British if things had been the other way round. But the French press never represented anyone in particular – certainly not the people like Dubocq and Elie and so forth, who could be really educational when they got abusive about the journals.

I remember that when I was a little boy at that school we were doing some middle-period history of the more elementary kind, and – as usual – the directeur brought up Joan of Arc, because I fancy he rather liked seeing me embarrassed. (I was an average smart lad there, as boys went, considering I didn't actually belong, and that was one way they could make me feel an awful fool, for no reason at all.) Anyhow, the master eventually said, as a kind of compensation: 'Joan of Arc was a saint. The English appear to have erred, from that point of view. But please recall that the English, although they may be somewhat barbaric in certain unimportant ways, are the only other people in Europe to whom a French commander has ever surrendered his flag – and the French flag is the only flag a British soldier has ever handed back. There is a lot to be said for being a gentleman, gentlemen.'

He called it 'avoir de la race', which is even better. And even if his facts were more picturesque than accurate, the spirit was there all right. And I didn't in the least mind his calling the English barbaric, because as I frequently pointed out, I was a Scotsman, and agreed most heartily.

M le Directeur may remember that himself. He has forgotten me, but I have not forgotten him. I hope he is nowhere near, when the R.A.F. bombs fall – knocking off the shackles.

But I think he would only say: 'Knock away. You in Britain are not the only ones who can take it – though perhaps you take it better than anyone else. Knock away, and we shall thank – those of us who know.'

And so, of course, we shall. And while we're doing it, I – who cannot do much more in the matter than look on – still insist on thinking of Armege, and these places, in terms of those chestnut trees, and the dusty white road south, and a barrel of cider coming over the pavé on a wooden cart, and the green sabots of Papa Dubocq. There will be no more river-fish cooked in the Hotel du Cerf Blanc – but we shall have it again, somewhere, sometime.

That is up to us. And to them.

Because I, for one, want to get back to see my friends again.

B.B.C. Radio,
20 January 1941

TO MY ENVOY EXTRAORDINARY
IN THE U.S.A.

My old friend Lou, who lives in New Jersey, but who once used to share a sombre lodging with me in faraway Dundee, Scotland, when he was learning to be a doctor in the University of St Andrews and I was learning to be a newspaperman – he is a good guy and an honest man and a first-class democrat, but he is an old sentimentalist when it comes to hard, hard facts. He uses the words 'freedom' and 'alliance' and 'solidarity', for instance, in a very loose way. He develops his politics as he develops his friendships. He is one of the Americans who like Great Britain. He is one of the Americans who say so.

Lou and I, now, we used to sit up o' nights in our third-floor room over the River Tay eating an original combination of our various familiar foods, maybe oat-cakes and gefilte-fish, and we would put the world straight between supper-time and sunrise. Across the landing was number three of the Little Entente – Michel, the Frenchman, who was planning to be a civil engineer. That was away back, when Munich was a place and not a curse, when Warsaw was a city and not an epitaph, when Scotland was a blue-grey railway-porter, and not an armed camp.

Say about 1934 or so, when we talked of wars and rumours of wars with that fine, smug detachment we all had around 1934, if you remember. The motto of the time was It Can't Happen Here. That isn't altogether fair to Lou or me, or to Michel either; we had a feeling it could. But we didn't do much about it.

However, Lou eventually went home with his degree in his pocket and his eye expectantly on the livers and duodenals of the fortunate folk of New Jersey, and there he is tonight, I think. He has always taken time off from that interesting study to write to me, spasmodically, as my own Envoy Extraordinary in the United States – the only one I have.

In that way things have rather changed. Lou is tapping stomachs in New Jersey, I am tapping typewriters in London, and Michel – Michel is dead, he died on the Meuse in 1940, trying to stop a German cruiser tank, I understand, with a 1917 rifle and five rounds of ammunition. Michel always felt it Could Happen There. He has established his point.

Well – Lou still writes me his letters. Some of them can be read now only by the spoiled and pampered fishes of the Atlantic Ocean, but most of them make the trip. They have become no matier nor warmer since last December – Lou is the kind of man who makes a poor non-belligerent and an even poorer neutral. As I say, he is a sentimentalist. He has his own ideas of what this war is all about. They are good ideas, to my mind. I share them, only more so, if you follow me. But he has lost touch a little with the country he is good enough to be fond of, now he's some 3,000 miles away.

Just a little while ago I split the censor's seal from his envelope – such a fine, quality envelope, and it hasn't even been used before! – and read his news from home and his enquiries for mine, and on to his comments on things in general. It seems he had been reading in his papers where Michel's home town had been jumped on by a posse of stormtroop thugs and a couple of streetfuls of citizens dragged away to jail over some difference of opinion with the Kommandatur. So, says Lou, in effect, over in Britain now you must feel pretty good, living in the only country in Europe where fellows are absolutely free, where there is no dictation, where you can do what you like when you like, and where you maintain those blessed ideals of freedom and democracy every minute of the day, and so on and so on.

It is a very nice idea. As an idea, it's about perfect. I would hate to deny it. I would dislike having to say that it is the bunk, that the Perfect Freedom of Democracy is a fine old-fashioned whimsy in Britain today – if it weren't for the fact that right now in Britain we perverse British are a little bit more proud of the rights we've lost than the rights we've kept.

Lou is thinking back to those salad days in Dundee when we had what we wanted when we wanted it, when we had so much 'freedom', in quotes, that we didn't know what to do with it, when we talked so much about preserving peace and did so little about avoiding war. That was then; this is now. Freedom – I'll tell my old pal Lou about freedom in Britain today. I know how he would hate to be taken so literally, but I still think he needs to know.

We'll talk about the Rights of Man, then, and here they are as applying in the year 1942 to us, the citizens of Great Britain. So what? We have none. It says a lot for the suave way things are run over here that a great many people can't really appreciate how few rights they actually have now, but there you are. Everyone in Britain – his person, his property, his time – are, technically, at the disposal of the Government. Anyone may be ordered to go anywhere and do anything – and that means anything – emergency statutes have made that clear. The Government can control people, banks, money, trade;

it can requisition land; if it thinks fit it can destroy anything it wishes. . . . So much for the broad outline of Freedom.

In detail you might not be too conscious of it; the bones are of the silkiest of rope, the fetters are made of the gentlest and most yielding steel, so far. But one by one they have been clamped on – not in the least furtively, but perfectly openly and usually with a fine blaze of publicity, and on the whole the people have accepted the sacrifice of so-called Perfect Freedom with much the same wry, humorous tolerance as they have brought to give up half their income in taxation.

The rights of the workers? That was our hobby once, in those days of everlasting talk and undirected theory. How do they sound now? Workers in essential industries can't be sacked, or change their jobs, even, unless the Ministry of Labour says so. Strikes and lockouts can be forbidden. The Unions have had to accept dilution of labour on a whacking big scale. Slackers or absentees can be, and often are, jailed. Inefficient managements can be replaced. Not all these things *do* happen, but they all *can*.

The rights of the home? Well, the Englishman's isn't his castle any more. His home can be broken into any time if he runs up against one of the many Defence Regulations. I am thinking somewhat of the fine which I expect very rightly and properly to have to pay for having a chink two and three-eighths of an inch wide in my bedroom blackout last week. And if I were suspected of hoarding food, say, my home can be forcibly searched any time. Does Lou, I wonder, remember the day we barricaded our door with suitcases to keep out the gas-meter man – once upon a time – and got away with it?

No, it wouldn't be much of a boast if we insisted that all we were trying to do in this war is preserve a glorious sort of Arcadia over here. Lou wouldn't know the old place now. After all, if you have twenty-two million of us fully mobilised in the trade of war it rather alters the social shape of things. There isn't a man of military age out of uniform, as you know, except the unfit and those who are doing what has been legally judged to be a necessary job. And for those, Civil Defence work is compulsory. It is all very obvious to us; is it so obvious, I wonder, to Lou?

We could make a long, and I guess a pretty tedious catalogue of all this. Going over it all is rather like telling your friends about your operation. Except that it isn't a question of being upset about things; it's a matter for congratulation. Self-congratulation. If you've developed a somewhat spreading waistline and things inside it have got a bit lazy and out of control, then it's very comforting and reviving to clamp on a girdle or a tummy-belt – or so I read in the advertisements. And we in Britain are very well aware that our own national internal organs right up to 1940 could do with a bit of dragging together. Lou, as a doctor, will probably disapprove of the analogy, but I can't help that. I would just suggest that wearing a strap round your waist for a while is better than wearing a ring in your nose – or a rope round your neck.

By this time, after nearly three years of war, the strap has become a little uncomfortable. We all know the state has several more notches it can drag in on us in case of emergency, but what we've got is tiresome enough for us. It's quite painful, indeed, to look back on the days when Lou was mugging up his Forensic Medicine with us here, to think of the days when we had a light in our window till four in the morning if we wanted it, to think of the car-trips to the Pass of Glencoe -- there are no car-trips now, except in earth-coloured Army trucks and lorries carrying things you can't ask about. It's even hard to think about the oat-cakes and the gefilte-fish. Anyone could eat half-a-pound of meat a day then – now, it's less than two ounces. No more white bread, no more cream, no more oranges. Well, well. Does Lou remember the tweeds he used to buy in the St Andrews tailors? Twenty-six coupons now, Lou – *if* you can get them.

Does Lou remember the landlady's young daughter – how old was she, about fifteen? She's now a soldier. She works a height-finder at an anti-aircraft gun-site in England. She wears a tin hat and battledress. She has seen more life and death since she joined the A.T.S. than Queen Victoria ever saw in Sixty Glorious Years.

Yes, there's been a few changes around here. The house we shared is still there, but I've never been back. The house where Lou sent his wife to spend a vacation with us in Glasgow has been wiped out by a little bomb. It was an old house, so maybe it didn't matter.

But above all I wonder if Lou remembers the typical aspect of those historic days, the interminable arguments around the town when Europe began to sizzle . . . no, no one will fight . . . sure, Mussolini's got his good points; he makes the trains run on time, doesn't he? . . . What did Marx say about that? . . . This guy Hitler, now, what's his big idea? Well, that Rhineland's his country, isn't it? . . . No, a rat . . . live and let live . . . talk and talk without end, amen.

My goodness, how quickly all that went. Nowadays, we know.

I've gone and denied my friend Lou's generous and comradely statement that Britain is a free country – but he knows that, really, I agree with every word he says. Lou knows that a country that can willingly buckle on a chain is no slave – that a people who can willingly throw up their freedom are free.

He doesn't have to tell me.

DAILY EXPRESS, 1948–9

My interlude with the *Express* was an eccentric affair, on the whole much more valuable to me than to it. It endured as long as it did, I suppose, mainly because half the time I was miles away out of reach of the paper, and really had but a hazy idea of what my masters had in mind. I got to know Lord Beaverbrook quite well only long after we had mutually sacked one another.

For example, one of my first jobs was to go to India to cover the negotiations for the Transfer of Power, as we called it then. I had great enthusiasm for the whole principle of Indian Independence. I considered M. K. Gandhi and Jawaharlal Nehru to be the most significant figures of their time. Nobody told me that to Beaverbrook both these men were anathema, and that the idea of Indian independence was a disastrous folly. (Much of this was certainly based on Beaverbrook's personal loathing of Mountbatten, the Viceroy who was to supervise the handing over. I knew nothing of this either; such was my 1940s naïveté.)

Consequently I filed back my stories of earnest optimism about India, and to the *Express*' credit it used them without comment or criticism, and when Gandhiji died I wrote the obituary reproduced here. Beaverbrook probably gritted his teeth, but he played fair.

When finally, at least for a time, I came back to Britain and was daily exposed to the prosperous and hugely-selling codswallop that was my bread and butter I was taken aback, to say the least. Quite soon thereafter the paper undertook a campaign (it was the one vilifying the late John Strachey) that was just impossible to stomach, and I resigned, with my heart in my mouth, since there were few dafter things a young reporter could do than publicly cross Lord B.

Until the break-point, however, he was most indulgent with me. Those were the heady post-war years, with newspapers swelling in both size and circulation and money coming in like billy-o, or so it seemed. It did not come in much to me, but I reaped the benefit of the Beaverbrook prosperity by being whizzed literally all over the world in some style on occasions both momentous and trivial; it seemed to make little difference which. I stored up experience like treasure, and have been drawing on it ever since.

When Lord Beaverbrook finally died, in his 80s, I wrote a memorial to him that was very nearly affectionate. But not for the *Daily Express*.

*   *   *

POWER WITHOUT THE SWORD

The last time I saw him, in that momentary Indian pause between day and darkness, was there on Birla's lawn where yesterday he died. 'I am a spent bullet,' he said, among the silent, white-clad congregation that surrounded Gandhi all his days, most of his nights.

A twin-engined transport came in low overhead, back from the Kashmir front. 'I asked for peace,' he said; the low, rather petulant voice of a very old man. He was still incomparably the most important person in Asia.

So that strange little man, the simple and subtle, meek and mighty, has had to go at last. Three hundred million people prayed it might never happen. Some thought it could never happen. But a crazy Hindu has done this thing; Gandhi died and left the world short of a legend.

Half his work was done. No man was more loved in his time, nor more loathed. He never got into the Bengal Club, but he may yet get into the Hindu pantheon of demigods. His work was twofold: not only to free India, but to unite her. His death may do what his life could not – that, or signal a disaster past accounting.

Who could compress the life and character of Mohandas Karamchand Gandhi into a handful of words? He did his best with self-analysis, self-revelation; no living man ever communed so publicly and frankly with his soul for strictly matter-of-fact ends.

The ends were politics. Everything in life was politics, from his Cabinets at sunrise to his evening prayers, from the milk of his goats to the 5s tin watch he slung at his waist. Politics equalled Faith plus Expediency.

He was seventy-eight; very old for an Indian. He was tough; the conventional picture of a bowed and skinny ascetic did no justice to that smooth and nimble brown frame.

That scrupulous personal honesty of an earlier day once forced him to admit that in certain circumstances even fasting could become a self-indulgence. By the same token it was clear he could enjoy jail, it punctuated a monstrously busy life with islands of privacy. Like Nehru, he wrote oceans of literature in prison.

It was obvious he could always get out of jail when he wished. The threat of a fast would be enough; the British could not risk Gandhi dying of starvation on their hands. But he never exploited that threat for himself; jail was far too valuable for him.

Examine Gandhi and you are beset and confused with paradox. He was the politician and philosopher, agitator and peace-maker, internationalist and patriot, religious leader and shrewdest of party men.

He was respected almost to idolatry by the practitioners – the Nehrus, Ghaffar Khan, Vallabhbhai Patel, Rajagopalacharl. He treated them like sons, and they called him Bapu, which is Gujerati for Father.

With age came a certain crotchetiness to sour that unbreaking patience – When, he demanded, will Indians learn love? I asked him a month or two ago for news of one of his talks with Mountbatten. He answered crossly: 'Nowadays I can give you nothing. Except' – with a sudden grin – 'my shawl, if you like.' Like a fool, I did not take it.

Gandhi was born in 1869 in the tiny state of Porbandar, to a family of the Valsya caste, the traders. When he was thirteen he married a neighbour girl, Kasturba. She died three years ago, old, kindly, still illiterate.

Although Hindu orthodoxy forbids the crossing of oceans, young Gandhi went to England in 1888, was called to the Bar and – as he wrily admitted years later – bought a top-hat and tried to learn the one-step.

South Africa started him. For twenty years after 1893 he stayed there, giving up a busy legal practice to champion the Indians there, founding farm colonies, propagating the gospel of the simple virtues. And in 1914 he came home to begin the biggest, longest, most enduring political campaign in Asian history.

After supporting Britain through the 1914 war he turned against her. In 1920 he opened the first All-India Civil Disobedience. A famous word was born – Satyagraha.

It was perhaps Gandhi's biggest contribution to language – It means, vaguely, 'the force of righteousness'; eventually it came to mean 'non-co-operation', 'passive resistance'.

Here was Indian nationalism's most potent weapon. Troops who could handle a shrilling armed mob were helpless against dark multitudes who stood wordlessly against the charge, allowed their heads to be beaten in, accepted death or injury without a cry, and were silently replaced by more.

It is fair to say that only Gandhi could have imposed Satyagraha on a fiercely resentful, bitter people. It worked.

Then came 1930 and a new rebellion, symbolised by the famous Salt March to Dandi. Salt was a Government monopoly, its tax was hard on the poor.

Gandhi – choosing, as always, the simple symbol for the complex issue – led his march to the source of salt, the ocean. Steadily, on foot, he crossed the enormous country, volunteers fell in; very soon India was alight from Karachi to the Bay of Bengal.

Gandhi reached the sea, lifted a handful of brine to his lips, India cheered – but the tax remained.

He went to London for the Round Table Conference of 1932. London smiled a little at the bizarre figure in the dhoti, who would break up any committee by squatting down to prayer halfway through, if it were time for prayer – or for a diversion.

He returned and fasted for twenty-one days that the Untouchables might be brought into the Hindu electoral body. For always parallel to his abiding ambition of Swaraj – self-rule – rode his obsession with the melancholy Untouchables, whom the British called the Scheduled Castes and Gandhi called Harijans, Children of God.

For fifty years he fought for them. His own paper was called the *Harijan*. The last copy I saw carried his plaintive editorial: 'Independence has brought them nothing. The Untouchables are still untouchable, shame to India.'

So the long life went on, illuminated always by the wild flash of the unpredictable. There is no way of saying yes or no about Gandhiji. (He was invariably called Gandhiji; the ji is the untranslatable Indian suffix implying simultaneously respect, devotion, admiration and homely friendship.)

He was old and young, solemn and humorous, profound and given to puerile practical jokes. He insisted that his own religion blended everything admirable of every faith, yet he was a Hindu of Hindus.

He disliked capitalism, yet lived half his time in the home of Birla, India's biggest industrial boss, and there he died. He disapproved of Britain and enjoyed the company of the British. In the midst of preparing a new campaign against the Raj he is said to have wept when he heard of the bombing of London.

One thing he would never tolerate nor countenance: that any man should lift his hand against any other man, for any reason. Peace was supreme and irrevocable. Non-violence was the one thing he became violent about.

He was a mystic and a mystery, a trouble-maker and a pacifist, a thorn in the side of Viceroys, who nevertheless went to great lengths to get him to dinner. He took on the greatest Empire history has ever known and beat it. He was human and irascible and a taskmaster, and perhaps as near a saint as any man has ever been.

Today he will be a handful of ashes on the burning-ghat, and that, of all his aspects, is the hardest one to believe.

Daily Express,
31 January 1948

THE NEW 'IDIOT'S DELIGHT'

Once again this evening as we stumble blindly home by candlelight, with aircraft rumbling incessantly overhead, it is all too like the days gone by.

Now, when the rumours start, and hate and pride and malice growl over the ugly rubble of Berlin, the present seems even more senseless than the past.

Of all the ghosts that walk this dismal realm of ruin, one at least is happy today – the wry shade of Goebbels, laughing merrily in hell to see his words at last come true.

The impending calamity with Russia, on which so many minds seem now so inflexibly set, has chosen a strange starting point.

For anyone whose senses are not yet numbed by this weary waste of debris, it seems very nearly incredible that Berlin, of all places – that broken monument of folly – could once again be talking war.

It is irrevocably apparent that the diplomatists on all sides have manoeuvred us into a situation from which no one can now expediently withdraw.

It is axiomatic that when the statesmen fail they shout for the soldiers. We are not at that point now. I think we may never reach it. But we are perilously near it.

The trigger-happy talk on the one side helps as little as the steely smugness on the other. In the middle, caught like a nut between Congress and the Kremlin, is Berlin.

Berlin today is, obviously, a city of wild and fanciful rumours, of nightly flaps and alarms among the maze of Informed Circles and Public Relations.

The Berliners, knowing the edge on which they live, inherit every fit and start. Interpret them variously with cynicism or despair.

But at heart they, rightly, care less than anyone. The Berliner, without resources, has little to lose now.

A war would at least rationalise an existence that has no future, anyway.

Already the West Berliner sees himself vaguely as a Free Fighting German, with old General Rundstedt resurrected in England and cast as a de Gaulle.

A black market boss I know, an urbane and comradely man, said: 'Business is dead. There is no material for my business under the blockade. Why, I am having to live on my rations.'

It is unlikely that he was telling the truth. There are leaks in the ring and black prices – £3 for a pound of butter, 12s for a loaf of bread – show no real signs of coming down.

My black market man said, with simple dignity: 'When the time comes I will stand by Anglo-America. I'll do my bit. Otherwise I guess I am a gone goose.'

The Berliner has fallen readily, emotionally, into his new role of Europe's gallant martyr, or Berlin Can Take It.

So he approves the sudden Allied discovery that Berlin is full of all the Christian and democratic qualities of resistance and constancy – 'Their courage, their fortitude, will see us through.'

Is not that what his masters have always told him, whoever his masters were? In this apotheosis of the Good Old Germany, no phantom memory of Belson or Auschwitz comes to spoil the theme. Indeed, to recall them is considered distasteful and impolitic.

The Germans now conceive the quaintest paradox of all: 'We may be the new Czechoslovakia.'

For so many Berliners life is indeed a painful dreamland today, with the deadening certainty that nothing within a measurable time can improve their state, that even war can scarcely worsen it.

The Berlin papers, dutifully exacerbating every disagreement with venom directed according to which side licenses them, can now get pretty well all the invective they require just from the official communiqués.

They are hireling instruments, without conviction or soul, just as the Berliners themselves are plain ballast in a struggle that quite obviously must reach its climax soon.

The blockade has made circumstances tougher, nerves tenser. Electricity is on for two hours in twenty-four, transport is closing down.

The air throbs and murmurs with the unending procession of planes bringing into Gatow and Tempelhof enough food, we are assured, to feed West Berlin's 2,500,000 indefinitely. No one looks at them any more.

Berlin continues its grotesque representation of rational life – shabby, dowdy, wan, ridden by day-to-day problems, flogging this and fiddling that, trying to turn a baffling confusion of currency into the odd pfennig's worth of profit to themselves.

Every so often the flat tones of drabness are pointed up by some nightmare burst of extravagant chic – a bizarre hat, a scarlet silken New Look against a background of broken brick, some desperate feminine challenge to the endless dreariness.

In the nightclubs, quarried from the cellars, you can (with enough of the right money) drink a glass of good wine and hear a song.

And late last night not far from the Hohenzollernstrasse, you could have seen a sight to divert the heart of a Balzac.

In a fragment of a bombed block a man and his girl were, as they say, courting, all politics forgot – and outside in the dusty wreck a guitarist singing, hired for the evening by the lover to strum a lieder and thus take something from the squalid misery of the scene.

Ever since the blockade began we have proclaimed that our air lift will keep our sector from starving.

Now the Russians say, with a rather studied casualness that they have enough and to spare for all comers who will go to their sector and pay in their East marks.

The East marks set no problem: everyone has some; our own employees are paid in large proportion in East marks.

It is more unlikely that weary Berliners will walk vast distances to do their meagre shopping in the Soviet zone; it might mean a ten-mile trip on foot.

Nevertheless, the move was efficient politics. It helps to devalue both the Allied Berlin mark and the Allied Berlin policy together.

The next move is likely to be the actual production of the food, and quite possibly the restoration of electric power, which might make our air lift look a little redundant, and would once again toss the ball back into our court.

Already the cigarette currency, so long a feature of the Berlin economy, has become part of the political game. Russia sells her cigarettes freely – but for Allied B marks only, so as to immobilise as much of the resented currency as possible.

The Americans are believed to be flying in untold numbers of cigarettes to meet the assault. The satirical Berliner could ask for nothing better than the stepping up of such a war with such an ammunition.

The menace has not yet ruinously affected life above-stairs – in the leafy Allees of British and American H.Q.s in the Grunewald and Dahlem, occupation officials still contrive a life that is only about four or five times better than in England.

It was still possible last night to hear one wounded complaint against the blockade, that there was no ice to cool the wine.

It is also possible in this Gilded Cage (one of the Liddle Jokes) to hear more earnest fighting talk than – one sometimes feels – can possibly be going on in Whitehall or Washington.

The official American point of view – that now is the hour to test the Russian will to war – has crystallised everything, for the Americans at least.

17

And there are Americans right here who are sincerely astonished that there might exist Englishmen who see the 'showdown' as the final conflict of two non-European Powers over a doomed and disintegrating Europe, and who somehow find it hard to regard that as an hour of glory.

The talk is of armed convoys, of Shows of Force, of Tough Notes, never of our unspeakable old argument that talks loudest of all. The Bomb.

Perhaps the same political delicacy that now keeps the name Buchenwald from the tongue inhibits the use of the simple word atom.

And, indeed, Berlin, poor dusty carcase, has little more to fear than Hiroshima. Yet I – perhaps the only one in this disputing multitude who ever saw that article in action – have an especial nightmare that populates these desolate streets with even grislier ghosts.

As for the Russians, no one knows. I have spent two afternoons walking and riding in and about the Russian sector. I met no Russian, hostile or friendly, fat or hungry, kind or cruel, democratic or tyrannical.

Outside, there is no link, no touch, no personal liaison, no point of even human rapprochement.

All communication is from the remote peaks of misunderstanding, at the top of one's voice. The line over which I am telephoning to England is under the control of the Russians.

Because it is presumably tapped (can you hear me, Molotov?) they say they like plenty of volume and good articulation. Anyhow, the line was never better in its life.

And now, of all Germany's 65,000,000, only half a dozen men are under Four-Power authority – Speer and Doenitz and Raeder and the other ageing war criminals in Spandau Jail. Four-Power authority now exists only there. And they, it is safe to say, do not care much either.

For the rest, Berliners know that, at least for the present, someone will feed them; right now it would seem to be a propaganda competition between the Russians and the Allies as to who shall do it.

That is the important thing – food. Not honour or liberty or democracy, or freedom, or all the shop-worn and devalued words which, in the mouths of angry men, send other men to war.

Food is the thing, the belly is the boss. Ideas belong to other races now.

The Berliners see the Americans, for all their dollars, and the British, for all their principles, out-manoeuvred heartlessly by the cold, unsentimental Power across the Brandenburger Tor.

They see all the good will and compromise disappearing in an accelerating mill of frustration and outrage. They see some sort of a crisis growing very near.

They see their old enemies stumbling, blundering into the final and definitive idiocy of the human kind, and they say, begging the question to the last: 'Can all this be for me?'

*Daily Express,
22 July 1948*

I'VE NEVER SEEN PEOPLE SO EAGER TO BE SHACKLED

This dismal city – the only one in the world, I should say, that can contrive to be hysterical and morose, furtive and arrogant, wealthy and bankrupt all at the same time – is now producing its most elaborate paradox.

Cheering and applauding, acclaiming and triumphant, it capers enthusiastically into the final condition of political servitude.

From noon yesterday to midnight tonight not a stroke of work is being done throughout all Argentina in honour of the great day and the new order.

In Buenos Aires, multitudes of well-fed *descamisados* gather gaily in the Plaza Congreso to watch President Peron take the oath under the new Constitution.

This is designed to perpetuate his rule, to outlaw all opposition, and to abandon at last the lip-service to Liberalism that has lasted for ninety-six years.

Never since the brave days of Nuremberg have so many people made such an eager fuss about putting on the shackles. Only the Opposition, which withdrew from the Assembly a week ago, stays out of the flag-waving and oath-swearing.

Peron, one would assume, is here to stay – he and his good lady, the fabulous Eva, Government Glad-Hand Girl No. 1 of the extravagant political novelette that is Argentina.

It is hardly right so far to call Peron a Fascist boss, since he has built his régime on a technically democratic constitutional basis. His programme of social reform looks pretty enlightened on paper.

On this basis, Peron has erected all the gaudy, silly trappings of dictatorship, all the oppression and deceit, all the hokum and eyewash, all the intolerance and espionage of totalitarianism.

One gesture now I shall always associate with Buenos Aires. Sitting in a friend's office one's talk moves round to politics. Automatically, and with a reflex long accepted, he unplugs the telephone.

That, of course, is old stuff now. Peron has had a couple of years of strong-arm administration.

For years past, Argentina has been a political madhouse, but until Peron it was at least rich.

If it squandered its patrimony on the masses, unnecessary, ostentatious imports, and army gear to reinforce its national pride, it was someone else's affair.

But how can you impoverish a country of such unlimited agricultural wealth – a country with twelve feet of solid alluvial topsoil where no fertiliser is ever used or needed, where cattle roam over endless prairies without shelter or need of it, fattening on alfalfa all the year round, a country the size of Europe supporting a population less than twice the size of London?

How would you ruin such a place? Well, Peron and his Government have nearly managed it.

Nobody knows the precise depth of the economic hole Argentina is in.

General Peron has a tendency in his splendid oratorical *tours de force* of using whatever statistics seem artistically most effective, propounding the twin arguments (a) the U.S. is a villain because it will not buy Argentine meat, and (b) Britain is venal because it does.

The rough position seems to be, however, that Argentina, which has done a nice job of international commercial exploitation over a period of years, is now on the rocks to a tune of some 400 million dollars owing to the United States. It is offset by a blocked credit in Britain of £60 million. It is this British debt which is causing so much eye-flashing and double-talk here today, with the perpetual demand all the time: convertibility, convertibility.

Argentina wants dollars, wants Britain's debt expunged in dollars (of which there is not the slightest, slenderest chance), and knows at heart that nobody but the U.S.A. can help her out.

A slender hope; Peron has already stood up an official loan by saying he would sooner cut his throat than take it, and no U.S. business organisation is likely to take the risk.

It is that unending dollars argument which obsesses the Anglo-Argentine economic talks which have been going on here since February 22, and which look as though they will go on for years.

The meat talks are frankly in a mess. Argentina is now 70,000 tons short of her commitments under the Andes Agreement and as certain to default.

Why? one wonders. There has been it is true, a good deal of jiggery-pokery in selling the meat ordered by us to other European countries. There has been a lot of short-weight killing.

But mainly there has been a lot of personal over-eating right here on the spot.

The Argentinos are the most fabulous and gargantuan meat-eaters in the world – something over a pound per day for every man, woman and child in the Republic.

But this, naturally, is only half the story. Much of the fault must be Miranda's – Miguel Miranda, the big tinplate boss whom Peron made economic adviser, and then fired not a moment too soon.

Miranda made a colossal and not unfamiliar Argentine error; he put his money on another world war to arrive shortly and do Argentina a bit of good, as most wars in the past have done.

So he haggled, tripped up and went, leaving Argentina in a chaotic economic mess.

Argentina's answer would be to do the same as Britain did: retrench, reform.

It is doubtful whether the Argentinos have the temperament or, in the present unconquerably glorious mood, the ability to do such a thing.

For the moment, it is fair to say, the *descamisados* – the once 'shirtless ones' so dear to the Peron family – never had it so good. Only the most politically astute community of workers could have resisted Peron's offers.

They have got their charter – thirteen months' pay a year . . . huge indemnities for dismissal, wage boosts up to 200 per cent, with milkmen now earning up to £65 a month . . . a lovely blonde running the Department of Labour and Welfare and ready to address them dramatically on high days and holidays.

They have all, but they have bought it very dear.

But what else in this uninformed and ill-traditioned country did they have to choose? What now opposes Peron and his chic and shrewd Eva?

Not, surely, the local *aristos*, the enormous *estancieros* – with their 100,000-acre ranches and their European education – who governed the land so arrogantly and selfishly before.

They hate Eva only because she is an upstart radio singer, not because she is politically smarter than they.

Not the army, always the big political force in Latin-America – at least not yet. It is only a little while since Argentina was stirring with rumours of a military ultimatum to Peron to get rid of Eva.

And when last week General Sosa Molina, the army's leader, made a speech of fulsome loyalty to Peron, and Eva too, the cynical reaction was only to wonder what sort of a deal had been made and by whom.

This is a strange and troubling city to live in just now. How prosperous it looks, sprawling beside its enormous cocoa-coloured Rio de la Plata.

But the stranger must beware.

The new Constitution – the biggest event yet in the history of Argentina – sets out to make permanent a system that bans unwelcome papers, that imprisons indiscreet speakers, that causes automatic censorship of B.B.C. relays by Senora Peron's own radio station quaintly called '*Libertad*.'

Yet – the stranger must see that Juan Domingo Peron, the thick-eared army colonel, took office not by force but by popular acclaim in one of the first fairly straight elections Argentina ever had; that Senora Maria Eva Duarte de Peron, the honey, is loved by the multitudes, and that this same Constitution is approved by the majority.

Politics are mostly Bedlam, as after all these years I am beginning to feel, but – South America, take it away.

Daily Express,
17 March 1949

OPERATION CROSSROADS

Now we have seen it. Down below the surface of the Bikini Lagoon this morning the first atomic bomb ever to be detonated under the sea has just gone off with what must and will surely be the most startling and extraordinary explosion ever contrived by the curiosity of man.

For those with eyes to see and sense to imagine this is worse by far than the bomb that split this same air three weeks past.

Less than five minutes ago, at 25 minutes before 9 o'clock, the young physicist called Marshall Holloway pulled the switch on the trigger ship *Cumberland Sound*, closed the radio circuit that started that fantastic and instantaneous process in the gadget suspended below the barge, and hurled what seemed to be half the horizon sky high.

I have at least seen something today that nobody ever saw before. Precisely at zero hour the bowstring line, where the sea met the sky, trembled and swelled in a vast gleaming dome of sheerest white.

Through binoculars – I am rather less than ten miles away and the morning is crystal clear – it looked for the minutest fraction of a second like a grotesque bubble, then forces inside it strained and burst through in the most enormous fountain ever manufactured.

At the very least a million tons of the Pacific Ocean leaped vertically in a sheer column more than half a mile wide, reaching up, it seemed, indefinitely into the clouds.

It climbed almost lazily up till in about a minute it was nearly two miles high, then it hesitated, and dropped like a mountainous snowman into the seething boiling cauldron that is Bikini Lagoon.

At this moment it is too soon to say what has happened to the eighty-seven vessels of the target fleet among which the bomb exploded as the entire area of Bikini Atoll has vanished into the grey haze. Whatever the bomb has done otherwise, it has created instantly out of the glorious morning a concentrated rainstorm falling and mingling with uprising steam, the whole confusion blending with the base of the familiar atom cloud.

First reports are again suggesting – and, this time it really seems incredible – that most if not all the guinea-pig ships are still afloat. This is only a few minutes after the explosion however, and already we can see on the television screen that the battleship *New York* has a list.

Now, out of the murk and fog on what moments ago was the brilliant Pacific horizon, the island of Bikini is appearing and now we can see the first of the waves beginning to break on the shore. We ourselves are in vivid sunlight.

The famous mushroom cloud is far slighter than in the previous test. The whole astonishing effect comes from the odd familiarity of the phenomenon. What has happened at Bikini is exactly what happens when a boy drops a stone into a still pool – the water is holed, and the inrushing water turns the crater into a spout which, falling back, sets up a turbulence sending outspreading rings of concentric wavelets.

Only here the hole was a chasm half a mile wide, and the spout was gigantic and wavering at the centre, probably 100 or more feet high.

More and more one grows sceptical of the omniscience of the scientists. For days they have been forecasting this phenomenon, but not one prophesied that the world's first submarine atom burst would look like nothing so much as a monumental cream coloured Christmas tree, that the climax this time would be not a towering monument of atomic particles, but a graceful, faint and delicate rainbow.

We on the *Appalachian* were this time only half the distance from the explosion that we were last time. From ten miles the rows of anchored warships stood out clear and crisp, and mingled superstructures not unlike the silhouette of a castellated city.

All around is the great fleet of observer and scientific ships strung out in a wide fifty-mile arc, and the flecked skies above dotted and murmuring with the ceaseless passage and re-passage of aircraft.

As the radio droned out the diminishing seconds to zero hour this time there was no suspenseful conjecture as to any bomb aimer's accuracy; the thing we knew was already there, hanging at some undisclosed depth between 30 and 150 feet, armed and established at some delicate fraction from the critical mass, awaiting Mr Holloway's finger on the button.

Then when it flashed into life the whole sinister and melancholy implications of the moment were lost in the momentary physical beauty of the soaring water and iridescent spray.

The report and blast of the explosion were more strongly marked than with the air drop. It took the best part of a minute to arrive. When it did the noise was that of an underground train passing under a house, more sensation than sound, and the shock wave absorbed by ten miles of sea brought a dull, almost imperceptible reverberation to the ship.

In the engine room, being below the water line, it was felt, they tell me, more strongly.

Surprisingly quickly the storm and confusion of the burst died away, diffused into the morning sunlight. Bikini island and the ships behind stood out again crisply on a completely dead-calm sea.

As we crawled in towards the rim of the reef we stared through glasses to try and see what, if any, hole had been made in the target array.

From one of the questing aircraft circling inquisitively overhead the first report arrived; the thirty-five-year old battleship *Arkansas* is at the bottom of the lagoon. So it seems are a concrete yard oiler and one L.C.T. The carrier *Saratoga* is listing to starboard and down by the stern.

Already I can see the little yellow drone boats, pilotless investigation craft, nosing busily with curiously uncanny perception among the ships gathering samples of radio-active water for the safety patrols.

That of course is the great unseen hazard of this experiment; Bikini Lagoon, as big in area as greater London, is at this moment in the process of becoming the biggest puddle of radio-active liquid ever known.

As we drift in towards this disagreeable neighbourhood, as the great fleet joint task force one gathers, concentrates and moves in on the experimental fleet, almost as a curious crowd gathers after a street accident every time, I tabulate a few of the most marked impressions of this most sensational experience – a remarkable comparison with the last experiment which somehow seemed a lesser thing than expected. This one is an infinitely greater one.

The abrupt feeling as the enormous water dome swelled and expanded in perfect symmetry to a monstrous bulb that it would never stop developing, that it would increase indefinitely and overwhelm us even at this distance, a genuine even if only a momentary feeling of fear.

Then, in a fragment of a second, when the outward movement became upward, the ineffable grace of the column, the weary slowness with which it dripped its million tons of water back towards the lagoon.

Then when the waves ribbed over the reef and were absorbed into the smoothness of the sea, the intense realisation of the enormity, not of the bomb, but of the ocean, this enormous expressionless Pacific Ocean which can take even the atom bomb, embrace it and forget it while one looks on.

Above all the feeling of surprise, perhaps disappointment, that the subsiding vapours revealed the fleet still in being. I do not at the moment understand how so many ships survived nor how many right now are preparing to sink.

It proves once again for any dumbbell who needs proof that atom bombs are not anti-navy weapons nor were ever intended to be, but if that gives rise to any more foolish misinterpretations, then Crossroads has been a terrible mistake.

Daily Express,
1 July 1946

PICTURE POST, 1950–52

The news magazine *Picture Post* was unique in its day. Its editor Tom Hopkinson was intellectual, popular, kind, generous and shrewd; qualities all unusual in the rat race of the Press. After the Beaverbrook débâcle I did not feel that I rated high in the Fleet Street popularity stakes, so when Tom offered me a job on *Picture Post* I grabbed it like a shot. I would have applied long before if I had dared.

The space! I thought. Two or three thousand words was nothing in a news magazine; newspapers began to sharpen their scissors after five hundred, and I was always a verbose varlet. I could not wait to start.

Nor had I to. Almost at once I was off to the Korean War. It had hardly begun, and already things looked black.

My photographer-companion was the great and good Bert Hardy, associate on many expeditions. Bert was no more than I brought up in the fearless buccaneering derring-do of the contemporary American cameramen, who later were virtually to take over the war in Vietnam, but we learned fast. Almost at once, it now seems, we were precipitated into the biggest seaborne invasion of anywhere since the Normandy landings, at Inchon, the story of which follows here. We were both, I think, equally scared to death, but Bert was perhaps less used to being scared to death than I, and it has to be remembered that while the writer can skulk in a ditch and think about his story the cameraman has to stand up and take pictures. I have never met a war-correspondent photographer who was not far braver than I. What *Picture Post* was all about, after all, was pictures. I mention this because in a textual book like this it can be forgotten.

On the way home we called to see Jawaharlal Nehru of India. I had had a tenuous friendship with him since the days before Independence; I can put it no higher than that, but it saved him from being as crusty as he usually was at these intrusions. Nehru could be terribly acerbic to journalists, for which he can hardly be blamed, but for some reason he was always comradely to me, not to say wise. In his dying years he became erratic and indeed downright eccentric; he outlived his enormous intelligence and died in the shadow of his useless war with China, but at his peak he meant more to me than possibly any man except my father. India could do with another Nehru – which, of course, they now have; but it's not the same; however hard they promote the Dynasty there will never be another Panditji.

*   *   *

INCHON

The challenge, when it came, was too loud, the effect too abrupt; it was not reasonable to fight a war so noisily. We had indeed been waiting for some time. Nevertheless, however you anticipate the stage revolver-shot, it always makes you wince; so I suppose invasions are always more startling and uproarious than you expect.

This was, after all, the biggest seaborne assault of all, after Normandy. This was the operation to end the war. This was the payoff to take the Thirty-Billion-Dollar Police Action out of the red at last. This was MacArthur's final argument in his personal one-man deal with destiny. This was the top-secret business for which we had been lurking furtively in Pusan, of which everyone in Korea appeared to know almost everything, even us. Then, when it came, it stunned, for a while. All the fear came first. Perhaps we shall never understand exactly how it came off as it did, nor why the enemy failed to do any of the three things that could have crippled the whole enterprise. Anyhow, God was on the side of the big battalions; they were even that big.

We had sailed out in a fat Naval freighter, full of stentorian metallic commands and whistles in the dark, deck-loaded with big and little landing-craft, nesting inside each other like Chinese boxes. We weaved in a curious pattern over the Yellow Sea until we met more ships, and then a few more, and in three or four days more yet, all in the silent off-hand manner of a casual encounter. Very soon there were a hundred and fifty of us, of incalculable variety of shapes and purposes, slowly converging on the port of Inchòn. I would never have believed how tedious it could be. It would not have occurred to me that a climactic moment of such emotional intensity and concentration of nervous activity could have been preceded by such days of numbing boredom.

Up until D-Day eve the Marines still kept up the jesting, the special exclusive badinage of soldiers before battle, the protective flippancies . . . this was of all landing-points the most unsuitable, with a thirty-foot fall of tide that, should anything upset our schedule, would give us a three-mile stumble through waist-deep mudflats under the shore batteries; the enemy was obviously prepared for us; the sea-wall on Blue Beach presented unmapped hazards. Everyone laughed briefly. Then at blackout they settled down to write to their wives. So we came in a great sombre regatta past the Tokchok-kondo islands and dropped anchor in the Inchon channel between the plains of silt, exactly one fortunate half-degree below the Thirty-Eighth. That night the thing happened as everyone knows – with a result, moreover, that everyone now knows, too, though as I write this I can only guess. On that evening of haze and filmy rain among the hills it was like an Argyllshire sea-loch, somehow steam-heated and washed with pastel grey. In no respect, and in no circumstances, can Korea be called lovely, nor even barely likeable; yet at this moment, in the especial dusk of doubt, it came more nearly to being beautiful than I had ever seen before.

The guns began erratically, an hour or two before H-Hour – half-past five – with a few crumps from the cruisers, an occasional bark of five-inch fire, a tuning-up among the harsh orchestra. At what point the laying of the guns merged into the final barrage I do not know; so many things began to take place, a scattered series of related happenings gradually coalescing and building up to the blow. All around among the crowded walls of the fleet the landing-craft multiplied imperceptibly, took to the water from one could not see exactly where, circled and wheeled and marked time and milled about, filling the air with engines. There seemed to be no special hurry. We could not go until the tide was right; meanwhile we lay offshore, in serene insolence, under whatever guns the North Koreans had, building our force item by item, squaring the sledge-hammer. The big ships swung gently in the tideway, from time to time coughing heavy gusts of iron towards the town. It began to burn, quite gently at first. What seemed to be a tank ashore sent some quick resentful fire back, but it soon stopped. Later, we found that one ship had tossed a hundred and sixty rounds of five-inch ammunition at the tank before it had finished it; the economics of plenty in action.

Quite suddenly we saw the floating tanks, those extraordinary seagoing hunks of amphibious hardware. They crawled awkwardly out of the hull of the mother-ship; she spawned them out in growling droves, a grotesque mechanical parturition. Like a flock of rattling turtles, they lurched out of the ship and began to crawl over the surface of the water; a spectacle utterly surrealist.

As the light faded the noise rose in key, the intervals shortened between the explosions, which now broke out from unexpected places; the din grew suddenly less discriminating and more vicious, abruptly hard to endure. We got into our landing-craft – by no means, as it happens, the easiest thing in the world to do, enveloped in rolls of lifejacket like the Michelin Man, with the helmet rolling over the nose, scuffling and dangling down a rope-ladder in the rising sea. When we headed for the shore, the concussion of shells and bombs was no

29

longer a noise, it was a fierce sensation, a thudding jar on the atmosphere, on the hull of the boat, on the body itself. The waterfront of Inchon began to disappear under a red-shot screen of smoke; it seemed to vibrate. Then the rocket-ships let go. That was the most appalling noise of all; the ships burst into violent pyrotechnics, with a new and ghastly sound, the sound of a tremendous escape of gas, the roar of a subway, the projectiles arc-ing through the air and crashing into the beaches; when soon one prayed for it to stop for just a moment it screamed out once more.

At last, as the hundreds of troops began to surge towards Inchon, with what seemed to be powerful express trains howling through the sky overhead, it reached the stage where individual sounds ceased, the bangs and thuds blended into a continuous roll of intolerable drums. The town, and what remained of its quarter-million inhabitants, was gaudy with rushing flames, with more explosive pouring into the flames; one more inconsiderable little city, one more punch-drunk town, one more trifling habitation involved by its betters in the disastrous process of liberation.

Now the twilight was alive with landing-craft, tank-landers, marshal-craft, ammunition-carriers, things full of cranes and guns and lorries and bulldozers and Marines, more Marines – forty thousand men on Operation Inchon, twenty-five thousand to be put ashore – tall boats and squat boats and bad-dream swimming tanks, all whirling round in an intricate minuet – and in the middle of it all, if you can conceive of such a thing, a wandering boat marked in great letters 'PRESS', full of agitated and contending correspondents, all trying to appear insis-tently determined to land in Wave One, while contriving desperately to be found in Wave Fifty. The L.C. bounced and heaved through the spray; I found to my bewilderment that I was not, as usual, rolling in nausea; I decided that I was too frightened to be seasick, the counter-nervous-irritant. It was a hard matter to rationalise at that moment.

We headed into the heavy bank of smoke, and there we were. By some extravagant miscalculation we reached the sea-wall ahead of the Marine assault-party, who came blazing in behind us, making retreat quite out of the question. I scrambled ingloriously up the stones and over the parapet and instantly fell flat on my face into a North Korean defence trench most happily empty of North Koreans. There seemed to be a field ahead, and a tidal basin, and beyond that the town, surging with smoke, jarring to the bombs; a place – it must have been – of stark despair. That was the landing, anyhow. The fact that in our flurry we had reached an unscheduled area, that we had in fact hit entirely the wrong beach, were considerations that moved us only when we were told, some time later. At the moment it seemed merely fantastic; the smoke and dust and flames on the one side and, on the other, picking that instant with outrageous theatricality, the sun set in a black-and-vermilion blaze that was too intensely dramatic, too exactly appropriate to be true.

In effect, that was the taking of Inchon, the hammer-blow to the heart, the smashing of the gate to Seoul, the turning-point. The rest was to come at next day's light – the consolidation, the flattening of ruins, concealment of corpses, tending of wounds, the turning of Red Beach into a fabulous marshalling-yard of heavyweight war-machinery. And, somehow, the handling of the Koreans who had survived that terrible night, the sifting of the friends from the enemies, the quick from the dead, the simple from the suspects. As we edged into the charred town they came stumbling out, some of them sound, some of them smashed, one or two of them quite clearly driven into a sort of bomb-happy dementia by the night of destruction. They ran about, capering crazily or shambling blankly, their only gesture a frantic hands-up; some calling their one English phrase as a kind of password: 'Sank you!'; a macabre piece of irony. It was the job of the R.O.K.s, the South Korean militia, to mop up and secure the town; this they did with violent and furious zeal, rounding up householders, searching them with great toughness, herding them around, ancient crones and baby toddlers too, with the strange venom of the Korean, which is that of the armed adolescent; the hoarded anger of the dispossessed returning. Once again there was the phenomenon everyone has remarked before in all captured towns: the inexplicable appearance of the victor's flag all over the neighbourhood; from almost every roof and window there was some version of the South Korean flag or the Stars and Stripes. One shopkeeper had gone so far in broadmindedness and lack of prejudice that already he had hung a sign 'Wellcom U.S. Forces!', while forgetting to complete the gesture by removing the Communist Red Star that hung beside it.

So began the drive to Seoul.

That was the taking of Inchon. Why the North Koreans did not resist more forcefully I do not know, unless the obvious reason be true; they had too few troops there and could not disengage forces quickly enough from the south. That they did not mine the channel, that they did not scrape together even a squadron of planes, however decrepit, to sprinkle bombs on that congested roadstead, that they did not send fireboats or saboteurs down that dense lane of shipping on the rushing ebb, that in fact they behaved with a hopelessness and irresolution they had never shown at any time before – these are matters that no doubt will be explained one day. They lost their beachhead, they lost their town, they lost their lives, in numbers, and with them the lives of many simple people who shared the common misfortune of many simple people before them, who had the ill-luck to live in places which people in War Rooms decided to smash. It seems clear they could have hurt us more than they did, but the hammer was too hard.

But there it is. Sitting here, one is glad to be alive – a bit ashamed, maybe, but glad.

Picture Post,
7 October 1950

A VOICE ABOVE THE BATTLE

This has been a good year for the political moralists, the international holy men in high places, celebrating hate and division to the tune of lofty hymns. Out in Korea, from which we came, desperate things have been going on, and continue to go on, in the name of honour and justice; sometimes the dark deeds have been less hard to bear than the pious talk surrounding them. Nothing has been done but in the name of this or that conception of truth, and the air is thick with phrases. Only one man in the business seems somehow to cling, angrily, to the simple ones, perversely pursuing the principle of humanity without appearing to mock it. It could be said that Jawaharlal Nehru can take the curse off moral platitudes by the curious method of believing in them. For that reason inevitably he is called Red by the reactionaries and Reactionary by the reds; a commonplace situation for men of goodwill, nevertheless remarkable for a Prime Minister of four hundred million people.

Because India's official line, under Nehru's persuasion, is that of settling the Korean war by negotiation, of treating with China, of limiting the destruction, he is attacked by Americans as misled, unscrupulous, and dangerous. Because he opposes Communism in India as tenaciously as he opposed Imperialism, the Russians assail him as a fellow-traveller of the Right. To many less articulate people he suggests an attitude that may be sentimental, even unrealistic, but that at least makes ethical sense. Coming home as we were from Korea, with the smell of Seoul still sour in the nose, still slightly punch-drunk from the crossfire of vilification from East and West, it seemed a refreshment to meet again a man so equally poised between the world's respect and abuse.

His argument has been re-stated so often. Our visit to Nehru was itself sandwiched between speeches patiently repeating the theme: the means are as important as the end, and there is such a thing as pushing victory too far. 'Every action has its reaction. It is the old natural law: a good action will result in good and a bad one will result in bad – maybe not immediately, but some time.'

This was the day the U.N. forces crossed the Parallel – wrongly, says Nehru. It is wrong to press military operations when peaceful methods could bring right results. 'When you enter the realm of warfare and the military mind there is always that impulse to go to the last limit, and possibly betray the object for which you are fighting the war. Wars are fought to gain a certain objective. War itself is not the objective; victory is not the objective; you fight to remove the obstruction that comes in the way of your objective. If you let victory become the end in itself then you've gone astray and forgotten what you were originally fighting about. Our objective here should be a peaceful and united Korea; of course, the Parallel should disappear. But if Synghman Rhee thinks he will win his aim by purely military means then I differ. I'm no great admirer of Rhee anyway. It seems to me that North Korea has been adequately defeated, and it should not be impossible to bring about peace on the lines of the United Nations objective. It's *always* wrong to assume you can succeed by pursuing military means to the utmost and the last. Every major war has shown this: the last one created plenty of new problems exactly for that reason. There have been many great soldiers who were great men, but I don't think the military outlook ever yet solved any major problem in the world. I believe in the old argument that war is much too serious a thing to be entrusted to soldiers.'

It is possible that there is more than homespun Gandhian simplicity to the Nehru line; through Red China's Ambassador Yuang Chung-Hsien the Pandit has the clearest pipeline to Mao Tse-Tung and to Russia itself. It is confidently said in Delhi that Nehru has been told that the Soviet Union will pay a price not to have the United Nations on their doorstep in North Korea, with American guns practically at the edge of Vladivostock. India, clinging to her political independence of both the East and the West blocs, would probably know more about that than anyone. But how long can India preserve this 'neutrality'; will she not inevitably be drawn into one camp or the other? Nehru spreads his hands. 'One can never say what circumstances may cause. One tries to heal the cleavage. By taking sides one might precipitate the thing one wishes to avoid.' Does he intend to meet the Chinese leader Mao, the only other Asiatic leader of comparable magnitude?

'At the moment – the opportunity is hard to envisage. It is a terribly difficult journey.'

The conflict within Jawaharlal Nehru is more than that of all the millions of liberal men who find themselves in a dilemma for which they feel partly responsible and from which they see no immediate escape. It has so often been pointed out that Nehru is too many men within himself: an Indian who became a European, an individualist who must identify himself with the world's most enormous proletariat, a Brahmin who became a socialist, an intellectual rationalist leading a land of monstrous mediævalism. At sixty-one he is still the most beguiling and sensitive of statesmen, a man to enrich any conversation; he is probably the most fatigued of politicians, ridden with the paradoxes that threaten all Asia.

'In India we have spent our lives,' he said in a speech that very day, 'trying very imperfectly to follow the spirit of our great leader. He talked of non-violence – and here today we are in charge of Government, and the Government keeps armies and navies and air forces and indulge in violence pretty often. What are we to do about it? None of us dare in the present state of the world to do away with the engines of organised violence. But we know it solves nothing, absolutely nothing.

'We feel that here in India we might be in a better position to understand our neighbour countries of Asia – to have, may I say, an emotional understanding of them which is much more important than any purely intellectual one. But what is nationalism? I don't know. In the case of a country under foreign domination it's easy to define; it is anti-foreign-power. But in a free land what is nationalism? It starts as a healthy force, a progressive force, a liberating force; then maybe after liberation it starts looking greedily at other countries just as other countries used to look at it. Where do you draw the line?

'But one thing is absolutely clear, and matters now – no argument in any country of Asia is going to work if it goes counter to that nationalist spirit, Communism or no Communism. I'm not arguing for or against it; I'm just saying that is how it is. Masses in movement – minds in movement. I am Prime Minister of India and I haven't the faintest notion what India or Asia will be like in twenty years. I know what I want it to be. I do my job with the best of ability and energy I have. If I succeed, good; if not, I have done my best. . . . If in the modern world wars have unfortunately to be fought (and they do, it seems) then they must be stopped at the first possible moment, otherwise they corrupt us, they create new problems and make our future even more uncertain. That is more than morality; it's sense.'

By contemporary standards, as one found them in Tokio and Taegu and the Imperial Hotel in New Delhi, that was heresy, if not sedition.

On the verandah of the Prime Minister's bungalow that, the last time I had visited it, had housed General Auchinleck, it sounded remote and rather sad. Pandit Nehru, after all, said little for the record, and generalities are generalities. It just reminded one momentarily that somewhere between the excesses and threats that hemmed us all around there was a point of view that put a higher value on principle than on expediency; one had almost forgotten that there was such a thing.

Picture Post,
28 October 1950

TIBET DISSOLVES

Over there to the west, the soaring extravagant horizon of Nepal, petrified melodrama; to the east, Bhutan; behind us the interminable plains of India. Not far away is the highest mountain in the world, invisible only because the second highest mountain in the world is in the way. A road clinging to the slope, the obscure sound of a temple gong; curious people on the edge of the Himalaya, panting a little in the thin air of eight thousand feet.

And over there to the north, just across the Pass, beyond the snows, lies Tibet – vagueness and silence, that preposterously eccentric country that was the final stronghold of mediæval exclusivity until history, to its astonished resentment, caught up with it at last. Shangri-la lasted a long, long time. Then the Red Star of China rose over to the east, and one dull growl from Sikang province jerked the Forbidden Country into the twentieth century – to the Tibetan social system, an advance of about six hundred years; a startling process. So now, in a dim and rickety village called Yatung, sits the refugee Court of Tibet, that ineffable coterie of mystics and monks and smart operators and near-divinities and anxious business men in braided hair . . . just in Tibet, and no more. Near enough, and far enough. For those who now feel the impression that we are shaping up for the first, unprecedented interview with the Dalai Lama let it quickly be said that they are labouring after a vain thing. No one in the world – no king, no pope, no potentate, nobody – is harder to get than a Dalai Lama, that unique immortal surrounded by a quite impenetrable curtain of holiness, sitting there on the roof of the world behind a wild grille of mountains twenty thousand feet high. His curious country, jarring for the first time under the impact of a rude intrusive world, may see its remoteness disintegrating; nevertheless Tibet remains Tibet – some get out, none gets in.

Right now the steep township of Kalimpong, hanging on the hillside of North Bengal, is the nearest any of us is likely to get to Tibet for a long time – probably for ever, the way things look now. We did, as a matter of fact, get a good deal nearer than that, plodding among the mule-trains up through Algarah, up through Pedong, up past the scarlet poinsettias and the lovely deodars to the rocks and winds of the Sikkim border. But no one knows exactly where frontiers run among these enormous hills, and here begins the great business of passes and permits and sudden inspections from the Government of India, already twitching with uneasiness at the dubious political situation on her most embarrassing boundary. Ahead, moreover, lay the Jelep-la, the main road into the peculiar recesses of Tibet – if you can call a thing a road that climbs to 14,000 feet and leads to a monstrous wilderness twenty times the size of England, where the depths of the valleys are higher than the summits of the Alps – an exacting stroll, we felt, for mid-winter. For all that, this trail is now the funnel through which Tibet is filtering what she can of herself and her property, the wool, the hides, the musk, the furs, the borax, and the other commodities less easily identifiable. Above all the wool. We shall come to that.

Meanwhile, there is Kalimpong. This simple town, main roadhead for the caravans from the north, has presumably existed for long enough without being distinguished for anything in particular; for some reason today it has become a rendezvous for the most impressive collection of human eccentrics in Asia. Wealthy refugees and peasant-dealers from Tibet, bumping south down the Chumbi Valley on their mules, curious personalities drifting north to see what is going on – a miscellaneous double stream of irreconcilable oddities has silted up in Kalimpong and turned it into a place where anything goes. There among a fluttering forest of Buddhist prayer-flags, a rickle of corrugated iron, a smell of incense and a mouldy statue of Queen Victoria, strange characters move around in concentric circles, eyeing each other sharply. To the ordinary background confusion of Nepali farmers, Indian merchants and Lepcha tribesmen has been added a rich seasoning of wizards and sorcerers, Tibetan aristocrats, political exiles from China, forgotten twigs from the minor European nobility, Indian yogi, Bhutani politicians, anthropologists, students, linguists, pilgrims, dealers in miracles, and a sprinkling of commonplace nosey parkers. There are European Buddhists trying to convert the Christians and Christian missionaries retaliating on the Buddhists, and itinerant abbots of indescribable piety and filth exorcising evil spirits by tooting on human thighbones. There is Prince Peter of Greece, who arrived on a research mission to Tibet in a gigantic air-conditioned caravan and has been stalled in Kalimpong for a year and doesn't mind if he waits another year. There are the remnants of the forlorn Tibetan Mission to the United Nations, burying their hopeless bewilderment in bouts of meditation and exercise on the prayer-wheel. There was one long rum-party among the refugee notables, to celebrate the Tibetan New Year, which is now the Year of the Iron Hare . . . a situation that comes back most surrealistically to mind as a welter of mad paradox, with a Tibetan lady of high degree giving out with 'Buttons and Bows'; with myself, a poor European primitive, being taken in hand by a lass from Lhasa and taught to do, of all things known to God, the samba. . . . Only the other day great resentment was felt in Kalimpong against an American correspondent who described the town, tersely, as 'zany'. Now, on reflection, the more rational inhabitants can only agree that the term was a feeble understatement.

Kalimpong has the additional peculiar atmosphere of all frontier towns at moments of the international jitters: a watchfulness, a coming-and-going, an embarrassment of cock-eyed rumour and a total absence of hard news. The Government of India, which knows very well that whatever goes on in Tibet may yet be her pigeon, keeps a tense eye on all the palaver. It has a job for itself.

Yet behind all this Mad Hatter business exists the deep and anxious preoccupation that has helped to produce it. What about Tibet? What about the Dalai Lama? How far will his flight lead him, and when? What, in fact, *does* go on in Tibet?

Four months have gone by since China invaded Tibet. By every account that can be considered even remotely reliable (which is about one in eighty) the attack has been no more than a loud saying of Boo! from the province of Kham. The Chinese have moved no nearer than 150 miles from Lhasa, where they remain, making frightening faces at the horrified lamas. Nevertheless it is an unprecedented matter for the Tibetans, whose considered foreign policy has always rigorously been to have none at all, to get mixed up in no way whatever with the antics of the outside world – in which, one is bound to say, they showed themselves no fools. Tibet, which has by now roughly reached the condition of social progress achieved by Britain in the fourteenth century, knows the Chinese could have a walkover any time they liked. Tibet knows that the days of isolation are over, emergency has finally arrived, and as is customary in such situations, the big boys tend to be most swiftly off the mark. Many wealthy citizens are outside already, with their portable capital; many more are fidgeting on the brink, waiting for the correct moment, and passing the time searching the scriptures in any of Tibet's 3,000 monasteries. The peasantry, having nothing to lose, are waiting to see what shows up – or so one supposes; everything in Tibet is a matter of supposition, since nobody knows.

Tibet, the final example of the completely feudal community, has no vestige of a middle class. On the top crust the priestly power and temporal authority are inextricably integrated; there is no simple way of explaining the wholly theocratic nature of a state where anything up to a third of the total male population are monks and where the ruler is God, and technically several centuries old. There is no short-cut definition of a religion which mingles Tantric mysticism, Shamanist cults and Indo-Tibetan demonolatry, tinged here and there with the teachings of the Buddha, involving a brain-reeling pantheon of godlings and angels, tutelary deities and canonised evil spirits. Above all there is no simplifying the creature who sits atop it all, the Fourteenth Dalai Lama, the living incarnation of all before him, free from human error, all-knowing and all-powerful, the man with the most exclusive job on earth. Now the present incumbent, who is fifteen – or rather sixteen, since in the Oriental fashion he was born a year old – waits, and ponders, and beats his gongs, just over the border at Yatung. Just how much this strange cloistered being is in control of his own behaviour no one knows. He is surrounded by a close entourage of ministers – called, rather ominously, Shapes – who have every reason to stay clear of possible Communist flying columns. He can skip into India any time he likes. Meanwhile he sits, and waits, and Kalimpong, full of tense surmise, can only say: He'll be coming round the mountain, when he comes.

The Dalai Lama may wait, but business will not. Of the great trade exodus out of Tibet there is no doubt whatever. All through the hours of daylight the rare Himalayan air echoes gently with the steady donging of the mule-bells, distant and near; the long caravans wind over the traders' trail at the deceptive crawl that takes them every day thirty miles along the road from Tibet to India. On the pack-beasts is piled the great Tibetan staple, the wool that is the source of what wealth they have. The Chinese alarm started the rush; now more and more wool – heavy, oily, grey, baled with thongs – is trundling over the border, to be out of harm's way should the Chinese move nearer. The mass is greater than ever known before – nobody in these parts knows anything about figures, but it is said that this year Tibet's exports will be a record of ten million pounds weight, maybe four or five times the usual. Most of it goes to the U.S., to make blankets.

With it come the drovers, the muleteers, extraordinary individuals to a man, quite extravagant swashbuckling picturesques in their embroidered fur hats, their kilted togas, their tall boots, their matted hair, their gorgeous broadswords. Some, indeed, have an air of almost contrived rakishness, like musical-comedy brigands, with a great jangling display of amulets and charm-boxes and phylacteries. They are a merry enough people. It is their custom to show respectful greeting by sticking out the tongue; a disconcerting matter to begin with. It is also against Tibetan rules to wash at any time between birth and death, a circumstance which tends to make their company oppressive. And day and daily they bring in wool and more wool, the skins and the famous yaks' tails (the big yak-tail market is again the U.S., where they are used – if you can stand any further fantasy – for the manufacture, exclusively, of beards for Santa Clauses). At night they camp, protected by groups of the world's most violent tempered dogs, and drink quarts of their appalling tea, made of Chinese tea-bricks stewed in salt and yak butter. For the machinations of Mao, for the fears of the Government, for the lunatic-gyrations of the outer world they have never seen they could not, one feels persuaded, care less.

So endeth the first lesson for Tibet. For months Peking radio has been announcing the imminent 'liberation of the Tibetan people'. Why the Chinese have not yet plucked the fruit from the tree is no doubt a matter for the inscrutable Chinese. That they will is as certain as anything can be in the East. That may or may not be a matter for regret among the Tibetans. For the world – if it has time to care just now – it is, one supposes, a sort of milestone. The one unique monastic kingdom is pretty evidently on its last legs; it suggests some oblique emotions. It was bad, it was dissolute, it was mediæval and idolatrous and about as democratic as Caligula's Rome, but is one more thing gone, and we shall not see its like again.

Picture Post,
24 February 1951

THE ILLUSTRATED LONDON
NEWS, 1952

The following piece you might think is included as an aberration, but not so. I have never been a zealous enthusiast of the monarchy; the institution has always seemed to me somewhat irrational and pretentious, not to say absurdly expensive. But every time there is a Royal occasion – a birth, marriage, or death – I am in such a minority that I accept that, democratically, I must be wrong.

Such an occasion came in 1952, when George VI died, and was buried in the sort of pomp and ceremony that would have made him, as a man, cringe with embarrassment. Of course I could never claim to know him, but I had been in his company when he had toured South Africa not long before, and I had a powerful impression that he was a good man, and every bit as reluctant to be a King as was I to be a Subject. I mourned his death with true sincerity.

I described his funeral for a magazine that very soon followed him into oblivion. It was a considerable challenge to me, as a journalist, as a citizen, and as a human being. I truly believe that I fulfilled the job in all three respects. Reading it again now, after all those years, I am neither ashamed nor proud of it; I am quite certain that it reflected precisely the mood of the time, and that was what I was employed to do.

*   *   *

THE KING IS DEAD

When a King dies, we, who have to put into words the strange grief and grievous strangeness of the time, then know how ill we have served ourselves over the years. While the King lived we spoke of him as this, and as that, endowing him with all the remote virtues of an infallible man; such men do not die. But the King died; and we found somehow a different thing: that we loved him. When the King dies, the worn words are empty; there is nothing left to say.

He died quietly, and without imposing his passing on the nation, as befitted a gentleman who was shy and considerate and shrank from the public drama of death. When it came, it came as he deserved, kindly – a good night, a book at the bedside, a little sleep. The least among us can ask no more, and no better.

But that was the end of privacy. The King was gone, but Kingship remained, to become for a while the overwhelming emotion of the land. The man who had been diffident all his life, who had dutifully permitted publicity about everything except his suffering, now stilled the noise and hushed the argument and silenced the affairs of State, and drew for the moment an inescapable curtain of mourning over the lives of millions who had never seen his face.

What is a King, that so many strangers should sorrow at his going? His title endures, work goes on, no crisis is changed, no personal problems eased or worsened, the harassed world outside is deflected in no way from its obsessions. Yet when George VI was known to be dead the sudden shadow fell momentarily across the heart of every man; loyal men and cynics, the rich and the dispossessed, reactionaries and radicals.

What is a King, then, a mortal man, who exacts this tribute from twentieth-century people? Constitutional lawyers will tell you what he was. Politicians will tell you what he was unable to be. A vast historic chronicle of precept will tell you that his position was most intricately poised on the peak of Government. It will say that the Monarchy this country devised for itself over the generations is like no other that ever existed, in its ancient root and its modern tolerance; its power without authority; its simple splendour and elaborate simplicity.

Only in a strange country like ours could an apparently indestructible fortress be built on such a slender web of compromise and affection, that no logic could create and no law enforce.

What is a King, therefore, that hundreds of thousands of strangers should wait all night in the bitter cold to file for a moment past his bier? That person cannot be an Office, or a Function; he must be a man. And there lies the simple truth: our people knew him for a good man. They knew him for a man without ostentation, without ambition doing an intolerable job, and doing it well. They know now, moreover, that the job was harder than they thought, and the end nearer.

We may not have known that as citizens – how could we? – but the ancestral memory of England knows it. The people of England have not always loved their Kings. Among them have been tyrants, conquerors, oppressors, imbeciles, and mediocrities. England has endured them, reviled them, deposed them, and, where necessary, executed them. Sometimes, only, have they loved them, and we think of this as such a time.

We never found it hard to understand a man who loved his family.

We do not find it hard, now, to salute a King who, inheriting a generation racked and anxious as no other before, did what he had to do with dignity, patience, and courage.

He, who had planned great voyages over the quarter of the world that owned him King, has done his best, and greatest – from Norfolk to London and from London to Windsor.

For many hours London had been listless and numb, drawing a curtain between this day and other days; not resisting the paralysing chill that seemed somehow to strike simultaneously at the body and the emotions. At the roadside people hunched their shoulders against the gnawing wind; even the policemen beat their gloves together in the empty expressionless streets of the route. Only the sentries, near the end of the journey that had now begun, remained rigid in the graven way of soldiers in exclusive regiments, their eyes buried in their peaks.

From King's Cross to Westminster is a long, slow walk; the gun-carriage would trail its lingering dejection behind it for an hour yet, but far ahead of the advancing silence London paused, slowed, and stopped.

All this we could feel rather than see as we waited in Westminster Hall. Funerals of kings are a deliberate, complex ritual, governed by precise and intricate protocol, day by appointed day; the tradition of State sorrow is not to be lightly changed. It was as though England were not burying a king but proffering once again a strange and somehow indestructible philosophy, as indeed it was.

Here, in this vast stone room, was to be the final formula, the last pause where the King, who by our custom belongs to the people, would remain among those people until the end. It is a grim, grand chamber; eight and a half centuries of English history have soaked through those smooth grey walls since the days of William Rufus. It was already three hundred years old when Richard II gave it the superb hammer-beam roof, scrolling its wooden way ninety feet above the cold flagstones. It is a stark place. For a while, as we waited in the aching cold, it seemed utterly without colour; a monochrome of hard, clean lines; it was as though one were existing in an etching.

Then, halfway down the two hundred paces of the hall, the eye caught the purple of the catafalque and the red of its dais; the four tremendous candlesticks. There, sixteen years ago, a King of England and a man who was to be King had stood and guarded the remains of their father, on just such a winter's day as this. One was now hastening back from America. The other was returning here, without haste, on a gun-carriage.

That was the stage, in every sense dramatically right, full of sombre overtones for the sense and the memory. Gradually the players gathered, and with them the overture to what was a moment of history.

First the King's Bodyguard of the Yeomen of the Guard, in the famous, odd, Tudor uniform that in some inexplicable way does not look ridiculous . . . a sudden red sprang into the composition and gave life to the pallid grey. They took up their stances around the catafalque, reversing that weapon which is not a pike, and not a halberd, but a 'partisan'. Behind them the Gentlemen at Arms, helmets topped with horsehair fountains, the most immense plumes of contemporary uniform.

And at last the two long processions of men who did not walk with precision or military bearing or indeed anything but a despairing sort of unhappy determination – Her Majesty's Lords, and Commons, one side led by the Lord Chancellor, the other by Mr Speaker, robed and bewigged. Across the width of Westminster Hall they faced one another, black-coated, sombre, unidentifiable. One had not imagined there were so many Peers. They lined the west wall many deep, shuffling a little in the cold – renowned and unknown, exalted and obscure, erect and bent, glossy and dishevelled, indistinguishable from the anointed of Democracy across the way. From time to time there would be a prolonged, old-man's cough; no other sound of any kind.

Then in the next moment this dark setting was transformed by something that could have been conceived in the brain of a ballet-designer: Enter the Great Officers of State. A streamlined world has not lost them yet, and so long as Kings are crowned and Kings are buried they will fantastically reappear – the strange titles and archaic functions of Pursuivants, Heralds, and Kings of Arms.

One would have thought them relics, or reproductions at the least – the tabards, the stockings, the brilliant heraldic designs – yet they were so palpably alive, moving through the hall like living court-cards. It was as though someone had abruptly turned on the lights.

It is an indescribable paradox that such a day, casting all London into funeral black, should be the day when the gayest, the most vivid and debonair costumes known should emerge from history and flourish their gay grief among the mourning.

Yet even here the Utility Century came creeping in. The order of march was printed for all to see: Norroy and Ulster King of Arms, Clarenceux King of Arms, Garter King of Arms, the Gentleman Usher of the Black Rod, the Lord Great Chamberlain, the Earl Marshal of England – and centre, between these quaint legacies of chivalry, the Minister of Works. As they paced silently to the door to meet the cortège, in the composition of that group was revealed something of England not easily analysed.

The time was not far off. From outside came the ringing of hooves, the bark of military orders. The pause that followed held an awesome sense of theatre.

Very slowly, with short hobbling steps, the eight huge Guardsmen moved through the door and up to the dais, bearing above them the Imperial Crown on a purple cushion, and below that the Royal Standard, and below that the oak in which lay all that remained of the King of England.

Here was, in fact, the moment of history, and here it was not proper nor yet possible to think of national bereavement, when amongst us now, behind the coffin, were those whose bereavement was real and personal, to be minutely recorded moreover by the camera, to be borne amid a press of work never so exacting as in the moment of loss.

At such a time one hates one's craft that has dwelt for years on fulsome overstatement and banal adulation of such people, so that now when something genuine cries out to be said, there are no words left that have not been debased before.

The Queen was courageous. That we have been told five hundred times, but she *was*. One's father's funeral is an ordeal at any time and for anybody; few people have to watch their father's funeral four times over, in every circumstance of high drama, before many thousand eyes that may be kind, but are also curious.

For two a father, for one a husband, for one a son. It was strange – almost incredible – to see these opaque veiled figures and recognise them for the ladies whose professional uniforms – that they may fulfil their duty and be conspicuous – are light pastels. It was difficult to adjust oneself to the new styles and titles: Queen, Queen Mother. And those who photographed them that day did a strange thing: they found for the first time perhaps in twenty years a picture of the King's widow without a smile.

Queen Mary stood like a figure of fate, like a matriarch – bent, frail, old, walking now with difficulty, but standing there as she stood before.

And the man on the catafalque? How was he to be remembered? We who did not know him, yet in our various professional ways saw much of him, could perhaps think of a quiet man who was greatly loved, in the end; who created in himself the strength for the task, ridden with handicaps, difficulties, inhibitions, mostly bravely and painstakingly overcome.

One remembered him eighteen – twenty? – years ago, as Duke of York, fighting through a Freeman's speech at Inverness. Or on his balcony at Coronation Day. Or craning a neck in the frankest curiosity as the car drove through Washington . . .

To me there is one recollection, and a long way, indeed, from the grey chill of Westminster Hall . . . an evening in South Africa, the White Train berthed on the verge of a broad beach near Port Elizabeth, for the King was to have a bathe. As the sun dipped the police swept down on the sands, opened a wide swathe of beach and roped off a vast crowd into two great halves. By and by a man came over the dunes; down the path from the Royal Train walked a solitary figure in a blue bathrobe, carrying a towel. The sea was a long way off, but he went. And all alone, on the great empty beach, between the surging banks of the people who might not approach, the King of England stepped into the edge of the Indian Ocean and jumped up and down – the loneliest man, at that moment, in the world.

Big Ben struck the quarter. As it did so, with all eyes still on the three Queens, there could be seen by the big door, for those who looked, a slim, tall, unobtrusive man – who again, for those who looked on public occasions, had never been many paces from King George. He was Detective-Superintendent Cameron; for so long his hands and eyes had held responsibility for the King's life. Somewhere there, it seemed certain, was an allegory, but who could say what?

And that was how the King came to lie in state in the capital of his realm.

From the next day on there was seen in the precincts of the Palace of Westminster a sight so extraordinary and unprecedented that many responsible people deduced a strange new trend in national psychology. The public, who were to be admitted into the hall to file past the bier, began to arrive in numbers so astounding that every plan was upset, every traffic arrangement entangled.

By dawn of the first morning many were already there – one man had waited thirteen hours through the bitter night – and the line grew instantly, prodigiously. By the afternoon of the third day 80,000 people were waiting in what was almost certainly the longest queue the world has ever seen. It crossed Lambeth Bridge, moved north to Westminster Bridge, doubled back on itself; the police, alarmed lest the queue begin to snake at random all over London, broke it in two. People were taking taxis from the head to find the end of the queue. The halves joined up, spanning the river, a vast strip of humanity over three miles long, stolidly facing a five-hour wait in the toothed wind.

There was even one preposterous man who, ultimately finding his turn through the hall, emerged, and joined the queue again. There was the depressing vulgarity of the hawkers with their 'Funeral Programmes' and 'Memorial Cards'; happily, practically nobody seemed to buy.

Inside, the hall seemed much as we had left it; the immobile figures at the four corners of the bier were not the same, but might easily have been. But where had been the still rows of Lords and Commons were the quietly, noiselessly moving rows of those who had waited so long, who were now moving past the dais at the rate of five thousand an hour, which was not fast. If they had been chosen as a cross-section of the random, heterogeneous mass of the peoples who called the dead man King, they could not have better looked the part. The old outnumbered the young, the women the men; there were black hats and caps, collars and no collars, cripples, blind men – as though it were a sort of shrine – there were nurses and Negroes and Indians and Asiatics: and as you looked at them in the candlelight you thought of them stretching backwards, out of the hall, over the river, to the far distance: an utterly unbelievable cavalcade that must, somehow, be Monarchy's gesture to all the forces of logic.

On the coffin the white wreath still rested, the widow's wreath to 'Bertie', the same that had been laid on it at Sandringham. The flowers were wilting and frayed, for the wind and the rain had beaten on them a long time, and the King had been seven days dead, and the new Elizabethan Age had begun.

The Illustrated London News,
23 February 1952

NEWS CHRONICLE, 1953–60

My years on the late *News Chronicle* were by far the most stimulating and rewarding of all – not materially rewarding, for the paper was not rich and its proprietor notably mean – but rewarding in variety, cooperation, comradeship, and a certain rather touching integrity. As far as I know I never changed my attitudes or trimmed my sails to accommodate the attitudes of any employer, but on the staff of the old *News Chronicle* it was accepted without question that *nobody* did, nor would be asked to; if he or she did not like being liberal he or she would not be there. We were a coherent and tolerant crowd. That is perhaps why we were done away with.

The pieces selected here – I do not know why journalists insist on calling their stuff 'pieces', when they are in fact little entities, attempting to have beginnings, middles and endings; I suppose 'articles' would be just as meaningless – came as you can see from all over the place – Europe, Asia, Africa. I had always spent much of my time on the road, and in those days travelling was both my pleasure and my education. It was sometimes numbingly fatiguing (no Concorde then, even if we could have afforded it) but how else, I sometimes wondered in tatty hotel bedrooms in tropical nights, could I be having such experience and such fun *and* being paid for it? It is true that the pay evaporated, but the experience endured. Still does, like the residual rays of the setting sun.

Some of these – all right, pieces – are dated, and obviously and properly so, since it is the nature of the reporter's job to define the character of that week, even sometimes that day. The message from Barcelona was, as it turned out, unreasonably pessimistic, but I doubt if any Spaniard would have disagreed with it then, when Franco was officially immortal. The story from Poland in 1956, on the other hand, could almost be used again today, with a bit of subeditorial updating.

Oddly, the most poignant personal memory for me is brought by the story of the Labour Party Conference in Brighton, in 1957, when Aneurin Bevan was forced to make what was certainly the most agonising decision of his life. As putative future Foreign Minister of a Labour government he had to define his attitude to the British Hydrogen Bomb, and he forced himself to conclude that he must accept it, 'writhing on the twin hooks of conscience and expediency'.

For most of the night before Nye Bevan was walked up and down the Brighton seafront by his good friend Vicky, the cartoonist – poor tormented Vicky, the little emigré genius who loved Nye Bevan as much as he loathed atom-bombs, as did I – and by me, imploring Nye not to commit this terrible apostasy. All three of us were almost in tears.

The next day Aneurin Bevan made his sad and memorable speech. He would accept the Bomb. 'I cannot,' he said, 'go naked into the conference chamber.'

The next day Vicky published his cartoon. It was a simple drawing of Mahatma Gandhi, on the floor in his dhoti. The caption only said: '*I went naked into the conference chamber.*'

And I wrote the article that you have here. It was the saddest I ever wrote, and the one most needful of remembrance, or so I feel today.

There was a brief postscript. That evening Nye Bevan came up to Vicky and me, sitting together in the hotel. He said, very softly and sadly: 'Boys, I shall never speak to you again.'

And he never did. Not long after, Nye was dead, through illness. And Vicky was dead, by suicide.

I must be the only one who remembers that.

*   *   *

THUMBPRINT AMONG THE MULGA TREES

We in Australia are today suffering the slightly sour post-atomic hangover that usually seems to follow the mushrooms.

The great Emu explosion is over; it did *not* bring about the end of the world, and already there is the familiar tendency to write it off as a disappointing something not fully understood.

Of the effects and results of this most highly important experiment not one word may be officially said.

The experiment had indeed been an unconscionable time arriving, through some freakish refusal of the upper winds to blow from the south-east quarter that would carry the dangerous fission products out of harm's way for the Australian cities.

But when the final moments ticked off on that enormous empty plain the tension was hard to resist, since even the world's fiftieth atom bomb is a visitation of the abnormal and a moment of personal drama for anyone who sees it.

The count down through the loudspeaker emptied the seconds away in the thin precise and very English tones of some disembodied scientist.

He said it in a detached, metallic way '4–3–2–1–zero' and then he had no need to say more, because the sky caught fire. The welder's goggles we wore changed the landscape to a bleak coppery green.

On the edge of the horizon, where the thing stood on its tower fifteen miles away, the fireball turned it momentarily to gold, and flung a brief wave of brilliance over the entire sky.

In that first fine edge of a second it was a pin-point crucible, a glowing spheroid full of forces that strained and split it in a perfectly visible haze of shockwave.

It is in the nature of things that expectancy does not endure so long without anti-climax; perhaps it was not as awful as we had thought.

I have seen three atom bombs explode and in each case there has been the same sort of acceleration of perception; in that first subdivided second you seem to see the gradual maturing of an instantaneous thing.

It was not hard to believe that this grim business had produced the heat of a million degrees centigrade, ten times that of the unscientific sun, and that this was the Penney-packaged version of 20,000 tons of T.N.T.

Then the flash was gone, and the cloud fingered its way upwards, bellied out as it struck the cushion of the upper air, insisted on another upward movement as some new impulse possessed it.

It stood over the desert like a grotesque tree and for a while, until the winds seized it and distorted it and sent it into a random shape there was an unwilling monstrous quality of grace about it.

So far the whole performance had held one especial aspect of fantasy; its utter silence.

It seemed that this gigantic release of forces produced no vestige of sound; even as we relaxed and studied the growth of the column the noise was surging towards us until – fifty-seven seconds later by my quite unofficial count – it arrived.

An abrupt and violent crack, a suggestion of blast, and a rumbling that crawled away and was lost in the plains.

Perhaps it was not a very big noise.

Perhaps the sound of a 25-pounder gun at a quarter of a mile would have been as menacing.

Perhaps, as I remember thinking almost ruefully at Bikini seven years ago, however long you wait for the stage revolver shot it is always less alarming than you expect.

But it was enough; it would serve.

When, a little later, we flew over the place where it had all happened there was little of any note at all to the unexpert mind – a great and horrible black scar on the face of the claypan, a circular burn, a quarter-mile in diameter with a pattern of blast extending all around.

No tower, no wreckage, only a great stark black thumbprint among the mulga trees and the saltbush.

But it was remarked that most of the scrub outside the zero mark appeared to be standing, and the guinea-pig, Mustang aircraft parked less than a mile away to receive the blast, appeared generally intact.

The site of the explosion is not to be revealed. It was somewhere in the abandoned hinterland to the far north-west of Adelaide.

We flew there through the night from Mallala to Woomera, from Woomera on for another two and a half hours, but what was happening underneath was none of our affair and the plane was sealed with long canvas screens obliterating every window – bar that, one hoped, of the pilot.

Before dawn we came down on what is known as Emu, an isolated airstrip in another of Australia's extraordinary landscapes – a flat emptiness of red clay dotted with saltbush and spinifex and the crimson-berried quondong tree, all the gnarled and persevering scrubs that somehow suck a living out of this thirsty land.

And it was here that we found our grandstand on a gritty little knoll to watch what was – it was repeatedly emphasised – not a bomb but a WEAPON.

It was just visible through binoculars on the far horizon, or rather its tower was, a remote and meaningless thing, with another not far away presumably an instrumentation point.

There was a feeling, from the complete invisibility of the large Boffin population that have been inhabiting the site, that this was the moment when the scientists had been handed over to their own machinery.

All around this wilderness they had planted their mechanical eyes and ears and memories, their instruments to record blast and heat-flash and contamination and gamma-ray flash, cameras capable of operating at the rate of one hundred thousand pictures a second.

Everywhere there would be some device to determine in the most scrupulous detail what happens when one explodes an atom bomb in a desert – a thing which in the last analysis can be established in one way only: by exploding an atom bomb in a desert.

Somewhere perhaps there might be a few imponderables in the way of moral issues, less clearly illuminated by a nuclear flash.

A makeshift loudspeaker system on the knoll announced itself in the voice of a schoolmaster who felt satisfied that he had a popular subject and would not therefore make things too difficult.

Each preparatory phase of this operation coded as X200 had been given the name of an Australian creature; there had been daps, dingo, emu, koala and kookaburra – 'You will I trust, forgive any mispronunciations,' said the voice graciously.

At the moment just after six, as the sun peered over the landscape, we were in Phase Opossum, when balloon ascents were being made to ensure that those perverse and pesky upper winds were not about to pull another fast one.

At 6.15 we went into Phase Platypus (the unshakable insistence of experts and military men on devising whimsical code names for perfectly easily numbered things is one of their more endearing characteristics).

Platypus meant they were evacuating the forward tower area. The final detonation is accomplished by an intricate series of links: the last man out carries the final link in the circuit himself, so that no straggler demented enough to linger around the bomb is accidentally atomised.

At 6.27 we merged into Phase Wombat, the checking of the instrumentation for the umpteenth hundredth and, they hoped, the last time.

We hung around in the growing day performing the inevitable rite of Anglo-Saxons at moments of crisis: drinking cups of tea.

Somewhere in this endless neighbourhood was Sir William Penney; one visualised him pacing the floor outside the overgrown delivery ward – almost certainly wrongly.

Somewhere here, too, were the shy and inscrutable family of 'ologists', as elusive as wallabies; the force of 180 troops under Brigadier Lucas; the splendid body of Corps of Ministerial Nursemaids, the Security Section, with whom our lives of late have been so jovially and intimately bound.

The chanted count-down changed from minutes to half-minutes and half-minutes to seconds. Precisely on the zero of seven it happened, the bullets face to face, the charges of plutonium on the edge of their disastrous embrace, the critical mass, a mass of banal metaphors culminating in this stunning flash.

Unfortunately, the sun was in a bad position to illumine the column effectively or perhaps the composition of the claypan was to blame; I recall the first Bikini bomb as a sculptured obelisk of white shot through with streaks of pink, a colossal raspberry icecream, this column was a dirty brown, somehow dripping a little curtain of vaporous grey at one side.

Very soon the winds at varying levels twisted the conventional mushroom into a heavily leaning tower, and into a shapeless spiral, and by and by it was gone, all but the pretty wisp of cloud that must now be tracked and charted and shadowed until the half life of its lethal radioactive particles has decayed.

We may, moreover, be sure that Sir William Penney's brigade will not be the only 'interested parties' (as they are demurely named officially) whose curious tentacles will be groping around the upper air looking for a smell of it.

Soon there was nothing left. And then came the realisation of the enormity not of the bomb, but of the desert, the vast, expressionless plain that, as the Pacific had done before, can take an atom bomb, accept it, and forget it while we look on.

There will almost certainly be a measure of disappointment over our X200; it did not, after all, blow a hole through Australia; the first guess that it might be heard for 200 miles is almost certainly exaggerated; no one was even jarred, as far as I know nothing has dropped off any of us.

Just as the city of Honolulu protested in fear at the Bikini test and then groused when there *wasn't* a tidal wave, so Adelaide and Melbourne may well feel cheated that nobody had to duck.

It is true that within ten minutes of the explosion the first exploratory parties in protective clothes were examining the zero point around that ghastly blackened scar.

Atom bombs, it is clear, do not damage deserts. It is equally clear that atom bombs are unlikely ever to be dropped on deserts, while there are houses and nurseries and factories and hospitals within simpler reach.

And that while we are at this moment flying south from the site suffering from not much worse than the hangover of a sleepless night, if that clay-pan were a village it would now be peopled with either corpses or maniacs.

It was, as they said, a long way to come for a loud noise. We are going home; we have seen our bomb; already we are thinking of something else, and that is perhaps the worst thing of all.

News Chronicle,
16 October 1953

HUNGER IS THE BIG PERSUADER

In the tangle of lamp-lit alleys behind the Ramblas life went on all night. On the corner a man was roasting a chicken on the kerbside spit, his feet comfortable on a dead cat.

Someone was thumbing a rough guitar phrase in the shadows; a blind man sold lottery tickets, calling 'Tomorrow is the day!'

The *vigilante* watchman thumped his staff and cried the hour: three in the morning, and all was well.

Yet the last time I was in Barcelona – almost to a week three years ago – an armed truck barred that corner and rifles covered the street; the jails were full and the Civic Guards fingered their guns everywhere among the scowls and shouting.

That was the time of the big Barcelona strike, the nearest thing the regime ever saw to a revolt. And even then the poor people were rebelling against hunger, not politics; the mob desperately shouting: 'Viva Franco!' like a nightmare, even as the shots rang out.

If today that armour-plated regime seems even more unshakably in power it is not just the guns and the jackboots that do it; that chicken on the spit was part of the deal.

Spain is still a land of bitter, grinding poverty among the flesh-pots. There is prodigious eating in the Parellada and Amaya, and much quiet unostentatious starving in the backalleys; the harrowing contrasts are as strident as ever.

But today Spain is no longer the desert island of Europe, Spain has the American grant and the U.S. bases; at last her flagging economy is getting the vital transfusion of dollars it has been promised so long. Franco has been riding a thin horse for three years against this very day; now is the moment of truth.

It was not an easy thing for this proud and dignified country, anyway, to abandon an historic neutralism for a hand-out, however ample. So many Spaniards said to me: Let us wait, and see what the dollars buy.

'A few more Packards for the Ministries,' said a cynic, 'one or two more half-finished skyscrapers and half-built roads. A few more pesetas in the barracks and a few more Chesterfields on the market. *We* shall continue to live on bread and oil.'

'In which case,' said a cynic of another sort (for there are indeed some 25 million of them in Spain), 'the Government has nothing to fear. Give Franco the means of providing cheap bread and cheap oil, and he need not worry for the rest of his life.'

Yet there are serious people who hold the contrary: that it requires only a small rise in the standard of living to give Franco's enemies just that extra physical strength and spiritual endurance to become again dangerous. Political resistance is very much a matter of calories: the dictator's dilemma.

But is there a 'Left' in Spain – and, if so, would one know? Barcelona – traditionally Catalan and individualist, traditionally distrustful of Castilian authority – could always be the flashpoint in what the Caudillo calls his Oasis of Ordered Peace.

Oasis of Ordered Peace or not, Franco must consider that at least fifty-one per cent of it is against him, or he would have risked at least one election.

Where is that fifty-one per cent? It is nearly impossible for a British person to find out; Britain has few friends in Spain. The Radicals feel that Britain let them down in 1936; the Francoists resent the years of boycott and contempt – and there is always Gibraltar.

All one can *see* is an apparently integrated oligarchy of State, Church, and Army, with the various stresses among them making the only political activity. From time to time, to be sure, someone goes to jail – in bizarre combinations; Anarchists and Monarchists mysteriously united in forlorn-hope undergrounds.

Franco would seem to take them all in his stride. He knows that his opposition is distorted by factions and feuds among its leaders, discouraged by apathy from abroad, bewildered by endless agents-provocateurs – above all, vitiated by the terrible memories of the Civil War.

But the Civil War has gone into history. 'There is still scarcely a family in all Spain that cannot count its dead,' I was told, 'but now those that mourn them are going too.'

There are therefore grown men today whose minds are not still numbed by those memories. But Spain has come now to that worst evil of long dictatorships: the loss of all political experience. I have spoken to nobody inside Spain who has any real understanding of how an opposition works, nor any faith in such an opposition's chances.

Franco, having no middle-class to worry about, knows that his workers are more concerned with keeping alive than overthrowing *him*. Since he reached power industrialists have been compelled to pay six times as much for 'welfare dues' as they did in 1936.

Everyone says – if not Franco, what? A Spanish Communism seems barbaric and paradoxical. A Spanish democracy – born of what, in a country that for sixteen years has had no free Press, no free unions, no elections, no freedom of worship or expression at all?

The biggest Spanish tradition of all is of bad government. It is not unreasonable to say that never has Spain been governed either democratically or efficiently.

Could it not be – I was told over and over – that the aloof Spanish philosophy answers it all: wealth, security, politics are fundamentally unimportant, what are important are courage, faith and grace. It colours every attitude, and even in the most ghastly slums and shanty towns around Barcelona it somehow manages to exist – superb, and sad.

The dollars will save Franco – but in the end it will be the Spaniards who save Spain.

News Chronicle,
3 March 1954

WHO IS TO BLAME FOR MAU MAU?

Some twenty months ago a new word broke abruptly and painfully into everyone's consciousness – a word with every undertone of horror and despair, yet for which to this day no one has ever found a meaning.

The word was Mau Mau. The agony it represents continues, at a terrible cost in money, life and human conscience. On the bitter misery of Kenya today has crystallised sometimes the best but far more often the worst of white-and-black relations; barbarism meets ruthlessness; atrocity begets atrocity; on both sides reason is lost in vengeance; nor is the end even in sight.

By now most people's conception of Mau Mau has hardened into various kinds of hopeless half-truth, writing it off as seditious gangsterism, nationalist martyrdom, or just orgiastic blasphemy. The name itself is, as it has always been, meaningless.

Only in the *Manchester Guardian*, over the weeks, have experts continued to debate the insoluble problem: *is* Mau Mau our fault? Or has Nature suddenly and incomprehensibly reversed the evolutionary pattern and produced in the Kikuyu tribe a race *deliberately* collapsing into magic and evil?

For anyone who has spent any time in that sad Kenyan climate of frustration and fear, any argument that takes the thing out of the machine-gun and cut-throat routine is something. Only the *Guardian* could so spaciously investigate Mau Mau as something not necessarily to be solved by the gun and the gallows.

It was Dr Max Gluckman, Professor of Social Anthropology in the University of Manchester, who produced the thesis that Mau Mau is not really African at all – that is, the complex bestiality of the oath is not a reversion to primitive savagery but a degeneration *from* it – and that part of the cause is an unhappy contact with the European. Or: Mau Mau is a result of colonialism.

There was a vigorous denial from Sir Philip Mitchell – a most distinguished ex-Governor of Kenya – who insists that since colonisation is beneficial and Settlers mainly good men, Mau Mau must spring from something basically horrible in the Kikuyu.

Both these writers are great and sincere authorities; by oversimplifying their arguments we are dodging a lot of sound technical reasoning. Once again it sounds like the pro-white Settler v the pro-African intellectual. The dreary fact is that this is pretty solidly the case.

There are two dilemmas:

(a) Without describing the intricate obscenities of Mau Mau ritual it is impossible to convey its abysmal nastiness; yet these details are genuinely impossible to print publicly, however objectively.

(b) A dispassionate account of some of the legal methods of repression used against the Kikuyu read like violent anti-European propaganda. It is a straight case of emotion wrecking everything – sense, decency, logic, and, for one lovely country, almost hope itself.

Professor Gluckman is a Freudian, and sees the Kenya horror in terms of men's minds; Sir Philip is a Civil Servant and sees it in terms of the Law.

To the anthropologist there *must* be some new and awful impact on a tribe to force it into bestial atavism. To the ex-Governor that impact has nothing to do with the fact that the Kikuyu have turned their clock back, maybe for ever.

Yet there are hundreds of Kikuyu who ask no more than to be rid of Mau Mau, of which they themselves are far and away the greatest victims – thousands of Africans killed against fewer than thirty whites.

There are equally European Kenyans whose hearts have been broken by the collapse of all their values of loyalty to both races. They will agree with neither the Professor nor the Governor, believing somehow that just as all Settlers are not monsters, so are all Kikuyu not animals.

Yesterday the *Guardian* ran yet another comment, from Londiani in Kenya. There, it seemed, the local Mau Mau leader was a Kikuyu with an annual income of £2,000, tax-free. His chief opponent among the anti-Mau Mau Kikuyu is a poorly-paid charcoal burner and lay reader of the Church of Scotland.

This is adduced to show that 'privilege' has nothing to do with racism – which is exactly what *both* the Professor and the Governor say.

Very soon the Kenya emergency will be two years old. During that time all the resources of the European – his guns and jails and bombers – have made only momentary imprints on the ill-armed Mau Mau. Therefore force is not the answer.

During that time increasingly more and more Africans have turned against their fellow-Africans. Therefore race is not the answer.

Somewhere that gruesome gulf between men's minds – which broadens daily – has to be bridged. Now, for the first time, Kenya has the makings of an inter-racial 'Cabinet'. On the heads of men like Michael Blundell and Benaiah Ohanga, spokesmen of their people and their colour, rests the *necessity* of making Kenya the home not only of the brutish Kikuyu and the vengeful Settler, but of six million human beings.

News Chronicle,
4 June 1954

HOW LONG CAN THEY WALK THE TIGHTROPE?

Hungary's hope lies dying in its brave and tragic ashes, lost in the international delirium, the great moment of Western history gone shamefully to dust.

No one can study everything at once; from London it might almost seem that the sudden flame of European freedom flickered out.

But what happened to the greater nation still, where indeed it all began – to Poland, her own half-revolution overwhelmed by a month of melodrama?

So much has happened and so fast, it is hard to remember that it is only twenty-six days since it all began – since Khrushchev and Kaganovich hastened to Warsaw, with the biggest Soviet entourage ever to leave Moscow since the days of Potsdam, to stop the leak already apparent in Poland.

While it lasted it was itself tremendous: the Poles had their way; they restored the discredited Wladyslaw Gomulka; they defied Russia's tool, Marshal Rokossovski.

Poland stirred, but Hungary fought. Hungary died, but Poland continued.

Yesterday the stirring began again. The Polish Politburo decided to dismiss from the Party's Central Committee Wiktor Klosiewicz, who is a Khrushchev man – a man of the pro-Soviet 'Natolin' group, an associate of the fired Rokossovski.

There is a tale behind that, too.

Mr Klosiewicz had demanded that the Government should dispel rumours that he had been conspiring against Gomulka.

This, said the Politburo in its strange and exclusive jargon, was designed to cause 'disorientation and confusion' – as well it might, when one reviews what happened.

The Polish revolt, unlike the Hungarian, was orthodox, devious, doctrinaire, conspiratorial. Rokossovski had ordered a coup; the arrest of 700 Gomulka men.

Things began to move like a Hitchcock thriller: the orders fell into the hands of the secret police chief Komar, who was faithful to Gomulka.

The workers of the Zeran car factory were mobilised – and every one of the 700 people was warned not to spend that night at home.

Every one escaped.

That was the end of Rokossovski: he went 'on leave' and has not returned.

Poland's destiny seemed, quite suddenly, changed to a new course.

Israel invaded Sinai. Britain and France invaded Egypt. Russia invaded Hungary. This was saturation-point for news, if ever there was one.

Poland faded out. For two and a half weeks we have heard virtually nothing from the State which – first at Poznan, then in Warsaw – rebelled against the Kremlin.

In circumstances of such foreboding there can be no state of suspended animation. The Soviet system does not accommodate fence-sitters. How long, then, can Poland walk the tightrope between two worlds?

There seems to be no sign yet that the abominable punishment wreaked on Budapest has scared the Poles.

They have, on the contrary, continued to print articles on democratisation and freedom: by reflex action they continue to use tortuous phrases – 'Down with conservatism and pusillanimity,' they say, 'and compulsive adherence to obsolete doctrine' . . . but they mean: Down with Russian overlordship.

We are now in the age of the finest paradox, when 'Conservatism' means 'Stalinism'.

But now Gomulka goes to Moscow. Gomulka the heretic, Gomulka ousted seven years ago for Titoism – but still a Gomulka who yet proclaims: 'Socialism cannot be built in Poland without the Soviet Union.'

Poland cannot yet be equated with Hungary.

They are both old and proud nations, both still full of memories of curious and peculiar patriotic and religious allegiances.

Both have shown signs of being puppets who turned into people.

Both in their widely different ways announce the renaissance of human personality behind the bars.

But the Polish movement against Soviet domination was led, and controlled throughout, by Polish Communists; until now its argument has been the dialectic, not the gun.

Hungary revolted against Soviet Communism itself. Hungary's own past was against her. Hungary had already killed off her Titoists.

When the time came the Poles could produce their Wladyslaw Gomulka from the shadows, active and alive; the Hungarians could produce only the poor exhumed corpse of their Laszlo Rajk.

And when the time came the Soviet could parley with the Poles; Hungary they rolled over and crushed as the old Russia did in 1849.

When Nikita Khrushchev wrapped himself in the bloody mantle of the Czars he broke Hungary, he broke the little communist parties over the western world, and he broke the hearts of many honest men who had trusted a little too far, a little too long.

Poland today, however, is juggling with liberal concessions on the edge of the abyss.

It is probable that Parliament is about to embody the Security Police into the Ministry of the Interior which would mean the virtual disappearance of the 'U.B.', the secret organisation.

Yesterday Rokossovski formally lost his job as Minister of Defence. Klosiewicz is going; the Stalinists diminish.

And yesterday it was reported from West Germany that forty Soviet armoured divisions were moving to the Polish border.

Wladyslaw Gomulka, symbol of the new day, will have to talk hard and quickly in the Kremlin. When he returned from obscurity (less than a month ago; how much has happened since!) he said, among other things: 'One cannot plan human consciousness.'

That we have seen; that we may yet see.

News Chronicle,
14 November 1956

AT NOON NYE BEVAN HEARD THE JEERS OF THE LEFT

By now the fierce television lights that beat all day on the Labour Party Executive have become so oppressive that all the Socialist leaders have taken to thick black spectacles. They stare out sightlessly at the rank and file down on the ice-rink floor, eyeless in Brighton.

The party hierarchy has found the unity of which it endlessly talks; one could almost call it the unity of the mask.

This is my first Labour Party conference; after many years observing the political antics of foreigners I have had the chance to see our own.

It is a spectacle full of sad surprises.

It was, perhaps, a sort of privilege to see for oneself the Labour Party enthusiastically rejecting – presumably for ever – what I had always taken to be its fundamental principle: the nationalisation of the means of production, distribution and exchange.

It was, perhaps, an historic day when Labour decided that its own funds and energies can best be spent in buttressing and supporting the capitalist system it deplores.

It was, perhaps, instructive to see that, while most of the arguments were against the Executive's strange and obscure declaration of policy, one of the modifications of conference democracy is that the block-busting union votes of Messrs Cousins, Carron and Cook could steamroller it through by three to one.

All this was important to observe. What one had not expected was that the Socialists should so triumphantly acclaim the destruction of the first article of their creed.

But the climactic privilege was reserved for today, when one was there to watch the metamorphosis of a great man, the very moment of transformation.

At noon today the star of Aneurin Bevan skipped in its course, the new man took over formally from the old, and at least one aspect of politics can never be quite the same again.

This finally defines the words 'agonising reappraisal' – Aneurin Bevan insisting on the hydrogen bomb; writhing on the twin hooks of conscience and expediency, passionately defending the American alliance; Aneurin Bevan, his face vermilion, hearing for the first time the jeers of the Left, producing what one had not expected from Bevan: Casuistry. And, of course, triumphantly, if that is what triumph is.

'I knew that today I was going to hurt my friends,' said Bevan. And he did.

'If we abandon the bomb, we contract out of all our alliances,' he said. 'That isn't statesmanship. It is an emotional spasm.'

Something like an emotional spasm did in fact go through that stark, crowded arena at these words.

The argument – that the H-Bomb is evil but that nevertheless we must retain it 'to save polarising the world' – is indeed an argument, or could be from someone else who had not in the past said so many other and different things.

From Aneurin Bevan it sounded to many people today like apostasy. I suppose it was only politics. Does the door of the Foreign Office look so soon ajar?

All week we have been enjoying a series of curious illusions in Brighton, of which the most beguiling has been that we are on the verge of a transfer of power, that Mr Gaitskell's foot is already on the threshold of No. 10, that the penetrating air of compromise over the conference is an immediate tactic, and that when Mr Gaitskell sets his sights on 'the ordinary decent people who do not think much about politics,' as he said, he is thinking of tomorrow, or at least the day after.

This has given great buoyancy to Brighton which is a pretty town between the subtopian stretches, though permeated everywhere by an inescapable reek of frying fish. (When the Tories come next week will it smell of port and pheasant?)

'We call ourselves democratic Socialists,' said Mr Bevan at the Tribune meeting. 'It's a new term. What does it mean?' What, indeed, we asked ourselves, basking in the Indian summer on the promenade, wrangling in the lobbies, commuting up and down the Brighton line.

'It means,' said Mr Bevan, 'active co-operation between the people and the Government.' It sounded oracular, but it didn't seem to get us much farther.

'We have our differences in the party,' he said. 'But we mustn't conduct them openly.'

Beside him Michael Foot sat pale and muted. Who are the Bevanites now, and what do they do, and where do they go?

Of course it was not all apocalyptic; even destiny falters a bit in Brighton.

Very soon we used up all the standard jokes about having the conference in an ice rink (cold feet, hot air, thin ice, the fact that the National Executive was perched on a stand over the 'sin-bin', to which defaulting ice hockey players are banished), and it was a pity when these feeble jests were exhausted, because after that there was not much to do except listen to the debates.

And it must be said that these were awful. I am personally a simple peasant in this context, but even I was numbed by the flood of anæsthetic oratory, the relentless march of the worn-out phrase and the cliché rubbed smooth by years of indefatigable use.

There were exhilarating exceptions – Manny Shinwell, who bitterly 'hoped he was not going to be expelled from the Labour Party by talking like a Socialist': Jim Campbell, who said: 'I belong to the Old Guard, but they won't send *me* to manage a hydro-electric plant in the

North of Scotland'; Harold Davies, Frank Cousins, Dick Crossman, Jennie Lee, Nye Bevan himself – people who at least suggested that they had given ten minutes previous consideration to their speeches.

But mostly it was the emotive stuff that should have been the blood of life, yet clothed in wordy periods almost too drab to be endured, while from the councils of state on the tribune came the quiet rasping sound of axes being ground, the gentle sigh of knives being delicately inserted into backs.

And faint and far away, the troubled whisper of Keir Hardie turning in his grave.

News Chronicle,
4 October 1957

THE GOD INCARNATE REACHES HAPPY VALLEY – BUT WHERE NEXT?

The great flight from Shangri-La finished today in a business man's villa with a potted plant in the front window. As far as the Dalai Lama is concerned the story is over now, the journey finished, the exile established.

The all-knowing and all-powerful joins the handful of refugee monarchs adrift round the health resorts as the jetsam of a changing world.

The exodus began on mule-back and continued in a jeep.

This morning it ended in a black Dodge convertible, snaking up from Dehra Dun Station, round the two hundred hairpin bends to the middle-class hill station of Mussoorie, which has juke boxes in the cafés and groves of deodars.

There in the place known as Happy Valley is the house of Mr Birla the Industrialist, a tidy property in the style of a stockbroker's villa in Sussex.

There is the new enthronement of Vice-Regent of Buddha on Earth, a suite on the top floor (since Divine protocol endures, and even in these reduced circumstances none may live above the Dalai Lama).

Into this curiously suburban atmosphere this morning arrived the PRESENCE, still in his very travel-worn rust-coloured robe, still beaming behind his spectacles and crew-cut, still looking much more like a successful Rhodes scholar than the fourteenth reincarnation of a god.

And still surrounded by his marvellous supporting cast of wild and wonderful men with braided hair and daggers – abbots and chamberlains and counsellors and transcendental legmen in various degrees of immortality.

'DALAI LAMA ZINDABAD!' chanted the rather sketchy crowd assembled to greet him today, but by and by everyone drifted back to work.

This has gone on too long; anticlimax hangs in the air.

The big drama is yet to come, and not in Mussoorie.

What's now needed is a sense of proportion.

Of all troubled states in the world today Tibet was, until now, internationally the least full of meaning.

The crushing of this peculiar system of archaic theocracy is a bitter spectacle just because it was so brutally unnecessary.

I think this is the first really damaging error the Peking Government has committed in Eastern eyes.

It now seems inescapable that China is prepared to risk almost a hundred per cent disapproval of her drastic pacification of Tibet for grimly practical reasons.

Her relations with Tibet have always been a long chain of conflict, but only now have these empty lands of China's outskirts been in any way necessary for the increasing millions of China.

The 'autonomy' guaranteed by their occupation treaty of 1954 was just for the books; what they needed was integration.

That meant communications.

What mattered to Peking was not that the Dalai Lama and his uncountable priestly aides and landlords were running their country by a picturesque system of demonology and the donging of temple bells, but that, in the last few years, the railheads of Lanchow, in Kansu Province, and Chengtu, in Szechuan, have been connected with Lhasa by the 1,300-mile long Tibet–Tsinghai road, and the Tibet–Sikiang road, finished four years ago.

What mattered, too, was that the tenuous track from Tibet to India, linking Lhasa with Kalimpong, is now reconstructed up to Phari on the Indian border for truck transport.

What also matters is that the planes are on the move even here.

For the first time in all its centuries, Tibet is not a forbidden country but a buffer State.

And finally, of greatest moment of all, is the fact that India and China, still slightly mesmerised by the last few years of 'indissoluble peaceful co-operation', are now inescapably rivals and now have a common frontier of 1,600 miles.

What is passing through the mind of the twenty-four-year-old Only Undefiled no one can possibly guess.

Not impossibly a piquant thought has occurred to him: that the tragedy that has befallen him, has, perhaps, saved his life. The succession of Dalai Lamaism, being not hereditary but by divination, has always been a complex business, and the search for the body which the Holy Spirit has chosen for habitation was the affair of the chutukus, the greater abbots and cardinals of the State.

It frequently took years, producing long and profitable regencies in which the whole bizarre system could be manipulated one way or another.

The transmigration of a Dalai Lama did no one any harm, except, perhaps, itself.

The fact is that of the fourteen incarnations of the Dalai Lama, all but three (including this one) have died before they reached their majority, all generations but three have perished in their early teens.

This Lama, this young tenant of Birla House, is presumably safe from the mischances that befell his earlier frames.

For should the Dalai Lama die in Mussoorie, here in Uttar Pradesh, how could his successor be divined?

How could the exiled oracles detect the new *Nirvana-Khaya*, the apparitional body with the sacred marks, who will be by then presumably living in some difficult Chinese commune and studying not Tantric mysticism but the ABC of Marxist Leninism?

It may therefore be – and this is generally considered here as almost inevitable – that we have seen today the last Dalai Lama of Tibet.

Even so, his presence here has so immeasurably complicated the whole Asian political scene that the effects will build up for a long time to come, and to an end we do not know.

News Chronicle,
22 April 1959

BATS IN MY BAGGAGE or WHY I CAN'T DO THE CHA-CHA-CHA

I am for ever impressed by the memoirs of those true adventurers who, caught up in moments of international drama, are able to recall the *big* things. My own recollections tend to be slighter and less cosmic, usually involving something vaguely inglorious.

I remember briefly liberating North Korea, for example, mainly because I was seasick at the landing, which could explain the impermanence of that victory.

The drama of Cyprus only came to life for me when I was chased round the Nicosia moat by two hundred furious teenage girls with carving knives.

I think of the last Summit conference only as the time when I set my bed on fire at Geneva. I am a lousy historian.

Thus I recall the last days of Saigon only in terms of bats. I refer to the winged mammals of the order Cheiroptera, not to the instruments used, I think, at Lord's. My bats hate people.

This tale has already gone into the folklore of South-East Asia, but it might as well be straightened out for the record.

In May 1955, you recall, the Indo-China War had been officially over for ten months, since Geneva, but you would hardly have thought so in Saigon. This pleasant city was still in the throes of a very bitter little secondary war, between the official army and a big private outfit called the Binh Xuyen, supported by the French.

I do not want to revive old complications, but that is the way things were: the American nominee, Premier Ngo Dinh Diem, ran the Government (as indeed he still does), but the Binh Xuyen ran everything else, including the police.

It was an intricate business politically, but my personal concern was mainly that they were burning the city down all around me, and that I was spending too much time being shot at impartially, and I was deeply weary of this nonsensical pursuit.

Anyhow, came the day for me to pull out, and I returned late at night to the truckle-bed I had hired in a small hotel in the Rue Catinat.

It was indescribably hot; I was immensely tired; I had to catch an early plane. I made up my baggage, ordered a thé-complet for dawn, opened the window and lay down under the pounding fan.

I awoke with first light, rolled out of bed and put my foot on a corpse. It squelched slightly, with a crepitation of collapsing bones.

Recoiling, I found I had stepped on a bat. This was the first time in my life that I had ever got out of bed and stepped on a bat. For others the experience may be commonplace enough; I found it horrifying.

Worse, however, was to come, because on the floor a few feet away I saw another bat. Nearby, yet another. And then – you must believe me – still another.

Nor was it yet complete; squatting there like some haunted thing out of Edgar Allan Poe I saw the floor was *littered* with bats, some dead, some only dying; each in its little pool of evil blood.

The normally robust, well-adjusted correspondent would doubtless have shrugged this off as one of the simple hazards of the craft. ('Bats, my dear fellow? I thought you said *Japs*.')

To me it was numbingly gruesome; to me bats are other-worldly things beyond definition, and I have lived enough in the East to have absorbed too many of its unreasonable superstitions.

I then recalled that it was Friday, the thirteenth of May, and that I had to catch some insecure aircraft to Singapore in an hour.

While I slammed up my valise, averting my eyes from the carnage all around, I rationalised the affair; of course, the flight of bats had swarmed in through the open window and flown into the whirling fan. (Another illusion gone: I had always understood that bats had some magical radar sensory gadget that preserved them from collisions. Untrue.) Perhaps, tired of life under Premier Diem, they had committed suicide. Anyhow, the fan had got them.

To my great surprise I arrived safely in Singapore. Back in the Cockpit Hotel I flung myself under the shower, changed, exorcised the nightmare. Then, half-dressed, I put my foot into my shoe and was bitten on the toe by a bat.

If I were to say that at this point I nearly had a terminal thrombosis I would be putting it too high; I nevertheless thought my time had come. My foot was bleeding from a bat-bite, though the bat to be sure had gone to its fathers.

And then as I glanced at my suitcase a bat flew out of it. Flew up, dazed and angry, made a tight circuit of the ceiling and flapped out into the sunlight of Oxley Rise.

But now I knew what it felt like to be the doomed central character of a Graham Greene novel. Here was the reward for all my shortcomings, minor sins, infidelities, lateness with copy, unearned self-indulgences: I was haunted by Indo-Chinese bats.

The answer was, I dare say, simple enough; when the squadron of bats had hit the fan in the Rue Catinat in Saigon most had fallen to the floor, but some, only winged, had fallen into my open valise, nursing their shock in my apparel; stowaways to Singapore.

What, I wondered, would have happened if the Customs officer had opened my case, and released a cloud of alien bats into the colonial sanctuary? What intricate quarantine regulation would I have infringed? *Where would I be today?*

That evening I had an engagement to dine at Prince's with an old school friend called Miss Chong. She had undertaken to teach me how to dance the cha-cha-cha. I arrived limping slightly. I said: 'I have been bitten by a bat. In Saigon. In the civil war.'

She said, 'What a misfortune,' civilly enough, but she began to look at me narrowly, and by and by she went home with an officer from the Commissioner-General's office.

When they tell this story in Raffles Bar now they embroider it in a very damaging way. I present the authorised version only to explain how it is I never learned how to dance the cha-cha-cha.

News Chronicle,
10 August 1959

THE SMILE ON THE FACE OF THAT LAOTIAN WIZARD

Every so often the wheel goes full circle and this, we say, is where we came in.

It chances that the first story I ever sent to this newspaper from foreign parts was from the Kingdom of Laos, Land of Ten Thousand Elephants and the Golden Umbrella – then, as again now, at war with itself.

It came to pass, then, that I found myself in a place called Luang Prabang, and if by chance you are not familiar with Luang Prabang I can define it only by saying that Siam was behind, Burma over the shoulder, and China straight ahead. It was uncommonly lovely.

I had come in some time before with an airlift of the French Foreign Legion, to which I had most improbably become attached.

At times I have been briefly and rather lovelessly engaged to all manner of forces; I recall this unit of the Legion as quite the most unattractive of all.

They were Germans almost to a man, full of Pernod, and given to singing *Tipperary*, of all things, *Wir Fahren*, and *Auprès de ma blonde*.

In their care was the preservation of the French colonial principle, frayed around the edges as it was.

It was an unfortunate moment to arrive, everyone said, since we were now wholly surrounded by the Communist armies of the Vietminh, who were (though I am glad to say we did not know this) rehearsing for the final siege of Dien Bien Phu.

I mention this only to show that my encounters with history have not always been as dotty as sometimes must appear.

However, there we were, on the banks of the great slow, tepid, cocoa-coloured Mekong River, which carries the silt of South-East Asia from the heights of Yunnan 2,000 miles to the China Sea, oiling past the drowsing buffaloes, snaking through the mountains.

In the mountains, some ten miles away, were 300,000 invisible Viets, drawing a little closer all the time. There was not much to be done about it. It was in any case ferociously hot.

A picture of Luang Prabang at this crisis in its destiny shows a township overcome with an unconquerable drowsiness, relaxed in changeless siesta all day long.

Here and there a few eight-year-old monks played desultory games on the pagoda steps; now and again a bemused Legionary would reel back to his tent; from time to time a turtle would rise lethargically to the surface of the river, sigh, and subside. For the rest, everyone slept.

Meanwhile the Viets pressed on.

The reason for this tranquil acceptance of the situation was quite simple: the good people of Luang Prabang were completely confident in their security. Not, you may be sure, because the French had told them so, since the French had told them very much otherwise. The Wizard had told them so, and everyone believed *him*.

This Wizard was the head necromancer on the staff of the monarch of Laos, King Sisavong Vong, and he had been in the business a long, long time.

He was very old, and blind, but he was recognised as an outstanding local prophet whose forecasts invariably came up. He announced with complete confidence that the invading Viets would come to within eleven kilometres of the town, would stop, and would withdraw.

This was good enough for Luang Prabang, which thenceforth put the war out of its mind. Morale was high, and when Laotians' morale is high they relax into torpor.

Daily the Wizard studied form, cast the hens' entrails and read the stars, and always the answer came up the same: the Communists would approach to eleven kilometres and no more. Far away in Hanoi the French headquarters hopped about in frustration, but Luang Prabang only rolled over on the other side.

Well – by and by the air reconnaissance helplessly observed the advance Viet-minh positions in the hills some eleven kilometres from the garrison. For a while they remained there, doing something inscrutable, then they withdrew. In fact, vanished. The siege was over.

This, of course, confirmed the Wizard in the top flight of sooth-sayers; he gained more face than ever; and when he ended his days shortly thereafter, old and full of years, there was a smile of crafty wisdom on his ancient blind countenance.

It was some time before we discovered what the Communists *had* been up to all the time. What they had been up to was getting in the opium crop.

Laos is one of the great opium-producing states, and the stuff that was worth 500 piastres a kilogram in Luang Prabang would fetch 2,000 piastres in Hanoi, 3,000 in Haiphong, and more than its weight in gold in Hong Kong.

So while our embattled township dozed the war away the Viets had been busy with the harvest. They cropped seventy million piastres worth of opium – about £1½ million worth – and when they were through they retired, and sold the lot to the Chinese in exchange for the guns with which, some time later and in deadly earnest, they destroyed Dien Bien Phu.

And the Wizard, of course, rest his artful old ashes, had been on a cert throughout, since as a leading agent of the Communist organisa-tion of many years standing his information was cast iron. Straight from the Ho Chi Minh's mouth.

Anyhow, as General Navarre said when the tricolour came down in the end, the Wizards are always on the side of the big battalions.

THIS MAN VERWOERD

It is interesting to imagine, if Dr Verwoerd's would-be assassin had been a better shot, the nature of today's obituaries – the faltering justifications, the far-fetched search for virtue, all the *nil nisi* bonumerie of the professional requiem.

Dr Verwoerd doubtless had his faults, we should have been told, but at least he was sincere. He was a bitter, brutish man, but he was at least a Christian. Even his enemies would agree that he . . .

We have meanwhile been spared all this canting humbug. Dr Verwoerd lives to fight another day.

He will, however, clearly not be coming to the Commonwealth Prime Ministers' Conference in London next month.

This drastic and unfortunate solution has got both him and the Commonwealth out of an intensely embarrassing situation.

We were committed to giving Dr Verwoerd an enormous security screen in London. In Johannesburg we are told, his personal body-guard was also carried out of the hall, having fainted clean away at the sight of his master's blood. No such contretemps can now arise in London; South Africa will be represented, as seemed probable all along, by a stooge.

That at least Dr Hendrik Frensch Verwoerd could never be called. He is no second-rater, at least by the debased standards of Afrikaner politics.

He is (as everyone over the weekend was on the point of writing) extremely honest – as the late A. Hitler was honest, as J. Stalin was honest; they had horrible notions, but they were not hypocrites.

Since the Union of South Africa was established in 1910, a simple half-century ago, it curiously enough has had only six Prime Ministers: Botha, Smuts, Hertzog, Malam, Strydom and Verwoerd; every one of them a Boer, every one of them going a little farther on the path of Afrikanerdom and apartheid than the one before.

Dr Hendrik Verwoerd is among the brighter of this set of granite patriots. He is unusual among his company of insular peasant-politicians in that he has at least seen something of the world outside South Africa.

Indeed, his father was not an Afrikaner but a Dutchman from Holland; he himself studied at German universities, specialising in – of all things – psychology.

When you meet this youthful, fresh-faced, grey-haired fifty-eight-year-old you gain the impression of a lively and considerable mind.

Only later do you realise that you have been judging him by the standards of the bucolic boneheads of his entourage; to be head and shoulders above them does not perhaps mean as much as one had thought.

Dr Verwoerd was Professor of Applied Psychology at the Afrikaner University of Stellenbosch, a stronghold of the Boer intellectuals.

For nine years thereafter he edited *Die Transvaaler*, which became the chief organ of anti-British opinion in the Union. (During the visit of the British King and Queen in 1947 not only did Dr Verwoerd personally boycott the event, but his paper never even mentioned it.)

During the late war with Germany the present Prime Minister of South Africa was among the many members of his Government who were vigorous and articulate protagonists of the Nazi cause.

He did not in fact enter active politics until 1948, when he was elected to the Senate and became Minister for Native Affairs, a key job in an Administration dedicated to writing Native Affairs out of the Bill of Rights altogether.

He was said then to be the best mind in the Cabinet.

Nobody was more passionately dedicated to the principles of *baaskap* and apartheid, and the definition of the Bantu as sub-human.

For this he has always invoked the authority of his Church (for he is a deeply religious man) – the Dutch Reformed Church, which long ago formally ordained that the place of the black man is on his knees, so long as it is not in a white man's chapel.

His election as Prime Minister, after the death of Johannes Strydom, was another victory for Transvaal rigidity over Cape flexibility.

He very soon made it clear that he intended to abolish all African representation from both Houses of Parliament – and did, with his removal of the handful of Native Representatives (who were by law all white, to be sure), who made some small expression of the Africans' view.

The next move to which he is formally committed is the Republic. A draft Constitution by the Nationalist Party is already in existence: it renders the President of the Afrikaans Republic 'responsible only to God'.

South Africa is soon to hold a referendum on this subject, and Dr Verwoerd has announced that he will institute the Republic whatever the result of the referendum.

He is not, as we have seen, a man of many nuances.

Further than that there is not a great deal more to say about Dr Hendrik Verwoerd, except that he is a devout Calvinist and a strong family man, with seven children.

News Chronicle,
11 April 1960

YEARS AGO I LOST A JOB FOR EXPOSING THIS MONSTER

The last time I saw Dr Syngman Rhee was nearly ten years ago, in the enclave of Pusan, to which we had uneasily retreated in the first dark summer of the Korean War. I didn't like him, and he didn't like me. The passage of time has richly ripened that feeling. The difference is that now it is kosher to say so.

In those days Dr Rhee was a comparative stripling of seventy-five, but he was every inch as offensive and dangerous a little despot as he is today. At the time, however, he was on the establishment as a Gallant Ally.

It was unfashionable, and indeed hazardous, to point out that he was, in fact, a cruel and arrogant oligarch who was dead certain one day to end up behind the barricades.

All appearances to the contrary, I do not live my life wholly on hindsight, and I have some reason to sound off on the question of this impossible man.

It was Syngman Rhee, after all, who brought about one of my several professional crises when I made the error of being prematurely anti-Rhee to such a tune that I found the rug smartly pulled from under my feet by the don't-be-beastly-to-Syngman lobby. (Not, I hasten to say, the *News Chronicle*.) The good doctor then declared me Undesirable, which was probably the only mutual sentiment we ever shared.

Still, any vexations he caused me were pretty small beer to a man who – I would like to repeat – was responsible for the deaths of uncounted innocent people, many of which I factually and personally observed.

With respect to one and all I am getting uncommonly tired in my old age of going out on a limb on issues that are officially defined as crackpot, and which turn out later not only to be true, but blindingly obvious.

Sharpeville didn't turn South Africa into a rotten State; it was that for years and years and years, as one tried unavailingly to make clear.

Shooting his civilian opponents last week didn't turn Syngman Rhee into a monster; he was that all along.

But when one pointed it out at the time one was derided, one lost one's job, one was called all manner of irrational names, and finally one packed up. One did? Several did.

In those days South Korea was a 'bastion of the Free World', and Syngman Rhee was a 'stalwart of democracy', though anyone who knew either it or him sometimes wondered if words had lost their meaning. The fact was, they had.

For twelve years Syngman Rhee ran his country as a police State of the most iron-clad kind, while his deluded patrons in the U.S. State Department drooled on about his 'staunchness' and his 'upholding of Asian liberties' and similar incomprehensible ramblings in cloud-cuckoo land.

Through the terrible years of the Korean War he conducted his domestic affairs on lines that made tough observers flinch.

These lines included concentration camps of an outstandingly gruesome kind for his political opponents and an awful custom of summoning local officials and Allied staff to ceremonies in which selected parties of men, women and children were produced and shot.

All this I found not to my taste. Furthermore I argued that if the Communist propaganda radio was forever going on about our condoning atrocious behaviour behind our lines the best answer would be that it was a lie. This was held to be a rather emotional attitude.

When, however, Dr Rhee took to crowning the scene of some of his nastier demonstrations with the flag of the United Nations I suggested that this was perhaps going a little far.

Some effort was made to discourage him. Even greater effort was made to discourage me, and with greater success.

So Syngman Rhee endured, still sponsored and subsidised by a State Department to whom anything was acceptable so long as it proclaimed its anti-Communism with a sufficiently loud noise.

This, to be sure, did Dr Rhee do, even to the extent of periodically threatening to drag us all into his own private war.

At home he ran his own organisation – called, with a mad irony, the Liberal Party – as a one-man military band.

Finally his own desperate people rebelled against the crookery of his rigged elections and the tyranny of his rule, and were shot down by the firearms so lavishly supplied him by America for the defence of freedom.

For ten years now South Korea has represented the basic fallacy of the divided world, with its symbol this obstinate and confident Syngman Rhee, who even now, driven into a corner, refuses to accept the inevitable and retire.

This extraordinary person still has the staggering crust to issue a statement saying: 'I can now join the people in encouraging political parties to purify themselves.'

The last week's work, anyhow, has finally aroused the Americans to the embarrassments of their problem child, now revealed as a senile delinquent.

What one wonders now is when we may hear something from our own international delegation on the spot – the United Nations Commission for the Unification and Rehabilitation of Korea, which goes by the unlovely name of U.N.C.U.R.K.

This body would seem to have been keeping its head well down during the recent carryings-on. Perhaps it is time for someone to uncork U.N.C.U.R.K.

What happens now is obscure. Dr Syngman Rhee, self-propelled upstairs, remains Chief Executive of the State, which I should have thought was a continuing affront to the unlucky Koreans who died in their protest.

He is an old and bitter man and he will not readily lie down.

I do not know if I have made it clear that my affection for Dr Syngman Rhee is less than fanatical. I hope so: it has been on my chest for some time. And so, dear doctor, you know what you can do with your visa now.

News Chronicle,
26 April 1960

DAILY MAIL, 1961–2

After the destruction of the *News Chronicle* newspaper I never joined the staff of any other, nor have I to this day. This was no sort of noble sacrifice by me; I just felt that I had reached the age when I could just possibly look after myself. There were times to come, only too often, when I reflected that I must be out of my mind, but Fleet Street was more generous to me than I had been to it, and I got by. I never prospered, but I survived, which is as much as most of our kind can ask.

A helping hand was offered by the *Daily Mail*, of all papers, largely I suspect because it was then edited by William Hardcastle, who had long been a friend and colleague of mine. Bill Hardcastle was an unusual phenomenon, an editor who had been all his career a foreign correspondent and working journalist, rather than being promoted from the ranks of management. He knew about journalism rather than business, which is doubtless why by and by the *Mail* got rid of him. He went to the B.B.C., where he untimely died, to my sorrow.

I wrote my stuff for the *Daily Mail* exactly as I had done for every other paper; it took me on my own terms, since by now I was too old and obstinate to change them. I recall it as what I used to call a 'sedentary interlude', which meant that I worked mostly from home, without darting all over the place in the old compulsive way; it was relaxing, if a bit self-indulgent. Now and again I surrendered to the urge and went somewhere – to Paris, where I had spent so much of my youth, to celebrate the ending of the horrible Algerian war. (I had watched a lot of that wretched conflict in Algeria: to this day I recall a moment of horror when I went to an Algiers hospital and found that the bitter departing *colons* had as a final gesture fixed a bomb *under an operation-bed*. I can remember nothing that so sickened me of the colonial human race.

Then I made this wholly fanciful and crazy trip to Albania. In those days nobody went to Albania; it was out of the question; we had long ago broken off relations with them and the place was as inaccessible as the moon. Then I stumbled on a small-ad in an East German paper offering a conducted tour for guaranteed anti-Soviet Communists, if you can imagine such a thing. I applied, and was cautiously accepted. I furnished myself with a very odd document: it was a British passport enclosed in a Russian-looking cover, by a conspiracy I still do not like to explain. In my innocence I supposed that arriving in this company I might just get by.

Of course my stratagem was spotted in minutes, and the indignant Albanians ordered me out. Unfortunately for them, however, the plane had by that time gone, and there would not be another for three weeks, so most reluctantly they had to keep me, in conditions of rather agreeable duress. Albania is a most beautiful boring country. I was happy to have got there, and shall be equally happy not to return. But that, today, goes for almost everywhere.

What a dismal admission.

Having made it I have already changed my mind.

*   *   *

DARKNESS AT NOON – AND YET I SEE SOME HOPE

A t least it can now be said for the late Joseph Vissarionovitch Stalin that he is, at last, turning in his grave.

Turning, indeed, or being turned, out of it altogether. In the deepest pit of hierarchical disgrace, yet with the biggest gun salute the world has ever seen.

Did it take the crash of the most enormous explosion in mankind's increasingly manic history to dislodge that brooding mummy from the Red Square tomb?

Or did they disturb those clasped and waxen hands, and the heavens consequently rock?

In a world that is rarely lacking some kind of desperate irony or other this is surely one of the maddest of all.

Anyhow, there is great theatre in it. The exorcising of the Wicked Uncle-figure could only be symbolically accomplished to the roar of fifty megatons – or sixty, or eighty, or whatever it was the Russians felt necessary for whatever it was they had to prove to themselves.

Did the final ignominy of Stalin, then, depend on the apotheosis of Kruschev?

Today there is only speculation. By blowing his vast and vile bomb Mr Kruschev has outraged both the conscience *and* the intelligence of millions who do not necessarily reproach him for other deeds.

How many people may one day die as the result of this day's work?

But by finally laying the ghost of Stalin with the cadaver of Stalin it may be that Mr Kruschev has stabilised himself for the next vital year to come, and that is important to the world.

We may denounce Nikita Kruschev for his cynicism and scientific irresponsibility with the bomb, but we need Kruschev in the Kremlin, since the one man in that obscure network who does not want war is Mr Kruschev.

He may have an odd way of showing it, but such is the case.

Last night, then, they lifted the shell of Joseph Stalin from its eerie bed below the Square, from the great glass box below the lights.

By night? By stealth? Through a subterranean passage below the Kremlin wall, or with a guard of honour of reversed guns, and solemn eyes staring from the windows of the GUM stores?

It is indeed, strange to see him go. Several times have I called on that terrible exhibition where Lenin and Stalin lay so permanently, so totally without life or mortality. It was not as though they were dead but as though they had never really been alive.

Rash tourists, to cover the *angst* that troubled everyone in that fantastic presence, called them the Gruesome Twosome. And the words would die on their lips.

Now that sardonic waxen face of J. V. Stalin will no longer stare upwards every May Day, presumably at the boot soles of his successors, jostling for position on the mausoleum above. Lenin will lie alone.

This terrible gesture – for necrophobia is as lowering to the Russians as to everyone else – must strike at the nerve-endings in a way even Mr Kruschev's most biting attacks could never do. Stalin was a wicked man; Stalin's body must be a wicked body.

And yet . . . J. V. Stalin was a mighty man; the disposal of his embalmed head can be of no meaning to the world, not now. The work he did was in his lifetime, and its shadows still walk the world today.

What, now, for Molotov? His impeachment is demanded; the calls arise for *his* head on a platter too.

He has been already humiliated as far as the step before the last – but he lives, he works, he draws his money. He sits in the Soviet atomic commission in Vienna in the last of the uncommitted Central European States. What sort of Darkness at Noon attends Mr Molotov?

If they kill him – after all these years – the world will know. If they try him – after all these years – the trial must clearly be as rigged as those he himself sustained in the days of Stalin.

Can they exile him further than he is exiled now? He is not even dead, to be disinterred.

One would not wish to be Mr Molotov today.

Would one wish to be Mr Kruschev?

He has exploded his bomb, just thirteen days after promising to do so. By those of us who hate his bomb, our bomb, anyone's bomb with an equal and disinterested detestation he will not readily be forgiven.

He is now, perhaps, the most powerful human being who ever lived. Could we ask him now – now that he demonstrably heads the megaton league, now that he can even brandish the bones of Stalin in the open air – to recall that there are 2,000,000,000 people in the world who deplore the first and admire the second?

Can these people now require of Mr Kruschev that he exploit his position, above all by returning *at once* to the Geneva Disarmament Conference – with what advantages he wishes to claim – but with the determination to give them, for once, real meaning?

The faults have not been by any means all on his side. From now on they may be. Today he has assumed the mantle of total force. To take the Geneva initiative now would prove him not just a strong man but a big one.

To everyone there comes one moment of truth – and this is it.

Daily Mail,
31 October 1961

WATCH THIS SPACE SHOT . . . AND I HOPE THAT'S ALL WE DO

The apocalyptic picture of Lieut.-Colonel John Glenn that haunted every front page yesterday should be (and probably will be) preserved as a symbol of man's endurance, desperation, courage, arrogance, and blind dedication to the awful rigours of international one-upmanship.

It looked to me like the face of *homo sapiens* pretty near the end of his tether.

It was more than enough, anyway, to put most of us off space-travel as a possible career.

That drawn and monkish head set in its metallic cowl, the dazed and opaque eyes – it was an expression of most cosmic significance even if, as I suspect, it symbolised for Colonel Glenn some even deeper human need, such as: 'My God, I could do with a drink.'

To anyone with even the normal claustrophobic fears the thought of those five hours rammed in a tin can is almost unsupportable; I, who have my imprisonment-crises even inside enormous aeroplanes, begin to sweat at the consideration of it.

On this indestructible human guinea-pig, then, the whole public image of America is focused.

It is hard to believe that such a man could be an introvert, yet probably no living creature has ever been made so wholly conscious of the biological factors that make him tick.

It has been pointed out in scores of P.R. releases that Colonel John Glenn is a man as other men, in that he is composed largely of carbon compounds and water, but no one was ever so mapped and charted within.

It is solemnly said that there are at least twenty eminent doctors who can recite Colonel Glenn's pulse-rate, respiration, bloodcount, sedimentation-rate, retinal reflexes, and digestive condition for any hour of the twenty-four, and that they can continue to observe these phenomena even as he careers through the empyrean at 17,000 miles an hour.

The only thing they cannot explain is the look in his eyes, after five hours in the capsule.

There was, at least, time to think. It might be unrealistic to assume that Colonel Glenn devoted those five hours to philosophical meditation (though it is hard to see what else he could do, unless he is a praying man).

But he must have wondered, as he faced the imminent possibility of an indescribably lonely death, whether it was all worth it.

There are those who now argue that all this – Cape Canaveral, the surrealist gadgetry, the Sputnik Motels, and the same sort of thing duplicated, more discreetly in Russia – does provide the 'moral alternative to war'.

This immense expenditure of men and money, it is said, keeps the Defence Departments out of worse mischief, and ensures that the rocketeers are at least ostensibly on the side of pure research.

Does it? Does anyone still believe that Colonel Glenn is to be shot among the angels in order to investigate cosmic rays and high-altitude meteorology?

Of course nobody does, and it is fair to say that few pretend to. Colonel Glenn's Mercury capsule is a military vehicle and his Atlas rocket is an I.C.B.M. Major Gagarin travelled in a machine of identical purpose.

Without a manic world situation how far would peaceful space-navigation have progressed?

The question is as unanswerable as it is banal. The compensation for the human race periodically going off its head is a consequential spurt in scientific knowledge, or so they say.

Yet the amount of energy, skill, devotion, and just plain dollars spent on Colonel Glenn's expedition must be enough to have re-dressed the national economy of many a small country.

If the mission fails again, it is lost; if it succeeds it will keep the U.S. up with the Joneskis, but it cannot advance research much more than the Russians did.

This year alone the U.S. will spend £1,700,000,000 on her space programme. The Soviets will spend at least as much, and some say far more.

That President Kennedy can balance his Budget is either in spite of or (more likely) because of the fact that fourteen per cent of the nation's income is swallowed in Defence.

The one thing both hot and cold wars have in common is that they sure give full employment.

It is I suppose a melancholy fallacy that if these measureless sums were *not* spent on absurd rockets they would therefore be spent on something more valuable – that £1,700,000,000 a year would auto-matically become available to feed hungry people and irrigate thirsty lands.

Freed from the imbecile compulsion to shoot people to the moon, we say, what could we not do for the many perfectly remediable problems here on the ground?

So we say, knowing that when the chips are down it is rhetoric. These mad costings are now built into the American economy perhaps inescapably. This need not be so in Britain. We have no Colonel Glenns, and I hope we never do have.

I hope he goes up to time, and comes down safe and well, to rejoin the human species, with all his red cells intact. But I would not be him, nor any part of him.

Daily Mail,
29 January 1962

HOW COULD THE WORLD COME TO
SUCH A LOOSE END?

The trade of journalism is rich in occasions for feeling foolish, but none greater than writing an article the day before the world comes to an end.

It is pretty much an act of faith at any time, without scratching away on the eve of oblivion at something for which one will never get paid and which no one will ever see.

Punch called me 'melancholy and disenchanted' last week; they should have a look today.

On the principle that prophets can be as fallible as politicians, one must nevertheless soldier on.

I agree that one cannot be too dogmatic about these things, but at the moment of going to press the world does not *seem* to have come to an end.

However, I have a very imprecise idea of what sort of end it will be, so perhaps it has.

As has been thoroughly rammed home over the weekend, a considerable body of informed astrological opinion read today's uniquely unpropitious conjunction of planets and computed global catastrophe, including total human dissolution, for around one o'clock this morning.

All the *saddhus* and soothsayers of the East have been busy with prayer and ritual to avert this untoward development, and to this we say: Well prayed, sirs.

We have also much for which to thank U Nu, Prime Minister of Burma, who activated Deterrent B, the propitiatory release of three bullocks, nine goats, 129 doves, and, I am happy to say, 218 crabs.

If we are in a position this morning to share another day of melancholy disenchantment, it may well be due more to this than, say, to Mr Marples.

As a matter of fact, I remember seeing the end of the world once before. It was around the summer of 1951 (graduate astrologers will correct me to the month) when a not dissimilarly inauspicious conjunction of the eight accepted planets threatened a total disintegration of the human scene.

I was at the time in the North Bengal foothills of the Himalaya, where these things are not taken lightly, and we had another such dicey day waiting for the ultimate celestial puff.

I took my defences into a spinney of prayer-flags and holy gongs, beyond the first impact of divine fall-out.

My lama gave me absolution, in exchange for a half-bottle of Solon gin. The next morning I rose from my truckle-bed in one piece to learn that the Chinese had the previous day moved into the heartland of Tibet.

'Do not proceed to Lhasa,' said my astrological advisers, and since it was still another 200-mile walk and 12,000-foot climb, I paid heed to them.

So it came to pass that I rejected this obvious opportunity of pulling history up by the roots.

After a lifetime of the I-was-there pitch it is pleasant to recall that once I was almost there, and deflected by Capricorn.

No such gentle drama attends the anticlimax of today. It would really be unforgivably clumsy if the world were to sign off on such a dying fall, amid such a wildly flapping jungle of loose ends.

It would be a *little* unsatisfactory to call in a zodiacal cataclysm to resolve so many local difficulties – to abolish all the nonsense, to put an end to a generation of Conservative Planning, to conclude the Algerian war, to rationalise the Rhodesias, to dispose of Senator Goldwater and Mr Molotov, to forget Cape Canaveral, Castro, and Christmas Island, and to find, at last, a place to park.

And yet there would have been something radically appealing in the disposal of all the howling bores that haunt the scene by such an act of necromancy. The eclipse – and an end to nuclear argument, an end to flannel about Gordonstoun School, an end to Sunday Supplements, an end to the I.C.I., to Lord Montgomery, and to the doomful prophets themselves.

Pity, in a way.

However – by my time it is not yet 1 a.m. The joke may yet be on . . .

Daily Mail,
5 February 1962

THIS STRANGE PARADOX THAT IS PARIS AT PEACE

It took President de Gaulle just as many minutes to intone the epitaph to the Algerian war as that melancholy war has taken years, and somehow the Olympian sonority of it all managed to make even this sound like a triumph.

It was a riveting performance: From the moment when the T.V. lens zoomed in on the Elysée window to the Marseillaise at the end the announcement was the inevitable tour de force.

No man can cram so few facts into so many resounding words and make them sound so prophetic.

But what he said meant so much less than the fact itself – the fact now blazoned on the special editions in the most enormous type I have ever seen: *'C'EST FINI.'*

For all Frenchmen of good will alive today this must be a moment of heart-catching relief.

Throughout this electric weekend we in Paris stood for the words that would tell us that the long night is over at last. Yet the promise of peace is like that of major surgery, equally full of hope and fear.

It really needs an effort of will tonight to believe that the thing is really over – those seven years, four months, and eighteen days (for someone has counted every bitter day).

The past years in France have not been lacking in paradox, and this is the final irony: that today ends the saddest of colonial wars on terms that could readily have been achieved in 1955, and that the man who has finally presided over Algeria's liberation is precisely he who was installed three years ago to prevent it.

Meanwhile 350,000 Algerians and 20,000 Frenchmen are dead in the struggle that corrupted thousands more, that caused two army mutinies, that destroyed the Fourth Republic and may yet, in its wretched aftermath, threaten the Fifth.

There is something characteristically perverse in the fact that Paris prepared for news of peace by putting herself in a state of quasi-siege, by mounting guns on the presidential roof, by banning aviation, by blocking roads.

That sort of perversity was born of the circumstances of the whole Algerian collapse, and is summed up in the wry and stale observation that it is now 'all over bar the shooting'.

It is perhaps true that nothing, good or bad, can happen in Paris without its touch of fantasy. What sardonic change or choice, for example, caused the French Radio to follow its first announcement of the ceasefire decision with a jaunty recording of *Bye-Bye, Blackbird*?

Whoever is supposed to look after the security of Paris is well advised to take a few precautions against a multiplication of the troubles they have tolerated, or even condoned, for so long.

No one of course knows what malevolent reaction the O.A.S. has prepared for this day, but their odious impertinences increase, the squalid treachery of these corner-boy commandos has become the reverse side of the Paris coin, and perhaps for a long time to come.

Even now it is recognised that the problem of the returning Algerian *colons* may produce something like an endemic O.A.S. situation for years.

The O.A.S. was formed with the declared aim of preventing an Algerian cease fire, which is now a *fait accompli*. They have therefore failed. They have now become merely instruments of frustration and hate.

In the past few days the counter-slogans have multiplied on the walls, saying 'O.A.S. equals ——' and a drawing of a swastika. There is something rather hopeless about this, too, as there must always be when democracy is reduced to scrawling on the brickwork.

The long night, then, has passed after all. Ben Youssef Ben Khedda will be Premier of an Algerian Republic.

This, said de Gaulle, was a victory of good sense – the good sense of the French people.

It remains now only for them to ratify the Evian decisions (when they know just what they are) by their 'approval and national confidence'.

'Frenchmen,' he cried, as he has so often cried before, 'I count on you.'

Let us pray that he can.

Daily Mail,
19 March 1962

SHQIPERI!
I WAS FLEETINGLY YOUR MAN IN TIRANA

The circumstances in which I became Your Man in Tirana bear some recounting lest this odd and unknown dateline be thought altogether too capricious.

For years Albania has been one of the hardest places on earth to get into (and, some say, out of).

Here was this fierce little Balkan nation, one of the smallest, and certainly the poorest, of States in Europe, of a Communism so fervent and dedicated that it denounces even Mr Kruschev as a revisionist backslider; a population the size of Birmingham's that has angrily challenged the whole world from Washington to Moscow, now acknowledging no friend on earth but China – yet so exclusive and inaccessible that scarcely anyone ever sees inside.

The penetration of Albania would obviously be a job of high adventure. In the event, it was almost uproarious.

It seemed there was a German Tour Party. Somehow one got on it. One made one's dispositions for anonymity. One hoped for the best of Balkan luck.

At the rendezvous in Munich Airport it at once became clear that someone had put a pretty liberal interpretation on the definition of 'tourist', since every man except myself was borne down with cameras, sound gear, tripods, typewriters, tape recorders and T.V. equipment of great complexity.

We travelled not by some furtive underground, but in a K.L.M. Convair called Vincent Van Gogh.

Thus, when our tourist group reached Tirana at last, it resembled less the wide-eyed arrival of those on pleasure bent than the annual outing of some eccentric Press Club.

This manifestly took the Albanians somewhat aback, though with great courtesy and composure they refrained from comment. You are, they said, tourists? Everyone nodded urgently, fiddling with their exposure-meters.

All around stretched Albania – mountains fading into the dusk, the silhouette of a mosque, a long and lovely valley, a place of disturbing beauty, smelling of cypresses and raw petrol.

On the airport stood some two squadrons of old-type MiG's and a rather rusty A.A. battery. Around them a shepherd grazed his flock. The hills closed in, range upon range.

The frontier examination was of the usual Eastern pattern, conducted with great civility, tough on details. The Customs lady accepted all the T.V. technology impassively (*she* knew what was going to happen to it inside); what she was looking for, she said, was weapons.

Driving into Tirana through the gathering twilight one saw the physical grandeur of the place, so like the neighbouring Macedonian mountains from which in the past I had looked with such curiosity into this State.

All around – since this is a fortified road – were soldiers, youngsters in the secondhand Soviet Army uniforms that were part of Russia's aid in the days when the two countries were talking to each other. It seemed on this first evening that Albania was populated entirely by soldiers in tall boots, and grey smocks with the Red Star.

That impression was soon to change, but this little nation is still the most over-armed I have seen for some time.

Tirana is a small city of immense initial charm, planned spaciously (by the Italians, to be sure) yet on a tiny scale, full of broad avenues and squares, laid out in little gardened piazzas under shade-trees, all with a nice air of elegant neglect.

The hotel, for all its glass and marble, has somehow acquired the antiseptic austerity of all Popular Democratic hotels. It is hard to define: a dim economy of under-powered electric bulbs, a fine lift that doesn't work, an excellent bathroom, complete with bidet (installed by the Italians, I'll be bound) whose taps emit more groans and clanks than water.

It is unfair to carp. To blame *Albania*, of all places, for an inadequacy with tourists – even tourists as bogus as us – is absurd.

And yet the curious thing is that Albania affects to believe it *is* a tourist country.

Presumably such visitors who do contrive to get in are East Germans, since Albania is barely on speaking terms with the rest of Europe, and it might be asking rather much to expect holiday-makers from Peking.

The Chinese, then – where are they? Since the famous quarrel with the U.S.S.R. they have been Albania's only allies. They are totally invisible. I looked in vain for the blue boiler-suits I had known so well in my days in Peking.

The Chinese are behaving in Albania as the Russians used to do in China: strictly keeping their heads down.

And then yesterday I blundered by chance through the wrong door into the wrong part of the restaurant, and there they were – some two dozen cadres, dining in discreet segregation. They looked up, startled, and I backed out in embarrassment.

Outside the pleasant streets teemed in the hot sun. Once off the main boulevard, the town is very nearly straight from a travel book. Here are the women in the enormous Moslem trousers and embroidered tunics, the men from the hills with the white felt tarboushes and blanket coats; splendid highland brigands.

These admirable people plod along among the normal shabbiness of an urban peasantry, and indeed you can see that though this nation is terribly, desperately poor, it has uncommon dignity and bearing.

Of course there is almost total absence of communication, Albanian is a language of great complication, bearing, it seems to me, precious little relationship to anything else.

Albania, for example, does not call itself 'Albania' at all, but 'Shqiperi', which seems unreasonable.

Stalin. He lives on here all right. Since the great row with Kruschev, the more the Soviets denigrate and denounce Josef Stalin the more does Albania extol his memory. His pictures proliferate, 'Rroste' (which means 'Hooray for') cry the banners everywhere.

The immense Stalin statue dominates Tirana's main Skanderbeg-square. But the new Soviet Embassy stands half-finished and derelict up beside the university. When the break came work on it stopped and the Russians left. The other Eastern Republics at least left chargés d'affaires, but the Soviets pulled out to a man.

If you stroll off the main boulevard somewhere among the trees between the university and the Fussbal Field, you will come upon a barred road, and behind the barricade a man with a machine-gun and behind him many more men with machine-guns, and you do not stand and stare because they advance on you with an air of very genuine menace, and then you get a rough idea of where the Central Committee is passing its time today.

Daily Mail,
4 June 1962

UP THERE THE GLORY,
DOWN HERE THE SHAME

The Seen and the Unseen, the Intangible and the only too Crudely Clear, the two faces of the East around us in Berlin – of Russia, which can soar so high, and sink so low.

Here, in this deplorable city, it is impossible not be utterly conscious of both.

Berlin, built on paradox, has it still today.

Somewhere circling overhead is the Triumph, at the same time wholly admirable and totally incomprehensible, the extraordinary Soviet technicians spinning through space in their mechanical magic, and long live their bravery and skill.

Down here, rooted in an ugliness somehow both pathetic and contemptible, is the Berlin Wall, with its cruel and desperate pretensions.

Every prick of memory insists that it was only yesterday, that it can surely have been at most only the other day, that the Wall appeared across Berlin.

But no, at two o'clock tomorrow morning is its anniversary; a year to the day since East Berlin sealed itself off behind that bleak and brutal barricade, and contributed a new dimension of desolation to the Cold War.

That fact hangs heavily in the Berlin air today. After twenty years of almost total unreality, Berlin has come to live on myths and symbols as nowhere else in Europe; they hold themselves to be symbolic, and everything takes on the character of an omen. It is almost as though the Berliners have lived so long in limbo that any fixed point achieves significance.

For the East, the 17th June. For the West, the 13th of August. The day the Berliners rebelled, and the day they were imprisoned. In a place as understandably neurotic as this, these things have immense meaning.

Only when you are outside Berlin are you permitted to believe that the world does not revolve on an axis pinned on Checkpoint Charlie. What are astronauts to Berlin? They have their Wall.

Today the papers are obsessed with the Wall; the space-ship is nowhere. By tonight they may change their mind.

It is said that tonight tension is building up fast on both sides of the Wall, since if West or East Berliners are to make a demonstration against it, now is the time. The East German army and police have been reinforced on one side. The same thing is going on here.

Mr Kruschev's Note denouncing 'Western-inspired provocations' against the Wall, has not helped. Yet nothing today could appear more tranquil than Berlin, both East and West. What preparations are taking place are certainly invisible to us.

I spent the afternoon through the Wall in the Eastern sector, after the tedious machinery that filters through foreigners and bars Berliners.

It was as I remembered it, as lifeless as Pompeii, a dreary uneasiness that seemed penetrated by an indefinable regret. All Berlin is a haunted place – on the one side dreary beyond description, on the other, brash and even bumptious, yet both sides sharing a common wretchedness that neither will admit.

The desolation of the East, the vulgar affectations of the West – in an inexplicable way they add up to a sum of emptiness that is probably unique in the world.

Until yesterday I had never, in fact, seen the Wall, and I believe that perhaps I had slightly discounted the dutiful expressions of pious horror that every Western notability has felt bound to utter.

If that was so, I regret it now, for I truly believe that Wall is one of the most shameful things I have ever seen in a life not wholly empty of disagreeable sights.

It is, indeed, of a monstrous and obscene ugliness, a thing not just outrageous and impertinent in its intention but vulgar and brutish in its execution, not just a violence to the dignity of human people but a crass and debased object in itself.

There are some twenty-five erratic miles of this unkind and ridiculous frontier – in London such a wall would stretch from St Albans to the Tower. It will be hard, tonight, to watch it all the way.

For the Germans I suppose it is a certain awful irony, that they, who created Buchenwald, Auschwitz, should now themselves have a Wailing Wall on which to lament their past, their present and the follies of the world.

For the East Germans, which inescapably here means the Russians, it is not a victory, but a pitiful defeat.

I have spent so much of my time for years trying to contest the greater absurdities of anti-Communism, the stupidities of Russia-hating, the meaningless surrender to total prejudice, that perhaps I can make a birthday protest without prejudice.

How great is one kind of genuis in the airless emptiness of space, and how squalid the other, here around me.

Can you, I wonder, build walls in space?

THE TRAP!

The small war between India and China on Asia's lost horizon is now a brutal and deplorable fact, sad and menacing.

For those of us who know and love both countries these are sickening days.

These frontier battles are archaic and absurd. To wrangle in these cosmic years over a meaningless stretch of empty mountainside is explicable only in symbolic terms that have nothing to do with the McMahon Line, or the Namkachu river, or the town of Dhola.

Nobody really gives a damn about these places, and everyone knows it. The trouble is in the heart.

Of all the conflicts possible in this imbecile world this is the most painful, exasperating and futile.

Nobody on earth can profit by it. No territory of any value can change hands, no ideology promoted, no cause advanced.

The whole situation was engineered to put the Indians on the spot, which has worked.

It is heartbreaking that in the twilight of his great authority Jawaharlal Nehru should be saddled with this intolerable dilemma.

The thing has, of course, been blowing up for years over the truly piffling issue of exactly where in that enormous Himalayan wilderness, India ends and China begins.

The fact that practically nobody *lives* in this vertical desert seems beside the point. This is nothing to do with a lump of land. This is nothing, essentially, to do with a handful of unhappy soldiers huddling on the snowline.

This operation is to drive India, morally and economically, to the wall. And the fact that the thing has begun at all is Square One for China.

Since the Chinese Army first nosed across the line in 1959 the quarrel has nagged away at Indo-Chinese relations, making a total nonsense of the *panch sila*, the famous Five Principles of Coexistence formulated by Nehru and Chou En-lai, which so many of us applauded for their enlightened realism.

There at least, we thought, the Asians could be above the battle.

But all negotiations over this absurd geographical misunderstanding failed, as – it became clear – the Chinese meant them to fail.

The Chinese moved into Ladakh, in north Kashmir, and occupied an area the size of Belgium. Now, moving far to the east, they have driven the Indians back from the Bhutan border.

Mr Nehru was goaded into an announcement that the Chinese must be thrown out by force. He had waited two years before making it, under every kind of pressure, partly because such an attitude is out of his character, partly because the Indian Army was in no shape to take the field.

It is pretty certain that he did not want to make it anyway.

In the event, he had no choice. The people of India were angered, his Congress Party was aroused, even the Indian Communist Party accused the Chinese of aggression and demanded that they be expelled.

But the moment that Jawaharlal Nehru proclaimed that he was ready for war the Chinese had won their first point. Nehru, the apostle of pacifism, had been trapped into bellicosity; the prime mediator of the world's disputes had been manoeuvred into refusing discussion.

Throughout the sensitive and vulnerable Afro-Asian world where China and India compete for influence, India could be represented as solving her disputes by force of arms.

Moreover Nehru has now been jostled into proclaiming that India's economy must be geared for war, to the immense disadvantage of her current Five Year Plan, to the interruption of the progress she has worked so bitterly hard to achieve.

If the border war goes no farther than sporadic engagements on the high tops, the Chinese have accomplished much, in sabotaging both India's international image and her finances.

Nobody, of course, can actually win this war. The idea of a Chinese invasion of India over these ferocious mountains is a macabre improbability.

I know that north-east region moderately well. I loafed around there for weeks waiting for the Dalai Lama to emerge from the mists.

It is indescribably beautiful, difficult, remote and useless. It climbs all over the place up to 15,000 feet, torn by ravines, locked in terrible winters. You would have a job to find a more hopeless place to wage a campaign.

But it is there that the whole northern wall of India meets its hinge, at the junction of the peculiar little kingdoms of Bhutan, Sikkim, and Nepal, intensely vulnerable to Chinese penetration.

There, too, India has her own troubles with the Naga tribes. Her situation can become politically dangerous as Peking works even harder to isolate her from her other neighbours, Pakistan and Burma.

There is a nice irony, to be sure, in the fact that it is Russia who is now supplying her with military aircraft. But even with these her chances of any kind of swift victory are small. The high Himalaya is no place for an aerial war.

The last time I saw Chou En-lai was in Delhi, garlanded and benign with his arm round Nehru. The only cry then all over India was 'Hindi Chin! bhai bhai!' – India and China are brothers, they shouted, and how splendid it sounded, and how far away today.

Daily Mail,
22 October 1962

HARPER'S BAZAAR, 1963

How I found myself in the pages of the August *Harper's Bazaar* I simply cannot imagine; I do not remember ever buying it or reading it or knowing the first thing about it, but it must have been quite otherwise than I have always thought, because it gave me much space for an article of which, after a long time, I am still not really ashamed. On the contrary; good old *Harper's Bazaar*, say I.

I wish there were still such magazines that would offer me that much room for that sort of idiosyncracy. What fun we used to have.

*   *   *

BRITAIN'S GRAND ILLUSION

Anyone proclaiming his intention of being blunt, brutal, bitchy, and beastly to the British, as I hereby do, must justify his intentions and declare interest. I argue that I have excellent cause to like and occasionally love my country, since I have spent so much time away from it; and a decent right to abuse it, since by so doing I abuse, if you will excuse the expression, myself. The failure of twentieth-century man is, after all, man's fault. Our own responsibility, that of the British, is modified by many things, but our showing is pretty abject.

I would say it is high time Britain made a new appraisal of herself. Not necessarily agonising; the adjective is tempting, but it supposes too much. To urge the British into agony is like asking a tortoise to do hand-springs; there are some activities for which nature has made no provision. Nevertheless, if we accept the fact that five comparatively unchallenged centuries have come to an end, there is no harm in asking why, while accepting the obvious corollary: why not?

A few weeks ago the U.N. Economic Commission for Europe reported, in its deadpan way, that Britain has 'the sorry distinction of being the only West European country whose volume of national output was practically unchanged from previous years,' and 'the one country where the unemployment situation has seriously deteriorated.' The economics of this are, to be sure, beyond our brief, and in any case are certain to be immeasurably dull. But if we have gone so badly wrong in this boring respect, which not one of us in ten thousand can understand, let alone check, could it be that we have compensated for our fiscal follies with some other kind of social advantage? Are we no longer a prosperous and dreary race, but a bankrupt and jolly one? Have we exchanged the solemn solidity of Edwardian security for the lighthearted insouciance of the New Elizabethans? Have we hell. Let us examine a few specimen attitudes.

I tend to see things through other people's eyes, since that is my function, and I can say that our 'image,' as they call it, abroad has wholly changed in the last ten years. It has not so much collapsed as decayed. Foreigners are fickle, after all; not all their conclusions are sound. But though many of their judgments are superficial they are nonetheless firmly held. Mostly they deal in paradox.

They see the land of liberty as the land that puts reporters in jail. They observe the country of craftsmen now noted for manufacturing cars whose door-handles are apt to come off. They note that the capital of a nation of Protestant moralists now flaunts more sleazy side-street sex than Saigon. They conclude that the Welfare State has now three-quarters of a million people out of work, and several thousand Londoners without homes; where even the jailbirds must sleep three to a cell.

While much of this is unfortunate, perhaps inevitable, it is made no better by the studious manner in which the anointed bumblebrains in high places affect to know nothing of these things, but continue to intone a ritual chant about the sort of National Destiny and Proud Heritage and Global Mission that came to an end with a resounding whimper around the early 1950s. The most visible thing today is the gigantic wall which the jackanapes-in-office have been compelled to build around themselves to exclude the view.

Thus we perpetuate a set of legends, the contemporary Anglo-Saxon myths. They are, in effect, that the enduring fortunes of this country are a fact of nature, occasionally and momentarily interrupted by circumstances that are invariably initiated by foreigners; that whatever befall we require only a slight increment of initiative and intelligence in Parliament to produce the built-in silver lining. Our conception of our institutions includes perfectionism, or nearly.

It does not accept the possibility that this may be at least partially an illusion; that all things (including good things) have a term on them; that for one sort of Great Britain this is the end of the road; that the future of this country may nevermore reside in power and glory of the kind our masters grew up with, but something far different – and no less admirable – if this generation must abandon the pretentions of the last.

Most people in Britain are in fact up against a situation they have never quite known before, and we haven't really got the psychological resources to face it even now. In any case the dilemma is far from easy for the ordinary man to define; it eludes him as it seems to elude the Government. The politicians tell us endlessly of the need for Britain 'to find a new direction,' to 're-assess her position in the world,' to 're-think her attitude to the Commonwealth,' to do all manner of things in the abstract which bring no particular consolation to the unemployed shipworker, whose 'new direction' now only takes him once a week to the Employment Exchange. If you have run out of fags on a Tuesday, how do you 're-assess your attitude to the Commonwealth'?

Whether we appreciate it or not, it is slightly traumatic to have all the old values undermined, the old acceptances shaken. Being kicked out of Europe was a chastening thing – even for those who had not wanted to go in anyway it was startling to have the rug pulled from under us so abruptly. It had therefore to be explained in all manner of complex political terms – de Gaulle's ambitions, the Franco-German conspiracy, and so on – if only to cushion the embarrassing conclusion: that Britannia no longer rules the waves, nor indeed anything else.

Being no longer a world power in a military sense – very well; we can live with that all right, though it is perhaps wearisome to have to put up with the myopic and costly pretensions of an Administration that still nostalgically clings to the illusion. Other things are tougher to swallow – the fact that not everyone in foreign parts is still in love with the pound sterling, for instance; even worse, that the pre-eminence of Britain in many traditional fields, of industry, of manufacture, of trading reputation, is no longer a sort of natural law. We no longer build what other people think are the best cars, for instance; we no longer make the finest ships – indeed, we scarcely make any ships at all. When the Australians want an Air Force now they buy it in the United States, just as when New Zealand wants railway trains she buys them in Czechoslovakia. Why not? There must be a reason. It need not necessarily be a consoling reason.

Not long ago the solemn and by no means carping *Guardian* devoted an entire editorial page to a long examination of 'What's Wrong With Britain?' It found, I am bound to say, plenty. It boiled down to the conclusion that Britain is not decadent but smug, refusing to accept that in the things she is good at she is otherwise than perfect. That both sides of industry, management and unions, are effete and mutually destructive. That society is bogged down with a hereditary archaism at one end and a bingo-parlour civilisation at the other, and that, as the paper roughly put it, in foreign affairs Britain 'is living in a fool's paradise, and at home in a fool's purgatory'.

That is tough talking, but maybe it had to be said. And maybe we can say even more.

It is supposed to be a reasonable axiom that the first thing to do about solving a problem is to look it in the eye. This is rarely done in our seats of power, at least not so the groundlings can notice it. The leadership of this country shows a truly professional dedication to the art of flannel, avoiding the harsher facts of life with an assiduity that makes the attitude of the ostrich seem vigorously watchful. Faced with situations that should embarrass a mule, they reply with slogans and clarion-calls of numbing banality, crying 'Think Victory!' and 'Talk Victory!' Confronted by slopes that are positively Gadarene, they riposte with daring and imaginative acts of statesmanship like bouncing American comedians out of the country.

They cling to the wild and pitiful illusion that Britain's diplomatic declension is some sort of momentary aberration, to be cured by gestures. They harbour the fantasy that there is still some place in the world for a British nuclear bomb; that is to say, against every kind of political, scientific, and military advice they believe that the temporary leasehold of a minimal share in a Western 'deterrent' is some sort of factor in the Cold War. Those who argue in the coolest and most objective terms that the notion is militarily a fallacy, economically a ruination, and morally an abomination, and who used to be denounced as (a) heretics, (b) idealists, or (c) Communists, now find themselves, rather unwillingly, upholding the formal doctrine of H.M. Opposition – which itself has somersaulted to reach this position, which it doesn't like anyhow.

When and where did the change come, and was it ever announced? Of course it wasn't. British politics are informed wholly by the pragmatic. Few people in British public life ever say *anything* that could risk a blowback, being now almost totally occupied in the business of proving that at least one or other of their previous miscalculations was sound.

So much for politics. Religion has also failed. Everything strongly suggests, indeed, that religion as normally defined will never reappear significantly in the councils of western man. However, the discarded lees of error, fable, and sentiment were not replaced by those elements of insight and logic which remain in the Christian teaching; the whole lot went overboard. Nor could the Church do much about it, since its bishops, priests, and apologists, with half a dozen exceptions, had neither the wit nor the integrity to accept the challenge, its component parts failing to agree on any basis, even a definition of terms. Their differences reached a peak of exquisite technicality on the question of whether God has a beard. Even when the Bishop of Woolwich decided to dip a toe in the cold waters of humanism and express doubts about Up There, and the cloudy heaven in the early Metro-Goldwyn taste, he was compelled for professional reasons to lard his doubts with the accepted jargon of theology.

Science did little better. Science took the atom apart. It greatly extended man's physical senses. Indeed, the degree of that achievement forms the most common case for the preposterous claim that we are civilised. No other attributes of man were vitalised by science. And when it became evident that a decaying society was hardly to be redeemed by putting a man on the moon, salvation was sought from a race of pseudo-scientific quacks labelled Economists, whose contribution to the general weal is to view men as consumers of goods, amenable to fixed trade rules. We see where *they* got us.

The social scene, then, started to liberalise itself. From being a nation of sexual second-division, for example, of gropers and figleaf merchants and dealers in undercover fantasies, the British suddenly became obsessed with the cultivation of Sex – that is to say, surrogate-sex: copulation by book and film and newspaper article; there is no firm evidence that the actual practice has become more accomplished or adroit. Nevertheless, the four-letter word abounds in the bookshops; the four-letter performance is a standard part of reel six in most feature films, or at least as far as Mr Trevelyan will allow, which is roughly up to the unhooking of the bra. One has nothing against this; what one winces from is the twenty-one gun salute of self-congratulation every time someone gets his hand above the knee.

At the same time, paradoxically, we have evolved a system of censorship that is uncommonly subtle, rarely revealing itself crudely for what it is. We have no political control of the Press, but we have D-Notices. We have the pressure of advertisers who – vigorously denying it the while – require a certain climate of journalism in which to flourish. We have an archaic and indeed ludicrous theatrical censorship in the ridiculous survival of futile feudalism, the Lord Chamberlain, who is not beyond banning for the tiny audience of a London revue a sketch already seen and heard by fifteen million T.V. viewers, and whose standards are as arbitrary as they are jejune. As far as sexual morality is concerned we are wholly schizoid; we do not know whose side we are on.

It has long been my view that a British University truly seeking to advantage the next generation would provide, along with its liberal arts and its science, such courses as: Adventures in the Larger Lunacy; With Rod and Gun in Darkest Greek Street; Christ and the Double Cross; How to Tell a Communist at Twelve Paces, Using Glasses if Necessary; Funny Peculiar: the Archives of The Establishment; Pedal Politics, or the Road from Aldermaston; The Private Lives of Ministers of the Crown; How to get On in Politics Without Even Knowing.

Students fully versed in such courses, and dozens more I shall be glad to list without charge to any accredited seat of learning, would at least be prepared to meet life head on, unwrapped in the Union Jack, the Red Flag, or the crisp cellophane of the P.R. boys.

Talk Victory! Think Victory!

Harper's Bazaar,
July 1963

DAILY HERALD, 1962–4

The next station on the line was the *Daily Herald*, a deeply-respected old radical paper rooted in the tradition of the Labour Party, which meant that it was earnest, well-intentioned, doctrinaire, and on the whole rather dull. This was always puzzling, because my colleagues on the paper were the reverse of all these things; it was just that some sort of Keir Hardie-ish ghost, or maybe just the T.U.C., somehow insisted that we be worthy rather than witty, efficient more than exciting. This didn't trouble me; I just plodded on regardless, as usual.

Like all my other masters the *Herald* gave me every sort of generosity and freedom, and I had a lot of fun. I believe that one or two of these pieces are as good as any I did. Again I came to work more and more at base, in London, although I did return to Cyprus. I had come for some reason to love that place, as one has to love or loathe places in which one has shared sorrow and conflict and death.

Long years ago I formed what could be called a friendship with the late Archbishop Makarios, who contrary to every public image was a very funny chap, and this was reinforced when we deported him to the then unknown Seychelles Islands, because I too had been exiled in those lovely islands years before, though by chance not design. When years later I became very ill he sent me an enormous telegram to the hospital, doubtless at State expense, wishing God's blessings on me a dozen times and hoping I was getting enough to drink.

The other pieces speak for themselves. The death of President Kennedy was a trauma: I learned of it in London at dinner-time; within two hours I was at the airport and the following morning in Dallas, with neither any luggage or any money. I fixed all that; in those days I was used to fixing things. If one meant it enough, one got by.

To this day I remember the death of Lord Beaverbrook. I had known him for some years; love-hate nearly but not quite defines our relationship. We had got rid of each other years before. I was in the pub opposite the *Daily Herald* office when somebody came in and said: the Old Man is dead. Everyone knew what the Old Man meant. I scrambled across the street to the office and wrote the obituary reprinted here. It was almost edition-time; I finished the piece in twenty-five minutes. It was the last service, or disservice, I could do for that lovable old villain. May he roast in comfort.

*   *   *

THIS IS THE YEAR WE MAKE OUR CHOICE

The human race, to which so many of us reluctantly belong, has now entangled itself in a fix that for self-induced contortion transcends everything since Houdini. Man is in a mess. His incompetence is abject. He has become accident-prone in an almost cosmic sense. His plans for redemption have all the stimulating clarity of a two-day hangover.

The latest imbecility, of proclaiming a British H-explosion precisely at the moment best calculated to rock the test-ban boat, is well in keeping with the times.

We are, in fact, so far round the bend of international confusion that it would not surprise me if we are about to emerge at the other end.

Historians of our age (assuming that any are permitted to exist) will say of 1962 that it was, for good or ill, the punctuation-mark in the records of mankind.

This is the year, they will say, when these people had their chance; in 1962 they made their choice. Quite arbitrarily that autumn they had the doors of the sepulchre opened for them; they stared inside aghast and recoiled.

They hated what they saw, but they did not shut the door.

The British, whose role in the big act had been that of a scandalised curate at a mobsters' punch-up, celebrated their escape from the big boys' crunch by suddenly deciding to brandish a popgun of their own, lest it be forgotten that they too retained some small potential for mischief.

Such groping impulses towards international reason as were induced by imminent catastrophe were sedulously sabotaged by an ancient German Chancellor, somewhat nearer the hereafter than the rest of us, who in his dotage contrived to retain a hypnotic ascendancy over better men.

The race, apparently despairing of both rationality and religion, began to invoke necromancy, and to babble of Black Boxes.

By and by, that year, they achieved for themselves a situation of such total desperation that – well, our assumption of historians to tell the tale implies that the shock-treatment worked.

It had to work. For 1962 was – is – the big deal and it may be that we who are putting up with it are the favoured few.

Meanwhile one watches the world scene as one is glued to a T.V. serial, in the mesmerised belief that since it can hardly get any stupider, it might just possibly improve.

Certain truths have at least been revealed, and fallacies exposed. The view that the nuclear stalemate was in itself a rational basis for the slow easement of international tensions had a kind of logic once; after Cuba it has no longer. Kruschev and Kennedy between them proved that the nuclear balance is not a balance, but a trap.

It has been established that the deterrent does not necessarily deter rash behaviour, but can itself cause it.

And the British bomb, which was to prevent us going naked into the conference chamber, merely (as Jo Grimond wrily observed) ensured that we didn't get into the conference chamber at all. I should say that from now on the politicians everywhere must stand by for far stronger pressure from the people for a new look at serious disengagement, for a clear-cut definition of the terms on which the two worlds can co-exist.

The age-old Geneva negotiations on a test-ban must be driven to a conclusion by January, and the clumsy arrogance of Mr Macmillan's Nevada squib must not distract them.

Above all, the issue must not shade off into the background – as it already is doing.

It is in the nature of our restless journalistic trade that it seeks uneasily to escape from the shadow of fear into all manner of pitiful irrelevancies, like the doings of queer spies and their silly political protectors, whose secret torments are a reflection of the society in which they live – they, and us.

On this note of somewhat qualified euphoria I take the liberty of intruding on this newspaper's soapbox, so that there shall be no misunderstanding about my capacity for rue.

I have nothing to offer but bile, gripes, fears and fret. We shall get along fine.

Daily Herald,
14 November 1962

TO WHAT SHALL A MAN BE TRUE?

The first recorded Chief of Foreign Intelligence, as far as I recall, was the prophet Moses, who sent the twelve undercover agents of Israel 'to spy out the land of Canaan – whether its people be strong or weak, few or many.'

They reported with great simplicity: that it flowed with milk and honey. More imagery, I fear, is required today, in a world of absurder doubts and fears. More detail, more data, more danger, and more despair.

This country today is infested with spies, says Mr Orr-Ewing, Civil Lord of the Admiralty, who should know. The spy-menace is 'the worst since Elizabeth I,' says Mr Deedes, Minister Without Portfolio.

In the Communist Embassies and missions, says Mr Orr-Ewing, thousands of operatives are keeping card-indices to suborn us on our personal addictions to drink, drugs, blondes or boys. It is, says Mr Deedes, the day of the Trojan Horse.

This is going to be a big and busy time, this heyday of the spy and the spy-catcher, each at work behind his different keyhole. I foresee tough days ahead for the bureaucrats, big and small; the heretics, guilty or innocent; all cranks and queers and nonconformists and obstinate adherents to lost causes.

There will be much turning over old stones, and gumshoeing around the private places where the ghosts live as a result of this past month's work, and that of the weeks to come.

We are going to hear much about treason, in these weeks. On specific cases we may not comment, through very proper laws, but we shall yet live awhile in a certain obsession with security – which means, paradoxically, its reverse: insecurity.

The Russians have always had it. The Americans have had it long enough. It makes for uneasy living, and we may not welcome the day when it comes to us – as now it inevitably will.

The land we live in, says the Government, is infiltrated with spies. Mr Orr-Ewing and Mr Deedes have told us so, in so many rather awful words. It could be that if they had been aware of this infestation of treachery they might have issued their warning a little earlier, when there were still a few secret drawers left unrifled.

But it is possible – or shall we say certain – that their brief arrived a little late. With junior statesmen, as with their leaders, the hour produces the mood, and the mood the phrase, and the phrase the panic.

Every nation has always had its infestation of spies, and agents, and researchers; what you will. It is the price a disordered world has to pay for the consoling and dangerous luxury of sovereignty. They occupy every sort of post from tycoon to tobacconist, from archivist to ambassador.

It is a hundred shots to one that there are no more spies, nor protectors of spies, in Britain today than there were yesterday, or last month or last year. But, brothers, how many more are there going to seem to be!

We are about to hear a great deal about the whens and hows of treason, its methods and mechanics, its orgins and aberrations, its follies and its fears. We shall hear it all, except perhaps the hardest definition of all: what it is.

What is loyalty? And to what shall a man be true? Sometimes it is hard not to suspect the theme of national loyalty in the hands of some whose own definition of personal loyalty has been so yielding – who would die before they sold their country, however readily they would sell someone else's.

If it is British to aim at the truth, to respect one's intelligence and that of the people, to put the welfare of the many above the advantages to the few, to recognise the indivisibility of human survival – then multitudes of the outraged loyalists are un-British, with whatever relief they may sacrifice the unlucky mate who got found out.

Loyalty, in its small but most valid sense, means regard for the security of the country to which we belong (since if we deplore it, we have only to leave it).

Yet security is a paradox, since all security is risk, or experiment – in the words of that great American constitutionalist Justice Holmes 'as all life is experiment'.

Indeed, OUR whole political faith rests on the most serious paradox of all: that the individual has a kind of dignity, irrespective of the rules, and must be permitted his measure of heresy if our excellent society is not to fall into the very thing against which we are trying to secure.

If I try to do commerce abroad with my country's nuclear posses-sions; I am correctly held criminal. If, however, to ask to abolish that country's nuclear secrets completely is treason, I am no more conspicuously treacherous than such fearsome conspirators as Jo Grimond, say, or even, nowadays, George Brown.

The difference between this country and Russia is that nobody prevents this curious band of brothers from sounding off where we like. This sort of security I value.

On the other hand, if I believed in the absolute values of our Deterrent, I should, logically, insist on revealing its resources to all available spies; indeed, force the information on them, so that they might more easily convey to their masters the terrible power at our disposal.

I should organise the Association of Secret Agents in great con-ducted Marches to Aldermaston, so that they might look upon my works, and despair.

All my life I shall never quite understand how you can threaten people with something they have never seen . . .

Unless, of course, it isn't there.

Daily Herald,
21 November 1962

BUT THE PLAGUE IS IN THE AIR AGAIN

Two sad but quite meaningless murders in three days brought the questing eye of the Press swivelling on Cyprus again for the first time for years, and how vainly.

There are, indeed, big reasons for worrying about Cyprus all over again, but the murders were not among them.

Nevertheless for a moment the Ledra Bar looked faintly like its old self, full of only too-readily identifiable sources talking nostalgically of Murder Mile.

There is a sort of illusion or tradition that nothing ever happens in Cyprus without involving mayhem.

This is very unfair, but understandable, for indeed there is some dark genius of pain and conflict that dwells here, and has nothing whatever to do with poor Englishwomen being strangled in their beds.

The people Cyprus tries to destroy are Cypriots. Today, the island never looked lovelier, but the plague is in the air again.

A day or two past, the President, Archbishop Makarios said: 'Things look dark, but I must go on.' Yesterday the Vice-President, Dr Fadil Kutchuk, who leads the Turks, said: 'I do not see how we can avoid great trouble, but I must go on.'

Four years ago almost to the week, the Agreements were signed that finally put an end to the brutal and wounding struggle here, and for the first time in twenty-seven centuries Cyprus ruled itself without a foreign master. It was a thing of great relief to many of us.

It is painful, indeed, to see the needless, perilous thunder clouds building up all over again, and so soon.

The infant republic of Cyprus began life with many problems, but none so intractable as the fact that eighty per cent of its people are Greek and eighteen per cent Turkish.

They differ in religion, in attitude, in standards of living. Above all, they differ in allegiance: the one to Athens, the other to Ankara.

The thing is of a complication that, were it not so menacing, would be hilarious. By the constitution so painfully hammered out for this mixed-up country, everything had to be shared between Greeks and Turks on a seventy-thirty basis.

For every seven Greeks in official jobs there must be three Turks. Every departmental chief must have a deputy of the other race.

Above all, beside the Parliament of the Republic there were set up two Communal Chambers, one Greek and one Turkish.

If ever there could have been devised an absolutely certain way of building the foundation for future trouble, this was it. And today's crisis stems exactly from this situation.

One of the more dubious provisions of the law ordains that each of the five main towns in Cyprus must have (or should have – it is madly ambiguous) twin municipalities, one for each race.

Last month the Archbishop declared that this was an absurd system. Henceforth, he said, the towns would be run like everywhere else, with one elected authority.

This has brought the Turkish community out in a white-hot rash of fury. The Turks are almost pathologically jealous of their minority 'safeguards'.

Their Communal Chamber decided to make a law of its own, restoring the municipal situation.

The Greek majority in Parliament cries that the Government's competence is at stake.

A quivering deadlock prevails.

It is the idea of Dr Kutchuk, the Turkish Vice-President, that the only thing to do with these five towns is physically to divide them up into Greek and Turkish quarters – a manifest impossibility.

Nevertheless the doctor has produced an extraordinary scheme actually to measure up the fronts of people's houses in 'inches', and divide the places up on that basis, which is a bit of a fantasy even by Cyprus standards. At all events we have now reached a pitch of mutual ill-will in which bombs have been exploded in the Mosque (though nobody knows by whom), telephones sabotaged and a frenetic campaign of vilification waged by the Greek and Turkish Press.

The very highest quarters here hold it extremely likely that genuinely serious trouble is on the way. It is, as we know, always latent.

It is monstrously unfair and disabling that this little nation's hard-won sovereignty should be forever bedevilled by the racial differences of its neighbour states, but everything in Cyprus makes the Greek-Turkish rivalry self-perpetuating.

Education does nothing to diminish it and everything to institutionalise it, since the schools are not a national responsibility but a communal one.

The Greek schools import their teachers from Athens and the Turkish ones from Ankara. The history they teach is angled exclusively in the interests of Greece or Turkey, and all the old rivalries are nourished.

This is unwholesome, in an independent state, even when Greece and Turkey are on relatively good terms with one another, but this state of affairs rarely lasts for long.

Agreement, tranquillity, the chance to settle down and build a stable economy – all these are desperately needed and desired by this little island, and require only two things; good-will and non-interference.

Yet whenever the Turkish Cypriots prepare to accept the proposals offered them by the Archbishop – as well they might, since they are offered from the republic's economy far more than they ever contribute – somebody nudges them from Ankara, and once again Cyprus becomes the instrument of purely Turkish politics.

The affair of the municipalities – and it is characteristic of the situation that the argument sounds pettifogging in itself – has now been angrily submitted from both sides to the Constitutional Court, a strange tribunal of three judges, one Greek, one Turk, presided over by a West German.

When it will give its ruling no-one knows, nor if the ruling will be peaceably accepted when it comes.

Cyprus today has not a good climate for resignation.

I know this place so well; I have spent here so many days of fun and sadness and hope and regret, and above all, comradeship.

I do not want to see the day when I ever have to return here for any other reason than to drink with my friends.

Daily Herald,
6th February 1963

WHAT AN EXCITING ASSEMBLY-LINE!

The Leader of the Tory Party looked across the House and said in his Establishment voice: 'I learn that in some quarters I am being likened to a boiled lobster.'

'Hear, hear!' cried the Opposition cordially.

'In view of the wet speech in which this House has been offered the thin edge of the Socialist wedge,' said the Tory Leader, 'I ask for the unequivocal rejection of this dotty Bill.'

'Oh, oh!' intoned the Labour benches dutifully, and sent their Leader in to bat.

The debate was on an Education Bill of some intricacy, which was appropriate enough in the circumstances, since for the occasion the House was sitting in the gym of Forest Hill Comprehensive School in South-East London, for whose Parliament I was briefly the sole gallery correspondent.

I know a bit about Parliaments, but very little about schools. My own schooldays were short, erratic, untidy and useless; they bore no relation at all to this great boy-factory.

Here eighty-odd experts in adolescence are dedicated – uncommonly cheerfully, considering – to the business of processing some 1,400 human males from puppydom to puberty, from shining-morning-face to five-o'clock shadow.

The institution is no Greyfriars. It made me feel not so much square as cubic. It wholly, though perhaps not permanently, disables one's literary style.

It is populated in the upper echelons by what are either very big children or very small giants. They say one is growing old when the policemen begin to look like boys; what when the boys start to look like policemen?

Teenagers: what a word! What a thing to be saddled with by second-hand sociologists and muscular Christians and T.V. knowalls. I think this decade's teenagers are strictly marvellous.

I have owned some myself, and they're nice too, though they did not go through an assembly-line as exciting as this.

To get back to this Parliament. It is part of the Sixth Form deal, and owes nothing to the dismal Debating Society of yesteryear. This is serious politics.

I am taken by the division of the place, not into Houses – that rather desperate togetherness of the smarter seminaries – but into Parties, duly elected along constitutional lines, with a slight edge to the Tories.

This may be an expression of the invincible perversity of the young or a touch of personality-cult around the Chairman.

This one was a knockout. A teenage Tory is always a rare and touching sight, being like all earnest political children, just one or two dialectical laps behind the times. But he knew his stuff.

The Labour Leader's motion had demanded the opening up of higher education to everyone. (*'Abolish the closed university scholarships, which go to the public schools and the rich! Equal competition for all places!'*) He had his facts both ample and right; he was lucid and persuasive.

I know that at his age I could no more have done it than the binomial theorem; the grim thing was that this stripling could probably do both.

The Tory's, however, was a virtuoso act. He was Hailsham seen through the wrong end of a telescope. Clearly he was a Character, and richly and ably did he ham it up among the claps and catcalls.

'Higher education may be all right for some,' he cried, as from some sixth-form Parnassus, 'but not for all. You don't need a B.A. to clean out lavatories!'

It was noble; it might have been Cheltenham. It brought the House down.

I cannot remember if they passed the Bill, which demanded also another £2 a week for the teachers. *('Not that they all deserve it, by any means.')* I went to do some research on the recording tapes of previous sessions.

I have not the remotest idea whether this comprehensive school differs materially from any other. It is the first I ever saw. If most are like it, there is some vague hope for a rationally-adjusted generation, though they would be the first to doubt it.

Despite the schoolboy Supermac, the place has clearly a pervasive Radical mood, a proper sense of controlled anarchy, tempered by the continual preoccupation of being on the edge of the incomprehensible.

It is unique to our times, compounded of restlessness and resignation, of acceptance of a manifestly-manic adult world, but under protest. There were plenty of C.N.D. badges. The debate, Right and Left, was real and uninhibited.

PRISONS: A debate on the Committee of a Hundred book about how lousy they are; a boy had been deeply outraged on holiday by the sight of Dartmoor.

POLITICS: Is the attitude of 'neutrality' in the school a façade, when the *Daily Worker* is excluded from the library? Conclusion: Yes. Up to the Fifth Form, political feather-bedding is O.K., but Sixth Formers should be exposed to everything.

RELIGION: An argument on whether Religious Instruction should be compulsory. *It is; you are not obliged to teach the two times table, but R.I. is a must.*

PATRIOTISM: A 1963 recap of the Oxford debate of the thirties – Would you be prepared to die for your country? Some indecision here; a laconic disinterest – how in these days can you die *for* anything? 'I suppose so, if everyone was doing it. If I could choose, I'd be a warden in a deep shelter.'

A DEFENCE debate, with the young Messiah of the Right almost inarticulate with indignation at someone's rejection of the Bomb. 'Cowards! Poltroons!' He adored it. So did everyone.

I asked a master: 'How do you discipline these debates?'

'Don't have to. Almost never. Unparliamentary language, of course, and personal abuse, of which boys are fond, and good at.

Opinions never. They're all right, you see.'

I don't know if I quite saw, but I nearly did. If this is comprehensive schooling, I wish I'd had some. Indeed I believe I have, now.

Daily Herald,
3 April 1963

THE POLITICAL OBITUARY OF
HAROLD MACMILLAN

Of all the ironies that haunted the last days of Macmillan's regime, surely the most pitiful is that he should finally collapse on an issue as oblique and ridiculous as adultery.

That *was* the issue, elaborately as it was obfuscated variously as Security, Probity, Morality, Honesty.

The abject fact is that after twelve years of a Tory rule vulnerable on all manner of really serious fronts, Mr Macmillan breaks over one man's fornication. There has been nothing in politics known like this since Cleopatra.

For Harold Macmillan this must be exquisitely, gruesomely painful. A Prime Minister who had with studied intent built up over the years an image of cultivated insouciance, of upper-class Edwardian remoteness, would probably have been less humiliated if Mr Profumo had been caught robbing a bank.

It is not all that much more agreeable for the Opposition. This was not the issue over which they would have wished Mr Macmillan overthrown, when so many better challenges abounded.

His Ministers had bamboozled the House before; his Government had been guilty over and again of wanton evasion and negligence and smugness, and much misrule.

It is not especially rewarding to see Mr Macmillan hooked at last because one of his men went to bed with a slut and owned up too late.

The showdown was reduced to a dilemma so elementary that it was bound to defeat the fabled ingenuity of a politician so crafty and elusive, simply because it was obvious enough for anyone to see.

Either Mr Macmillan had been covering up a colleague's lie for the sake of the party, or he had just not known what was going on under his nose. In one case he would have been a knave, in the other a fool.

This was Nemesis for the man who had given the impression of being the first by pretending to be the second. In the end, he continued to seem both at once.

Thus the paradox of Harold Macmillan endured to what was, indeed, a bitter end.

His famous grip on the Tory Party faltered over something the Tories value beyond most things: political acumen. The legendary Tory coherence and solidarity in the face of danger, forever embodied by himself, was the very rock on which he foundered.

The Leadership on which he based his confidence in political immortality will, in the end, be remembered by the memorial of one public scandal and an anthology of bad jokes.

It seems that, after all, and in spite of his talents, Harold Macmillan in the statesman-stakes was never really leader-like material – not in a world that grew increasingly real and earnest as he grew increasingly unreal and self-hallucinated.

Towards the end, in fact – how readily one drops into the obituary theme – he seemed disinclined to accept that the world was other than the odd thing he had made of it for himself, in which he could drift and posture in a succession of mesmeric characterisations: Trollope-reading, grouse-shooting, cardigan-wearing; urbane and rich and clever – but uncomplicated; forever the simple Highland crofter from Eton and the Brigade of Guards.

It was not a world likely to be much disturbed by the Christine Keelers of the other, the real world.

The Image was all: that the son-in-law of a Duke of Devonshire should wear patched trousers was a diverting eccentricity; just as the air of quizzical detachment could conceal a biting ambition. The more he looked like Tenniel's White Knight the more one overlooked the sophistry and the rotten values.

It was not surprising that the P.M. decided to ride out the Profumo crisis on the golf-course at Nairn – after all, had he not successfully ridden out the 1961 Berlin crisis on the golf-course at Gleneagles?

But then the quirks and gimmicks began to overtake their own shadows; daily the idiosyncracies sounded more like self-parody; latterly one began to think the thing *was* Beyond The Fringe.

And, indeed, so it was.

What a loss were those gifts and talents. What a vacuum in the real event was that good mind, that commercial acumen, the groping good intentions of 'The Middle Way', the dedication to a picture of Britain that had died with Baldwin.

Mr Macmillan was the first Prime Minister since Asquith to be called an 'intellectual' – but it seeped away in the Carlton and the Beefsteak, the stately homes and the old illusions. When he recalled that politics was, in fact, about people, he could debase himself to the abysmal vulgarities of 'You Never Had It So Good' – and worse, justify it by electoral results.

In his various roles he was Supermac and Plastic Mac and Mac the Knife, and he will haunt the Tory subconscious for a long time yet.

The reign ends in conspiracy and deceit, and the spurious excitement of the second-rate. The issue that destroyed him was squalid rather than dramatic; even the knockout blow was half-hearted; a majority exactly the sum of his years, sixty-nine – not an inappropriate symbol.

Perhaps the real valedictory was given years ago by Aneurin Bevan, when he told a Labour Conference:

'We do not say that the Tories are bad men, or wicked men, or even that we are better men than they. We merely say: they are irrelevant.'

Thus it shall be remembered.

Daily Herald,
19 June 1963

DON'T REJOICE AT THE MOSCOW ROW

The picture of Mr Suslov and Mr Ten Hsaio-ping, leaders of the Russian and Chinese delegations, greeting each other at Moscow Airport was one of the major documents of our time.

When two major Communist statesmen survey each other as though they both wanted to be sick, then has the world skipped in its course.

We are now embarked on the most glorious guessing-game of the generation.

For four days every political microscope and hearing-aid has been turned on the talks between Russia and China; all the professional seers, clairvoyants, soothsayers, telepaths and diplomatic dowsers have been gyrating in well-informed circles to divine the development of the most resounding quarrel of our times.

Let no one underrate this Soviet-Chinese duel; it is surely the most tremendous political event since the Bolshevik Revolution.

It has qualities of terrible drama, and a certain clumsy poignancy, like the death-grapple of mastodons. From now on things can never be quite the same, and we who watch are privileged.

113

A year ago – even six months ago – the thing that is going on in Russia would have been barely credible. The Soviet-China row in the arena for all to see; Chinese being expelled from Russia as unceremoniously as Americans; embassy windows broken; a batting back and forth of insults hitherto reserved only for the most odious of fascist beasts; a ferocious split in the Communist world – who, until the other day, could have believed it possible?

The epithets slung back and forth have reached almost capitalist level.

Daily I wait to hear from Peking that Mr Kruschev has been found *in flagrante* with a boy ballet-dancer, or from Moscow that the Mayor of Peking is a secret Texan.

What is this thing called hate?

The ideological chasm now formalised in Moscow is a confrontation not merely interesting to diplomats and Kremlinologists; it is immeasurably the most important event for years for every living soul from Mac to Mandy.

There is not one of us who will not feel the consequences of this week's work, and maybe sooner than we think. When we look back, this may well be another ten days that shook the world.

We are today at a punctuation-mark in the development of socialism. From now on the world can never be simply divided into those who are Marxist-Leninists and those who are not.

From now on, it necessarily consists of the haves and the have-nots, the arriving nations and the arrived, the rich and the poor – and the dividing line is not Communism.

For good or ill Mr Kruschev has been driven on to the side of the big providers; when he talks today it is to Kennedy. Chairman Mao invokes the rest.

The blocs are breaking up. We are on the edge of strange events. Some will rejoice. Myself, I am afraid.

For those who sniff the troubled air of Communist affairs, the Peking-Moscow feud began in 1958.

Its origins have been defined and analysed a thousand times by the necromancers: Mr Kruschev, alive to the awful dangers of war, is prepared to treat with the West to avoid it. The Chinese, boasting the world's hugest population, are not.

In consequence China must denounce Russia as a backslider. This is near enough to the truth, but it is far from the whole story.

For five years, then, the quarrel grew, expressed in the mysterious, convoluted, almost coy code-language of Communism, invoking as Aunt Sallies two little nations both remote and meaningless: Jugoslavia and Albania.

When the Chinese denounced Kruschev they called him 'Tito, the Revisionist'. When the Russians denounced Mao they called him 'Hoxha, the Dogmatist'. [General Enver Hoxha is Albania's Communist Prime Minister.]

The words were as obscure as the issue.

It was one of the odd formalities of Marxist-Leninist feuds; whether it was really meant to deceive anyone is hard to say, but at least the Communist conventions were observed.

One of the mysteries of our time was why everyone went to such complicated lengths to disguise a situation of which everyone was aware.

The watershed was reached in 1960, at meetings in Bucarest and Moscow, when Kruschev personally condemned the Chinese in the presence of eighty-one Communist Parties. Still it was reported in oblique terms, using the dotty double-talk of 'Albania'.

But the crunch was on the way – and now, here it is.

For this year, after the Russian withdrawal from Cuba under pressure from the U.S., and the Chinese invasion of India, the thing could no longer be denied; at last they began to refer to each other by their own names. And from that moment on, the breach can never be healed. If Kruschev goes, if Mao goes; the breach can never be healed, for this conflict has nothing to do with individuals.

Whatever formula is found at the talks to paper over the cracks, the schism remains.

For good or ill, the fact exists that Russia as a great industrial society *must* associate herself with the other great industrial societies, like America; and China – still fretting outside the U.N. – must look elsewhere.

China in Asia. These things transcend the ideological jargon of 'revisionism' and 'dogmatism'; these are the facts of life.

'What is at issue here, fundamentally, is whether there is to be any future for a unified Communist movement; whether there will be two Communist Popes, one in Moscow, one in Peking.'

I take the words from Edward Crankshaw's new Penguin book, *The New Cold War; Moscow v. Peking*, which by a fabulous break in timing appears today.

'Are we out of date,' he asks, 'in continuing to arm ourselves against what we take to be a dynamic and monolithic force inspired by an untouchable ideology? Should we stop thinking in terms of the Communist menace and more about balances of power?'

In such a rotten world as this, he is probably right.

THE GREAT MARCH FOR FREEDOM

Here in the capital of the Free World, or whatever, the President has returned from the seaside to the White House, and the medieval court that is the United States administration functions again in the vapour bath that is a Washington summer.

Everything steams. Indoors the grumble of the air-conditioning contends with the endless, inescapable, emollient moan of the Muzak. From six T.V. channels dribble half a dozen T.V. quiz shows, interspersed with occasional desultory practice air-raid alarms.

The Gay Girl Club have a fall-out shelter. All round, in the rows of olde countrie-style eateries, pale, square men ruminate food-style food, variously described, all identical.

Today in my highball I found a cherry with a plastic stalk.

When all else fails, an advertisement offers a telephone service called Dial-A-Prayer.

Here is life on the edge of the biggest precipice of social change since the Civil War: the eve of the Great March. After tomorrow it will be just the same. But not, perhaps, for long.

Tomorrow the tens of thousands – possibly, they are now saying, a quarter of a million – who are gathered now for the Civil Rights protest will advance on Washington in what cannot now fail to be the most enormous civil demonstration ever known.

Over the months it has been scattered and sporadic – Alabama, Mississippi, Tennessee; the dismal, humiliating contests over schools and States rights.

Now it has abruptly become national, universal; the open demand at last for a square deal for the American coloured man *everywhere* in the land of the free.

From tomorrow nineteen million semi-citizens will have formally insisted through their physical symbols here in Washington that in future they must have the vote where now they have not, and the right to work where now they have not, and the right to send their children to school where now they have not, and that this future shall not be years away, but tomorrow.

For a nation, well-meaning though it largely is, that has shuffled this immense problem under the rug for so long, the experience is astonishing, even unnerving.

I described it all yesterday – the vast preparations all over the Union, the trains and buses and planes converging on the capital, with extraordinary precautions that have practically put Washington in a condition of siege.

President Kennedy, one may be sure, could well have done without the embarrassment of a Freedom March at such a time as this: his Administration have dragged their feet over Negro rights as long as they could, since this troublesome business is the canker at the Democratic Party's soul.

Now, however, he must make like a liberal if it chokes him. He is committed; the blacks have committed him. But his Civil Rights legislation is hopelessly stalled in Congress.

Perhaps he hopes that 200,000 multi-coloured faces on the parliamentary doorstep will force the diehards' hands, and save not only the Government's face, but the integrity of the United States, for nothing less is now at stake.

Consequently we have the situation most piquant to anyone British, adjusted to the obdurate inflexibility of Tory-type rule – of a Government responding to a really basic challenge by embracing all its human principles, by snatching the words of freedom from its mouth, by proclaiming that the right of protesting by public assembly is guaranteed to all U.S. citizens under the Constitution, by turning Washington inside-out to accommodate them, by insisting how impossible this sort of jamboree would be in Russia, making it clear that if you can't lick them, you join them – and even, perhaps, use them.

And yet, despite it all, it *is* the spearhead of the contemporary American revolt. From now, things must change, and every thoughtful American knows it. If for nothing else, the saturation publicity that tomorrow will get must make America pause.

At least 2,000 journalists are already baying at the barricades, with sixty-eight radio circuits and twenty-seven television pick-ups, including the invocation of Telstar.

Here is by far the most sensitive point in the international American image, and the world is, for once, on its doorstep.

The March is pledged to totally pacific non-violent aims with the minimum of partisan politics.

But the problem remains; if the Great March is too peaceful, dull, inconclusive, many Negroes will be dissatisfied and resentful; if this huge multitude is too greatly stimulated, there may be terrible trouble.

It is recognised that recently the racial cause in America has been nagging too much about smaller discriminations; this march is to restore the validity and dignity of the big issue.

Yet the Civil Rights measure may still stay bottled up in Congress; at the very best, Senate couldn't react until the end of the year.

Here is the signal test for those Negro leaders who have advocated negotiation and non-violence as the way to promote the black man to a decent way of life. When nothing happens they will be denounced by the extremists.

If there is violence, there will be a bitter price to pay. Can the United States at this moment afford to let the world know that ten per cent of their population have lost faith in their democracy, and can no longer accomplish anything through peaceful means?

Today, waiting among the simple, tedious luxuries of Washington, the polythene pleasures of this clean-hearted, kind and totally ignorant civilisation, so rich and so generous and so uncomprehending, petrified in its ironed-out acceptance that here, at least, all is okay is the okayest of possible worlds – I truly wonder what there is to say.

Tomorrow there will be a gigantic movement of racial protest, with all the resources of government, troops, and Press to see that it comes to no harm.

Only the other day, it seems, I was in South Africa, where racial hate is institutionalised, graven forever in the legal fabric of society; where, if this multitude of Negroes marched on the capital, they would be shot.

Here they will be marshalled, ordered, directed to their stations, provided with toilets, formally interviewed by the President – and sent away.

What then? And how may I define this impossible situation?

From Dr Kenneth Clark, Negro Professor of Psychology at City College: 'Equality, as defined by law, is exactly what it says. Equality is not qualifiable. For the Negro to postpone further the attainment of his rights would be to accelerate the moral erosion of America and to deny validity to Democracy.'

From Dr Martin Luther King: 'The non-violent revolution in America, with all its drama and conscience, is just coming of age, moving the Negro a giant step forward – now.'

From Mr James Farmer, Leader of the Congress of Racial Equality: 'It was Gandhi's teaching that the extension of love in a fight for freedom struck deep into the heart of the oppressor. Yet I fear the Negro will not wait much longer.'

Tomorrow morning the marchers arrive. As marches go, it will be short indeed – the mile between Washington Monument and the Lincoln Memorial. It will, nevertheless, take all day. Nor will the day end it.

Daily Herald,
28 August 1963

THE AMERICAN TRAGEDY

Now the American Tragedy is complete. Nothing like it has been seen before. There is room for no more drama. The wheel has come full circle.

The American nation is almost tangibly in a state of shock – stunned by the size of its own violence, by the picture of its own excesses.

Two dead men have made this day traumatic.

It was electric enough to hear – just as Washington was freezing into immobility for the passing of John Kennedy's body – that the man accused of shooting him had himself been shot.

Then, just as Jacqueline Kennedy knelt to kiss the coffin, we learned that Lee Oswald had died in the same hospital as the President. This brought the situation to a pitch of incalculable intensity.

Lynch law has followed assassination. The corruption of high tragedy by the personal vengeance of a Dallas club-owner has brought total fantasy to the American scene.

While Lee Oswald lay dying with a bullet in his belly and as Jack Ruby, the self-appointed executioner, was held in Dallas City Jail, the immense formula of pageantry went on here in Washington.

Thousands watching it did not even know how this new mad Texan melodrama had intruded on their grief.

The American people have been spared one terrible legal trial. But there will have to be another, and how does one try a strip-club proprietor for usurping the function of the nation, and doing for his own awful reasons what the State would almost certainly have done for its own?

Meanwhile there is the spectacle of Washington in mourning – a city almost supernaturally silent.

Crowds stood blank-faced under a brilliant, bitter sun as Kennedy's coffin was borne from the White House to the Capitol.

There, in the Rotunda of the seat of Government, people are filing past the bier all night.

Tomorrow, proclaimed a day of mourning throughout half the world, there will meet in Washington the most immense and solemn gathering of world leaders ever brought together in one place.

It will indeed be the strangest of days that links such men as Charles de Gaulle and Anastas Mikoyan, Sir Alec Douglas-Home and Eamon de Valera, Prince Philip and the high, exotic dignitaries of fifty States – the great and the little.

Only one thing could have united them: the common mystery of death.

At first sight the American nation seemed today to be still in a condition of anaesthesia, an almost visible combination of outrage and regret, and a sort of incredulity – *how could this ever happen to us?*

It is the reaction of all human beings to a brusque bereavement, multiplied 100 million times.

Quite suddenly, the United States feels itself simultaneously horrified, guilty and vulnerable. It is a hateful sensation, and there is nothing one can say.

The assassination of the thirty-fifth President of the United States has suspended all values. I was here only a couple of months ago, when the great Negro freedom march was underlining both the good aspects of the Kennedy optimism and its helplessness.

My coloured maid today recalled it. 'How much has been wasted,' she said. 'I shall never know why it happened.'

How John Kennedy will rate historically as a president after only two years, ten months and two days – the goodwill, the energy, the image of vigour and the achievements that did not come off – will be argued for years. But not today.

Even at such a time the American sense of drama has heightened everything. This is the first presidential assassination in the television and popular newspaper age, and the impact is numbing – even without the new violence that has followed.

Yet it is perhaps true that even the most authentic emotion is crude.

The papers that exploit the haggard misery of relatives, photographed in unwillingly public grief, are themselves grieved.

The circus parade of human sorrow, the day-long keening on television, is America's true trial of mourning.

Even when all the big advertisers turn their displays into black-bordered In Memoria, it looks less cynical than you might suppose.

Every society expresses itself in its own idiom. Public relations lamentation need not necessarily be insincere.

But the other mood is uglier. In Dallas a little while ago we got a glimpse of how ugly.

Whoever shot President Kennedy – and unlike the United States Press, we have been trained to await at least a trial – the political theme was bitterly thrust forward today.

'Kennedy slain by Red,' the banners shouted. 'President dies by Commie bullet.' 'Red killer held.' Jack Ruby became the symbol of violent reactions.

The former General Edwin Walker, of the John Birch Society, has said Kennedy's death was 'tragic, but not surprising. This internal threat must never be underestimated.'

Lee Oswald's association with the Fair Play for Cuba Committee has pricked that boil again. This morning they dragged the wretched Cuban delegate to the U.N. on the television and rubbed his nose in it.

'Aren't there Castro-lovers in Cuba who would want Kennedy's death?' they demanded. And he could only cry: 'No, no – for so many reasons, no. You will never understand.'

Today the whole apparatus of United States Government is in abeyance. President Johnson has returned to his home in Spring Valley, to the house that used to be the scene of the hostess Perle Mesta's celebrated parties.

Now it is ringed with police and secret servicemen.

The roaring tide of speculation and pressure that will descend on the new President is momentarily held back. It will not be for long.

Today Kennedy's family flew in from Hyannis in Massachusetts – all but his father, crippled with a stroke.

Joseph Kennedy, one-time Ambassador in London, is not ordinarily an easy subject for sympathy, but it is impossible not to flinch at the many blows fate has dealt him.

His first son, Joseph, vanished during the war on a bombing flight. His second daughter, Kathleen, married the Marquis of Hartington – killed in Normandy – and herself died in a plane crash.

The eldest daughter, Rosemary, is at forty-four, still in a school for the retarded in Wisconsin. And now this – in the last days of his life.

Tonight the late President's coffin lies in the Rotunda, surrounded by marble statuary and vast ceremonial paintings.

Nine soldiers and sailors – including two Negroes – brought the body in.

The official mourners stood around in the bleak empty way of those who must listen to the official eulogies.

Among them was Jackie Kennedy, two days widowed, looking very erect and slim in black.

She stood there with every smallest change of expression brutally exposed to the zoom lenses of a dozen T.V. cameras.

On one of her hands hung her son John, three years old tomorrow. On the other Caroline, who will be six two days later.

They know of the tragedy. But they cannot know the full drama of the youngest man ever elected President of the United States – and the youngest ever to die.

Now two men lie dead, one in Dallas and the other in the Capitol, for a purpose no one will now ever know.

Daily Herald,
25 November 1963

NELSON'S DESPERATE MESSAGE

The African wheel is coming full circle at great speed. When I last saw Nelson Mandela, in the days when he led the African National Congress, he spoke of boycotts and protests. Now, from the dock at Pretoria, he admits fighting apartheid with sabotage – 'the only way' – and virtually asks for the gallows.

If they do hang Nelson Mandela it will probably be the point of no return in South African affairs.

For while Mandela was formally stating his own despair, the U.N. special committee on South Africa offered that bitter, tragic country what is tantamount to a last chance.

They urge a National Convention of all South African peoples, including the Government, solemnly and reasonably to reconsider the nation's future before it is too late.

The argument is simple: Whatever happens, the cruel anomaly of white domination is doomed and *must* sooner or later come to an end; the one question left is how many shall die with it.

'What is now at issue is not the final outcome but the question whether, on the way, the people of South Africa are to go through a long ordeal of blood and hate. If so, all Africa and the whole world must be involved.'

This proposal for a South African Convention stands roughly the same chance of being accepted by Dr Verwoerd as does Martin Luther King of becoming President of the United States.

It will be furiously rejected as an interference in South Africa's internal affairs, as has every other expression of international disgust at her own especial racist tyranny.

It is quite on the cards that if the point is pressed South Africa may finally do as she has often threatened and become the first member-State to quit the U.N. altogether.

The U.N. committee members were a Swedish chairman, a Moroccan, a Ghanaian and our own Sir Hugh Foot. To anyone but a South African Nationalist their findings must seem moderate and rational, even cautious.

Their suggestion of an amnesty to opponents of apartheid to attend a Convention is only fair and logical. Their belief that the future of South Africa must be determined by South Africans is sensible and humane. But the proposals are addressed to an administration that is neither fair nor logical, that does not understand moderation, reason or humanity. Implicit in the offer is the hopeless certainty that it will be refused.

There follows, therefore, the threat.

The threat is for the rest of the world to send South Africa to Coventry – but seriously and effectively, to isolate her politically and economically from the transactions of other peoples everywhere.

The U.N. group want the whole logistics of sanctions to be examined by the Security Council. This would be an official and extremely solemn extension of the International Conference on South African Sanctions held in London last week.

It would be the battle-plan for an impending non-military World War on the Republic of South Africa.

And this must mean the co-operation – indeed the leadership – of Britain and the U.S. with whom South Africa does most of her business.

This is a uniquely serious proposition. It goes immensely further than a refusal to buy oranges and sherry or to sell Buccaneer aircraft and Saracen troop-trucks.

Sanctions against a nation (as we learned with Italy twenty-seven years ago) mean nothing without a blockade, and a blockade can be argued an act of aggression (as Cuba argues today against the U.S.).

Vast interests in this country are already denouncing the notion of impeding trade with a country in which £1,000 million of British capital are invested, to whom we export about £150-million-worth of goods a year, the making of which employs 130,000 people here.

There are many hard and specious reasons made (and many more to come, when the crunch arrives) why it is bad business to invoke commercial pressures for moral reasons.

Britain's Tory Government oppose sanctions, the Labour Party hedge hard. Have we not, they say, made our disapproval of apartheid known?

We have; and the result is that after twenty-nine resolutions in the U.N. formally denouncing apartheid, after sixty-five nations announce their individual boycotts, after ten years of international denunciation, the only effect upon the South African state at the moment is her exclusion from the Olympic Games. *Nothing else*. The enormous Anglo-U.S. investments in South Africa are the *reason* why the principle of apartheid works.

The first crisis may come in the Security Council quite soon. If sanctions are put to the vote, we shall presumably once again side with Portugal, our oldest and probably only ally in this matter.

The second and inescapable crisis will come in rather less than a year.

Then, after four years of consideration, the International Court must produce their decision on South-West Africa, the great territory that South Africa has for ten years refused to hand over to the U.N. Trusteeship Council.

The Court are almost certain to rule that this must now be done, and that apartheid must be withdrawn from its people. The Republic are almost equally certain to refuse again.

And the Security Council will present the world with the equation of survival – either White South Africa, or the United Nations.

By then it may seen a long way back to Nelson Mandela, the black lawyer in the Pretoria dock, and his flat words: 'I had hoped to live to see my idea realised. But, my lord, it is an idea for which I am prepared to die.'

Daily Herald,
22 April 1964

AN EMPIRE – AND A TRAIL OF LOST CAUSES

So he has gone at last, eighty-five years and a fortnight old; he outlived by some fifteen years the allotted span ordained by the Book he quoted so vigorously. Doubtless he insisted on doing so; he was one man of whom it was claimed that he had a hot line to Heaven. He will be immeasurably missed.

Only two weeks ago 700 people, gathered to wish him well on his birthday, heard him announce that he was 'entering his apprenticeship'. Everybody nudged; 'The old man has done it again!'

And now he really has. Rest him, wherever he is.

I worked for Lord Beaverbrook for many years; I left him in circumstances of great and mutual disaffection. In later years I came to know him again, and found in him as a man all the qualities there were not in the tycoon.

I do not think anyone got to know Beaverbrook by working for him. Between him and the Beaver boys hung the impenetrable barrier of a common purpose.

He did not believe anyone could possibly disagree with him and still be sane. Not when you took his money. When you stopped, then you found the charm. How he could charm!

The obituaries today will most certainly vary from the adulatory to the waspish. This is reasonable; it was virtually impossible to come to terms with Lord Beaverbrook in any sort of *medium* emotion.

He was genuinely hated by some, and genuinely loved by some.

Others can adjudicate on his life and works as a politician. I can only consider him as a newspaperman, and at that he was a terror. He loved being a terror. He loved stimulating his gifted flock by keeping them forever on the edge of phobia, showering them with bounty and abuse, scaring them to death and giving lavish parties for them.

It is true that he bought men's souls. It was not always done with money. The man who could charm a bird off a bough could certainly charm left-wing journalists into the fold, sometimes before they knew what had hit them. What had hit them was the most galvanic personality in the business – a business that is that much shorter of the quality today.

But journalism to Beaverbrook was merely an extension of politics. He did not hide it; he proclaimed it. He told the Press Commission: 'I run my newspapers solely for the purposes of propaganda.'

The business of garbing that propaganda in the most highly-professional of expertise he left to his technicians. He pressed the buttons.

The paradox (which he wryly appreciated) was that the means came off and the ends didn't. He finished with a brilliant and prosperous newspaper empire, and a trail of lost causes. 'I keep telling 'em,' he once said, 'and they pay no heed, but continue on their way like brands to the burning. Still, I hammer 'em.'

On his eighty-fifth birthday two weeks ago he made a speech, vitally articulate for a man so frail, and that was his theme. He had accomplished everything, and nothing.

He had made a million pounds, or maybe several, and that was all. No Empire Free Trade – for that matter, no Empire. None of the causes for which he had laboured so long invoked so much talent, including Holy Writ itself.

All he had left was a scintillating example of daily journalism – and, he proclaimed, a sense of humour.

All his life, especially as he grew old and exhausted, he thought back wistfully to the days when he had been a small-shot tycoon but a big-shot politician – the brave days of king-making in 1916, when the Beaverbrook homes at Cherkley and the Hyde Park Hotel were the hub of the splendid machinations to get Asquith out and Lloyd George in.

It is pretty sure that he loved the machinations more than the objective. 'I laid my web,' he would say with relish, 'how they needed me!'

If he could be less than honest with those he disliked, he was completely candid about his own character. It seemed there was nothing he enjoyed better than explaining how he was tricked into his peerage.

He had anticipated its bestowal, and when he wanted to reject it he couldn't, to save his face. 'Thus was vanity my downfall, or up-fall,' he would say, with pleasure. But he genuinely regretted being shunted upstairs, far from the splendid scheming of the Commons.

In that last speech – which was, I see now, a farewell – he explained how first New Brunswick had become too small for him, then Ontario too small for him, then London too small for him. 'They say,' he mused, 'that I may well find the same trouble with hell.'

That we shall never know.

Goodbye, Max Aitken, you leave a mighty gap. Already down Fleet Street they are hearing the echo of a mocking laugh.

Daily Herald,
10 June 1964

FRONTLINE HARLEM

Wherever you walk, the broken glass crackles underfoot, unswept, and the shopfronts sag. It is like the morrow of a blitz – except that the brass mementoes in the gutters are the empty shell-cases from the policemen's guns.

From the number, you would think they had been defending Stalingrad.

The air still carries the overtone of cordite among the garlic and herring but mostly it reeks of bitterness.

Harlem is charged with hate, a thing as tangible as fear. The battle of Lenox Avenue is momentarily halted by a sort of truce; it will not last.

The frontier of white Manhattan is now roughly along 110th Street, just north of Central Park. No cabman will cross it today – 'except I go in with a machine-gun mounted,' one told me, 'and I can mow down every black bastard I see.'

Already, with the first riots barely subsided, the posters are out on the Harlem streets: 'Organise and mobilise now against the enemy.'

The enemy means *ME*. Every eye and every glance, every thrust in the face and shove off the sidewalk proclaims it. The billboards say: THE DAY OF RECKONING IS AT HAND.

A long row of steel-helmeted policemen stand restlessly across the intersection, fingering their guns.

'You don't want to come here, Bud,' said the tall Negro, flitting by like a shadow. 'This isn't your war, Mac.'

At the end of the street, a dozen shots crack out. Everybody ducks.

The 'Long, Hot Summer' of angry omen, so long forecast for the coming American race crisis, has now brought the first rumbling thunder of the gathering storm.

This week's riots in Harlem have left this wretched coloured ghetto of New York consumed and tormented with a baffled, vengeful uneasiness.

What has been implicit in the American Negro struggle for years is now without its disguise.

It is completely certain now that war has been declared, and those who were shot and bludgeoned and outraged this week in Harlem – those, both black and white, who suffered in this senseless skirmish – were only the first.

Jesse Gray, the Harlem evangelist, has now called for 'a hundred skilled black revolutionaries ready to die' in the coming guerilla campaign: 'If we must die, let us at least die scientifically.'

When Bayard Rustin, the Negro patriot and organiser of last year's Freedom March, called once again for moderation he was screamed down with the Negro militants' bitterest epithet – '*Uncle Tom*'.

All Harlem, from 131st Street to the Park, has lost the mood to listen to moderation of any kind.

There are Malcolm X and the Black Muslins on the one side, and Commissioner Murphy's cops on the other.

The Harlem riots were not just one more link in the chain of civil disturbances now spreading steadily throughout the United States.

They are probably a turning point in the whole story of the American Civil Rights struggle.

What everyone has so long feared has finally come about: *there has been organised violence and racial street fighting on a mass scale, and in a northern and vaguely liberal city.*

The New York police, under stress, proved as indiscriminately brutal and trigger-happy as any in the Deep South.

The Negroes of Harlem, provoked by years of frustration, proved as hysterical and destructive as any crowd can be.

The deadly, inescapable, steamy heat of this endlessly oppressive summer has reduced everyone's temper to rags and blown up both white and black uneasiness into neurosis.

The theme of real violence that lurks forever a millimetre under the urbane surface of this harrowed and hapless American society has proclaimed itself, momentarily subsided, and now awaits its greater opportunity.

The provocation of this crisis would have been trifling otherwise than in this long, hot summer of the racial crisis.

An off-duty New York policeman fired three shots into a fifteen-year-old schoolboy and killed him, explaining later that the boy had threatened him with a knife.

Why a trained policeman had been unable to handle a recalcitrant schoolboy other than by shooting him dead is so far unexplained, though now a New York Grand Jury are investigating.

The occasion, and the boy's funeral – with suitable stimulation from the Negro activists – was enough to fuse off the tragedy we see before us in uptown New York today, with Harlem resembling a city in the grip of civil war, which is virtually what it is.

It is difficult to overstate the extraordinary perils of this situation, which cannot be appreciated without understanding what Harlem actually is.

This place which has gone into legend as a sort of market place of jazz and bonhomie is in fact the most festering enclave of urban squalor, with a quarter-million people, almost all Negro, jammed into three and a half square miles of hopeless and unredeemable decay, which itself has been defined as 'a product of violence whose existence is a symbol of neglect, inhumanity and injustice.'

Harlem is the northern ghetto of Manhattan in which black people are confined because they cannot escape, a racial colony within the most liberal, sophisticated and cosmopolitan city of a great nation.

It is inhabited by citizens who, paying the same taxes as everyone else, have not the political or economic power to gain even the minimal services in housing, health, sanitation, education or even police protection.

It is, when you look at it, a horrifying anachronism, a quenching environment for the human spirit in which violence has been accepted as normal for years, since nothing else is possible.

Its index for juvenile delinquency has for ten years been consistently twice as great as the city rate; its proportion of narcotic addicts nearly eight times; its venereal count six times and likewise its homicide rate.

It is in fact a loathsome slum which was destined to be, and has become, a social volcano.

The Harlem riots which have happened, which continue to smoulder tonight, and which are inevitably bound to develop, are bad enough in terms of their simple human suffering alone.

Their political implications are, if possible, even worse. An election campaign is now beginning in which one Presidential candidate, for the first time in living memory, is an avowed racialist, who himself voted against the Civil Rights Bill.

He and his Southerners, who have resented the Civil Rights struggle and its emphasis on Southern outrages, are now vindicated by these troubles in the North. Their ranks are strengthened.

The 'white backlash' (as it is called) of resentment in the Northern cities against Negro advance is immeasurably reinforced.

Every disaster in Harlem is a magnificent bonus for Senator Barry Goldwater, who is now assured of the whole-hearted support of everyone, Republican or Democrat, who fears and opposes the huge Negro drive for equality and justice.

Every white-hating Negro fanatic, every wog-clobbering Irish policeman, every snarling bigot of a Jewish New York taxi driver, is a vote in the bank for the dreaded Goldwater.

Did he not himself only a few days ago announce that 'extremism in defence of liberty is no vice'?

Will that not be requoted for ever now by every black man with a Molotov cocktail, every dumb and angry New York copper with a blackjack and a gun?

The implications of this go much deeper than Harlem, beastly though they are.

'If racist hatred, violence and resentment are capable of electing a President,' says the *New York Post*, 'then Goldwater has a right to be hopeful now.

'A few more such riots will create the spectre of violence in the streets of every city, so that neither white nor Negro feels safe. Goldwater has been preparing the ground for exactly that.'

We are facing bad days here in the world's greatest democracy, and the end is not yet.

Daily Herald,
22 July 1964

EVENING STANDARD, 1965–6

The *Evening Standard* developed the trick of adding after my byline 'the dissident voice'. I never quite understood this, since I was not markedly more dissident in the *Standard* than anywhere else. I imagine it was merely the paper proclaiming: Lo, see how liberal are we; dissent flowers and freedom prospers! It was all a bit embarrassing.

One column remains memorable to me: the obituary of the cartoonist Vicky. Vicky, Victor Weisz, the little Jewish German genius, was for years a very close and beloved friend, we met almost daily. Every new aspect of political or diplomatic folly and peril – and God knows in those days there was almost one a day – he took as a deeply personal emotional commitment; he was a dedicated worrier, he revelled in despair. The worst part of the day for Vicky was the very early morning, before the papers had arrived to tell him what he had to weep about that day; he fretted inconsolably until he had the bad news in his hands; then he would visibly brighten up, and shift gear into whatever realm of misery was appropriate.

Michael Foot, another of Vicky's great chums, wrote not long ago that Vicky grew very weary of people trying to cheer him up by insisting that things were not all that bad. Only I evolved the right trick: I would mourn and repine even more desperately than he, until in self-defence Vicky was forced to think up some cause for hope.

He was forever threatening, with relish, to take his own life. It could be a tedious topic, and once I was stern with him, and said: 'For God's sake, old pal, don't go on and on about it – if you really want to do it, do it.'

Soon after that I was very ill, in south France, when the Editor of the *Standard*, Charles Wintour, telephoned me to say that Vicky had poisoned himself.

The Wee Man, we used to call him. After all these years I miss him still.

One other item of huge importance – I mean to me, not necessarily to anyone else – is the story about the birth of Bangladesh. When the Indo-Pakistan conflict began I was on holiday in the South – indeed, on my honeymoon, if you please. Nobody asked me to do anything about the war. But I became the usual Pavlov's dog; I sent my wife back to London while I went to Bengal, for I argued that it was against the rules for anyone to have a war without me.

131

I had been there but a week when I was badly broken up in a military jeep smash. I was in fact the only survivor. Fearful of going to hospital in Calcutta, bursting with refugees and threatened with typhoid, I got myself sellotaped together and freighted home. I do not remember the journey.

In the London hospital I became obsessed with the need to write something about this stupid war, if only to justify to myself my broken ribs and knees and back and, as it turned out later, heart. I asked for pencil and paper and – it seems, for it is not even a memory to me – wrote the *Evening Standard* story reprinted here.

Later, when it was shown to me, I read it with a rather eerie wonder, for I had never seen it before. To this day I have not the slightest recollection of writing that story of Bangladesh. That had never in my life happened to me before, and I pray it never will again.

*   *   *

ON THE WAY

At five in the morning Peking has a disembodied air; its strange pearly quality achieves no sort of shape in the half-light; its outlines are blurred and misty; it is rather like existing within a seventeenth-century Chinese water-colour. It is lovely, but eerie.

It had been years since I had last been in Peking, which is a city with uncommon charm for me. I was so entranced at being back again, if only momentarily, that I could hardly bring myself to go to bed. In any case the plane for Vietnam was to leave at dawn. I fussed and wandered about imprudently for hours. I thus missed, though I did not know it, the last chance of any serious night's sleep I was to have for weeks.

You have to be up extremely early in the morning to beat the first Chinese; in fact I doubt whether it is possible. Long before dawn there is always someone about sweeping the streets or pushing a barrow or shuffling stuff behind the shutters of a shop. Peking is a curiously un-animated city, but it never really goes to sleep. At five that morning the blue lines of workers were already lining up for the early buses. A few zealots writhed about under the trees doing their obligatory morning P.T. The public loudspeakers that are the one indefensible curse of that agreeable city were already in business, braying out

Slavonic martial music and the erratic wail of Peking opera. It was all very like it had been in the old days.

By the time I got to the airport the day was fully under way. Peking airport is a place you seem to be at only in the middle of the night or at the crack of dawn; it has the vaguely neurotic feeling of those sections of a Communist city that are used almost wholly by foreigners. All airports have a queer dissociation from the ordinary life of the cities they serve; Peking's could be in another world.

By some sort of Oriental paradox it is a big job getting one's *dokumenti* attended to in China. It is necessary to stand around in great echoing halls under immense busts of Chairman Mao, apparently cast from one universal mould in some pallid material resembling lard, until someone comes and asks you, almost diffidently, for your passport. There would doubtless be the most unholy trouble if you contrived to miss the formalities (as most fearfully did I find out on the homeward trip) but the administrative procedure seems oddly casual. At that time of day nobody speaks English, and there is much cordial misunderstanding. The only thing to do is to produce every kind of form and document in one's possession and proffer the lot; the official accepts them with a puzzled air and goes dreamily away into invisibility, leaving one rooted to the spot, not daring to move in case he apparently never finds one again.

Eventually one is always rescued by a very young woman with her pigtail in a bow, who copes with the situation. Contemporary China gives the impression of being managed entirely by very competent schoolgirls.

My flight was going to Wu-han and Nan-ning and thence to Hanoi, which caused a certain interest; it is not every day that British passports go to North Vietnam. My immigration official was suitably inscrutable; he took the thing as no great drama (which it certainly was to me), rather did he appear to regard the trip as a quaint eccentricity.

'Hanoi, ha-ha,' he said. 'You go wrong way.'

I had a moment of great alarm, thinking I might be mistakenly embarking on a flight to Vladivostok, until I remembered the Chinese trouble with the letter 'l'.

'Yes, a long way,' I replied.

'Don't mention,' said the officer enigmatically, and gave me a card that said 'Valid for One Muslim Meal.'

They soon forgot about me, however; they became too busy with the Russians.

Somehow the departure lounge had become full of Russian experts (every Russian outside Russia is by definition an 'expert') who were milling about in a kind of disciplined confusion, shouting loud instructions at each other and pacing about in all directions without at any time ceasing to be a cohesive group. This is a procedure which in my experience is peculiar to Soviet travelling parties: that of separate people busying themselves in intensely individual activities while never for an instant losing touch with the *ensemble*.

They were a group of Soviet technicians bound for North Vietnam – almost certainly mechanics for the anti-aircraft missile-sites with (as it turned out later) a few advisers in civil engineering. It was one of the hazards of their exacting trade that to reach their destination from Moscow they were obliged to travel through Peking. There was no welcome for them there, and they knew it.

As we entered the aircraft we were presented with handfuls of small, densely printed, and very hostile booklets. There are many delights to be found in the People's Republic of China, as well I have found, but the distribution of public reading-matter is not one of them. It has been a frequent penance for me to be left with nothing to read but the numbingly boring propaganda pamphlets that abound, and which are even less rewarding when all that are left on the stands are the versions in Swahili or Albanian.

I found myself left in the plane with only a booklet crisply called: 'We Shall Fight to the End against Khrushchovism, Soviet Revisionism, and Moscow's Betrayal of the World-Wide Struggle against Imperialism.' The alternatives were 'Down for Ever with Moscow's Philosophy of Splittism,' or 'The Soviet-U.S. Conspiracy: a Study in Treachery.' They seemed flashy things to be reading in a planeful of Russians, even though it was a Chinese plane; it is curious what a sense of ideological neutralism comes over one, surrounded by Soviet citizens ten thousand feet above Shansi Province. The Chinese had considerately provided every Russian with a selection of the most vigorously anti-Soviet literature in stock.

My seat companion was very civil; he was thumbing without excitement, since he could not read it, through 'Le Trahison des Héritiers de Khrushchov.' He was an extremely huge man; I wondered what service he was going to render to the people of North Vietnam. Then the comrade stewardess brought the tea round; the glasses were so horribly hot that I nearly screamed, and dropped mine on the gangway. My companion reached out a hand that must have been made of the material of a hoof, enveloped the almost incandescent glass, and sent the whole boiling lot down in one.

There was one great diversion. Soon after take-off a fly appeared, wandering distractedly around the cabin. This, in China, is always a great event, as I remember from early days in Peking; I was gratified to see that things had little changed. The great phenomenon then had been the famous 'fly campaign', part of the great drive for the most un-Chinese cleanliness and hygiene, when no fly's life had been worth a moment's purchase. For years thereafter any stray fly that had somehow escaped the original purge was harried remorselessly, and such was the case with this one, entrapped in the Hanoi plane. The anti-fly attitude has clearly become a conditioned response, and the comrade stewardess reacted dead on cue. Magically there appeared in her hand a People's fly-swatter, and the hunt was up. As the fly felt obliged to settle on the back of a seat it was taken out, as the Americans say, with a deft and practised forehand flick, and its remains wrapped in a piece of paper and taken away to wherever Chinese flies go after death.

This caused a great flurry among the Russians, who had clearly heard all the funny Pekinese fly-stories; they applauded loudly, with what I could not help feeling was a strong undertone of satire. Then they affected to find flies everywhere, and for a while there was much happy horseplay, with the Soviet passengers scrambling about and swatting each other on the head with rolled-up sick-bags. This was their revenge for the pamphlets. The comrade stewardess looked on impassively, but I saw she kept her own professional swatter at the ready from then on.

'The intractable divergences between the Marxist-Leninists and the schismatic faction of the C.P.S.U.,' I read in the Peking pamphlet, 'rest on the question: do we ally with the labouring people of the world against the American Imperialists and their lackeys, or do we ally with the American Imperialists and their lackeys against the labouring people of the world? Among the many acts of betrayal committed by the Khruschovian revisionists the most flagrant was the conclusion with the U.S. and the U.K. of the shameful Treaty on the partial cessation of nuclear tests, the great act of treason against the peace-loving peoples of the world . . .'

I read it once, and twice, and indeed again; it said the same thing every time.

We were over the Yangtze Kiang; we were over Hunan Province into Kwangsi, over the lush and abundant South China; invisibly down there were the patchwork fields of rice and sugar, the buffalo drowsing in their pools and the farmers turning the irrigation treadmills. For a moment I wished I were going back there, and not going into the unknown bafflements of Vietnam.

At Nan-ning is the frontier. I still had in my possession twenty-four pieces of People's money – twenty-four yuan, Y24: about £2 10s. It is illegal to export the smallest amount of Chinese currency; I deposited the money in the Nan-ning airport branch of the Bank of China, against a receipt that took ten minutes to prepare.

'I am now,' I said, 'in a sense, a capitalist of China.'

The man smiled wanly, and returned to his abacus. In China there are things too trivial even for jokes.

A couple of hours later I was in Hanoi.

In such a mood shall men land on the moon.

---

* Editor's Note: In December 1965 James Cameron became the first Western correspondent to be admitted to Hanoi. A series of articles which appeared in the London *Evening Standard* became the basis of the book – "*Here is your Enemy*."

VICTORY IF IT TAKES FOREVER

When the sirens go these days there is a difference: the shelters are made of earth and seem built for children, the loudspeakers chatter their warnings and exhortations in Vietnamese, so I am unable to distinguish whether I am being urged to run like hell or merely improve my production.

Moreover, the men in the aeroplanes overhead are surely called Bill or Joe, and are already thinking about getting back for lunch aboard their carrier in the Seventh Fleet. Maybe they will and maybe they won't.

I am ill-accustomed to being bombed by Americans.

Not so the people here in North Vietnam; indeed they are obsessed by it. Every aspect of life is dominated by this mood of embattlement and siege. It is tangible everywhere in the eerie emptiness of the daylight countryside, the emphasis on darkness, the air-raid shelters and foxholes, the rifles stacked at the corners of paddyfields and the edges of desks, the great painted posters everywhere proclaiming bitterness and defiance.

'We are, as you know, in a state of war' – it explains everything, excuses everything: the hardships, the rationing, the endless repetitive hours of civil defence rehearsal, the A-A drill, the anger that keeps breaking through the gentle courtesies. Sometimes, as with ourselves in wartime, it excuses too much – the regimentation, the sudden bursts of suspicion, the barrenness of everything, the exaggeration of both suffering and success. But no wonder, you say, as you look at this unhappy and furious country, no wonder; no people in the world have been so continuously at war as these small people of Vietnam.

One feels extremely alone in Hanoi. Among its 600,000 inhabitants there seems to be nobody like oneself – nor is there, nor has there been for years. It was far from easy to get here; the thing is virtually unprecedented, and feels it. This is not a place where non-Communist Westerners are welcomed, since recently the only ones who have come here have come in B50s and F105s and blown things up, like bridges and people, which is not agreeable when you see it, nor very persuasive.

My European face is accepted so long as I am taken to be a Russian technician or a Czech diplomat; when they learn who I am the reaction is astonishment, curiosity, and doubt.

But one is through the looking-glass at last, in the capital of North Vietnam, and as far as most Westerners know today it might be in the moon.

This is Hanoi, which the Americans will say is full of demons and the Communists will say is full of heroes. It seems to me, on the contrary, to be very full of people, largely indistinguishable from those of Saigon except in the bleak austerity of their condition.

The important thing is that one is now *through* the looking-glass, and everything outside – you and home and London and New York; everything – is a sort of mirror-image, where black is white and white is black, good is bad and bad is good, defence is aggression, military efficiency is wanton cruelty, right is wrong. It is not the first time this has happened to me, but more strikingly now than ever before. Once you turn all the political value-judgments into terms of people, they become both simpler and more difficult.

Hanoi is unrecognisable. I had not been here for twelve years or so, when the French were bleakly and blindly sweating out the last days of their empire, already on its deathbed at Dien Bien Phu. It was then what the French made of all their colonial garrison-towns: a sort of provençal prefecture with Asian overtones; the French were said to create their colonies of boulevards and brothels. Hanoi had never had the sophistication of Saigon, but it was a pleasant provincial city, built around lakes.

The Communists have had it for eleven years; the old Hanoi has vanished. It had a wayward charm; now it has an anguished efficiency. No more brilliant girls floating like butterflies in their gossamer *ao dais*; the black and white trousered uniform of the workers is everywhere.

The shops have the battered empty drabness of State stores everywhere, for these are hard times; outside the ration there never seems much to buy, except an occasional plastic comb, an enamelled bowl, second-hand spare parts of unidentifiable machines.

It is a fact that the economy of Vietnam, decaying in the South, is immensely increasing in the North, but not much seeps through in consumer-goods. 'We are, as you know, in a state of war –'

I looked vaguely for things I had remembered – where was the Restaurant Manoire, the little Bar Paradis, where the taxi-dancers sat embroidering, demure as schoolgirls; what had they become? They had become nothing, it seemed. They had not just been transformed, or closed; they had become eliminated; they had ceased ever to have existed, and nobody remembered ever having heard of them. What of the dreadful Camp de la Presse, where I had so distressfully lodged as an appendage of the French Army, longing for the forbidden luxuries of the Metropole Hotel? It, too, had become a non-thing; it had never been.

Instead, I now inhabit the Metropole. It has become the Thong Nhat, the Unity Hotel, and whatever were its glories in the days of General Navarre, they have departed. At its sombre bar, the only one in town, brood a handful of expatriates – Roumanian attachés, the Soviet cultural officer, a few East Germans, the man from Tass, drinking the Vietnamese vodka called Lua Moi and dreaming of the *dolce vita* of Omsk or Riga.

I have one friend: a splendid unsinkably sanguine Bulgarian, who introduced himself: 'I have just heard the radio: the news from the West is disastrous, catastrophic!' Aghast, I begged to be told. 'It is the European Cup. My Bulgaria has been beaten 5–0 – *imaginez-vous, par les Belges!*'

My room is vast. The bath had five taps, all unmarked except one, which says *Froid*. This is the one which emits hot water for an hour each day. Luxuries of this kind are permitted only in the 'foreign' hotel: it is oppressive. Elsewhere there are only Vietnamese, who are infallibly charming and patient.

The war hangs overhead like a brutal cloud. The schools have been evacuated from the towns, so has much of the plant from the few industrial enterprises. Basic food is not especially scarce (Vietnam is a fertile country) but there is a rice ration of five kilos a month. Cloth is rationed to five metres a month; there are coupons for soap and meat. There is practically no private civilian motor traffic in the North, but what exists is like all military transport, heavily camouflaged under piles of branches, palm fronds, banana leaves. Even in the towns this phenomenon continues, cars and lorries buried in greenery; Birnam Wood forever coming to Dunsinane.

The people too – every citizen goes for his military exercises with a cape of vegetation hanging about his shoulders. It is, perhaps, taken slightly to excess: the cult of camouflage has become in a way modish, and the new standard hat for everyone of importance is, paradoxically, a sort of topi of marked colonial appearance, garnished with little fronds of green cloth. The buses have rationalised the whole thing by being spray-painted in a formal pattern of foliage, like Oriental wallpaper.

Maybe the thing has become a little theatrical – but whom could it be supposed to impress, in a place that sees almost no strangers?

The fact is that this is a land where everyone considers it necessary to live in disguise, to inhabit their own country pretending they are not there, but invisible, resentfully. Rifles abound in the most improbable places. There is a strong feeling of the early days of Israel, the same sense of wariness and never-ending siege.

You can call it what you like, but it is a war, an enduring war and a special war, a dedicated and within the limits of workable society, a complete one. There are many arguments about its righteousness; they come as a rule from people 10,000 miles away. I just happen to be where few of the politicians or the soldiers or the statesmen who talk about North Vietnam have ever been – that is, in North Vietnam.

I have now been a good deal about the country, from what are called the 'fighting areas' towards the border to the north-east coast on the China Sea. I have talked to as many people as I can communicate with, including the President and the Prime Minister. They vary greatly in their persuasion. This is often a matter of linguistic limitation; too many officials speak an English or French that was actually *learned* in slogans – the only word for American is 'rabid-imperialist-aggressor'; the only word for Vietnam is 'heroic-valiant-resistance'. It is understandable but tedious.

What is taking place in Vietnam, both South and North, is an offence to international decency, both disgusting and absurd, and one of its chief wrongs is that it is corrupting both the assailants and the victims alike.

However, what is quite clear in this lunar landscape of North Vietnam is that the people have a totally unshakable determination to win the war, on their terms. Not to make an end to it, or find a way out of it, or 'conclude an agreement' about it. They have the extraordinary and rather impressive nerve to insist upon winning it.

Victory, however, has a strict definition, which is the implementation of the Geneva Agreement of 1954, which requires a Vietnam united under popular elections, and the elimination of all foreign troops from both South and North. To Hanoi, winning the war does not mean the crushing or destruction of U.S. forces; it means their departure. This they will achieve, they say, if it takes forever.

The thing is militarily illogical – a poor and small Asian country convinced it can successfully challenge the richest and strongest nation on earth – but the mood is extremely pervasive. It is a fact (as everyone from Mr Davies* to Mr Kosygin now knows) that they reject the machinery of compromise categorically. Indeed the word 'negotiation' has become an emotive, even offensive, word, in the way words these days acquire unreasonable connotations, as 'appeasement' did in the '40s, as 'peace' did in the '50s. 'Negotiations' to Hanoi merely mean some devious stratagem to get the U.S. off the hook, to rescue her from a cruel and intolerable situation.

'The negotiations are over,' they repeat. 'The negotiations were concluded in 1954, at Geneva, by international signature. There is more to say – except when they shall be made good.'

It is nevertheless true to say that Hanoi now requires something more than that; it wants to see the U.S. chastised for her behaviour in the way especially punitive in Oriental eyes: by shame, by loss of face. It is not pleasant, but when you see what has been done to this place it is at least comprehensible.

The painful thing is that this attitude, this emotion, is almost impossibly foreign to the normal character of the Vietnamese, who are probably the most gentle and diffident of peoples, nervously courteous in ways of considerate formal civility that makes the average Caucasoid feel like an oaf. The photographs one sees from the South, the stories one reads of Vietnamese barbarity to their countrymen, their disregard for human pain (those terrible spiked mantraps, the routine acceptance of torture) are in some tormented way a charade of our times.

If this bloody war has done no worse, it can be condemned for currupting a quiet and tranquil Asian atmosphere into a contest of beastliness, and it should not have happened here, for these are among the most quietly cultivated people in the world.

I hasten to say this is not brainwashing. I have known the South-East Asians for twenty years, and I might well wish Vietnam had found another road than Communism. But they chose it, and I would argue that it is their affair. Many may disagree.

I think it is a fact that on the whole the Western industrial societies have a very imperfect notion of the nature of Asian Communism, for which there really should be another and less emotive word. It is a specially local product of a peasant economy, the most obvious factor of which is that it caters, for the first time, for hopes as well as for

---

* Mr Harold Davies, M.P., visited Hanoi in July as the Premier's peace emissary. He was not allowed to see either the President or Prime Minister of North Vietnam.

needs. I should guess that you would have to look a long way outside
official cadres in Vietnam for a truly doctrinaire Marxist. But everyone
trusts Uncle Ho.

Evening Standard,
7 December 1965

A NORTH-VIETNAMESE COLONEL TALKING

It is endlessly and formally insisted in Hanoi that the Republic of
Vietnam, North and South alike, is one State, temporarily divided
at the 17th parallel, and that this fact is acknowledged at the Geneva
Agreement of 1954, which was accepted and signed by Britain,
France, Vietnam, Laos and Cambodia.

The implementation of this legal fact is what, they say, the war is all
about. Only the United States impedes it, by force of arms.

The United States equally argues that if this unified State comes
about, by the elections required by Geneva, Vietnam will become a
Communist country overnight. This is almost certainly true.

I talked for an hour with a lieutenant-colonel in the Vietnam regular
army in Hanoi, whose name was a delicate matter since his function
was head of liaison with the National Liberation Front of South
Vietnam, elsewhere known as Vietcong. His headquarters, with a nice
irony, were in a villa of surpassing ugliness that had formerly been the
property of Madam Nhu,* the 'dragon lady', who may be half-
forgotten in the West but who is remembered with a special loathing in
Hanoi.

'This war is often described as one which nobody can win,' he said,
'you have used the phrase yourself. I would dispute that. It can be
won, in the sense that our objective can be attained. That is, as you
know, no more – but certainly no less – than the implementation of
the Geneva Agreement. That entails the withdrawal of American

---

* Madam Ngo Dinh Nhu is the former 'first lady' of South Vietnam, now in exile.
Her brother-in-law, President Diem, and husband, the secret police chief, were
assassinated in a South Vietnam coup in 1963.

troops. When it comes about, it will constitute what our Government will regard as victory. We require nothing more of the Americans than that they go home.

'The fighting in the South will inevitably grow fiercer and more bloody, and I do not by any means reject the possibility of its escalating far more directly in the North. In a word, the war is going to get far worse. But Mr McNamara has miscalculated in several important ways.

'It is argued that for regular forces to cope with guerrillas requires a proportion of five to one. If you assess the Liberation Front as about 180,000, which is more or less correct at this moment, that would need the best part of a million men. Yet Mr McNamara reckons he can turn the tide with about 200,000 American troops and 500,000 puppets.' In the accepted vocabulary of the situation 'puppet' means South Vietnamese troops. [Recent indications are that the U.S. forces may be increased to 350,000.]

'Furthermore the guerrilla forces are also increasing, and very fast. This is of course not difficult, as already most of the South has been liberated.

'On the accepted proportion, the Americans would soon need about 2,000,000 men in the field, which is preposterous.

'This is not to take into account the difference of fighting spirit. Our people know what they are fighting for, which is simply their homeland. The American boys do not. I don't blame them; it must be extremely hard to die for a concept that just says "anti-Communist", especially when it must be obvious to the intelligent ones that by no means all the Liberation soldiers are Communist at all. Of course the leadership is Communist, and we who sustain their struggle are Communist, but we could hardly require party allegiance from people who only want to be patriots.

'The nature of the fighting in the South has greatly changed. It has become inaccurate to refer to "guerrillas". What is happening now is that the Liberation people are meeting the enemy in genuine battles on a conventional pattern – Plei Me, Van Tuong, Do Bac and so on are examples.

'Naturally the United States forces have an enormous superiority in weapons and equipment; in no circumstances could we ever begin to match them in resources.

'But in the new phase of the struggle we, that is to say the Liberation forces, are putting a strong emphasis on what we in our language call "catch-and-grasp" – hand-to-hand fighting, you would say.

'It is fair to say that in this sort of thing the Americans can always be defeated – they dislike it, and they are untrained for it. It is intensely disagreeable, and you have to have a particularly good reason to be able to do it at all.'

I am not a military expert and do not know whether the situations are comparable, but this kind of fighting has become more and more widespread in Vietnam. Most recently, for example, in the Iadrang River valley, where American forces and regular North Vietnamese troops savagely mauled each other during a week-long battle when although it is safe to say that they did not like it – nobody in his right mind could – the Americans stood and fought in hand-to-hand combat in terrible intensity and confusion.

Their casualties in dead and wounded were very high, higher than in any other week in the war, but when the vicious battle ended and the two mauled and exhausted sides drew apart, the Americans said they had hurt the North Vietnamese even more than they had been hurt themselves.

'Another miscalculation of Mr McNamara,' the colonel said, 'has been his reliance on his superiority in firepower; he put too much trust in the effect of the B-52 bombers. It is true that for some time they had a very destructive effect on the Liberation soldiers, but they learned how to cope with them.

'It is a question of effective sheltering. The Liberation people have become extremely skilled at the business of deep shelters. They have clearly no means of opposing the bombers in fire-power, therefore it is necessary to survive it, wait until it is over, and return at once to the attack. There is a great emphasis on the practice of scattering and concealment and swift regroupment. In this it is even an advantage to be short of mechanical transport; the guerrillas hardly ever use anything but their feet.

'There was a good example of this the other day, in what we call Resistance Zone D. After sixteen B-52 attacks the U.S. command declared the area a white zone – that is to say, wholly devastated. In point of fact our total casualties were eight oxen killed. The Liberation men are still there today, and somewhat reinforced.

'Mr McNamara has recently put much confidence in mobility. He has described his new 1st Mobile Cavalry Division as the strongest and swiftest division in the history of the nation, and he is probably right. He has about 1000 helicopters. What he always forgets is that in three years the Liberation forces have learned how to handle helicopters, which can be very vulnerable at between ten and twenty metres up. You can safely say that we no longer fear helicopters.'

[It was interesting that throughout he referred always to 'McNamara', never to Johnson, personifying the U.S. through the Pentagon rather than the White House. I believe the reason for this to be quite simple: Mr Johnson does not go to Saigon and Mr McNamara does; he is recognisable as a personal factor in the U.S. operation.]

'We are now well into the dry season, when the Americans reckoned their superiority would begin to tell. The idea was to scatter the guerrillas with the air force and thus prevent face-to-face encounters, while the big military waves penetrated into the liberated areas. But it is now two months since the dry season began, and the Liberation people are still in the ascendant.

'The new strategy of our people is: to ensure both a concentration of force and guerrilla tactics; to attack in the mountains, and also in the enemy's rear, and to attack in many places simultaneously.

'They are now occasionally contriving to do all three at once. It seems that the dry season favours us, too.

'It is the case that the present resistance fighters are incomparably better than we were in the French time, and we were clearly not bad then. We have, however, grown more mature.

'Our own help, from the North, grows; this I do not conceal from you. The Americans claim that three divisions of our regular army have been identified in the South; I can assure you that this is nonsense. To send so many troops from the North is just unnecessary; there is more than enough manpower already there; we provide training, cadres, equipment. Not so much equipment as you might think; the Americans and the puppets are good providers. I cannot, of course, inform you of the strength of our aid.

'We are well aware that the forces against us are stronger, and richer, and infinitely more powerful. We have already had great losses, and I am afraid we shall have greater yet. The price of all this is horrible. But quite honestly I do not see how we can lose. How long it will take I do not know. I may not see the end myself. But I expect my children will.

'I wonder where they are. My family is from the South. I have not seen them for ten years.'

Evening Standard,
8 December 1965

144

AND BEHIND EVERY DRAWING,
SUCH ANGUISH

If Vicky is dead – and I am obliged to believe it, here in a house where he was himself not long ago, and now too far away to say goodbye – then a chapter has ended for him and for me, and for the craft he had made almost into a folklore.

I suppose no man is indispensable, but I do not know how we shall do without Vicky. I know I find it hard to imagine how I shall do without the man I counted as my true and beloved friend.

At this moment I selfishly think of that rather than of the catastrophic loss to the trade we both served.

Vicky and his work were always indivisible; he lived for his work more than any human being I have ever known: more than I, more than the politicians he mocked and glorified. More than the journalists who so laboriously tried to supplement in words what he so readily accomplished in a rectangle of line and tone.

So readily! It must have seemed so to those who were not sometimes compelled to share the ferocious anguish that went into the conception of those tidy and tormented drawings, the doubts and uncertainties and second thoughts, the very real concern that he might have gone too far, or not far enough.

He was secure and successful, but never could bring himself to believe that he was either: he had the endless *angst* of an artist who believed he was staking the career of a lifetime on every cartoon, every day. I know so well how he felt: a thousand times we have argued it out: we have lasted long enough, is this the moment we are bound to fail?

Victor Weisz was a German refugee from Fascism, with the Hungarian background he loved to satirise, and the cynical Jewishness he for ever made his jest. He and I had laboured in this newspaper vineyard for some twenty years together, but Vicky never ceased to be a refugee in his heart.

And since his heart was by far the most important and meaningful part of him, that was the key to his nature, and he went through life, prospering, enveloped in the endless anxieties of the expatriate.

Vicky could never identify himself with certainty or success. At the height of his renown he felt the compulsion to reassure himself every day of his usefulness – which is how he came to be the craftsman he was: he tried so hard, and today harder than yesterday, and tomorrow harder than today. How well I understand that need: I cannot believe it has come to an end.

People who never knew this gentle and generous little man could sometimes hate him: that was good. They flinched from the abrasive cruelty of his criticism – often not realising, I think, how singularly was Vicky's anger free from malice.

Behind every one of Vicky's most waspish comments was an implied positive; it is thus, he would say; I wish it were otherwise. It is possible that this alone – which was the compassion, expressed in bitterness – separated Vicky from every other political draughtsman in the whole world.

He not only drew better than anyone else – and in that alone he leaves a gap that will not be filled in this generation – but he minded more. I never in my life knew a man more dedicated in his personal life to the daily political implications of our distracted world. I suppose that is why he is dead.

Poor Vicky. He really meant it.

Evening Standard,
24 February 1966

SOMETHING IMPORTANT, POSSIBLY DRAMATIC, IS IN THE AIR

Those transatlantic jets will kill me yet, but not by having their tails fall off, only by accumulated disorientation. One day this week was thirty hours long; the next but eighteen. I leave London at noon to lunch in New York. Six hours of borrowed time: what might one not do with it! I pay it back when I get home to London at teatime, to find everyone in bed.

But those six hours have nothing to do with the changes that have come over the United States in the few weeks since I was last there. The mood over the one thing that matters, Vietnam, has gone through, and is going through, a change so palpable and at the same time so subtle that the Americans themselves are finding it hard to make adjustment.

The old certainties are being undermined every day. The old confident voices are speaking with a new uneasiness. A feeling of extraordinary confusion reigns. Something important, and possibly dramatic, is in the air.

The people of the U.S. have caught on to the fact that almost all their assumptions about Vietnam have suddenly become invalid, that their credit account of Asian friendship has virtually evaporated, that they can rely on no one – except perhaps the British Government, which is an irrelevancy.

They are faced with the extreme probability that an elected government in South Vietnam might choose to negotiate with the Vietcong and demand that U.S. troops leave the country. The question of what the U.S. would do in that case poses a dilemma so acute that few people are talking of anything else.

Coming from a London where the dialogue on this huge subject is officially so vapid and half-baked, I was very strongly affected by this change. The vocabulary has altered. The roles are shifting. This time, I suspect, there is more on the stage than the old familiar conflicts and we are about to witness something that one man's decision can steer between redemption and disaster.

How President Johnson must curse the melodramatic impulse that took him to Honolulu to give his official endorsement to the mountebank General Ky, Prime Minister of South Vietnam, so soon to be obliterated in the rising wave of Vietnamese discontent. To spite the face of Senator Fulbright and the Foreign Relations Committee he has cut off his own nose, and the whole U.S. is feeling the pangs.

Almost overnight, since it became clear that most of South Vietnam is furiously tired of tyranny from both left and right, powerful attitudes have changed. Secretary of State Dean Rusk has told the Senate that the U.S. administration would be obliged to honour any decision made by an elected Saigon Government.

Vice-President Humphrey has endorsed this. Even Senator Russell of Georgia, until the other day a Right-wing hawk of hawks, agrees there is no other choice. So do Senators Cooper of Kentucky and Javits of New York.

Senator Mike Mansfield, the majority leader, now suggests 'direct confrontation across a peace table' with Hanoi and Peking. Senator Fulbright says 'the Vietnam struggle would have been settled long ago if the United States had only kept out of it.'

Judge Edgerton of the U.S. Court of Appeals writes publicly: 'I see no remaining reason why our fighting men should not be brought home as fast as our ships and aircraft can carry them.'

All this a few weeks ago would have been unimaginable.

Part of the symbolism of this is that I just spent a day taping an hour-long television show to be carried by 102 stations through the U.S., the sole and total theme of which is that Vietnam, both North and South, is inhabited by human beings and rational citizens and that the war against them is an imbecile cruelty. This was performed at American invitation.

The last time I played this theme on U.S. television, not long ago, I was thrown to the lions and chewed up. This time I was given no lion, but Jean Lacouture, of *Le Monde*, now lecturing at Harvard, whose book *Vietnam Between Two Truces* I only wish I could have written, and which (another sign of the times) is going like – well, like a bomb.

Strange things are on the move.

Congress is reassembling after the Easter recess. Tuesday's *New York Times* said that its mood is that 'the administration's conduct of the war in Vietnam has spread confusion and discontent among the American people . . . that our deep and growing military involvement reflects a colossal blunder of statesmanship.'

To face up to the present riddle of statesmanship, said the *Times*, 'would require the substitution of candour for the official evasions and outright misrepresentations of current and prospective conditions of the war. It would also require the admission of gross miscalculations of the military situation by Secretary of Defence McNamara.'

The dialogue is now out in the open with a vengeance. The most responsible people are now pointing out that after having for so long rejected any United Nations participation in bringing about a cease-fire in Vietnam, Washington suddenly back-tracked on that decision – precisely when it resumed the bombing of the North, so that the U.N. function was simultaneously solicited and paralysed.

They point out that Secretary of State Rusk made a statement before the Foreign Affairs Committee prophesying and encouraging eventual friendly relations with China – releasing this for publication on the day that U.S. bombers hit the Hanoi suburbs for the first time.

Yet when Senator Mansfield proposed a Summit conference in Asia (he suggested Japan or Burma) with everyone interested in the Vietnam war, he had just returned from a trip to Mexico with President Johnson, who inferentially must have given his approval.

Those who know most insist most categorically that this is President Johnson's war, his decision, his commitment, his responsibility; his and nobody else's. He acts on a synthesis of information available to nobody else in its entirety. He may know some of the answers. But until he gives them, the United States will not know whether the strange and eerie new chemistry at work today will lead to reason, or to perils yet unknown.

But from now on things can never be quite the same.

*Evening Standard,
21 April 1966*

LORD MORAN AND CHURCHILL: WHAT A STORM IN A TEACUP!

We are becoming a race of querulous, niggling, objurgatory, carping and censorious old scoutmistresses; nothing seems to happen that someone doesn't denounce.

There is this queer covey of ladies and small-time parsons who insist that the telly is lewd. There is Mr Wilson's other cabal that says it is partisan. There is pusillanimous old B.B.C. itself, which has no sooner to commission a film with any guts – like *War Game* or the bullfight film – than it gets cold feet on transmission.

Now we are asked on all sides to jump from a great height on Lord Moran, otherwise the former Dr Charles Wilson, for having written this enormous book on the declining years of his distinguished patient, Sir Winston Churchill.

The bitter controversy about Lord Moran's book may have escaped those who do not follow, as we are obliged to do, those daily columns of oleaginous auto-praise which pass for letters in the posh dailies.

The idea is that Lord Moran not only violated his Hippocratic oath by turning a bob out of his association with the late Prime Minister, but had been especially caddish in explaining that Sir Winston Churchill passed his final years in a condition of incapable senility.

There are other inferences that even in the later years of his public life Sir Winston was not on genuine terms with reality. These vagaries a doctor would understand, and for that reason, it is argued, the doctor should not sell his intimacy.

What a lot of nonsense: what a storm in a teacup! I know little of the professional *mores* of doctors, nor of the mysterious sanctions their closed shop passes on each other, and I imagine that Lord Moran, in his late eighties, cares as little as I.

Lord Moran has written a picture of Churchill as an old man. He has not argued that Churchill was a Negro, or an Anarchist, or a card-carrying homosexual.

He shows him, with love, as an old gentleman, full of days, who worked incalculably hard for what he held to be the salvation of his homeland, and whose duties taxed his mind into deliquescence long before his splendid and obstinate body surrendered to death.

What is there to make a fuss about in that?

Can there be any moderately well-informed person who is not aware that Sir Winston Churchill's body continued to endure many years longer than his mind? He was sixty-five when he became Prime Minister. The task thereafter was, to say the least, exacting.

Did it need Lord Moran to inform us that after 1945 Churchill was a similacrum of a great political leader? Other great leaders have had matters more under control: the ageing Mao Tse-Tung and Ho Chi-Minh have made no public appearances for nearly a year: their image is untarnished; Churchill was subjected in his infirmities to publicity wherever he appeared: his public accepted his decrepitude with understanding, even gratitude.

In Lord Moran's diary there is no entry for the month of January 1960. The immediately previous entries record a successive decline: indeed, indicate a total absence of volition. I am interested, because it was in that month that I first met Sir Winston Churchill: a poignant time in which to meet such a man.

It was at dinner in Lord Beaverbrook's house at Cap d'Ail.

There was myself and my host and Aristotle Onassis and Churchill, and the whole occasion was invested with so many secondary dramas that its true meaning was obscured. I am always speechless in the company of celebrities: with Sir Winston that night it mattered not: he slept throughout the whole occasion.

But once he roused himself, to break across the financial arguments of Beaverbrook and Onassis. Suddenly and apropos of nothing at all he awoke from slumber and said 'Max – did you ever go to Russia?'

To which Lord Beaverbrook said with some reason: 'Of course – you sent me: Aircraft Minister, mission to Stalin. Don't you remember, Winston? It was *you* sent me to Russia.'

'To be sure,' said Sir Winston, retreating into his dream, 'but did you *ever go*?'

To which there was no answer: even Lord Beaverbrook must needs accept that impenetrable reverie.

That is the stuff of which history is made: that is why I rarely trust history.

Evening Standard,
5 May 1966

THE SIX DAY WAR

We stand on the edge of a truly tragic absurdity. The Middle East war which now seems inevitable must surely be recorded as the most stupid, meaningless, wholly political and indeed preventable war of all time. If we start blowing each other up here, as doubtless we shall, then the whole proposition of homo sapiens is in question. In a lifetime of describing the human aberrations I have never been involved in anything as senseless as this – and yet I comprehend the folly only too well.

For all their posturings and demonstrations each side of the border nobody really wants to fight, and to carry their attitudinising to the point of getting painfully killed – as they will be killed, as we may all be killed.

The whole thing is technically ridiculous. Yet the mad thing about this Israel-Egypt confrontation, which by definition is a local row, is that it puts the whole world once again on the barricades, and for an issue that few understand. The blockade of the Tiran Strait means something to me – ten years ago I was with the Israeli group that 'liberated' it, in the accepted phrase, which meant that the Egyptians should no longer throttle Israel's one passage to the east. To have access to the outer world is of importance to Israel; to them it is as though somebody had told Britain she had no longer access to Liverpool. This is the issue over which Israel could go to war, and almost certainly will. Going to war is in most circumstances fatuous, but we are no longer talking of rational considerations.

I am obliged to say that I have known this improbable country since the day of its birth, and am only too aware of its Jewish impatience, chauvinism, and arrogance. Nobody should know better; I was part of that early exhilarating nonsense. It is still fair to say that this crisis, which may embroil us all, is none of Israel's choosing. This is probably the most vulnerable state in the world – fewer than three million people in a country about the size of Wales, surrounded on every landward side by fifty million Arabs dedicated to its destruction. It is totally crazy, for no one can readily comprehend the extraordinary coherence and discipline that overcomes in time of trouble a people ordinarily the most anarchic and self-destructive.

At this moment Tel Aviv is a city transformed. I was here only a matter of weeks ago – it was gay then, and merry; it is not so now. The mobilisation has taken away one's friends, reduced our taxi-ranks; the nightclub bands thump glumly to empty floors. It is at such a time that you remember that every citizen of Israel is in fact a soldier, and that every vehicle is a hostage to war, that every single concern and aspect of this extraordinary society is part of a psychology that is on the defensive yesterday, today, and tomorrow. I remember it so well from the old days; one had hoped those days were done. One was foolish; they will of course endure forever.

Nobody knows from moment to moment what will happen. We are allegedly waiting for the return of Foreign Minister Abba Eban, who has been whizzing round the world canvassing support for Israel – an easy enough assignment in the U.S., with three times as many Jews as Israel, but possibly less so in a London whose last public face was that of obsequious welcome to that prince of antisemites, Feisal of Saudi Arabia.

Lord knows this world has crises enough; it is somewhat absurd that it should now be preoccupied by one as silly as this. Nevertheless one listens for the roar in the sky; one has heard it all before.

Evening Standard,
28 May 1967

CATASTROPHE UNLIMITED!

The catastrophe that is about to befall Bengal, inevitable for years and now imminent, gallops in with the rain clouds.

The monsoon which brings life to India must first bring death. One of the Four Horsemen is of course Pestilence, but he is only the outrider.

The awful paradox for the millions of Bengalis, threatened for so long by their own perversities and contradictions and hopeless politics, is that they are now stricken most terribly, and probably lastingly, by something that is not their fault.

This is the great Bengali irony; for once they did not ask for it.

Mrs Gandhi has said that the Pakistan–India exodus is 'history's biggest and cruellest migration,' and I believe that for once she is speaking the literal truth; without rhetoric or second-guessing.

This is the most massive and unmanageable refugee influx there has ever been anywhere.

I have been looking at refugee situations all over the world for twenty-five years; I have never seen anything comparable. It is infinitely more than the two-way nightmare in India of 1947, and that was unspeakable enough.

I have no faith in the guesswork figures of three to four millions; I believe it to be 5,000,000, and by the end of the month it may well be 10 million. Of these a fair proportion will be corpses.

Moreover the political circumstances of this exodus are uniquely unexpected and tragic, and the implications are uniquely ominous.

I was in the border area just a few days ago, before I was unlucky enough to get chewed up in an accident.

This brought me back to England rather hurriedly after three months away from the British news scene, but with much exposure to the calamitous affairs in East Pakistan and the explosion of what now must be called Bangla Desh.

I was truly rocked in England to realise how small it had appeared at first, how little the story was valued or understood, how indifferently the western world had reacted. Press, governments, the U.N., everyone – to something that was, and is, a really shattering and perilous event.

It is presumably irrelevant now – since the Powers considered it irrelevant at the time – to consider the wholly outrageous origins of this tragedy which has sent millions of people into exile, destitution and death.

If the U.N. chose to condone them there is no more to say, except that it is condoning the administration of the world's largest Islamic state on the political principles of the late Al Capone.

Leaving that aside, it has taken us some time to appreciate that right now in Bengal, where the British Raj was born, the Indian Raj is faced with something that is probably going to be far too big to contain – physically, medically and politically, and perhaps even militarily.

This may well be one of the most important crises of Asia, but I don't think it got much thought until the cholera story broke a couple of days ago.

The cholera story which is only a fragment of the whole was there a couple of weeks ago; it was there when I was with the exhausted and near-demented district magistrate at Sirkarpur, with the refugees coming over at the rate of 18,000 a day and one doctor to give inoculations and 200,000 Hindu escapees making a vast infected lavatory of the region, and no food, nor shelter . . . how could there not be cholera.

By now it has reached the fringes of Calcutta – Calcutta with its 10,000,000 denizens of a conurbation that at the best of times is a corrupt and ungovernable urban sink forever poised between pestilence and anarchy. The omens are very bad.

Poor Bengal, doomed from one agony to another. How selective we are in our responses!

It is interesting to compare this with the dramatic comparison and interest shown to the same place only months ago with the cyclone and the floods.

How we sympathised with them; how we shelled out!

(The fact that a million pounds of that shelled out charity still hangs about in London banks because Pakistan didn't know what to do with it is, I suppose, another irrelevancy.)

The fact is that the typhoon got the ratings: the Purge of Bengal didn't. Presumably it is easier to feel the impulse of outrage at an act of nature, which however awful has no special political implications or strings.

God sends the typhoons, but God is not, as far as we know, a member of S.E.A.T.O. nor a debtor to the World Bank.

So God's vengeance can safely be deplored without diplomatic kickbacks; President Yahya's is more delicate. Let us, therefore, wait a couple of months or so until nature helpfully takes the heat off the politics with a neutral epidemic, and then let us think about unwrapping the blankets and the vaccines and console our consciences with discreet lamentations over the misfortunes of those for whom our kind consideration will as usual, be too late.

If, as I believe likely, this month will end with some 10 million refugees in West Bengal territory, the military government of Pakistan will have achieved a remarkable thing. It will have virtually eliminated its Hindu minority and adroitly saddled India with an almost insuperable problem at her most vulnerable and dangerous place.

Bengal – tense, overcrowded, desperately poor, politically hysterical, forever on the verge of some disaster or another – cannot cope with this situation: there is no hope whatever of absorbing the refugees.

The State Government has virtually no existence. Mrs Gandhi's Central Government is under tremendous pressures – from well-wishers, ill-wishers, patriots, opportunists, sentimentalists and conspirators – to solve this almost intolerable problem by exploding. That is by making war.

She has successfully resisted this crazy counsel so far. She knows only too well that Bengal is a nation of a strange kind, that a Bengali is a Bengali before he is an Indian – or a Pakistani.

She may feel Yahya's methods of holding his country together more odious and contemptible – but she may also feel that if Yahya fails to hold his Bengalis, she may fail to hold here.

But the tensions are tremendous – more so than London seems to know. A week ago in Bengal the bazaar talk was not whether war, but when.

Perhaps we are a bit late to worry about the cholera.

Evening Standard,
28 May 1967

NEW STATESMAN, 1965–7

Every now and then I was asked to write a centrepiece for the *New Statesman*. In those days this was fun; it was before the magazine had turned into an economic tract. It was enjoyable to have a whole page in which to ride one's hobby-horses that had absolutely no relevance to anything remotely topical.

The one about Malcolm Muggeridge is the best. I came to know Malcolm in an odd way. He was then editing *Punch*, whose office in Bouverie Street adjoined the *News Chronicle*'s. One week he did something that made me very angry, a thing that practically never happened to me.

It was at the time of the conference in Geneva that was supposed to bring to an end the French colonial rule of Indo-China, after the French had been finally clobbered to humiliation at Dien Bien Phu. Having been personally mixed up in that Asian débâcle I went down to Geneva to see fair play. The conference was presided over by Anthony Eden, and very successfully. The French, with a fair amount of grace, or at least resignation, accepted surrender.

Punch then marked the occasion with a full-page Illingworth cartoon depicting Eden with bowler hat and umbrella, recalling the poltroon Neville Chamberlain at Munich. I called my column that week 'Punch Below The Belt', suggesting that it was unfair to deride what was probably the only useful and constructive thing Anthony Eden had ever done. Mr Muggeridge's *Punch* made some sort of reply, and I had another go at it. The episode began to develop into a sort of private war disguised as low comedy.

I wrote to Malcolm suggesting that this nonsense could go on forever, and since we were virtually neighbours in Bouverie Street we couldn't go on not meeting like this. So we did meet, and became – as we remain – the very best of friends. So Anthony Eden can be said to have accomplished two things in his life.

*   *   *

A QUESTION OF IDENTITY

The card of identity: I seem to have lived with it forever, yet its meaning continues to elude me. I cannot remember how many I have had, and carried about the world, and still carry – the name, the definition, the picture, the antecedents, the accreditation, the purpose, occasionally the fingerprint, always the number; the piece of paper that establishes one's right, in certain absurd and special circumstances, to work or even to exist.

Without the piece of paper one is reduced to ordinary proportions, groping outside; one cannot, for example, use the Delegate's Toilet. I look at about 200 cards of identity: buff and blue and white and laminated and endorsed and bedraggled, scrupulously and meaninglessly explaining in a dozen recognisable languages: this is Mr C; he works in the world; allow him to do so.

The common denominator of all these passports and permits and *laissez-entrer* should amount to a kind of certainty and confidence, you would think; if so many vigilant authorities have sieved one through and found one real, one must surely be so: distilled to the bone. The Russians let one into Russia, the Americans into America, the Chinese into China, the Jews into Israel, the Arabs into Arabia, the newspapermen into Fleet Street, one's friends into their homes, one's acquaintances into their confidence, one's lovers to their beds; some require more endorsement than others, but everyone wants something.

What a piece of work is man! Observe his photograph, his number, his code-index, his yellow-fever certificate, his sign-manual: that is he. Thus I am inscribed on the filed and forgotten registers of something like seventy countries, sovereign states to a man, and every time I turned my head there was another one, demanding even greater abundance of identification. Personally I never knew yet quite what I was nor where I slotted in; I suppose I was ready for total identification somewhere, but never where I happened to be. *Cogito, ergo sum*. That satisfied Descartes; it never satisfied the lowliest immigration clerk of the meanest of states. It never satisfied me.

In the first waking moments before the dawn the great thing is to remember first who you are, then where you are; for years this has not always been easy. It seems to me that I was quite young when these eerie moments of suspense first came, unanchored and adrift in the dark, groping through a helpless sequence of reasoning to resolve the supreme problem of where I was. These moments still come at the precise transition from sleep to life, lying there in a trance of doubt: what is this bed, where is this room, what lies beyond it, when must I move and what must I do? London, Cairo, Peshawar, Peking, Damascus, Moscow, Chicago – there have been so many places so often; any of them could be the best background for this foolish vacuum.

In the next moment, of course, it is a room by a familiar sea, or a taxi mourns by in the ruined street; here we are and off we go. I have no roots at all.

I am the end-product of one exiled and disorientated tribe of an anarchic aberration of the middle class. In my mind I identify myself elsewhere, but this fact cannot be denied. I would far sooner have been the by-blow of a ducal tyrant, or the honest end of eighteen generations of persecuted ploughmen, since either of these backgrounds would have helped me to rationalise my tiresome but incurable dissatisfaction with both the rich and the poor. I deplore my equivocations; in self-defence I become dogmatic. I should have been reared in either a Stately Home or a slum; instead I am the eventual residue of a decently eccentric Scottish family who, as far as I can discern, asked little of life but rather more than enough to read and drink. It produced at least two exceptional men, who will be remembered awhile where quality is valued, but that process stopped with my father.

I have no religion, and I am bad at politics. I can recall no time when I was not a socialist; that is to say I can remember no conversion from anything else; from the moment when politics were anything more than a word I accepted socialism without any particular reasoning or argument. This was commonplace and inadequate, and all my life I have been exasperated at an insufficient grounding in the scientific basis of what I profess to believe. I imagine it is true that most people feel no compulsion to define what they intuitively comprehend, but they are better off if they can.

I survived part of adolescence in the despair of Dundee, that industrial graveyard of the Thirties. All I could grasp, or more accurately assume, was that this sort of class structure was unnatural, and therefore to be rejected – not at the time necessarily to be opposed! I knew no way of opposing it. I could only equate class with poverty – not individual poverty, not the knock-kneed hunchbacked poverty of one old jute-mill reject in the Overgate, but the poverty of what seemed an endless background of morally exhausted people: the poor who were always with us.

Class existed, and was expressible in material terms, which were hateful. What made my own indignation especially feckless was my inability to establish myself in the pattern at all. I was extremely poor, frequently to the point of desperation and hunger, but I still lived in the part of town inhabited by the less-poor; I had few friends, but those I had were not millworkers nor foundrymen. If the conditions of one's life counted for anything I was working class, since I worked excessively hard for little pay; so much so that it left me forever thenceforth with a nagging compulsion to work, a dread of being hard-up, a self-defeating inability to relax. But it did not give me entrance to the confidence of true workers because – for one thing – I spoke wrongly.

The epithet 'education' was ironical indeed, since there was, and is, no company anywhere in which I am not invariably and technically the least-educated of all. Such schooling as I had was sketchy and erratic to the point of fantasy, taking place as it did (for reasons too complicated to explain) in a series of French village schools, where I learned probably less than the ordinary pupil of today, however deprived, would believe possible. I will not go into the bizarre processes of a rural Breton *externat* between the wars; let it be enough to say that I emerged from this process knowing virtually nothing about everything. I am not exaggerating. My ignorance of all the conventional matters was truly outstanding. Of history I culled a few myths about Charlemagne; from time to time I was persecuted and beaten for having been party to the burning of Joan of Arc; sometimes we prated doggerel about democracy; current affairs were defined by a madly schizoid *mutilé de guerre* who once, to make a point, hit me on the head with the artificial arm he had acquired at Verdun; a memorably traumatic event.

I there developed not just an ignorance but a positive, active horror of mathematics; I never learned even to multiply; I still recoil from the very *look* of figures. I think I must be the last person of my generation who did sums on a slate. I can smell the bloody thing still.

Even this barren business came to an end when I was fifteen, when I entered the great world of letters filling paste-pots in the branch office of a very provincial newspaper. It was inevitable that someone of my abject and total non-scholarship should finish up in this undemanding trade, and there, for thirty years, I stuck.

Education my backside.

All these considerations are hard to define on the card of identity. Even the straight facts are suspect. For example: my mother had the unusual feminine name of Douglas; on every occasion when I have been obliged to nominate my parents and fill in: son of William, and Douglas, it has raised conjectures so peculiar that they have been inexplicable, and I soon learned to call my mother Margaret. Nobody ever knew or cared. Indeed I was myself twenty-five when the first sight of my birth-certificate revealed that my own first name was other than what I had supposed all my life. So much for the fiddling accuracies of the bureaucrats.

An inability to define oneself makes it nonetheless interesting to observe the manner in which one is defined by others, I have a ticket from one Asian country calling me a 'Sojourner'. Another, with cryptic intent, calls me: 'Male, for a week'. A South American passport clerk stamped my page: 'Admitted, he is Passing On'. The worst is a document from Ethiopia cataloguing me for all time in the chilling phrase: 'Temporary Person'. I feel these things to be true.

Once I reached Dar-es-Salaam on the day of a census, the only time such a thing befell me; it is therefore a fact that the only place on earth in which I have become an official statistic is Tanganyika. And even that, as a state, no longer exists. A Temporary Person, sojourning in a vanished country; male, for a week. But ah, what a week! It is part of the whole sad business that I have already forgotten where it was.

New Statesman,
7 May 1965

CONFESSIONS OF AN ADDICT

It is known that for those who have been for some time on the bottle, pot or needle, and who for some reason have to be deprived of their crutch, the withdrawal process can be extremely painful. If the subject survives, however, he is supposedly cured. I can perhaps be informative about this, since the de-junking experience is comparatively new to me. I can say that neither of the above propositions is necessarily true. This could possibly be a comfort to others.

I had been for many years – it is fairly well known, and I am no longer especially shy about it – a registered addict to a certain fairly familiar drug. It is probably correct to say that I was seriously, and it was clinically believed incurably, dependent on this substance for some thirty years. It was not generally realised even by my friends to what degree I was dominated by the commodity I was obliged to use. I was in fact breaking no law, since long ago I was given legal access to the prescription, it being held that my system required it for the continuance of my normal activities. It was expensive, but it was not beyond my means. Anyhow, I had to have it. I need not go into the origins of this addiction; it was partly hereditary (at least two of my immediate family had been similarly addicted) and partly caused by the singular pressures and tensions of my work. It invaded my metabolism quite early, but in recent years it had become necessary for me to reinforce myself with this drug literally before I could get up and face the day. That is to say: I had to have the bloody newspapers.

It started innocently enough, as these things do, when I was quite young and uncorrupted, for I was brought up in a home where the substance was not only openly consumed but frankly displayed. My father actually showed a sort of perverse pride in proclaiming that he was hooked on the *Daily News* and was – I recall it clearly – shameless enough to try to proselytise weaker-minded acquaintances to fall victim to the same fell influence. I grew up in an environment of extraordinary permissiveness. Newspapers abounded. Even as a child I was fed with small paragraphs with the morning coffee. My mother, who was a sweet and wholesome woman in every other way, would move furtively off after breakfast with her share of the Satanic mischief from the laboratories of Fleet Street. Small wonder, then, that I grew up to believe that this was part of life.

As the years went on the dosage, inevitably, had to be increased. The occasional paragraph grew into the complete news-item, magnified itself imperceptibly into the Article. In no time at all I was ingesting a whole Editorial. I soon became such a slave to the commodity that I could absorb two whole *Telegraph* leaders before nine in the morning and feel virtually no reaction at all, other than the customary slight nausea. My level of tolerance grew alarmingly; I had to explore more and greater varieties of the daily hallucinogenes to achieve my release.

The time came, inescapably, when personal gratification was not enough; I was tempted to exploit the public vulnerability. There is no point now in concealing the fact that I myself became a pusher of the stuff. Worse still, I learned how to manufacture it. The process is fatally easy for anyone with access to a few simple ingredients and a pot to boil. The product can be put together in a room or even a telephone-box. Soon I was driven to expand my activities; by and by I was travelling the world to establish wholesale sources of raw material. People would comment: 'Off on another Trip, eh?' little knowing how poignantly right they were.

The trouble was that the more I pushed the stuff the greater became my own physiological involvement. Ever-increasing quantities of the drug became necessary to satisfy my personal craving. All secrecy had to be abandoned. My family looked on with growing despair, exactly like the helpless families in Victorian temperance-warnings. Their life became a torment as the toxic stuff poured into the house. My own capitulation was now hopelessly apparent; until the first delivery from the Agent was in my hands life had little meaning. In the late stages of my illness the house became knee-deep in the crumpled debris of the unconsumed portion of the day's ration. In my terminal condition I was demanding eleven daily doses, in English and foreign brands, eight weekly boosters, six massive Sunday injections, and unspecified numbers of paper narcotics that would arrive unasked from subterranean hash-hawkers in Soho and the university towns. My need for the fix of Fleet Street fantasy was so notorious that every oddball print-peddler had me down for the first push. As for the Audit Bureau of Circulations, I was the last digit of every figure.

I pumped my system full of the lot. I mainlined them indiscriminately into a small hole in my head – a few grains of hempline here, a trace of poppycock derivative there, a dash of the old country Simple and a measure of gall and worsthorne to levin the lump. As they became absorbed the tensions would slacken, the nerves relax; soon I would be ready for the hard stuff – my Lou Heroin and my Robert Potman, my Stephen Barbiturate and my William Hookey and my Morphine Cleave. Without them, in the dark days, it is hard to say what I would have done.

My attitude to this sorry stimulus was the same as my attitude to tobacco; I get no pleasure from smoking, indeed more often than not it makes me sick, but it is far worse to be *not* smoking. I derived no happiness from my daily print-fix, but the deprival symptoms were worse. I had to feel that first stab of the 42-point, the sudden swift pinch of the chapman, the blessed connection as the noxious chemistry of the three-column intro coursed through my bloodstream. Only then was I capable of facing a day's work – which only too often, alas, was the secret manufacture in my own laboratory of the self-same baneful dope for the use of others.

It was obvious that this could not go on. I was not only destroying myself, I was perpetuating a grave social wrong. How many people were there like me, I wondered, whose lives were being made desperate by this daily necessity of so many column-inch intakes of Common Market, acts of violence, freezes, royal romances, protests, Mr Wilson, first nights, comprehensive schools, skirts? How many faceless men in high places were prospering from this pitiful addiction of the groping multitudes, themselves almost certainly immune? In how many stews and all-night coffee-bars were the sordid long-haired merchants of melancholy selling their midnight copies of the next day's early editions, so that teenage parties could roister through the night on sneak previews of tomorrow's *Hansard*?

Thus I got off the hook. I became one of the rare company who has drunk deep and long of the public prints and who has broken free. The transition was made somewhat easier by a two-month spell in Asia, where the drug is less pervasive when it is presented in a totally incomprehensible literary form. The emancipation took some time – for weeks I would lurk around the bazaar bookshops for an unordered *Daily Mirror* or a dogeared *Economist*. Yet the urge faded. A sense of proportion imperceptibly prevailed. And on my return to Britain I found that the trivial tidings of the previous night were of no greater interest nor importance than the boring lucubrations of the previous month.

So I went to my pusher, whose front is a celebrated newsagent's name in SW3, and said, quite bravely: I am through. I am dried out. You may cancel that order of opiate wadge with which your persecuted little hireling has been for so long battering my door. The late-night T.V. news will inform me of the graver and more immediate events, such as forest fires in the King's Road or the descent of Space Men in Sloane Square; the eye-witness description of these events I shall take on trust. The analysis of the political situation I shall either do for myself or, more probably, ignore. From now on I shall be conducting small ad-hoc meetings at the corner of Smith Street with the theme: Shirkers of the world, unite; you have nothing to lose but your brains.

I am not totally apostate. Just as the reformed alcoholic will keep an untouched bottle in plain view, to prove his liberation, so do I permit a copy of *The Times* (or whatever it is called these days) to lie at my bedside unopened. Sometimes I may glance fleetingly, to see with a casual curiosity if some new great and celebrated name has been bought over to write the Births and Deaths. Perhaps some currently resounding television personality has been engaged to edit the Weather Forecast. For the rest, I can take it or leave it alone. I get my news from the datelines; and my opinions from the crossword. Thanks to Antipress, I am a man re-born. Three regular applications and the urge dies.

And yet . . . I wonder how they got on at those elections?

No. Absolutely no.

Pray, sir, how are things at Barchester Towers?

New Statesman,
12 May 1967

DON QUIXOTE ANSWERS BACK

When my learned leader Malcolm Muggeridge throws up the sponge then is indeed time for general re-examination, since neither by word not act is he given to unreasonable repining. I have in my time learned so much of value from Malcolm M., both in the pursuit of our mutual trade and in the more oblique considerations of life, that my first impulse is always to respect his reproof as readily as I value his praise. It is true that some thirteen years ago we had a bit of what the late *News Chronicle* called a Fruckus over a small difference of opinion in *Punch* (in which I found myself somehow defending, of all people, Sir Anthony Eden), but that only taught me that one does not lightly take on one's *guru*.

He has now, with his exasperating charm, likened me to Don Quixote – 'wandering about, as Cervantes's hero did, espousing good causes, championing the downtrodden and oppressed, etc., etc.' – and in general making rather an ass of himself by failing to come to terms with the real old rough-and-tumble world whose temporal values he doesn't accept.

Well, maybe. I have indeed over the years become reconciled to this, as I see it, strangely mistaken view of my character, which I have always innocently felt to be quite otherwise. Where in my mind's eye I see a vivacious, convivial, even sanguine figure, bringing heart's ease and merriment to all, others apparently see a demeanour of settled melancholy and built-in *angst*.

I am pretty sure it must have something to do with my face, which is, I grant, cast in a lowering mould. Moreover, I have got somewhat type-cast as a Jeremiah largely because the last twenty-odd years of my work have on the whole involved a number of highly discouraging events and situations, and it became oddly rooted in many people's minds that I did not merely *report* the occasions, but in some way brought them about. Mr Muggeridge would be surprised at the number of people who share his illusion that 'the arrival on the scene of Cameron and his mates usually presages conflict and chaos.' Nothing could be further from the truth; not only is it many years since I disported in congeries of cronies, but my arrival on the scene has more often than not, as many a Foreign Editor can testify, coincided with the total evaporation of the story.

However, the difference between what I imagine myself to be and what other people, including Malcolm M., consider me to be is something I am obliged to live with. I am still not sure that I can agree with Malcolm Muggeridge's despairing definitions. I don't think, for a start, that Don Quixote was all that ridiculous a figure; he was probably less of a fathead than many people suppose. In our own day his successors in naïveté, of whom I am represented as the last (stuff: there are dozens of me), are reproached for their nostalgic belief that something can be done to modify the sombre state of affairs that Malcolm holds to be incurable.

If I really shared his resignation to the inevitability of decline I am fairly sure that I would not be in this business at all; there are easier ways of making a living. In fact its only compensation these days, in the age of chainstore newspapers, is the very occasional opportunity of hopping on one's Rosinante (provided by the firm, of course) and deliberately seeking out a windmill or two, not because one expects much success but because it is in fact rather more interesting than wringing one's hands. I would argue that it could even be marginally useful. I am *not* an idealist; I have had too much of this 'crusader' stuff slung at me of late (the word has funny implications for me). I only feel that if one's business is to write about affairs and the antic life around one, it is not only more interesting to take sides, it is very difficult not to.

We have a society admittedly in a bad way, indeed a depressingly and probably perilously bad way, with remarkably little to hang on to politically or otherwise. Change and decay in all around we see. Illusions topple, loyalties are betrayed, white hopes turn grey. Mr Muggeridge believes that this is an historical inevitability, and that anyone who still finds the energy to protest is either an idealist or a simpleton.

He finds it touchingly absurd that 'there is a good guy to be supported against a bad guy, a happy outcome to be expected.' Well, the simple fact is that unless we surrender all values in all circumstances there usually *is* a good guy to be supported against a bad guy, and if a happy outcome is not necessarily to be confidently expected it can always be hoped for, and even occasionally promoted. Of course 'history is a drama of the human will pursuing power'; that can surely be no revelation even to political Pollyannas like me. The only function we have is to watch it, write about it, wherever possible anticipate the fallacies, foresee the consequences, once in a blue moon activate the seats of authority to do something about them, mitigate where we can't cure, and to continue to shout when we fail.

It seems to me that Malcolm Muggeridge, in his criticism of the journalistic 'carriers of the liberal plague', falls into the trap (easily done, I agree) of stuffing us all into the same indiscriminate pigeon-hole, that of self-deluded hero-worshippers forever being let down by history. This is not strictly the case. Mr Muggeridge cites examples. Yet Redeemer Nkrumah disliked me only slightly more than did Dr Banda; I think it is fair to say I was hardly starry-eyed about the Congo; Mrs Gandhi has no reason to extol my uncritical support. Still, Ghana today *is* a better place than was the Gold Coast; I don't regret the passing of the Union Minière (if in fact it has passed; I'm unsure); and I would sooner have Mrs Gandhi running India, however inadequately, than Lord Curzon.

The trouble is that it is a bit too easy to present this familiar predigested concept of the 'boozy, noisy company' of the press (I must with respect protest that while I am boozy I am rarely noisy) forever in search of simple images capable of encapsulating in a 42-point headline, without any absolutes of our own at all. Dear Malcolm, you cannot really believe that. After all, you were one of us. You still damn well *are* one of us. To be sure, you no longer tilt at windmills; you sit inside them, out of the rain.

At this point I always feel that somehow I have gone through all this before. I remember another bit of a Fruckus with *Horizon* as long ago as 1948, when Cyril Connolly, then its editor, sombrely surveyed the existing world of collapsing values and from his unquiet grave foresaw just two more years of existence, in which he could 'enslumber the arts, like a skilled anesthetist, into final oblivion'. At the same time Bertrand Russell, surveying *The Outlook for Mankind* in a mood of logical despair, informed us that the end was at hand. (What a dirty trick it is, to have access to the files.)

Now I was, as I am, a moderately well-practised pessimist myself, but even I considered no disaster inevitable, and rather resented the tendency of intellectual people to say that it was, however tough on the arts it might be. If respectable and experienced thinkers believed in the inevitability of disaster who was I to challenge their assessment? Well, I didn't, and don't; I only challenge their right to load the negative balance by the weight of their reputation.

I don't think Malcolm Muggeridge should do it either, honestly, not even in a review of a book (to which he was, if I may employ the dread word, quixotically generous). What he was really reviewing was an attitude, or what he held to be an attitude – that of the dinosaur utopians who still blunder about the planet looking for causes and pretending they can still be won. This may well turn out to be good pragmatic criticism. I will agree that a good many of the causes that seemed to have importance to me have turned out to be lost ones; that in no way persuades me that they were not worth pursuing.

What's gone wrong, then? asks Malcolm Muggeridge. Why have all the newspapers and mags (*News Chronicle*, *Picture Post* etc.) 'folded'? That is a dead easy one. They both folded because they surrendered precisely those attitudes that Malcolm finds so fruitless, because they drifted into default and timidity, because they sacked their Don Quixotes. The *News Chronicle* allowed its radical traditions to wither on the bough just when its public were ripe to appreciate and value them; it died not because of its liberal cause-making, but because of the absence of it. *Picture Post* expired similarly: as soon as it abandoned all the radical values and purposes that had made it noteworthy and strove instead to win the witless market of cheesecake and crumpet, its public rejected it, and by and by it passed away. That's why they folded: because they ran out of blood.

In the same *New Statesman* of last week was an article on sleep in which Donald Gould wrote: 'We need to dream just as surely as we need to eat and breathe, and we abstain at our peril.' This was a scientific and not a metaphysical conclusion, but not without application. It is a phenomenon of my life that my sleeping time is virtually dreamless, except for the occasional nightmare. I never dream anything that I can remember. Perhaps Malcolm Muggeridge is right, and I do it all by day. Don Quixote, says Malcolm, 'gave every intimation of being off his head'. For that reason he remains vividly after the centuries in Malcolm Muggeridge's mind, which he would almost certainly not have done if he had been sane enough to accept that the game was up, and to have settled for a decent pad in an ivory tower – or a windmill.

New Statesman,
28 July 1967

B.B.C. RADIO AND TELEVISION, 1968–72

What follows now is not really writing at all. Except for the more solemn and mannered sound-radio broadcasts wireless is fairly often a matter of hit or miss, and television even more so. And the apotheosis of this sort of improvisation was the weekend show on the B.B.C. called 'Up Sunday'.

This was a sort of inheritance from 'That Was The Week That Was', much less intricate and far cheaper. It was an anarchic irreverent commentary on the passing show, peopled by the like of John Wells and Willie Rushton and Eleanor Bron and Kenny Everett and an occasional naked lady, to raise the moral tone. My bits, reproduced here, were supposed to bring the programme briefly to earth, to suggest that we were not as daft as we seemed. I played straight man to the stars.

It was not all that easy; the show was contrived with a pressing sense of immediacy and above all topicality. The mainstays of the programme were expected to be, and were, frivolous and funny; I was shoved in half way through to give the customers a rest, or so I suspected. Nevertheless I was supposed to be as up to the minute as everyone else, so it was impossible to prepare a script long in advance. I used to drive to the B.B.C. forever wondering what the hell I was exactly going to say, scribbling mad notes to the bitter end. The results you see here, with the hiccups and groans omitted.

The major television pieces were in a totally different key. 'Cameron Country' emerged from an unexpected situation. In the very early days of B.B.C. 2 I suggested to its head David Attenborough that what a new, and almost certainly minority, channel wanted was a theme that would break all the B.B.C.'s rules of objectivity and neutralism, and give a monthly opening for different people to articulate their prejudices with all the prejudice and personality they felt like. If their attitudes were sufficiently varied and opposed, I thought, in the long run a kind of consensus would emerge.

David was discouraging; in no way would the Corporation abandon its lifelong loyalty to the anodyne and the on-the-other-hand. Yet some time later they abruptly changed their mind; they would run a series called 'One Pair Of Eyes', and I could do the first one, like a good boy. They gave me a crew, a director, and a budget, and we were on our way.

I did the first one in India. Because we were fairly expensive, by the excessively modest standards of the time, we were asked to use up our air-fares by doing a couple more on the way home. We did a couple more in, I think, the Middle East.

So the first three 'One Pair Of Eyes' were all mine, which was directly in contradiction to my plan, which had been for a widely contending variety of views. When I returned to Britain I pointed this out to the B.B.C. and asked to be fired, in the interests of the programme. They saw my point and obliged me. But because my shows had not been bad and I was beginning to get the hang of this peculiar medium they gave me a compensation prize; the series called 'Cameron Country', which was exactly the same thing under another name. These are the transcripts you have here. They are not 'scripts'; they are the recordings of what actually happened on the spur of the moment. They are of great interest to me, revealing how differently things turn out in reality from what had been planned in solitude.

*   *   *

HO CHI MINH

So goes the senior Communist of them all, the strangest and most quixotic, far and away the most attractive, perhaps because so few are left in the western world who ever knew him. Ho Chi Minh belonged to a different theme to the men of today. It was possible to oppose him, vilify him, even try to kill him, but it was impossible – everyone who ever met him agrees – not to like him.

I encountered him three years ago in Hanoi, when even then most of Asia was ringing with rumours of his grave illness, or even death. Hanoi was the other side of the moon; nobody knew the truth. Then that evening, while I was talking to his Prime Minister Pham Van Dong, he came shuffling through the door, padding along in the extraordinary sandals everyone wears in North Vietnam, made of old motor-tyres. He laughed at my surprise.

He had categorically refused to see me, after all. Now it seemed his old man's curiosity had changed his mind. But he refused at first to talk seriously. 'Let's leave that to the Prime Minister,' he said, 'Instead, tell me what the Haymarket looks like these days.'

Long years ago, one recalled, he had achieved part of his Marxist education by working as a pastrycook, of all things, in the old Carlton Hotel. That, and being a darkroom assistant in Paris, and a revolutionary student in Moscow, and a hundred other things. He asked if we could try speaking in English: 'As you can imagine, I get little opportunity to practice.'

But he spoke better French, and Vietnamese, and Mandarin, and liked to write quatrains in them all. This was the odd impulse of Asian rebels, like Ho or Mao Tse-Tung, to pass their leisure hours (which were mostly in jail) by writing inconsequential verse.

In Ho one came to terms with a Vietnam whose whole history was that of shaking off intruders. The Chinese had ruled it off and on for a thousand years, the French for eighty, the Japanese during the war; all long before the Americans. Somehow this had thrown up the young Vietnamese scholar called Nguyen Tat Thanh, later to be known as Nguyen Ai Quoc, which means Nguyen the Patriot. Deciding that any successful revolutionary must be a man of international experience, he left to travel the world. It turned out to be an exile of thirty-five years, until he returned to his country at the end of the second world war to organise the uprising of his people against the Japanese invaders and their French helpers. He was now a veteran Communist, with his third and finally celebrated name: Ho Chi Minh.

It is curious to recall how in those days Ho had such faith in the United States' sponsorship of Vietnamese independence. When he wrote his Declaration of Independence he lifted it largely from the American phrases: 'All men created equal . . . inalienable rights . . . life, liberty, the pursuit of happiness.' There was virtually no Marxist dogma in it at all. To Ho Chi Minh Moscow was the cradle of the revolutionary movement, and that – or anything else – he would use to promote his obsession: a free Vietnam.

There were so many occasions when his patriotism manifestly transcended his ideology. The most extraordinary was in 1945, the thing unprecedented in international communism, when he actually dissolved the Indo-Chinese Communist Party he had formed in order to facilitate national unity. But that was long ago.

There in that ornate room in Hanoi from which the French Governors had ruled, he poured some more beer, lit his fifteenth cigarette from the stub of the old one, and laughed. He was, in fact, rather funny. He was the only top-level Communist leader I ever met who had a recognisable sense of fun. He could even be sardonic about holy writ. 'You ask the P.M. that,' he would say, 'he's a better Marxist than I am. After all –' pause ' – he has to be.'

With his wispy Asian beard and glinting eyes he had the air of a gnomish ivory miniature. I must say it was something to see him there: the man who had held the limelight over so many years while never consciously appearing in it: the elusive father-figure whose unseen presence dominated every move in this most brutally tragic situation of our time.

Not exactly a father-figure; it was subtler than that. His odd position was illustrated by the quaint title he had chosen for himself, which was not Chairman Ho, nor even Father Ho, but Uncle Ho. Thus did he sign all announcements and demands to the people: It is required by Uncle Ho. Thus, it seemed to me, did the people accept him: this or that is a damn nuisance, the Government is pushing us around again, but Uncle Ho says it is all right so we suppose it must.

His trouble was he fitted into no accepted picture of Communist hierarchy; he was far too debonair. He could be, naturally, immensely ruthless, wholly arbitrary, and many a sombre deed was doubtless done by Vietnamese in his name. But he retained this queer quixotic detachment, his private fantasy: that unique role of the Universal Uncle. And for the future of South East Asia it is ten thousand pities he has gone, for he who follows will not be another Ho Chi Minh.

B.B.C. Radio, 1969

ARAB–ISRAELI PEACE TALKS

You know I'm not a Diplomatic Correspondent, nor a diplomatic anything, really, so nobody will mind if I say that I'm impatient and troubled and anxious and fed up, as so many people are, about this political folk-dance on the Middle East peace talks – even though it is a bit presumptious to be irritated over other people's life and death. The fact is it's no longer a middle-eastern thing, this Israel–Arab business; it's everybody's thing, and that's why I have the impertinence to intrude on it. The situation has a rather special meaning for me – and because I've been personally mixed up in all three of the Israel–Arab wars I had hoped to get myself mixed up, however marginally, in the Israel–Arab peace. I still hope so, though with diminishing confidence, I must say. These talks should have been off the ground a couple of weeks ago; and now what seemed like a great chance is slipping away already into a semantic quagmire in which I'm bound to say nobody's showing up too well. This is really a hellish waste of time. When you think that for twenty years we have been waiting for the Israelis and the Arabs to get the world off this tragic and dangerous hook, and then the argument stalls and fiddles about and becomes more and more of a bore, though that's a terrible thing to say. And then before we know where we are the three-months Cease Fire will be over, and off we go again. If not sooner. All this is putting a bit of a strain on the *goyim* and the infidels, whose sympathies with either side may be different, but who badly need an end to this 8,000-day war, which is what it is.

I have an involvement in this Israel–Arab thing – simply because it's happened; even reporters have involvements. I'm not going to contribute any more to the obfuscations that are obsessing everyone to the point where they just can't understand that if there is to be a Peace Conference it has primarily to be about peace. Boundaries, yes; aspects of sovereignty, yes; security, yes; dignity, yes. But these are things of which peace is made: peace isn't just a by-product of its own conditions. That is to say, the means for once are not more important than the ends, though if you listened to some of the people in this deal you might really believe they were. Not everyone, I think. A week ago on the telly I saw Abba Eban, the Israeli Foreign Minister, saying more or less this: what on earth *are* we supposed to be talking about – geography or peace? That of course is just the thing that doesn't endear Abba Eban to politicians, on either side, because Abba Eban is highly articulate and polyglot, and that in a statesman makes people uneasy. My trouble is that I've met such a lot of these quarrelsome gentlemen over the years. It's true I worked a lot in Israel, which I suppose colours one's thinking a bit. Yet I met President Nasser many times, after the Egyptian revolution of the 1950s; he won't remember but I do, and I liked him quite a lot then; though I like him a lot less now, simply because he isn't the same man. I think Gamal Abdel Nasser has a great potential for Egyptian good in him – and a surprising number of Israelis think the same thing. I'm personally supposed to be an Israeli-supporter, which I am – but I know which Israelis I support. Taking sides racially is a preposterous position. In any case we know perfectly well that even if any accommodation were made, or forced upon, the Jews and the Egyptians and the Jordanians, it still leaves hanging in the air the biggest factor of all: the Palestinians themselves, who aren't represented at any peace talks and who not only have the biggest personal stake in the argument – since they argue it's their land we're talking about – but who are also aware of a bigger international understanding than they've had for years, if perhaps they were not so crude and opportunist in their methods. They say the world hasn't listened to their arguments for years, so maybe they'll listen to their bombs. It isn't exactly my scene, but I can see what they mean. So can the intelligent Israelis, of course. I assure you it's a great error to assume that there aren't multitudes of Israelis who understand the Palestinian dilemma very well; they'd be fools if they didn't. There are, I am sure, Arabs who comprehend the dilemma of the Jews. But to solve one dilemma – as things are now – you must negate the other. We live in a barmy world of bogus absolutes.

I think in one thing the Israelis are right: the Talks shouldn't be in

New York, and they should be at Foreign Minister level. But we're stuck with what we've got, which is better than nothing.

I must say I never saw a Peace Conference get off to a more bloody-minded start, and I've seen some bloody-minded peace conferences, let me tell you: the only thing in the world I'm an authority on is the diplomatic double-cross. Mr Heikal in Cairo, who speaks for Nasser – a journalist, and once an acquaintance of mine – says flatly that Israel doesn't want peace and is only talking because of American pressure. That's a hell of a way to start a conference, since it's blindingly apparent that Egypt is only in on the deal because of Russian pressure. I don't mind in the least; there are many worse ways the Big Powers could behave than propelling their pensioners into peace talks. We shouldn't grouse about this, you know; we should make it a habit. If we only could.

Do you know that just twenty-two years ago on the island of Rhodes we were doing exactly the same thing, negotiating the first Armistice after the first war – with everybody being dragged struggling out of dreamland into reality, with the Israelis and the Arabs pretending they were never consulting each other at all, which was bunk. I only hope the same sort of face-saving melodrama is going on now.

I've spent such a lot of my life embroiled one way or another in this Arab–Israel thing, and frankly I know too much about it to be glib. There's a terrible tendency to say: very well, gentlemen: it's your trouble and not ours. But alas, we know now that we don't have that luxury any more. And nor, I'm afraid, do they.

B.B.C. Radio, 1967

THE BOAT PEOPLE

It was a dishonest journalistic compromise to call the Vietnamese refugees the 'boat people', which has an almost comfortable sound, like people on a holiday cruise. Refugees by definition seek refuge; they leave because they must. They are fugitives, escapers, victims, the lost and the lonely. Refugees have been a large part of the life of anyone who has travelled in this generation as much as I. They have nothing in common; they have everything in common.

Jewish refugees, Arab refugees, German refugees, Indian refugees, Pakistani refugees, Russian refugees, Bangladeshi refugees, Korean refugees. One of my childhood memories is of sharing our home with what were known as Belgian refugees, fugitives from the First World War. It seems a very long time ago, but I remember it. I think I have lived too much among the dispossessed.

But only comparatively recently have they become a kind of integral community in themselves: the society of the rootless. The Refugee Camp is a new and sad phenomenon of politics. In fact the Refugee, of whatever tribe or race, is in a way the symbol of our century.

Not of our century alone. In the seventeenth century there were the Huguenots, the Protestant heretics of Catholic France who emigrated to most European countries, notable England, in many cases, as it turned out, greatly to the host country's advantage, because not all history's refugees have been beggars, far from it. Many of them brought talents and skills and indeed resources that enhanced their new land's society, and we may well find some of the so-called 'boat people' doing just that, since it is obvious that many of them have fled from politics and not penury.

At the turn of the century how many persecuted Jews fled from Eastern Europe to America? Can it be said that America's cultural and commercial life was not advantaged from this extraordinary influx, which has left America with a far greater Jewish population than that of Israel? What would Canada and the Carolinas have done without the importation of destitute but industrious Scots after the Highland Clearances?

For that matter where would the United States be without those Eastern immigrants, the Founding Fathers? Who in America today is not a refugee or the descendant of one? Ask the Sioux, the Navajo, the Cherokee; only they will tell you.

It is so easy to be wise after the event. In those days the world was a pretty empty place; there was room almost everywhere for the homeless stranger. Everywhere to which an alien might wish to take refuge is now overpopulated, and already with problems of its own. Hong Kong is practically in a standing-room-only situation; one can understand its difficulties. Malaysia has always been uneasy about its delicate racial balance between Malays and Chinese and is wary about introducing more ethnic Chinese, which is what basically the Vietnam refugees are. The British have never quite come to terms with the differences between 'refugees' and 'immigrants'.

But what about the French, who started the whole colonial principle, or the Americans, who finished it? What, for that matter, about the Chinese themselves?

The Prime Minister of Singapore, Mr Lee Kuan Yew, has firm ideas about the whole thing: the Vietnamese refugees are a Communist plot to overcrowd the democratic parts of South-East Asia, thus to embarrass and de-stabilise their economies. It is a simplistic theory. It presupposes that tens of thousands of people are willing to risk getting drowned in unseaworthy hulks for the sake of Mr Brezhnev's blue eyes, and that six- and seven-year-old children have lent themselves to a great Marxist conspiracy. In the International Year of the Child we could perhaps give them better credit than that.

Of course it is true that not all refugees escape for the best or purest of motives. Some are avaricious, some are saving their skin, some are on a bandwagon. But I have yet to meet a refugee baby who left home other than because he had to.

Up to now the world is a fluid sphere; there is no divine ordinance that says you must stay where you were born. Talking of divine ordinances: what about Exodus – were the followers of Moses not refugees, as they continued to be for 2,000 years, until they replaced their exodus with someone else's?

One day the world will be a nation, but that is a long way off. Meanwhile we who are fortunate must help; one day we may need it ourselves.

B.B.C. Radio, 1976

NIXON'S VISIT TO CHINA

If there were any justice I would not be mouthing away here tonight but sitting down in Peking to a splendid dinner of lacquered duck and mushrooms and lotus seeds in a restaurant called Fong Tze Yuen, which is by far the best joint in Peking – at the end of, ironically enough, the Street of the Coal Merchants. There I would pass the night carousing with my philosophic friends and exchanging epigrams and awaiting tomorrow's arrival of Mr Nixon, the first President of the U.S. to visit China. Everything is all teed up for the big day, even to the tons of imported television equipment and the chaps to work it and the custom-built satellite that even now hovers expectantly over the Pacific. The great cavalcade wings its way from Guam in what is called the Flying White House – and indeed technically is, because wherever the President of the U.S. goes becomes the White House for the time being, and a rum sight it is, with its built-in Zieglerphones and Kissinger-machines and as many of that famous band of brothers, the White House Correspondents, as can climb aboard. You may have heard that for the purpose of this China operation the gallant company has been called the Peking Toms. For twenty-five years there have been no Americans in China, now the place will be stiff with them. It's a big deal, just to make sure Nixon wins this year's election. There may be another purpose behind this extraordinary safari, but it isn't easy to learn what. Mr Nixon himself has been about as cagey as a man can be who practically never stops talking; there's no agenda for the talks as far as we know and we're warned not to expect miracles – other than the minor miracle of the thing happening at all, of course, and we're not cynical about that, I promise you. Still, we're told that Nixon's landfall in Peking is going to have the biggest T.V. coverage since the men landed on the moon. One almost expects to see him coming out of the aircraft in slow motion, and bobbing and floating about in a symbolically weightless way. How far the cameras will be able to go outside the airport I long to know, since I love China visually. To tell you the truth I once went to dinner with Chairman Mao Tse-Tung some years ago for a bit of a chat; it was in an intimate little place called the Hall of Purple Light, only about three times bigger than the Albert Hall, and there were another 2,700 guests. Maybe Mr Nixon will get a bit closer than I did, which was about 800 yards. There was a scholarly article in *Punch* the other day explaining some of the Chinese protocol – for example the exigencies of the Mandarin pronunciation, which can't cope with the 'X' sound, means that the President will have to be called Mr Knickers On. 'Welcome to the Celestial Capital, Mr Knickers On; we accept your homage.' 'Glad I could make it, Mr, er, Mao. Or may I call you Chairman?' 'One day, perhaps. You know my Prime Minister, Joe?' 'Funny, I always thought he was Chou. Chou En Lai.' 'Chow is a dog. Joe is a Prime Minister.' 'Well, hi Joe, whaddya know?' 'As a matter of fact, Mr Knickers On, I know a hell of a lot. Like, for instance, that third Secret Service man from the left in the back row, the one that's made up to look like Madam Chiang Kai Shek; he's showing his flies. In China flies have been abolished since 1953.' 'Okay, Kissinger'll fix it. Tell me, Mr Chairman, been having any good Thoughts lately? For the Little Red Book, I mean.' 'One or two have occurred in the last few minutes.' 'You know, Mr Chairman, sir, confidentially you do get away with a lot of crap on those Thoughts, don't you. You could almost think they were ghosted by Clifford Irving. I mean, things like "The corn grows quicker when it thinks of Chairman Mao"' 'How do you know it doesn't?' 'Because I'm cornier than thou, Mao; ha ha. Credit two dollars Bob Hope please, Mr Ziegler.' At this point the Chairman mutters: 'My God, the inscrutable West; you can see there'd be a problem having a Cultural Revolution with these chaps; where would you begin?' And off he goes into the perfumed darkness, leaving the boys to their nightcap. This is a ferocious stuff called *mao-tai*, which is put up in bottles made of granite, because it's liable to dissolve anything else, and it's guaranteed to make a thousand flowers bloom. Imagine what the I.R.A. would do with one or two of these. . . . As I say, if there were a divine providence I wouldn't just be talking about it, would I? I wouldn't be sitting *here* wondering what was going on. I'd be sitting *there* wandering what was going on. Waiting for the cut-price millenium. . . . When I think of that delicious duck . . .

B.B.C. T.V., Up Sunday,
20 February 1972

MARTIN BORMANN

If it turns out this chap they have caught in Colombia, in Central America, *is* Martin Bormann, what happens now? What should be done with Adolf Hitler's number two Nazi who got out of Berlin one jump ahead of the Russians twenty-six years ago, and who vanished without trace ever since? Does it in fact matter what's done with him? And who is going to decide?

If this man who calls himself Johann Ehrmann is Martin Borman, and not just another false alarm, he is a fascist murderer and a very serious transgressor indeed. But he can't very well be tried as a war criminal, because he has been tried as a war criminal, and he was found guilty at Nurnberg, in his absence, and he was sentenced to death. I don't think there's any precedent for arresting a man for crimes for which he was already condemned to be hanged a generation ago. So: this is going to be a very real dilemma.

All war crimes trials are dilemmas, it seems to me. The trials are as a rule as unpleasant as the crimes, or nearly so. I sat through a lot of Nurnberg, and a more sickening charade I never saw in my life: smug victors sitting in judgment on quiet unspeakably nasty prisoners, charged with offences that had been legally invented in order to condemn them, so full of humbug and yet so inevitable, in the mood of the time. Of that infinitely depressing chamber of horrors two living ghosts remain of that stinking Nazi past, two ruined and forgotton old men: Rudolf Hess, still in Spandau jail where he waits for death; and Martin Bormann in the Putamayo jungle. If it is Martin Bormann, Deputy Fuehrer of the Last German Reich. And if this sick old septuagenarian crook is the man, does somebody take him back and hang him? If so, who? And where? And why?

I'm no sort of a jurist; I don't in fact know if there is a statute of limitations that would apply in this sort of context. In any case I would imagine that statutes of limitations apply to accusations, not executions. But there's something so peculiarly horrible about these overlaps of history. I had to spend quite a long time at the trial of Adolf Eichmann in Jerusalem, which was no fun at all, I can tell you; this prim little bureaucrat sitting behind the bullet-proof glass in case somebody shot him before they had time to condemn him; a pedantic functionary correcting people's figures on the numbers of Jews he had arranged to be killed. . . .We had endless arguments with my Israeli friends: he's responsible for four million murdered Jews, so can you hang him four million times? They didn't really care what happened to Eichmann; they wanted the atrocious facts on the record; and by and by they had to hang him because what else could you do with him? Once you make people into symbols, even monstrous symbols, you're stuck with them. And until the very last of the Hitler gangsters is underground, and seen to be underground, this is always liable to happen again. As with this so-called Bormann.

Now this Martin Bormann has been reported – indeed perhaps even known – to be in this strange Nazi camp in Paraguay for about twenty years; I know at least three people who claim to have identified him there, and this gruesome Josef Mengele, the Auschwitz doctor. And one or two more. I remember that shortly after the last War I was sent chasing all over South America because Adolf Hitler himself was supposed to have landed from a submarine at Mar de Plata in the Argentine; thank God I never caught up with him, since he wasn't there. But Martin Bormann is different, having turned into a legend, or a phantom, like Prester John, that extraordinary will-o'-the-wisp of the early Christians. If Prester John had ever been identified he would have been canonised; if Martin Bormann is identified I suppose he will have to be hanged. Which seems a very meaningless thing now, after so long. It would surely make far too big an end to an unpleasant and secretive life, which at the age of seventy-two is coming to an end anyhow, I imagine. Still, there have been fifteen Martin Bormanns discovered since the war, popping up among the undergrowth in all sorts of places. The great authority on Martin Bormanns and the like is of course Dr Simon Wiesenthal, of the Jewish record centre in Vienna; he says prosperous ex-Nazis don't turn up in South American jungles, they turn up in places like surburban Argentina, as Eichmann did, highly thought of by the local cops. Or, to be sure, occasionally in Bonn.

I must say I hope this old bloke in Colombia turns out to be false alarm number sixteen. A Frederick Sewell *and* a Martin Bormann would be a bit much for one weekend.

B.B.C. Radio,
12 March 1972

'CAMERON COUNTRY'

'POINT OF DEPARTURE'

Producer: Richard Marquand

(NB: footages in script are 35 mm)

VISION	FOOTAGE	SOUND
MCU JAMES CAMERON at wheel of vintage car	1 5	CAMERON (COMM.) My name is James Cameron.
TITLE SEQUENCE – Passport stamps, stills, series title 'CAMERON COUNTRY'	8	MUSIC: 'The Garden of Delights' from 'MILLION DOLLAR COLLECTION' John Dankworth and his Orchestra Fontana TL 5445 (35″)
CU heavy rain on pavement, pan up to LS CAMERON walking towards camera from Dundee Railway station	64	
S/I 'POINT OF DEPARTURE'	89	CAMERON (COMM.) Long ago, in the golden days of Stanley Baldwin and the League of Nations and all that, I came as a young man to the city of Dundee, where I had reason to believe I should make my
MLS CAMERON goes up steps of footbridge	94	fortune – which at the time was marked up to five pounds ten a week.
LS CAMERON walks through rain down narrow alley	112	It is always a risk to go back. Sometimes it can also be an impertinence.
Exterior: entrance of the Royal Hotel, CAMERON approaches and goes in	125	After 40 years it is evident that not only does that Dundee no longer exist, but neither does that young man.

Interior: lobby of Royal Hotel. CAMERON comes through revolving door, gazes round, goes to reception desk	132 153	CAMERON (SYNC) Yes – this is the place right enough –
CU his signature in register	163	
CU CAMERON gazing round lobby	171	
Exterior: Law Hill. Pan round view of Dundee to CU CAMERON	175 180	CAMERON (SYNC) How often I used to look out on this and say – is it possible? This is one of the great locations to put a town on, this estuary, this Firth of Tay, this nice little hill behind us – it's almost Neapolitan geography. And look what's been made of it. Look at all this sprawling, brutal, meaningless building that's secreted around this lovely river. It was pretty grim in the days of the Depression and the poverty, and it's not much prettier now. Bonnie Dundee – my God!
MLS CAMERON walks away down hill	229	
Top shot: the Howff cemetery. CAMERON walks through among gravestones	244	CAMERON (COMM.) One memorable thing endures: a convivial old graveyard, smack in the middle of town. It must be an immensely valuable site now, in these new booming days. It is called the Howff: the meeting place. In my day it was the meeting place both of the dead and the half-dead, the debris of the Depression, mooning their idleness away among the wealthy phantoms. I passed them every day as I went to work, for I at least had work.
Facade of the Dundee Courier building, pan down to CAMERON approaching along pavement	282	How many thousand times did I slip cautiously through these doors, the office of the Courier, where I first fell addict to the curious compulsions of the

Interior: LS CAMERON comes into office entrance hall, walks towards camera	304	newspaper trade. Now, a generation later, something of the same peculiar uncertainty suddenly returns: what foolish error shall I make today?
Various shots: machinery room and presses	318	
	327	Anyhow, for good or ill, here I was enmeshed in the inky, edgy, clattersome and voracious occupation that was well called the Press, since with the name we acknowledged the domination of the machine over the men. Thud and thump and grind and roll; out come the thoughts and the non-thoughts, the ads and the agonies. All the truths and trivialities of great importance to us if to nobody else.
Papers taken to delivery vans	367	
Delivery vans loaded	385	So we spread the word to the waiting public of Dundee and Dunfermline, Coupar and Carnoustie, Leuchars and Lochee.
Driver gets into van and drives off	400	
CU CAMERON, zoom out to show him sitting at desk with newspaper file	423	CAMERON (SYNC) We are now approaching the touching scene that is the standard component of all these television nostalgia corners – whether it be elderly gentlemen returning to Calcutta, or middle-aged gentlemen coming back to Dundee. These little trips down memory lane can be very rough going for the ego. Still it can be very wholesome. I think everybody should be obliged from time to time to examine the pretensions of his youth. It's very good for the soul. In those days it was the custom to have nobody write under their own name, but under a great variety of whimsical pseudonyms. In this way I changed my role and character completely from week to week, assuming sometimes the nature of this and sometimes the nature of that – male or female – animal, vegetable – mineral.
File open at page dated September 1939	521	

180

MCU CAMERON at desk	528	Oh yes – sometimes I was also a reporter. This is November 1939, that's Armistice Day. That's always a very serious trap. Nor do I appear to have totally avoided it. 'At 11 o'clock I stood in George Square, there was an air-raid shelter on one side and a girl selling poppies on the other.' Well that's reasonable objective stuff so far. 'Yesterday was Remembrance Day.' So it was – it was the first Armistice Day after the war had been declared.
File open showing article and wartime map of Europe	599	'Yesterday was Remembrance Day. In Holland they are flooding the meadows and mining the roads. On the fields of Lorraine they are laying tank traps and waiting in the mud. The German losses are described as appreciable – unquote. Hitler confers with his staff. A wreath of poppies beside a surface shelter. You can ration even sentiment.'
CU CAMERON	623	Well it could have been worse. It usually was I must say. At times I reached a genuine mastery of the banal. I will forbear to quote. But this sort of reporting was quite big time for me, and it had taken me ages to graduate up to actually writing anything, from the long periods of pastepot filling and filespiking and all the other menial jobs that probably on the whole did a great deal less harm.
		CAMERON (COMM.)
Various shots in sub-editors room	667	Not that one's opportunities for doing harm were very great in those days, or good either, for that matter. That came later I dare say. Here among the undistinguished certainties of a provincial society I attempted to remedy the confusions of a dotty childhood.
		One laboured on in the subs' room as they labour on today.
		The place is still full of echoes of the past.
2/s and then intercutting: CAMERON talking to ALF ANDERSON in his office	712	**ALF ANDERSON (SYNC)** – that Press Club was quite a place in

Glasgow of course Jim, wasn't it?
(OH, YES –)
Remember the night you fell out of the
taxi going there?

CAMERON (SYNC)
I do not remember that night.

ANDERSON
We'd been to the . . . Jack Hylton was
playing at the . . . and we came out at
the side from the press conference, and
we got this taxi, all piled in, you sat
down on the small seat and leaned on
the door and disappeared. Well the taxi
was going, so we just closed the door
and carried on. But when we got
upstairs there you were sitting at the
bar. You'd decided you'd beat us to it
and you'd run like the wind down that
lane from Sauchiehall Street into West
Regent Street and foxed us all.

CAMERON
You're a truthful man Alf, otherwise I'd
have said that was a highly unlikely
story.

ANDERSON
It's a true bill – a true bill.
What about you Jimmy? Did you find
what you expected to find? Did you find
it worthwhile?

CAMERON
Yes – I think I expounded a little
bit more than I really intended to
do – but – I no longer believe in logic,
anybody's logic. I think everybody in
life now makes so many errors that it's a
fulltime job trying to prove that even
one of your previous judgments was
sound. Me most of all.

ANDERSON
But you're not dissatisfied about the
way things have worked out for you?

CAMERON
Not for me personally – no – no – you
make – you pay a price for it, of course.

ANDERSON
Of course, of course –

CAMERON
We've all lived a long time since then
and nothing is any longer easier to
explain or to define. I don't know. I was
just a campfollower of the age I lived in.
I don't think I really had much choice.

MLS CAMERON standing on dockside beside jute storage shed	883	
CU man on ship directing unloading jute bales from hold	891	
	904	CAMERON (COMM.) Dundee was made by jute, and Dundee was ruined by jute.
Bales of jute taken into shed	923	Jute is now restored to Dundee, but no longer can its fortunes destroy the people as they could then. Now there are other things to make: watches and cash registers. In the Thirties the watches were all in the pawnshop, and
Man throwing jute on spreader machine in Manhatten jute mill	938	we had no cash to register.
CU girl at loom	964	
Draffens store: various close shots, women in the Coffee Lounge	972	But downtown things were always completely different. And the morning civilities of the teashop still continue. Stands the church clock at half-past ten? Has coffee-time come round again?

WOMEN IN COFFEE LOUNGE
(SYNC)
Well I don't know how Jane managed to
see coming up the road . . . I never
even heard his car stop at the door . . .
Oh, she says, you must have had a
wonderful day. She says, yes, we had
quite a good day . . . rubbing it into
Jeannie – you needn't think you're
impressing me because you're not . . .

Jute thread spins off, leaving empty spool	1034	CAMERON (COMM.) Meanwhile our staple trade was running out.

Empty slum street	1044

Deserted harbour, Tay Bridge in background Various shots, slum houses and streets	1050	I don't suppose I shall ever really disentangle myself from this place. I don't think I ever loved it – but one wasn't critical, one lived there. At the time, it was all the world I had.

MCU CAMERON standing outside Dundee Labour Exchange	1068	CAMERON (SYNC) Today I think there are about two and a half thousand unemployed here, which is well under 3%. In my day there were 27,000 of them who just had no work at all. And this corner would be always populated by men just hanging about, endlessly, waiting for the days to pass.

Stills sequence: unemployed men during the Depression (Radio Times Hulton Library)	1098 1108	CAMERON (COMM.) If I had lived there now, instead of then, I would probably have been very different. I knew little about politics in those days. All I could grasp then, or more accurately assume, was that this sort of thing was intrinsically bloody awful, that there should be well-off merchants at one end of town and an aching economic emptiness at the other. It was obviously an unnatural state of affairs, it seemed to me, and therefore to be rejected. Not exactly opposed, not at that time, simply because I knew no way of opposing it. I became a socialist intuitively because I didn't see how one could reasonably be anything else. I hadn't the kind of education to equip me to define it in proper political terms.

The beach at Carnoustie: slow pan from waves along beach to CAMERON walking along sand towards camera	1180 1190	CAMERON (SYNC) I just really couldn't bear it, nor could I bear it now. One summer, with the help of a good friend, I went to live in a caravan which we pitched here, on the beach, just where the river and the sea and the sky are almost exactly the same thing. It was remote and awkward and inconvenient, and full of pleasure and

diversion. There was sand in the
sausages, and every evening there came
in this ocean mist, this Dundee Haar,
that enveloped the beach and the
caravan and me in this miasma of the
North Sea.

Then at the weekends I'd shove off in
my little car.

Various shots, CAMERON in the Trossachs at the wheel of a 1926 two-seater Morris	1268	MUSIC: Ian Campbell Folk Group 'Across the Hills' TRA 118 (1′ 00″)
CU CAMERON driving car	1364	I think my car cost me £17. It was neither new nor very smart even then. But it was the first car I ever owned – if you really want to know, it was the last one too. Very difficult to get a good £17 car these days.

Sometimes my father would come along
with me – he was persuaded to come
occasionally. My father had very little
confidence in the ability of the human
race to look after itself, and he'd never
travel without his own individual and
personal motor horn. The thing worked
with a bulb like this (HORN). With this
motor horn, which he held in his hand,
he would alert the pedestrians from
afar. As soon as they came into
sight – he'd honk at them sternly
(HORN) – saying 'Beware'! And even
when we'd passed them – if we did pass
them – he'd turn round and honk at
them backwards, retrospectively as it
were, to reassure them of their
fortunate escape. My father was the
only known virtuoso on the solo motor
horn.

More car shots	1528	So we would chunter along behind our 11.4 horses, through Angus and Perthshire, even further afield if I felt brave – decorously with dignity, a slow and moderate speed, and without frivolity.
Top shot from hillside, car stops, CAMERON climbs out, takes off jacket, starts climbing up hill	1598	

MCU CAMERON climbing hill	1639	CAMERON (SYNC) I was never particularly romantic about the hills, but I used to climb them whenever I could. I suppose that in my time I did almost every considerable peak in Scotland that there is.
CU CAMERON walking through woods	1662	
LS CAMERON, stops and blows nose	1681	
CU CAMERON climbing rocks, zoom out	1693	
MCU CAMERON sitting on rock, shakes stone from shoe, speaks to camera	1748	Nowadays I must say I rather wonder why I did it. I don't think I enjoyed it all that much. I was either scared or exhausted. I still think mountains are things best seen from underneath.
CU Highland cattle		(CATTLE)
CAMERON r. to l. across field through cattle, sits down on wall, speaks to camera	1793 1803	It wasn't very difficult. I'm glad I did it though – but I wouldn't do it again. Except to show off, like this.
CAMERON gets up, goes away towards hill	1818	
CU Highland cattle	1823	
CU CAMERON's feet walking	1827	
LS CAMERON climbing rock to top of hill	1835	
MCU CAMERON comes over top of rock, flops down, speaks to camera	1862	They were great days too, in a way. This was my ancestral country, and by God I made it mine too. Not really. If this were mine, my goodness, I'd have the whole place rolled out flat!
CAMERON standing on hilltop, zoom out	1887	

Heavy rain on pavement	1912	(THUNDER)
Exterior, Royal Hotel, Dundee	1926	CAMERON (COMM.) Back in Dundee my father would be writing away for his living in his hotel room.
2/s CAMERON and barman talking in a bar in the Royal Hotel	1931	BARMAN (SYNC) Yes I remember your father. I remember him coming round corners and saying 'Don't forget the inspiration now – remember, you forgot the other night' – (LAUGHTER) – we were boys, we made mistakes. CAMERON (SYNC) What was his inspiration? BARMAN One pint – (REALLY?) – Yes, a pint a day. CAMERON That fuelled him up with inspiration for another day did it? BARMAN Yes, it fuelled him up – not for the day, let's be honest about it – but fuelled him up – when the bar was closed – (LAUGHTER)
CAMERON walks along passage and down stairs	1978 1980	CAMERON (COMM.) It is odd to be moving back in time like this. It was indeed here that my father lived alone, battling with his terrible asthma like the brave old professional he was. Nobody realised how hard writing can be, when it's work.
MCU CAMERON sits on bed in hotel room, picks up phone	2004	CAMERON (SYNC) And he certainly had got work to do. Those novels and serial stories he wrote – they weren't literature, but they were very well thought of in their time, because they were by Mark Allerton. That nom de plume somehow invaded his whole being. Nobody in Dundee ever thought of my father as Cameron, he was always Mark Allerton the author. (RECEPTIONIST ANSWERS PHONE)

Yes – could I have a whisky and water, please? Room 85, thank you.
Yes, even his friends never called him anything except Mark – which is rather odd because that's really my name too.

CAMERON reflected in washstand mirror, pan to him as he continues 2075

And so he lived here alone – never very prosperous, never very well, never very lucky, but never out of temper and never impatient – and never, towards the end I suppose, never very sober. I saw that in no way as a wrong-doing or a weakness but as a perfectly understandable response to very great pressures. I rationalised my father's dependence on the bottle as later I suppose I rationalised my own. He was always very gentle, and he was always extremely good company, and we had a lot of fun.

CU snooker balls arranged for start of game, cue scatters them 2130

LS CAMERON playing snooker with MATT WADDELL 2134

2138
CAMERON (comm.)
During those last days we had a very special relationship, very meaningful to me, and, I believe, to him.

Closer shots of game 2153
His friend Matt Waddell was very much part of those days, and these ones too, luckily.

2166
MATT WADDELL (sync)
Your father was a man who didn't make friends easily did he? But he was a very staunch friend once you had made a friend of him.

CAMERON (sync)
He was quite an institution though wasn't he, while he was there –

WADDELL
Yes, but one never got into his inner soul, so to speak. He had his own private life tucked away inside him and no-one ever got in there. And he never encouraged the use of Christian names to himself, he rather resented people calling him Mark. And all the time we knew him, and we were very close

friends as you know for roughly twelve or more years, we never were on Christian name terms. Never. He was just that little bit always within himself – but kindness itself and most considerate to everyone. But it's one of those little things that one remembers about a man.

CU tap dripping into basin in room 85	2257	
MCU CAMERON sitting in chair	2260	CAMERON (sync) Then one day my father had to go to the nursing home. He was terribly ill, but under the deep sedation he didn't know it, and he was beset by the strangest of imaginings. It was characteristic of my father that even his hallucinations had this flavour of the fantastic and the slightly preposterous, probably his last joke. For example, he was very puzzled, and at the same time quite amused at having been obliged against his will to spend the previous night with Queen Victoria. 'Why,' he wanted to know, 'do the doctors impose this on me? It was very convincing,' he said, 'but surely everybody knows the poor old soul passed away years ago – didn't she?' He got the idea that all manner of extraordinary people were being sent in to vex him. 'Soldiers and lawyers and musicians,' he said, 'all total strangers to me. What on earth good they're supposed to do I can't imagine. How I could do with a little peace.'
CAMERON gets up, goes to dressing table, starts packing	2364	He didn't have long to wait. He died the next morning, still puzzled no doubt at how much more extraordinary his fact was from his fiction. He was quite the best man I ever knew, and it's absurd to say so, but I miss him still.
CAMERON picks up bag and coat, goes out, leaving the empty room	2412	
Exterior: Riverside Drive beside the Tay at night.	2430	

CAMERON walks towards
camera through mist

CAMERON sits down, speaks to camera	2457

CAMERON (SYNC)
This used to be the place to come of an
evening, probably still is, this long
esplanade beside the river leading up to
the elbow of the Tay Bridge. You can
still see how beautiful Dundee might
have been. But if possible you got here
before the arrival of the cold haar, the
seamist that still brings out these dismal
foghorns.
But the mist itself of course had some
advantages, if you had a girl, as most
people seemed to have – as indeed I
had myself, by then.
There was a very pretty art student with
whom I went out, as they used to say.
Which gave quite a new glow to the grey
edges of Dundee. And by and by we
were married here. My daughter looks
very like her.

Exterior: LS CAMERON walking through George Square, Glasgow	2535
Various shots, people in the streets of Glasgow	2550

CAMERON (COMM.)
By and by I was sent away to work in
Glasgow. For my wife and me Glasgow
was the start of a sort of liberation, a big
deal. Here I would set up the first family
home I ever had. Here in this Eldorado
of the West Coast I should perhaps
learn how to write. Glasgow was very
much on the way to somewhere, I
thought.

Tracking shots, CAMERON walking through the Cowcaddens district of Glasgow	2570
	2578

CAMERON (COMM.)
What can one say about this great and
gruesome city that hasn't been said a
thousand times before? This was where
I lived for years, and I imagine accepted
for years. Around this neighbourhood
was where I came to work every day, to
write my little feature pieces of such
insufferable pretensions I can hardly
bear to remember them. I didn't
complain. I really didn't notice it much,
not then. I notice it now, all right.

For all that, this was where I at least
learned to grow up.

Top shot from crane as CAMERON walks through Glasgow Botanic Gardens	2642	It seems curiously irrelevant to learn how to grow up in the Botanical Gardens – a bit eccentric really. I was obliged to be eccentric. These Botanical Gardens are another kind of time-machine for me. People usually remember where they met their first lover, or wife, or friend. This was where, in a sense, I met my first child. Botanical Gardens – what an absurd term it is. What can gardens be, other than botanical?
CU CAMERON to camera on seat in the Botanical Gardens	2691	CAMERON (SYNC) Just up the road there was where my daughter was born. We lived just down there somewhere, and up there, the other side of the Gardens, was the hospital where my wife went to have her baby. It was great days then. But it all went wrong. There was the war, there was an air-raid emergency – God, it was a long time ago wasn't it – anyhow, when the time came there was this little margin between life and death that always comes at such a time, and – we lost. That's to say when it was all over I had got a daughter, but I hadn't got a wife, because she had died. Nor was I by any means the only young man this had ever happened to. It's a bit of my life that's wholly mine. I very much wish it had happened otherwise, but it reaped a very big reward too. I broke my heart in these bloody Botanical Gardens once. It's a very strange thing – I never thought I'd ever come to see them again. But I don't mind. I can cope with them now. I can cope with Glasgow. I can cope with anything. The following years have taught me that much.
Dundee University: CAMERON with students	2828	CAMERON (COMM.) Well now – 30 years have passed. And it happened that the other day some of the students of Dundee paid me the quaint compliment of proposing me as Rector of their University – thus putting me fair and square into another generation. I was deservedly beaten by

CAMERON towards box	a strolling player of wider fame (SYNC: – get off my ad lib please –)
CAMERON gets up on box to make speech	Nevertheless I rather rudely turned up.
CU CAMERON addressing students 2873	CAMERON (SYNC) Right – ladies and gentlemen. I propose to keep you here about five minutes. If you had elected me Rector it would have been at least fifty. (LAUGHTER) Now this is a splendid example of how a political failure for me has turned out to be a social advantage for you. (LAUGHTER) Now I am told that I am committing a very serious solecism by being here at all, which is the intrusion of the rejected suitor into the truly integrated marriage bed. Now fortunately the successful bridegroom isn't here at the moment – (LAUGHTER) – or my chances would be very small, because to ask an ageing juvenile of a journalist to compete with the elegiac excellencies of a Mr Peter Ustinov is a little unfair. Personally, and to be frank and between ourselves, I don't think you got the best Rector (APPLAUSE AND CHEERS) – on the other hand – on the other hand, you are certainly going to get the best possible Rectorial Address. I lived in this city before the war, when it was a very different place than this, when it was an economic wasteland that made a tremendous – (IT STILL IS! LAUGHTER) – it isn't as it was. But it made a vast impression on a very young and inexperienced reporter, even though this man was learning his trade on a paper, your paper (SHOUTS) – nonetheless it was a paper that could never be accused of imposing an intolerably radical point of view. (LAUGHTER) I gather that its views have not particularly changed any more than its technique has. (LAUGHTER) Things around here, ladies and gentlemen, have changed however. Compared to the Dundee I

knew, this is a swinging city.
(LAUGHTER AND GROANS) Well
perhaps that will give you an idea of
what the Thirties were like.
Ladies and gentlemen, dear fellow
toilers in a barren vineyard
(LAUGHTER) – you've been kind
enough to entertain us here, and for me
this is something that's as new as it's
gratifying. I've spent my life going
round the world trying to find out
what's going on in the minds of people I
don't know, and trying to explain it to
the minds of people I don't know either.
As far as I know it never came off, and
the one ineluctable rule of my trade has
always been, say what the hell you like
behind the shelter of the printed word,
but never let the customer see the
whites of your eyes (LAUGHTER).
Well now I'm very gladly breaking that
rule. The world has spun around a
million times since I was last in Dundee,
I've argued the arse off a hundred
donkeys since then, and almost
everything I have foretold has come to
pass (GROANS) – and nothing I've
been able to do has ever stopped it
happening. Now will you do better
perhaps? I hope so.

Now some of you were kind enough to
want me to represent you. Why? Why?
I thank you again most warmly, but I
am obliged to put the question, why?
And that's the question that you had
better, I think, ask me. (APPLAUSE)

CU student	3245

STUDENT (SYNC)
They said in the Rectorial campaign,
Mr Cameron, and you said in your
autobiography that you were never
more glad to leave any city in the world
than you were to leave Dundee. This
includes Hanoi, and it includes Korea
and it includes half the capitals of the
world. Did you think of Dundee in
terms of the long dole queues and soup
kitchens, or did you look on it as merely
a representative function of a political
nature?

CU CAMERON	3290	CAMERON (SYNC) No of course I thought of it as Dundee. There are about ten logical fallacies in your question – (LAUGHTER, CHEERS) – I could not conceivably equate the Dundee of the 1930s with Hanoi or with Saigon or with anywhere else, places that in those days I'd never even seen. All I knew in those days was Dundee. I didn't know what had happened to Dundee until I returned. The metamorphosis has been complete. STUDENT Was this lack of interest that you didn't know what had happened to Dundee?
MLS CAMERON, zoom into CU	3359	CAMERON (SYNC) To some degree, yes. To be absolutely honest, it was a certain amount of lack of interest. Dundee has produced very few plebiscites, revolutions, wars – or any of the sort of things that I have been obliged to use as my stock in trade over the previous 20 years. It is quite true that Dundee faded from my mind. Quite true.
CU STUDENT	3393	STUDENT (SYNC) Mr Cameron, you've partly at the same time chosen to eschew any direct involvement in this environment in order to change it, and implicitly you do believe it can be changed for the better, yet you've never chosen to do so. Would you care to express your viewpoint on this?
CU CAMERON	3420	CAMERON (SYNC) Do you know, for about 20 years I've been asking myself exactly that question – (LAUGHTER) – I'm not joking about this. If this question hadn't been asked I would have had to ask it myself. Why do you sound off all the time and never do anything? Why do you urge attitudes upon other people and never express any yourself? Why do you never take the risk of going into Parliament or something? I suppose – it's a silly answer – but I suppose the real reason is that I didn't

think I'd be any good at it. I thought
that within the framework of the
medium in which I work I could
possibly do better, and I would do
better to be a successful polemicist in
print than a frightfully unsuccessful
back-bencher.

CU STUDENT	3512	STUDENT (SYNC) Mr Cameron, you have had vast experience of man trying to destroy himself. Do you think he will eventually succeed?
Pan to CU CAMERON	3525	CAMERON (SYNC) In a short answer – yes. And before too long I think. I wish it would be as abrupt and magnificent and marvellous as they tell us the Creation was, but I fear it won't be. But certainly in the end – there's no doubt about it, we shall. It's not an argument one can continue, because one gets into philosophical depths that would take a year to adumbrate – but I think so, yes. I am a pessimist. (Do you care about that? Does it worry you?) It doesn't worry me personally in the slightest, but anybody who's got children, grandchildren and things like that – it's bound to worry them. (You have children –) I have children and I have grandchildren – three of each.
Tracking shot from front of train crossing Tay Railway Bridge	3620	
CU CAMERON sitting in carriage	3635	
CAMERON speaks to camera, Tay Bridge girders pass in b'grd.	3644	CAMERON (SYNC) Well that's a second goodbye to Dundee. I must say it's not a trip I particularly want to do again. All I'd have to say I suppose is I won't. But how would I ever know? The world's full of places I hoped I'd never go back to, and had to. Something always happens.

Tracking shots from window backgardens, etc.	3683	If you have to keep on the move, there's something very appealing about a train – to me that is. I do millions of miles in aircraft, that isn't travel at all really, it's just a positional transfer from A to B – going to get worse too I'm sure. There's much more reality in trains, they're hooked on to the earth and on to life, and fields and coal depots and gasworks and backgardens and the secret regions of towns. Trains are decent slow things that inhabit the valleys and the backyards, and move in two understandable dimensions.
CAMERON comes along corridor	3752	
Restaurant car	3762	
CAMERON to camera sitting at table in restaurant car	3765	It was on a train that I first met Gandhi, surprisingly enough. That was just before the Simla Conference in 1946, the year before India's independence. It was very exciting for me because I was quite new to India in those days. As it turned out we didn't make history. It would have been great if he'd let me in on the big Indian political strategy of the time, but not likely. What he did explain on the other hand was his own personal private way of eating a mango so that you didn't get yourself drowned in the juice. It wasn't epoch-making, but it was more than some people have had.
Tracking shots from train	3850	
Corridor		
Forth Bridge from front of train Forth Bridge girders CAMERON in corridor Tracking shots over bridge	3879	My God I've been on some lousy trains too. What about those awful wartime days, those endless hours under those beastly little blue lights in the blackout, jam-packed like pilchards, lucky to get standing room in the corridor, luckier still to get a little rest crouching on a kitbag – wondering if you're ever going to get anywhere.
CU CAMERON in carriage, eyes closed, then open	3929	

196

CAMERON to camera	3946	The thing about a train is that if it's a long enough ride you can settle down and sort of institutionalise yourself. In a train you can't be got at. They don't have phones in trains, the income tax can't pursue you there, women don't happen on trains – it's a sort of retreat. I remember a good long one once called the Crossroads Special. Five days and nights across the United States from the Atlantic to the Pacific, when I was on my way to Bikini and the atom bomb. That was one occasion when to travel hopefully was certainly a great deal better than to arrive.
Tracking shots out of window	4007	
CSS CAMERON	4018	
CAMERON to camera in corner seat of carriage with newspaper	4027	Trains have, or they used to have, this romantic and literary thing. They had names – the Trans-Siberia, the Orient Express, the Santa Fe, the Flying Scotsman. Nobody ever heard of an aeroplane with a famous name. Aeroplanes are things that take you to work. Trains are things that take you home, or on holiday, or to some sort of non-work – I think – they lead one into green pastures and the non-political –
Looks at paper as he speaks, marks passage with a pen		
Looks up at camera, shrugs	4107	
		COMMENTARY I should know better by now than to look at the papers.
Tracking shots from train. Railway track	4113	Well – we shall see.
		(TRAIN SIREN – MIXES INTO TITLE MUSIC 33″)
Top shot, CAMERON sitting in corner seat of carriage (held under credits)		
'FILM EDITOR HOWARD BILLINGHAM'		
'PRODUCED BY RICHARD MARQUAND B.B.C.tv'	4171	(MUSIC ENDS)

B.B.C. T.V.,
14 September 1968

'CAMERON COUNTRY'

'NOBODY EVER ASKS WHY –'

VISION	FOOTAGE	SOUND
CU JAMES CAMERON in the astronauts' launch position of an Apollo Spacecraft Orientation Trainer (at the Manned Spacecraft Center, Houston, Texas)	1	INSTRUCTOR (THROUGH CAMERON'S HEADPHONES) At lift-off indication all of your timers within the Command Module will reset to zero and start counting up – JAMES CAMERON (COMM.) My name is James Cameron. INSTRUCTOR – the propellant dump auto R.S.C. command switch should go into the R.C.S. command position. Can you locate this? CAMERON (SYNC) No – I can't find it. That's a great way to start a space flight – Never mind – let's pretend we've done it –
SERIES TITLE SEQUENCE – Passport stamps, stills, title 'CAMERON COUNTRY'	38	MUSIC: 'Garden of Delights' John Dankworth 'Million Dollar Collection' Fontana TL 5445 (33″)
Simulated nebula, dissolve to –	90	COL. FRANK BORMAN (V.O.) 'In the beginning God created the Heaven and the Earth. And the Earth was without form and void, and darkness was upon the face of the deep.
Still – the Moon, photographed on Apollo 8 mission. Zoom in and past it	109	And the spirit of God moved upon the face of the waters, and God said – Let there be light. And there was light. And God saw the light, that it was good. And God divided the light from the darkness –'

(Voice of astronaut JAMES LOVELL continues Bible reading under the following commentary)

Dissolve to still of the Earth, then to second still showing the southern part of North America, zoom in. (Both stills also from Apollo 8 mission)	136	CAMERON (COMM.) Thus the astronaut Frank Borman, reading Genesis from his American spacecraft 200,000 miles away on the frontiers of the moon. It's Christmas 1968. Already it seems long ago.
		JAMES LOVELL (Fade up V.O.) '– and let it divide the waters from the waters. And God made the firmament and divided the waters which were under the firmament from the waters which were above the firmament. And it was so.'
Rubbish dump beside fruit store on the Old Spanish Trail, Houston	177	(MUSIC – recorded live from car radio: 'God is alive and well' sung by the Stonemans – 53″)
S/I TITLE 'Nobody Ever Asks Why' Pan to car, driven by Cameron Interior and exterior, CAMERON driving car, listening to radio	203	'Well you see it in the magazines, You read it in the papers, The story that God is dead – And some scientists on the mountain tops Don't believe what the good book says. Well don't you listen, and don't you be swayed, They're just a-preaching the Devil's ways. Keep the faith, 'cause I'm here to tell – God is alive and well.
Tracking shots from car – downtown Houston	235	'God is alive and well, brothers, God is alive and well. Pray for that sinner who don't belive, God loves him like you and me. The truth is ringing in the Sunday bells, God is alive and well.'

	268	CAMERON (COMM.) The reassurance comes not a moment too soon. If God is alive and well on Highway 59, this must be the right road. When God created Heaven and Earth, as we've heard, He then produced the State of Texas – and in it Houston, this rich place with its feet buried in the oil below, and its hands now groping among the stars.
TS along perimeter fence of NASA Manned Spacecraft Center	298	What sort of a place should a Space City be, I wonder? That is what we've come to find out.
Car turns into gate	315	Behind the gate lies NASA, the National Aeronautics and Space Administration. Where else but in Texas would men set up to administer space? If there were a tangible symbol of the American dream I daresay this is it.
CAMERON passes security guard, checks his pass. Car drives past man admin. block of MSC, into car park	347	The powerhouse of the new prodigies is the Manned Spacecraft Center itself, the heartland of the 30 billion dollar investment that is the monument to President Kennedy's commitment to put an American on the moon by 1971 – the Apollo programme. Men have made many temples of Apollo in their time – but none as big as this, and none as costly.
Party of tourists boarding MSC bus	387	CAMERON (COMM.) By now this Spacecraft Center, all 30 billion dollars worth of it, is part of the American tourist trade. So might it well be. It is, after all, their commitment, their investment. It's an investment that overtops the budget of many a whole country. But the moon doesn't come cheap. Once it was free – but not now.
Interior of bus	416	GUIDE (SYNC) We have three major functions to fulfil

at this Center. The first of these is the selection and training of all of the astronauts – and we will deal with this in a little bit more detail later in the afternoon. Secondly we're responsible for the initial development and the overall management of all manned spaceflight programmes, and finally we're responsible for the dynamic Mission Control. This will be the first area that we'll visit.

Tourists outside Mission   454
Control building

Tourists and Guide in the   466
observation gallery, Mission
Control

On the floor there are about 17 consol positions. Of course each area is divided according to its specific function, and basically the entire back row, here closest to the windows, is all managerial. Now on the extreme right, where you see the red telephone, this is our Department of Defence representative. He of course is the liaison between this Center and the military who are utilised for the entire recovery operation – because they already have the personnel, ships and planes and whathaveyou, and so they can economically effect a rapid recovery of the spacecraft and the astronauts.

CAMERON (COMM.)
And somehow, as the science fantasies are patiently explained, the questions are always – How big? How far? How much? Nobody ever asks – why?

Tourists board bus again

GUIDE (SYNC)
– covers the entire rear portion of the chamber –

Tourists and Guide in the   538
observation gallery, centrifuge
area

– and for most of our manned tests we operate within a range of about 3 G's to about 12 G's, which puts us within the limits which our astronauts experience during a normal Apollo mission.
Now if you notice right at the shaft end of the arm, there's a television camera mounted at that location, and looking out of the window and up on the wall is another television camera mounted that looks at the gondola from this angle.
Now the reason for this is that it allows our medical monitors to watch the facial

expressions of each of our test subjects and gain a little deeper insight into what they're actually experiencing at any given time.

TS CAMERON walking into and through the MSC exhibition hall: passes Moon Landing exhibit, Apollo 6 spacecraft, Lunar Module model, rocket engines, spacesuits, etc.

610

CAMERON (COMM.)
How very strange it is to find that already this extraordinary business has moved into a sort of mythology, has created its own folklore. Could you believe that in this tiny space of time, less than 10 years, the technology of space travel has produced its own museum. Is it credible that today there should already be veteran spacecraft, publicly displayed as interesting curiosities – the old crocks of empty space. And that among these ancient pioneers of only yesterday there are empty showcases even now ready for the rocks and trophies to be brought back from the moon.

CAMERON walks upstairs   654

Passes 1:10 scale model of Saturn V

In this space musuem I personally really find it hard to accept that these prodigies should so soon be enbalmed in exhibition – Lindbergh's aeroplane or Stevenson's Rocket – and how strange that today that same word 'rocket' is given substance by a scale model of Saturn V. How soon will it too be a curio, a relic, an interesting memento of these primitive groping days when even the moon seemed far away?

Reaches end of model –   717
spacecraft and escape tower

2/s, then intercutting,   735
CHRISTOPHER COLUMBUS
KRAFT, NASA Director of
Flight Operations, talking to
CAMERON in empty Mission
Control room

CHRISTOPHER C. KRAFT (SYNC)
There are really two basic reasons for the space programme, I think, and –

CAMERON (COMM.)
How seemly it is, how proper, that the exploration Director of Flight Operations should be called Christopher Columbus Kraft.

KRAFT (SYNC)
– I think that we're trying to provide an impetus in the space programme for the development of technology. There has to be something that does that in any nation, and if we want to remain a great nation we have to remain great in technology. The science is the other aspect of the lunar programme, and the scientists are very interested in finding out the geology of the moon – how is the moon made up, because by finding out really how the moon was made up we're going to find out a great deal more about how the earth was made, and therefore know a great deal more about its resources.

CAMERON (SYNC)
How does advancing the frontiers of knowledge of lunar geography advance other branches of science?

KRAFT
No, but – that's the whole point. It isn't lunar geography. That's only something that we get out of the project that we're developing. The electronics, the use of new medical techniques that we use with the astronauts – almost every walk of life is being affected by the advancements in technology that are being made in every industry in the United States, which are being pushed forward by the space programme.

CAMERON
Now – as we force out the frontiers of our knowledge and the scope of our understanding isn't it possible that this may tend to diminish what we romantically call the human values of people on earth?

KRAFT
No – I think that's age coming out in you. I think that the romance of today's children is a little bit different from the romance that you had in your day, and I think that that's inevitably so. However I would believe that you couldn't – you just can't say that there's any limit on

knowledge, because if that were so there's no need to press on at all. Everybody's life is going to come to an end – knowledge has got to be boundless. I can't conceive, and I don't – it's hard for me to visualise why people can't see the space programmes as I see it, and I admit most people don't – even here in the United States. Because I'm convinced that what we're doing is the salvation – *(PA pageing system interruption)* – is really the salvation – *(PA call again)* – to our way of life. And when I say our way of life, I mean everyone's way of life, because people are going to try and take it away from us – and that's what I think the Russians are trying to do. And the only way to prevent that is to stay better than they are, stronger than they are, in every walk of life.

CAMERON (COMM.)
Even in this walk of life.

Henry Wadsworth Longfellow   990
School, Houston: children
salute the Flag in their
classroom

SCHOOLCHILDREN (SYNC)
I pledge allegiance to the flag of the
United States of America – (FADE
UNDER COMMENTARY)

CAMERON (COMM.)
Here in Space City the day begins as it
does throughout America, where no
one may be too young to forget the flag.

SCHOOLCHILDREN
– indivisible, with liberty and justice for
all.

Classroom, teacher addresses   1025
children

SCHOOLTEACHER (SYNC)
– Marilyn mentioned NASA in her
report – how many of you remember
what she said NASA means?

BOY (SYNC)
National Aeronautics and Space – oh –

SCHOOLTEACHER
Help him out a little bit, Roy, please,

ROY
National Aeronautics Space
Administration.

CAMERON (COMM.)
Only perhaps in Houston can children
repeat a space catechism, with its
invocation of the new pantheon of
saints. Are they doing the same thing in
Russian schools today? I expect so.

ANOTHER BOY
– Frank Lovell – or – Frank Lovell,
Jim Anders and Bill – Lovell –

SCHOOLTEACHER
Help him out Andy, please.

ANDY
Bill Anders, Jim Lovell and Frank
Borman.

SCHOOLTEACHER
Can you tell me what impressed you
most about this flight? Marilyn?

MARILYN
Yes – on Christmas Eve they read the
first chapter of Genesis in the Bible, and
it was the most dramatic moment of the
flight.

NASA OFFICIAL FILM 'APOLLO 7'
Saturn V blast-off, rocket   1124
passes fixed camera position

(ROAR OF ROCKET BLAST-OFF)

First stage separation   1186

CAMERON (COMM.)
One thing we know – that the fuel that
powers the vast engines of space, the
driving force of the great phallic
emblems of patriotic virility, is only
partly chemical. The true motive power
is conquest. This charting of the
firmament is history's great
contemporary joust, where men are
making holes in the sky in which to
plant a flag.

NASA OFFICIAL FILM
'GEMINI 4'
Edward White's first   1216
'walk in space'

(CONVERSATION BETWEEN
GEMINI 4 AND MISSION
CONTROL)

		1255
'APOLLO 7':	Docking in space	1260
	Interior of Command Module	1282
'GEMINI 4':	Earth, seen during orbit	1296

NASA OFFICIAL FILM 1309
'APOLLO 8'
Astronauts' helmets and gloves
put on – CU Borman, Lovell,
Anders

'APOLLO 8':	Earth, seen during orbit	1322

(END OF NASA FILM
SEQUENCE)

Houston: welcoming parade for 1341
Apollo 8 astronauts.
Various shots – drum majorettes,
children watching, bands,
news cameras, flags, etc. 1366

Col. BORMAN arrives by car 1403

CAMERON (COMM.)
Is it smug to wince at pride? Rivalry has probably been the seed of most human endeavour. Perhaps this whole space business we're looking at is necessary for all man's self-examination. And perhaps it's not.

(FADE UP GEMINI 4
CONVERSATION AGAIN)

So man escapes the playpen of the earth and lives his fragile hour swimming in emptiness – before the cameras. That's the difference. We say these explorers are in line with Magellan and Columbus, but to the old adventurers everything over the horizon was mystery. They didn't know their destination, they didn't even know if they had a destination. Now man at least knows the way, and has the means. We say 'man', but do we really mean just man? Does it matter who is the first man on the moon?
You bet it does.

(FADE UP BAND PLAYING AT
APOLLO 8 PARADE, HOUSTON)

CAMERON (COMM.)
This is the beginning of January 1969, and the spacemen Borman, Lovell and Anders, fresh from the edge of the moon, are being given a parade here in Houston. They have been given bigger ones elsewhere, and bigger ones are to come – but this is the traditional expression of the American scene, the heroes' hometown welcome. Local astronauts make good. I daresay Drake was given something just like this when he got back from the high seas.

(FADE UP MUSIC)

Shorn of the astronauts' armour and brought only too literally back to earth, the spaceman moves back from legend into the folkways of his tribe, for it's part of the story that inside every lunar superman is an all-American boy.

Astronauts together on podium	1444	(FADE UP MUSIC AGAIN – GOVERNOR CONNALLY WELCOMES ASTRONAUTS AND THEIR FAMILIES)
Highschool band marches past	1467	
	1492	CAMERON (COMM.) America may be claiming this moon flight as a national conquest – in Houston it's a Texan triumph. No one indeed could grudge them that – it's as good as winning the World Series, or the Olympic Games, or a medal in Vietnam.
Astronauts given medals by Mayor Welch of Houston	1510	

(FADE UP MUSIC AGAIN)

They are brave men, and their enormous journey had started here. Everyone knew how, and how far, and how much – nobody to be sure asked why, this was no time for asking why.

Col. BORMAN addresses the crowd	1558	COL. BORMAN (SYNC) Governor Connally, Mayor Welch, distinguished guests and all you fine Houstonians – thank you very much for this wonderful day. I – Jim and Bill and I – have had the opportunity in the past three days to participate in some fine events, but of course it's just wonderful to be received like this at home. And I'll tell you – I'm grateful for many things in my life, the successful completion of this mission, and I'm very grateful to you people who might have had something to do with putting the Manned Spacecraft Center in Houston –
CU JAMES STRONG	1610	CAMERON (COMM.) Of course, not everybody went to the parade. Some were like Jim Strong, a student at the University of Houston.

JAMES STRONG (SYNC)
Well if you live in the American culture
you've got the difficulty of having to get
'the space programme funded, which
means you have to sell it to the people,
which means you have to sell it in terms
of personalities, I guess – personalities
and an American conquest of the moon,
or an American conquest of the solar
system – That's not the way I relate to
it, that's the way it's packaged. As far as
its purpose – I guess its purpose should
be to obtain scientific knowledge,
knowledge about physics, knowledge
about the origin of the earth, maybe the
origin of the universe. It's like selling a
product, they want to put the maximum
in and get the maximum PR out of
it – you know, if you're selling
cornflakes, you want to sell all the
cornflakes you can and you do the most
effective thing to advertise it. So – you
know – they have these people, they
televise back prayers from outer
space – people shaving in the space
capsule or something like that, which
is – the actual hardcore data that comes
out as far as scientific knowledge – it's
buried in some scientific journal, maybe
on the back page of some newspaper.
They name craters after their little girls.
I'm not – it's a facet of our
culture – I'm sure it's very interesting
and entertaining to a lot of people, but
as long as we can admit it and live with
it – maybe there's hope for changing it,
I don't know –

Manned Space Center Real Time
Computer Complex:
Various shots – printouts and
close shots of computers

CAMERON (COMM.)
In this headquarters of mechanical
mystery there's a place enigmatically
called the Real Time Computer
Complex, which is inhabited by the real
technocrats, the metal minds without
which it seems there are no solutions.
The computers – already now so
intricate they can be understood only by
their own kind.
This is the dominion of the computers.

TS CAMERON walking round
IBM 'Software' area – long white
corridor with cubicles opening off
it

This is 'software'. In this curious world
the actual thinktank is called the
hardware because the stuff is made of
steel. This is the software because it's
made of people. The special people,
who are the halfway stage between men
and machines – literally, actually so.
They are the middlemen between the
human requirements of this wild place,
and the boxes that give the answers.
These people, you see, can ask the
questions. They know the words, the
symbols, the arcane jargon these things
understand and to which they respond.
These software here, they can translate
what has to be done into the creepy
conversation of the computer. When
the day comes that they don't need
software they won't need anyone.

What a piece of work is software – what
an impertinence!

Texas Instruments Inc.,
Houston:
Various shots in Electrical
Assembly area, then very close
detail shots of computer
components

1882

(RADIOPHONIC
MUSIC – CONTINUES UNDER
COMMENTARY)

But computers even now are not born,
but made. Or at least brought somehow
into the world, and by the very people
who obediently assemble the things that
will no doubt one day enslave them.
How long before the electronics take
over? Already they supervise our
spacecraft, construct our cars, bake our
bread, regulate our taxes. How long
before they determine our dreams?
How long before they start demanding
their rights, with the first eerie crackling
calls for Computer Power? Not long I
fear.

(FADE UP MUSIC)

CAMERON (COMM.)
Meanwhile this hallowed hardware
bides its time, growing and multiplying
in its twittering, transistorised
infallibility. There's an awful brainless
certainty about these things, that know
everything – and understand nothing.
Or not so far.

209

These are the things that the astronauts find reassuring, all-protective. To me they are a sort of nightmare.

(RADIOPHONIC MUSIC FADES UP AND OUT)

CAMERON (SYNC)

CU CAMERON in Apollo Orientation Trainer, in the launch position

If you can imagine anything more preposterous than me in an Apollo spacecraft – I can't. The antics they make one get up to –
It is like – it is like being enclosed in a sort of demented telephone box, with two other men for probably a couple of weeks – out of the question, I assure you. In front of me, or rather on top of me, in a bank of uncountable and equally incomprehensible switches and dials and compasses and indicators of one kind or another – I can't even read the language they're written in – oh yes I can, there's the ABORT button of which they spoke so much. Then there's – oh yes, there's the MASTER ALARM – I think I'd have my finger on that little titty for the entire run of the trip –
No – I don't think I have the makings of an astronaut. I always thought I hadn't, but now I'm absolutely certain. You'd need to be mothered by a computer and have an acrobat as a father. My respect for the men who ride in these things, my respect for their courage and their endurance, is tremendous. I must say – nothing in the world would get me in one of these things,
operationally – nothing in the world, or out of the world either –
I shall come back – I shall come back – I shall never be in another one of these things – ever –

Various shots – CAMERON driving car   2230

(MUSIC: 'Something Extra'
                Ornett Coleman
                Contemporary LAC 12170
                40″
                CONTINUES UNDER
                COMMENTARY)

Topshot – from bridge across the Gulf Freeway, Houston – several lanes of traffic	2250	**CAMERON** (COMM.) Suddenly the one imperative is escape – at least into a recognisable world. But the only formula for escape from the machine is, of course, another machine – what else? In America, more than anywhere, the car isn't so much a machine as part of life, the fifth limb. Escape from what? And to what?
Old Spanish Trail, Houston: various shots (through telestigmar lens)		(MUSIC FADES UP AND OUT)
	2290	Here is the real domination of the automobile: this Moloch of machinery, forever grinding down the highway – which by some Texan irony is called the Old Spanish Trail. It is neither old nor Spanish – but trail it surely is, the long long trail a-winding into the land of bad dreams – saturating the air with its own thick breath, oil. What is Texas if it isn't built on oil? – suffocating in its own prosperity.
	2312	(MUSIC: 'Coltrane Time' John Coltrane United Artists ULP 1018 37' CONTINUES UNDER COMMENTARY)
Man cross O.S.T., through dense traffic	2531	In a moment of mad cult of personality somebody crosses the road. An insolent intrusion, at his own risk. No good can come of this. (MUSIC FADES UP AND OUT)
Car graveyard, on Gulf Freeway, Houston: various shots wrecked and derelict cars	2371	
CAMERON to camera, walking among the wrecks	2384	**CAMERON** (SYNC) This is the end product of the mechanical revolution, in its very primitive sense, of course, because the more advanced a machine is the easier it seems to be to dispose of it. When you've finished with a billion-dollar Saturn rocket it's quite easy – you just lose it in space. It's less easy here below, when you've

got something that won't go and
nothing left to sell.
I wonder whether one day there'll be a
bit of the moon that looks exactly like
this – with all the bits of lunar modules
that nobody wants anymore.

CAMERON (COMM.)
Sooner or later we'll muck up everything
we've been to such trouble to create.

Car headlights, dissolve to traffic on the Gulf Freeway at night	2436	

It is, surely, the genius of our species to
invent our own anarchy, our own
self-cruelty. Expensively and earnestly
to torment our environment into
exquisite inelegance. And then, when
things become insupportable, to shout
for the scientists – or call for the cops.

2456

MCU Houston City Police
Sergeant in patrol car   2485

TS through downtown Houston   2497
at night

In a city that can send a man to the
moon the old Adam hasn't abdicated
down below – far from it. The city of
the future hasn't achieved the civic
conscience of the future – or maybe it
has. There's no reason to believe that
even the computers will ever manage to
programme us into perfection.

Flashing red light on police   2514
car

Police officers and woman   2520
witness on the sidewalk

(SYNC between Police officers and
distressed woman:

– did they take him inside the building,
or did –
– I didn't want to look –
– did they let him out, or just take him
that way?
– they took him up there – he looked
like he was drunk and droopy –

CU man bleeding from a head   2552
wound, lying in an alleyway,
police round him

SYNC between Police and wounded man:

– What's your name?
– call an ambulance yet? – we just did –
– now what is your name?
– John L. Robinson.
– Robinson?
– yes sir –
– How old are you John?
– I'm about 40 years old –
– where's your home?

– I don't have any – home –
– Do you know who did it John? (No –)
Do you know the people? Were they
friends of yours? Have you ever seen
them before?
– I wasn't hurt –
– you weren't hurt! Now how did you
get that?
– they hit me –
– they hit you with a bottle? – with
their feet – with their fists, or what?
– I don't know –

CAMERON (COMM.)

Man on stretcher, put into ambulance, which drives away	2635

So they take him away. He'll never get
to the moon. I don't suppose he'll ever
get anywhere. We've lost him
now – everybody's lost him now –

(AMBULANCE SIREN – CLOSE
THEN FADES INTO NOISE OF
TRAFFIC)

Neon Pepsi-cola sign, pan to crescent moon	2662
CU James Strong	2676

JAMES STRONG (SYNC)

A man can sit in a factory and feed
something into a machine – they've had
case studies of this – for 10 to 15 years,
and then all of a sudden he'll go up to
the machine and throw a wrench in, and
just stop the machine. And he'll just sit
down there for the next seven hours,
and look at that wrench.

Alienation – if you have technological
promise, and people know this, and you
have the capacity to correct all these
things, and to begin solving these
problems, and you don't – then a
feeling of alienation is created. I think
that has already started. I think it goes
from the problems in the ghettoes to
every problem we have.

Houston Museum of Fine Arts: people looking at abstract exhibits	2738
	2748

CAMERON (COMM.)

What does this fashionable word
'alienation' mean? Perhaps all it really
means is a truly terrible need for
reassurance. Yet this seems to me a
desolate way of seeking human
security – in a gallery, beautiful and
expensive, and profoundly well meant,

I'm sure – where the arts not only share the bleak values of their environment but insist on even bleaker statements of their own.

I suppose it's easy to read too much into this, but this uncomforting art obliges one to be pedantic. It may well be that this is the right proposition – or so it's argued by Sebastian Adler, director of the Houston Contemporary Arts Museum.

SEBASTIAN ADLER (V.O.)
Twenty years ago you wouldn't say a car was a work of art, or a jet was a work of art, or a can of soup – and today we look at it altogether differently.

MCU Sebastian Adler, talking to Cameron   2821

(SYNC) Art is moving into factories in this country now, and working with the scientists on projects. And being considered a true partner, where they never were before. They're learning all the processes and the fabrications, and techniques of a company, and they are contributing things to the company that the scientists didn't see – the scientists didn't see, the technicians didn't see, but the artist saw.

CAMERON (SYNC)
There'll be a sort of cross-fertilisation there, won't there?

ADLER
It's already happening, it's already happening. We have a group in New York called E.A.T. – Engineering, Art and Technology. And – I think the show's still on in the Brooklyn Museum in New York – where there were some 200 projects of collaboration between artists and scientists.

I'm amazed, I really am, when I think back to Stonehenge and where we've come from there. How man has ever managed to get where he is – because people are always refuting the new and reminiscing and thinking of the past.

Pictures by Al Held, on exhibition in America-General Insurance building, Houston –	2924	And I think somewhere we've failed in education on this. If everything is moving – science is moving medicine is moving ahead, city planning – the whole of society is moving at such a clip – how can you expect art, whatever it is, to stand still?

(RADIOPHONIC
MUSIC – CONTINUES UNDER
COMMENTARY)

CAMERON (COMM.)

2949 I think he missed the point altogether. It isn't that one asks art to stand still – it's just that one asks it to stand somewhere, if only to compensate for the computers.

(FADE UP MUSIC – THEN
CONTINUE UNDER
COMMENTARY AGAIN)

2980 To me this doesn't compensate for the computers. I think it's in league with them – like every other damn thing –

New buildings in downtown   2993   (FADE UP MUSIC – UNDER
Houston – enormous,   COMMENTARY AGAIN)
geometric and impersonal   3021

I think this has a kind of manic beauty of its own, until you remember that this is a living landscape – not for robots but for people. Here is something that was once a village, and became a town and became a city and became a symbol, a place that assumes this grievous mask of mathematics because the calculating machines said that this was right, this is the way you live – in a concrete theorem. And let's be realistic. This has only just begun. The daunting prophecy of when the urban spread of a great nation becomes a series of ever more titanic super-cities hundreds of miles across – one immense town from Boston to Baltimore, another from Chicago to Pittsburgh, another from San Francisco to Los Angeles – each of them with scores of millions of people imprisoned in asphalt forever. This is not a fantasy. Any expert will tell us

that this is the shape of things to come, and that there is nothing, but nothing, to be done about it now.
So we go to the moon.

Interior: man walking down empty corridor, track back along its length	3119

(MUSIC FADES INTO SOUND OF FOOTSTEPS, THEN INTO MONTAGE OF RADIO COMMERCIALS, JINGLES, ETC.)

CAMERON (COMM.)

The sea – at Cocoa Beach, Florida	3160

After a while, you know, you just start running away again.

A thousand miles from Houston is the sea, and the Atlantic coast. Is this far enough to escape from the machine?

MCU CAMERON on Cocoa Beach, car passes him, driving along the sands	3178

(SYNC) Not quite, I'm afraid, the machines pursue you even to the water's edge.

This is the famous Cocoa Beach, in Florida – miles and miles of expensive sand.

Way down the coast that-a-way is Miami Beach, where the rich vacationers do sport and play. And away up the other side behind me there, that is where the technologists and the scientists do sport and play. That is the launching pads of Cape Kennedy. It's just a bit too far away for us to see from here, but still you've seen it a dozen times on the television before – the great firework display of the twentieth century, the airline terminal for the longest trip humanity ever does – 'Universal Airlines announce a delay in the departure of their flight 2001 for outer space – passengers will kindly remain – on the beach.'

John F. Kennedy Space Center:

LS Launch Pad 39A, with Apollo 9 Saturn rocket in position, seen through window from Launch Control, pan round to show Launch Control and observation gallery.	3279

CAMERON (COMM.)
This is the object this is the place. This is Cape Kennedy at the start of 1969, at a moment already erased by history.

And the moment erased by history will be repeated by history, again and again, as one rocket is replaced by a better rocket, as one ambition overtakes the last one, as the immediate past and the pressing future merge into an endless now.

Interior: handheld shots among technicians at work in Launch Control	3324

Nothing matters here except this moment of time, whenever it may be. How odd it is that this picture of Launch Control already seems banal. I suppose we're surfeited with miracles. This is a place the old magicians should have marvelled at. And what is it now? – the old television picture.

CU technicians at Launch Control consol positions	3358

(SYNC among Launch Control technicians –

Zoom into CU Firing Command button	3379

– would you check the fuses in J 32 W to X-ray and J 32 Zebra to Little A? –)

CAMERON to camera, outside Vehicle Assembly Building	3392

CAMERON (SYNC)
Even in a country of superlatives, this is a bit much to take.

It's the Vehicle Assembly Building, called the V.A.B. – or Apollo's garage. It's seriously claimed to be the biggest building, by volume, in the world. It's where they assemble the vehicle, and its parent tower, and the mobile launching platform – until the whole lot is carted away by crawler to the launching site three miles up the road.

Meanwhile the whole paraphernalia lives in this monstrous place. You could put all of St Paul's Cathedral inside it with still room to spare.

Interior of the V.A.B.: man walking across catwalk in the roof, tilt down to floor	3452

CAMERON (COMM.)
It is part of our time, and I suppose our needs, that the biggest building in the world should be not a cathedral – nor even, surprisingly, a lunatic asylum – but the labour ward of an engine to put a man on the moon.

It could be, one day, any one of the fifty-one hostages to fortune, whose life is to train for only this.

2/s Astronaut JOHN L.
SWIGART and CAMERON

Among them John L. Swigart – with three science degrees from three universities, test pilot, and astronaut.

3496

JOHN L. SWIGART (SYNC)
I first started flying when I was – I had my first flight when I was 14, and it was very much of a thrill. And do you know that it's – I've been flying now for 23 years, and it's still a thrill, and the magic has never gone out of it.

CAMERON (SYNC)
If we were to suddenly learn next week that the Russians had landed on the moon ahead of us – would you feel that's a triumph for man, or would you just feel hopping mad?

SWIGART
Well – I think that there's a definite pride, that I would like – I want our country to be first. And – this is a pride I think anybody has in the achievements of their own nation. And – I wouldn't be hopping mad – we set a programme, that started with President Kennedy's commitment for us to land – to land a man on the moon within this decade, and the programme that we outlined and have followed has been a suitable programme, both from the standpoint of the safety of the crew and the accomplishment of the mission. And I wouldn't feel hopping mad – I feel that we are doing what we set out to do, and – but of course right now I don't think the Russians are going to be first. I think we're going to be first.

CAMERON
Don't you feel a kind of ambassadorial status in yourself, as one who's going to colonise a satellite? When you do go there you'll probably be one of the half dozen most famous men in the world – you really will.

SWIGART
Well I – this is something – that I hadn't really considered. You know there is so much in – er – so much – so

many of the things that are planning for the flight, I had never given that part of it any consideration. It's just that – regardless of whether I am one of the ones that is selected – we're all working together toward that common aim, putting that first crew on the moon and getting them back here, and this is what takes up our time. And I hadn't really considered anything beyond that, or the attendant activities that go with that.

Pad 39A, with Apollo 9 in position CAMERON to camera in foreground	3728	**CAMERON** (SYNC) I suppose this must be one of the famous places of the world – the celebrated Pad 39A, from which by and by this enormous thing will leave the Earth, as others have preceded it, and as others will I suppose, follow it. For just a few minutes the greater part of that thing will ignite and burn away, and fall forever into the ocean – leaving three men in a little metal box, driving on to – God knows where. All that resource, all that ingenuity and skill and expense, all for – what I wonder? For the kids of today I'm quite sure all this is dead familiar – if not commonplace. If that is so, I'm sorry, because if this isn't a thing of mystery and dread, what is? Well I'm very glad I came and saw it – but I don't think I want to come back.
Pan away to Apollo 9 on pad	3823	(MUSIC: Balletsuite 'Gayaneh' Aram Khaschaturian Deutsche Grammophon 136414 CONTINUES UNDER COMMENTARY)
Close shots: Pad 39A and Apollo 9	3838	
	3888	**CAMERON** (COMM.) How easy it would be, indeed has been, to draw facile moralities from this strange trip, this confusion of dimensions. I confess it is not my scene. In consequence I've been glib.

But man, whoever man is, hasn't lived all these thousands of years for nothing. He's made plenty of things he can be pretty proud of – made them, written them, painted them, carved and composed them. He did well enough in his time. He'll endure.

Once upon a time the world was a realm of unanswered questions, and there was room in it for poetry. Men stood below the sky, and he asked why – and his question was beautiful. The new world will be a place of answers and no questions, because the only questions left will be answered by computers, because only computers will know what to ask. Perhaps that is the way it has to be.

NASA OFFICIAL FILM
'APOLLO 9'
Apollo 9 astronauts in   3952
spacesuits, at the beginning of the
mission (slow motion)

Apollo 9 – ignition and   3975
lift-off

(FADE UP MUSIC – THEN IT IS LOST IN THE ROAR OF THE APOLLO 9 BLAST-OFF)

Freeze frame on launch   4072
pad after lift-off S/I end titles –

(END TITLE MUSIC – 'Garden of Delights')

'PHOTOGRAPHY
GENE CARR'

'SOUND
DEREK MEDUS
ALAN DYKES'

'FILM EDITOR
PAUL CARTER'

'RESEARCH
CHRIS COOK'

'ELECTRONIC MUSIC
DELIA DERBYSHIRE
BBC RADIOPHONIC
WORKSHOP'

'PRODUCED BY
RICHARD MARQUAND'

'DIRECTED BY
DON FAIRSERVICE
B.B.C.tv'

4119   FADE SOUND AND VISION

B.B.C. T.V.,
12th July 1969

'CAMERON COUNTRY'

'THE GUNS OF APHRODITE'

VISION	FOOTAGE	SOUND
Shots of Sea	(35 mm gauge)	
Ancient Columns at	0014	FX: SEA WASH
Salamis	0025	
SERIES TITLE SEQUENCE:	0071	(MUSIC: 'Garden of Delights' by John
Passport stamps, stills, title		Dankworth (30″)
'CAMERON COUNTRY'		
Mount Hilarion		
		JAMES CAMERON (sync)
James, to camera, in	0085	It's often quite hard to remember when
ruins of Hilarion Castle		a love affair began or sometimes even
		why. My affair with Cyprus, so
		improbable and perverse, began with
		impatience and regret and even fear
		long years ago in the colonial days when
		the Cypriots were British and all they
		wanted to be was Greek, or most of
		them. Things have changed today.
		(WALKS)
	0142	In all its history Cyprus had been ruled
		by foreigners, Roman, Byzantine,
		Lusignan, Venetian, Crusader,
		Turkish, and then for 80 years the
		British. We were very foolish about
		Cyprus. Well intentioned and clumsy,
		the way we so often were when colonies
		wore out. We forgot that we were ruling
		romantics, and they fought us,
		romantically, and bitterly, and
		successfully. And we gave their country
		back to them. And for the first time in
		twenty-seven centuries Cyprus became

Long shot of mountain, Pan L to James	0194	a free nation, in a way. One conflict vanished. Others followed and followed and remain. It's like being love with a beautiful and generous woman who just can't stay out of trouble. The affair continues, but sometimes one wonders why.

Sea shore, zoom out to reveal rocks

SUPER: 'THE GUNS OF APRODITE'   0218

(MUSIC: 'Le Ragazze dell'Oceano' from the film 'Africa Addio' 45″)

Sequence of shots of peaceful Cyprus, intercut with brief flashes of soldiers

C/U Alex Efthyvoulou   0285

ALEX EFTHYVOULOU (SYNC)
I would say I feel proud about one thing, about being a Cypriot. About being an inhabitant of this wonderful place called the 'Island of Love' where Aphrodite was born: where St. Paul came along one fine day and spoiled it.

Car track down waiting convoy of private cars   0304 0306

(MUSIC: 'Return from the Ashes' by John Dankworth) (1′ 41″)

Sequence of United Nations convoy along Turkish held road from Nicosia to Kyrenia   0328

JAMES CAMERON (COMM.) (over music)

The people of Nicosia, the capital of Cyprus, are going for a day at the seaside in Kyrenia. A curious sight it is. Driving through their own country over their own roads, they must now travel in a military convoy escorted by an armed guard of the United Nations. This is because for a dozen miles the road goes through what is known as Turkish territory. Almost 80 percent of all Cypriots are Greek by definition, but nearly 20 percent are Turks, and there's the rub. For 300 years, before the British came and went, Cyprus was part of the Turkish Empire, and they don't forget it. In 1963 there was a brief and bloody civil war. Indeed, it very nearly brought war to Greece and Turkey themselves. It was so near a thing that the United Nations Emergency Force was hurried into the island – so newly

independent – to separate these
unnaturally quarrelsome brothers.
There the UN remains to this day, after
six uneasy years. And now a Greek
Cypriot driving from one Greek Cypriot
town to another, must travel as it were
in a kind of quarantine, under the blue
flag of the United Nations, protected by
Canadians, and Austrians, and Danes.

I have known Cyprus in good times and
bad. And here we are back on the
border.

(MUSIC ENDS)

James standing some 0465 distance from the barrier between Greek and Turkish Nicosia	**JAMES CAMERON** (SYNC) Just down the road here, a couple of hundred yards or so away, the Turkish quarter begins. It's always been there but now it's separated from the rest of Nicosia by a very ugly, built up barrier of which everybody is so ashamed that we can't film it from any closer than this.

It's a sort of second division Berlin Wall
which has separated two essentially nice
and decent peoples completely since
1964. Like Berlin, I can cross it any time
I like because I don't belong here, but
they who do belong here, can't.

James standing some distance
from the barrier, intercut with
closer shots of the road barrier

JAMES CAMERON (SYNC)
Its maintenance is now a responsibility
of the United Nations, if you can
imagine anything so preposterous. Over
there are a number of very nice,
agreeable, courteous and hospitable
people who happen to be Turkish in
origin, and over here a considerably
greater number of people, equally nice
and gentle, who speak Greek. For
generations they've lived together and
worked together and understood one
another until suddenly they discovered,
or somebody told them, that they
weren't Cypriots at all, but Greeks and
Turks. And that's what all the fuss is
about. Now those people over there
can't, or won't come here, and these

223

people over here can't go there. They
need each other, economically and
practically and they reject each other
emotionally because somebody,
whoever that may be, tells them they've
got to. As though the world didn't have
enough frontiers they have to build one
here.

Intercutting between Greek and   0600
Turkish villages

JAMES CAMERON (COMM.)
Some quirk of history required this
island of Cyprus to be inhabited by
neighbours, Greeks and Turks, whom
that same history turned into
opponents, God and the politicians
know why. These villages were always
there. They were friends or they were
not friends, as people are, but until the
last few years they were not enemies. In
a village of Greek Cyprus they grow
their crops and they tend their flocks
and they worry about the future when
they have time. In a village in Turkish
Cyprus they grow their crops and they
tend their flocks and they worry about
the future when they have time. Today
they survive, mutually, next door to one
another. And they might as well be in

Sequence of landscapes,   0664
Kantara and St Hilarion Castles,
James wandering in mountainous
region, etc.

different countries.

                                 0688

Independence came to Cyprus ten years
ago – but hedged around and qualified
by conditions, as it has been for
thousands of years. Everyone, in the
ancient world, took Cyprus, absorbed
it, contended for it, exploited it, and
abandoned it. And when at last the
island got its freedom from its final
landlords, the British, it was the
freedom of a probationer, a liberty
legally to be supervised by its
neighbours Greece and Turkey. You
can't have a crossroads without
policemen, they said. And this form of
independence specifically denied to
both communities what each had
demanded for years – for the Turks,
partition; for the Greeks, union with

0761 the land of Greece, which is called 'Enosis'. Remember that word, 'Enosis'. It haunts the history of Cyprus like a phantom.

C/U of Spyros Kyprianou 0769 **JAMES CAMERON (COMM.)**
Spyros Kyprianou is Foreign Minister of Cyprus.

0775 **SPYROS KYPRIANOU (SYNC)**
During the First World War when Turkey was on the side of the Germans against the Allies there was never any problem in Cyprus between Greeks and Turks. During the Second World War when Turkey followed a sort of hostile neutrality and did not participate in the war there were Cypriots, Greeks and Turks, forming the well known Cyprus Regiment fighting side by side against . . . against the common enemy.

At the beginning of the struggle against the colonial occupation in Cyprus, I'm referring to the arms struggle now, again there was no problem between Greeks and Turks. This came about suddenly and in circumstances well known and since then Turkey has been pursuing a policy of trying to set foot in Cyprus through various means.

Exterior shots of Mr Denktash, and Mr Clerides walking, intercut

0892 **JAMES CAMERON (COMM.)**
Mr Rauf Denktash is the principal representative of the Turkish community of Cyprus; he speaks for them.

0901 Mr Glafcos Clerides is President of the House of Representatives; he speaks for the Greek Cypriots. They know each other very well, as indeed they must by now, since once a week Mr Clerides and Mr Denktash formally meet, as they have done for two solid years, to discuss the impasse, to debate the anomalies, to drink coffee and to mark time.

Meeting between Mr Denktash 0928 and Mr Clerides in Turkish area of Nicosia, outside Mr Denktash's house. Both

JAMES CAMERON (COMM.)
And once a week the hopeful Press seeks to distil some drop from the

225

surrounded by members of the Press.

0962

desert. And behind it all, the emotive word 'Enosis', the ancestral and maybe irrational compulsion of Greek Cypriots to unite with Greece, which they incurably feel is home. And which the Turks will never, never accept.

SYNC from Meeting with Press.

MR CLERIDES: I wouldn't say in the next few weeks, but eventually everything will have to be retackled.

MR DENKTASH: I have never been briefed. I have had several talks, but I have never been briefed . . . neither before.

General SYNC

Interviews between James Cameron and Mr Clerides, in his office, and between James and Mr Denktash in the garden of the Vice Presidency INTERCUT.

0997

JAMES CAMERON (SYNC)
The whole basis of the Turkish cause is the shadow, as they call it, of Enosis and yet Enosis seems to have been drifting out of the political scene now. But is there enough pro Enosis feeling among the Greek community to justify this Turkish settlement?

C/U Mr Clerides

GLAFCOS CLERIDGES (SYNC)
I think it would be misleading public opinion both in Cyprus and abroad to say that amongst the Greeks the idea of Enosis has been given up.

C/U Mr Denktash

RAUF DENKTASH (SYNC)
Any agreement which we reach now will be a temporary agreement and when they find a time proper again they will attack us again and this is a genuine fear, a genuine anxiety in our minds. We don't ask too much we believe. All we seek is to keep a Cypriot State going, a Cypriot State which has no

doors open to Enosis, and which treats the Turks as equal partners.

C/U Mr Clerides

MR CLERIDES (SYNC)
When you consider that Cyprus is only forty miles from the Turkish coast and that there is a Turkish nation of about 30 million people, just forty miles across, very often the Greek Cypriots feel that with the support the Turks are getting from Turkey, the Turkish Cypriots are really the majority and that the Greek Cypriots are the minority.

C/U James Cameron

JAMES CAMERON (SYNC)
The Turkish leadership claims that it's being discriminated against by having civil servants' wages withheld and social amenities denied to them. Is that right?

C/U Mr Clerides

MR CLERIDES (SYNC)
It is correct that the Turkish civil servants who have abandoned the service of the Government since 1963 who are not reporting for duty are not being paid. But that's hardly a deprivation. Cypriots, Greek Cypriots also who do not report for duty do not get paid.

C/U Mr Denktash

MR DENKTASH (SYNC)
Turkey has been the only country which has saved us from the Greek onslaught, and is the only country which has paid for our upkeep for the last seven years. It is the Greek side which has pushed us so much into the laps of Turkey by refusing to pay the salaries of four thousand civil servants.

C/U James Cameron

JAMES CAMERON (SYNC)
Obviously the two communities are moving apart year by year, socially as well as politically.

C/U Mr Denktash

MR DENKTASH (SYNC)
Our youth, for instance, since 1965 have not met. They don't know each other.

C/U Mr Clerides

MR CLERIDES (SYNC)
One may say that the only contact they have is looking through a gunsight at

each other. Each one is being trained in military camps in the arts of war but we all know it's not enough to train people how to use guns. You have to create the psychological conditions that they would be ready to fight each other.

Sequence of sombre landscapes, ruins at Vouni, Paphos mosaics, ancient columns at Salamis	1261	**JAMES CAMERON** (COMM.) It must be nearly 20 years since I first started coming here, to Cyprus – because I suppose it was beautiful, and unhappy. Why else do people like me go anywhere? Today I don't know how long this state of affairs goes on; I truly don't, and nor does anyone. No sooner had they got rid of us, the British, than they were plunged into their own feuds and follies – in which we, the big nations, were far from blameless; we could perhaps have known better. I suppose we undertook something that was rooted too long ago, that was embedded in a culture that was old when we were young. We would have a bit of a nerve to patronise these people now.
Cricket being played at the Sovereign Base Area, at Dhekelia, by British servicemen	1331	Out of all those thousands of years, just 80 were British. Some of Cyprus still is British – quite a lot of it, in fact. Very strange, this durability of institutions, for this in a way is the very thing the militant Cypriots fought us to overcome.
Queen's Birthday Parade at Happy Valley, R.A.F. Episkopi	1355	Not the cricket, but the soldiers, the military dominance. The soldiers are still here in Cyprus. But now they don't dominate anything, nor do they try, except the old nostalgic rituals of the parade ground, threatening no one.
Firing of the Feu de Joie at the Parade	1375	(FX: Rapid gun fire.)
Contre jour shot of mysterious mountainside	1380	**JAMES CAMERON** (COMM.) I remember when it was otherwise indeed, when it was called the

Emergency, and the sad and secret war went on and on all over the menace of the mountains: the days of the guerilla army called Eoka.

Rapid C/Us of details of State of Eoka fighter throwing grenade	1399	(FX: CLAP OF THUNDER)
	1408	JAMES CAMERON (COMM.)

People in village street, C/U of Eoka graffiti, car tracking shots through Nicosia in the dark

One thing I can't forget was the night in August 1956 when three young Eoka men who had been caught were to be hanged. They made no protest at their sentence, and indeed by the strange rules of that time they were guilty, and seemed content.

Car tracking shots through Nicosia in the dark

But that night all Nicosia was quite eerily silent. Everyone under 27 was confined indoors. The cafes were shut; the streets were empty. Outside the prison there gathered a huge quiet crowd, no one saying a word. An hour passed in the darkness, or maybe two, and then gradually we heard the whole population of the prison beginning to sing gently – hymns, and marching songs, and Greek ballads. It grew louder, till you could hear it almost all over the city, and old people on their doorsteps were dropping to their knees and singing quietly too. Just after midnight, when the men were being taken away, there was a great shout inside the jail, and you could hear seven hundred prisoners singing the Greek Anthem. When the first drop happened the singing abruptly stopped, and there was an absolutely tangible silence over the city, over us. We could just hear the dogs barking far away. Everyone in

Present-day, daytime shots

those days lived somehow in the company of death – not wildly, and noisily, as we had it in wars, but in a terribly sad and erratic uncertainty, because the thing about a secret struggle is that you can never for a second be sure of anything.

Present day, daytime scenes in Nicosia	1520	Everybody was on one side or the other, and sometimes both at once. We

all had our networks of informers, honest or venal. At least once I had a new assassination breathlessly reported to me – a soldier has been killed in Ledra Street – and hurried to the scene just in time to hear the shot ring out: my spy in his zeal had been a little too previous. Where was the division between patriotism and professionalism? In that sort of Greek tragedy one never knows – not then, not now.

Exterior shot of Ledra Palace Hotel, Nicosia	Everybody seems to believe that all journalists' work is done in pubs and to some degree this is true.

Inside Ledra Palace, James reading newspaper at bar   1610

It's not quite true but still every foreign correspondent knows that everywhere in the world there is some bar to which he feels he belongs. It isn't necessarily the best bar in town, nor the most famous it just happens to be the one place where he knows he has to be.

James, at bar, turns to camera   1639

JAMES CAMERON (SYNC)
This is such a one, the Ledra Palace Bar in Nicosia. For so many years the rallying point, focal point, meeting place, trysting house, whatever you will for the journalistic Middle East. I know it very well indeed and it knows us too, the scores of newspapermen who passed through, took their dram, heard their gossip, wrote their pieces and went their ways. These are the real Press Clubs of the world.

Turns towards the telephone

This telephone has probably seen more momentous business than anyone I know in the world. Sometimes it was a big story. Sometimes it was a simple assignation. Sometimes it was Randolph Churchill insisting on a line to London in the middle of the Suez crisis in order to put a bet on a horse. It certainly had its share of expensive trade. And here I am back again with nothing to do. I suppose for poor bagmen of ill-tidings like me there's no other place where we feel really at home.

Car driving down road, sequence of shots from air of S.B.A. Dhekelia	1756	(MUSIC: 'With a Song in My Heart' by Richard Rodgers (50″)) JAMES CAMERON (COMM): (over music) Today part of the price of Cyprus independence is the existence in the south of the island of a hundred square miles that are British. The Sovereign Base Areas belonging to the Forces that are as much British as Wimbledon and strive to look like it. British manners, British customs, British law. It's a situation, as it happens, unique in the world. Dhekelia and Episkopi are in Cyprus but they are legally as much part of the U.K. as Kensington. Here N.A.A.F.I. land listens to the Forces Network. (MUSIC ENDS)
Scenes in the N.A.A.F.I. area of S.B.A. Dhekelia	1849	STATION ANNOUNCER (OOV) And now tonight's local announcements. Firstly a reminder to all wives of 259 Signal Squadron that Mrs M. Sinclair warmly welcomes you to Mrs Kelsall's Tupperware demonstration to be held at the Two R's Episkopi on Wednesday morning, June the 10th from 9.30 to 11.30.
Further scenes in the N.A.A.F.I. area at S.B.A. Dhekelia		STATION ANNOUNCER (OOV) Also Mrs Lowry will be contacting all 259 wives regarding the proposed formation of a figurette class to be held in Episkopi in the very near future.
C/U of Station Announcer in broadcasting studio	1888	STATION ANNOUNCER (SYNC) And finally a Parade to mark the official birthday of Her Majesty the Queen is being held on Saturday, the 13th of June at 8.15 a.m. at Happy Valley Stadium, R.A.F. Episkopi.
Band at Queen's Parade Happy Valley, R.A.F. Episkopi, followed by scenes from the Parade.	1904	(MUSIC: 'Goodbye, Mr Turnbull' from film 'Africa Addio' (50″)) (MUSIC ENDS)

James and Alex Efthyvoulou in long shot, in countryside	1984	**JAMES CAMERON** (COMM.) I have an old comrade and colleague in Cyprus called Alex; a famous man. I asked: these bases, the 100-square-mile British enclaves in your country, don't they inflict a certain sense of imposition?
C/U Alex Efthyvoulou	2002	**ALEX EFTHYVOULOU** Very much so, because nobody asked them at the time whether they wanted to cede a part of their country to Britain or to anyone else. This was the source of the trouble that's continuing today. Because in 1959 Greece, Turkey and Gt Britain go together and they decided 'This is the settlement that Cyprus will have'. And they said 'This is a force majeure and you will have to accept this'. I think if the Cypriots had been asked they might have accepted it, they might not. The fact is that they were never asked and they resent this.
Interview between James and Alex continue in C/Us on Alex and two-shots of James and Alex		**JAMES CAMERON** (SYNC) Nonetheless it is a very considerable economic asset to the Republic isn't it? **ALEX** You know, it is and it isn't. Because if the people who are employed in the bases were used somewhere else they would earn more money for Cyprus in a different way. It's true that the British soldiers who are based here spend money but I also feel at the same time that the existence of a big military complex on the island detracts from the tourist value of the island. And if there were no soldiers around they would be replaced by, the flower people. And what's wrong with that? **JAMES CAMERON** (SYNC) Well, look, however, Cyprus is part of the Middle East, whether we like it or not, and the Middle East is the great arena of competition among the great big powers, and there's always a feeling here, at least I feel it, of being

manipulated by other agencies, and for other people, and this I would find, if I were you, a slightly unnerving situation.

ALEX (SYNC)
It has been the tragedy of Cyprus for thousands of years from prehistoric times till today. Some Big Brother has always come along and grabbed Cyprus for his own use, and this continues to be happening today. The most frustrating thing is that in our time and age when we believe in principles and the United Nations, and this, that and the other, we Cypriots say, 'Well, look if the Big Powers believe in what they preach why don't they apply it in the case of little Cyprus. Leave Cyprus alone.'

Jets taking off from the airfield of R.A.F. Akrotiri	2201	(FX: Jets taking off)

Greek village: peaceful scenes – children leaving school, man and woman cutting corn, shepherd pumping water for his sheep, etc.

2259

JAMES CAMERON (COMM.)
The British jets howl and growl over the Mediterranean, because that's what bases are for. They are one factor of Cyprus, but this, surely, is another. There is a village; there is a school; there are children; this is what life is about whether it's Cyprus or anywhere on earth, or ought to be. This is sentimental stuff, of course, and verging on the documentary; still, somebody has got to cut the corn, whether it's a Greek or a Turk neither you nor I would know, from looking.

I said I am in a way in love with Cyprus, so I claim the self-indulgent privilege of dwelling for a moment on something disarmingly without drama, something that seems to me too decent and too basic to be bitched up by remote international considerations of which these quiet and durable people are hardly aware half the time, I dare say. Everyone's got their finger in the Cyprus pie: Greeks, Turks, British, I suppose the Americans, but I don't imagine it bothers these people very often. The pace is pretty slow here;

there isn't really any hurry, or not today
there isn't.

Two Cypriot women in farmyard, stoking open air oven, dog panting	2375	(FX: Women chatting in distance)

Men playing cards
in an open air taverna, Priest
drinking coffee   2417

JAMES CAMERON (COMM.)
What is life if full of care we haven't
time to sit and stare, and play a hand of
cards in the taverna, as one did
yesterday, and as one doubtless will
tomorrow. After all, the women will be
taking care of the work in the house,
and in the fields, and in the farmyard.
No hurry. One doesn't admire the
philosophy, but by God one envies it.

U.N. hilltop positions,   2470
from helicopter, and
from ground. Zoom into
Turkish held hilltop
position

Someone, however, is minding the
shop, and that is by inference, us, the
world outside. High on the hilltops, in
the strategic positions where the Greeks
confront the Turks, and vice versa, the
United Nations is holding the ring. A
few years ago the Cypriots were
shooting each other just here – because
the Turkish people of Cyprus felt, or
were told to feel, that the Greeks had
unfairly changed the law to undermine
their privileges. Small though their
numbers are, they had once ruled the
place for three centuries. So both sides
took to arms. Turkey herself intervened
with air raids. It was controlled just in
time. And here today a handful of
soldiers from Finland – of all
places – are seeing that they don't start
again. If you really want an
international paradox here it is: that a
few young men from the grey
Scandinavian north, the Finns, should
find themselves stuck here in the hot
hellenic highlands, pacifying two
peoples of whom they probably never
heard until somebody sent them here.

JAMES CAMERON (COMM.)
Finland, putting a muzzle on Athens
and Ankara. It's almost a diplomatic
fantasy, but I suppose that's what the
United Nations is all about. It costs

millions of pounds a year; it takes 4000 able-bodied young men out of useful circulation; it has gone on for six years and could well go on forever, as far as most of us can see.

James and Alex talking together	2602	But how – I asked Alex – does this endless tension affect personal relationships with fellow-countrymen of another kind?
C/U Alex Afthyvoulou	2613	**ALEX EFTHYVOULOU** It's not so easy to break a friendship that you've had since childhood days. There may have been political differences and a mutual disgust at the turn that things took but you don't blame each other personally for these things. You rather blame the politicians for the situation. And I think that in time if the artificial barriers that are put up now are taken down then everything will revert to normal. I think there are a great many Turks who feel just as frustrated as the Greeks because they don't feel any happier than we do about the turn of events. We're all Cypriots and we want to have a united house. But these things are not insurmountable. Other countries had the same difficulties. They had the same historical background in the sense that they were part of the Ottoman Empire and these things were settled in a . . . in a more civilised way, should I say? But they have been settled. The thing that's holding back settlement in Cyprus is the Big Power involvement, I feel.
Shots of opencast copper mining at Skouriotissa	2706	**JAMES CAMERON** (COMM.) The question is: how can Cyprus manage without the involvement of other people? Cyprus isn't rich. To be sure they still mine the copper that gave the land its name and for which it was famous 2000 years ago – but it is the Americans who run the mines, and the resources diminish. Meanwhile they gnaw out great iron mouthfuls of Cyprus and sell it to the Germans. It won't last for long.

Orange picking sequence	2752	**JAMES CAMERON** (comm.) There are always oranges. The citrus industry is the great money-maker of Cyprus today; people grow rich on oranges. It is not an unimportant thing to notice that here around Morphou the Greek orange-farmers employ Turkish women for the harvest. They've always done so. The point is that they still do.
Dried-up stony river bed, bridge and village	2783	But orange-groves are hungry for water, and so is all of Cyprus. There's never enough water. One rainless season and the place runs dry; the river-beds revert to stony deserts, with bridges crossing nothing but rocks.
Tourists on the beach at Famagusta	2816	Tourists, of course; the invaluable by-product of the sun. Everywhere in the world now seems to argue: the tourists will pay; the holiday-makers will see us right. I am not so sure, in the long run. But it's working now. I'm
Shots of hotel development	2839	bound to say, with Famagusta sprouting flats and hotels on the very beach that brought them there, and which thus grows smaller every year. For some people now, Cyprus is a substitute Greece. And all the time there remain
U.N. soldiers walking in Nicosia	2857	the Permanent Tourists – 4000 soldiers of the United Nations, who are not there wholly for fun.
Presidential Palace, zoom into Cyprus flag, flying from roof	2872	My involvement with Cyprus was not about Greeks and Turks, but with the independence struggle against us, the British.
James in front of statue of young freedom fighter	2882	**JAMES CAMERON** (sync) The strange thing was that even in the times of the greatest stresses and cruelties on both sides there was very little real hatred of the British, as people. Of the British Administration, yes, to be sure, for its obtuseness and its obstinacy and lack of imagination. But not for the people because the Cypriots seem to like the British for some reason. Some of us remained on very good terms for years with people whom we later discovered to have been what

they call patriots and we call terrorists. I know some of them still. Some of them who survived became high officers in the Government and one of them at least, Polycarpos Gheorgiadis, was this year himself shot and killed by the very people he had once inspired. And who loved him. He died of politics. In the new Greek mythology that's the occupational disease.

Exterior Archbishopric, zoom into window, and cut to interior. Archbishop Makarios with his Synod of Bishops

2957

JAMES CAMERON (COMM.): (over low SYNC)
One man, of course, dominates this situation as nobody else could ever do – Makarios, President of the Republic and Archbishop of the Church. Nobody on earth holds two tenser jobs. And to both he was elected. Here, in the Archbishopric, he is a priest for the day and not a politician, with this convocation of Bishops, all of them men of power in their own right. This is again a unique situation: a man elected as leader, as Ethnark, both spiritually and politically – but unique as it may be it is accepted and customary in the Greek society; the head of the Church is the leader of the people in whatever activities they find proper, whether they lead to redemption or revolution.

And this is what Makarios is – at least now – doubly pre-eminent. That is what nobody ever understood about Makarios and the Eoka fighters. That is why we exiled him to the Seychelles, thinking he was only a turbulent priest. Now we know better.

Exterior of village church

3056

And when the President of the Republic of Cyprus becomes the Archbishop of the Autocephalous Church of Cyprus, coeval with the Patriarch and the Pope, then the smallest village church becomes a cathedral.

Scenes inside and outside village church during service conducted by Archbishop Makarios

3074

(MUSIC: 'Soldiers' Song' from 'The Decembrists' sung by the Red Army Choir 2′ 30″)

237

James Cameron and President Makarios walking towards camera and chairs, prior to interview in garden of Presidential Palace	3303	**JAMES CAMERON** (COMM.) This had been the residency of British Governors; it was strange to find it a Presidential Palace. But I had known Makarios before. I asked him how he reconciled these two great offices of Church and State. Didn't he find some sort of professional conflict there?
C/U President Makarios	3327	**PRESIDENT MAKARIOS** (SYNC) I accepted the office of President at the request of the people when Cyprus became an independent state. I thought it was my duty not to refuse to offer my services during the first difficult steps of the new state. I consider, however, my Presidency as temporary and I hope that circumstances in the near future will allow me to be relieved of my duties as President and devote all my time to the Church. I am now for the last twenty years and I will be for life Archbishop. Acting under two capacities I have to divide my time between the affairs of the Church and the affairs of the State. I do not feel, however, any conflict of conscience or any dichotomy in this for the simple reason that the principles in which I believe and which motivate my actions are the same whether they are viewed from my position as an Archbishop or President.
C/U James Cameron		**JAMES CAMERON** (SYNC) The existing state of affairs between the Greek and the Turkish communities is wasteful and it's sorrowful and indeed it's absurd. Have you any optimism for its solution in our time?
C/U President Makarios		**PRESIDENT VAKARIOS** (SYNC) I think that we are both still young enough and I hope that the Cyprus problem will be solved in our time. I cannot say that I am very optimistic for the present, but I am hopeful for the future.

C/U James Cameron

JAMES CAMERON (SYNC)
When did you begin completely to reconsider Enosis as the basic principle of your politics? I know the tremendous troubles you had at the signing of the Zurich Agreement because I was involved in the situation at the time and I was very well aware of your really horrible difficulties. But in the light of today what are your feelings about the Greek Motherland?

C/U President Makarios

PRESIDENT MAKARIOS (SYNC)
I have always been in favour of Enosis, but due to many difficulties, and mainly to external factors Enosis has not been possible to attain. As to my feelings towards Greece as Motherland – they remain unchanged.

C/U James Cameron

JAMES CAMERON (SYNC)
That strange, historic bond that has existed for so long between the Hellenic and the British cultures have survived some very testing times, including the agonising times in the Fifties. Do you think it's a reality, or is it an illusion?

C/U President Makarios

PRESIDENT MAKARIOS (SYNC)
The bonds between the Greek world and Britain have always been very close, despite some temporarily disturbing circumstances. I feel that this is not an illusion, but a reality.

Sequence: 3683
Empty landscapes and solitary people

JAMES CAMERON (SYNC)
President Makarios believes in reality, which is a great act of faith in Cyprus. To most of us it's more elusive. How many places in the world have been contended for and fought over, for no other reason than that they were there? Cyprus isn't much *use* to anyone, except as a cross-reference on a strategic map. It once was, to be sure, before the ancient world stripped its forests and exhausted its mines. But now – how oddly empty it seems. How rich in spacious beauty, how thinly-spread with people. Do you notice the curious absence of crowds, the echoing elbow-room? The population-explosion

239

of the world somehow passed Cyprus by. Two thousand years ago there were a million Cypriots; today, half of that. Today there are about as many Cypriots in London as there are in Nicosia. And those who remain in the island are always wondering. Its two people are both homesick in their ways. When they think of home, both think of somewhere else. How strange, because I, who don't belong there, think of Cyprus.

James and Alex talking together in countryside	3791

JAMES CAMERON (COMM.)
Now does being a Cypriot mean frustration?

C/U Alex Efthyvoulou	3797

ALEX EFTHYVOULOU (SYNC)
Well I'd phrase it differently. I'd say it's all about allowing the people to have a say in their own affairs. And if they decide on one thing let them have it.

JAMES CAMERON (SYNC)
Therefore the sensation in the country largely is that if Cyprus was allowed in fact to resolve its own problems in its own way without interference it would not be really such a very serious difficulty?

ALEX EFTHYVOULOU (SYNC)
Not at all. All that the Cypriots want is to be left to themselves just like everybody else.

C/U President Makarios	3847

PRESIDENT MAKARIOS (SYNC)
It can be said that the ties among the Commonwealth family are perhaps not very close but there are some advantages for its members – exchange of experiences and mutual help in the cultural, technical, trade and other fields are some of the advantages. Irrespective however of the degree of benefit I believe that the institution of the Commonwealth is serving a useful purpose and I do not see any advantage at all for Cyprus to have been outside the Commonwealth.

Shots of convoy at the checkpoint	3935	JAMES CAMERON (COMM.) These are the ironies of Cyprus – the rebel country now committed to the Commonwealth; the little republic longing for the dignity and functions of true independence, whose citizens must be counted and checked by the U.N. on their own roads. Yet all its Government wants – the Foreign Minister repeats – is to be left alone.
Convoy at checkpoint	3975	SPYROS KYPRIANOU (OOV) We see Cyprus as not being part of any military blocs. We see Cyprus as one of the small countries which afford to stick to principles in – in its international relations and it is only through this approach that we can play within the framework of our limited possibilities a constructive role in world affairs.
Sequence of landscapes, Pan L from road to mountains, shots of brooding and sunlit mountain scenery	4031	JAMES CAMERON (COMM.) I seem to have been tangled up here a long time; in a life like mine you make unpredictable associations – or as we said, love affairs. I had hoped for Cyprus independence – and when it came it wasn't independence at all. I don't know why – Cyprus argues that if we, the world, left it alone it would solve its frustrations. But we can't leave it alone. And the more we worry about it the more we have to worry about it: the classic vicious circle. Today the little island of Cyprus has more varieties of foreign soldiers on its soil than anywhere else on earth. Canadian, British, Greek, Turkish, Finnish, Austrian, Swedes and Danes. It does
Pull back from the rocks of Aphrodite, to reveal whole bay		seem a bit much for the Island of Love. I often think I must have imagined it.
Shot of Kykko Monastery		(MUSIC: 'Return from the Ashes' 48″)
Door opens to reveal monastery courtyard and James and Alex walking away from camera	4132	

The Best of Cameron

SUPER END CREDITS:

'PHOTOGRAPHY
KEN WILLICOMBE'

'SOUND
ARTHUR CHESTERMAN'

'DUBBING MIXER
RON EDMONDS'

'FILM EDITOR
DAVID THOMAS'

Shot of misty landscape	4176	

SUPER CREDIT:

'PRODUCED AND
DIRECTED BY
MICHAEL ROBSON
B.B.C.tv colour

PICTURE FADES	4184	SOUND FADES

B.B.C. T.V.,
24th October 1970

'CAMERON COUNTRY'

'PREJUDICE ON THE FACE OF IT'

VISION	FOOTAGE	SOUND
SERIES TITLE SEQUENCE: Passport stamps, stills, title 'CAMERON COUNTRY'	0000	MUSIC IN: 'Garden of Delights' John Dankworth
H.A.S. tube train passing below – tilt up along rails	0022	FX TUBE TRAIN
	0029	DARCUS As a person I feel extremely violent.
Black and white people in streets of Notting Hill	0031	This is not part of a congenital or inborn trait. It is the conditions under which I live. I'm very conscious of that.

CS man in street talking to cam.	0036	**VOX POP** It doesn't matter how much you want to integrate, how much you want to be my friend, you're still coloured. And this is a bias which is an unfortunate bias and it's causing a great deal of unhappiness amongst these people.
Black people in streets	0043	**DARCUS** That is the position that British society has placed me in.
CS Man in street talking to cam.	0045	**VOX POP** Well, I haven't noticed it a lot myself, not actual discrimination. I mean, they're free, they go about, they're welcomed by everybody.
Track behind black man in street	0050	**DARCUS** You know I want to fight. I need to fight to express something.
CS 3rd man in street talking to cam.	0052	**VOX POP** Well there are one or two agitators amongst them who are causing the trouble. That's all I can put it down to. I leave people alone. They don't interfere with me.
Series of fast zooms in to houses	0058	**DARCUS** I need to fight to express something. I need to argue, I need to scream.
Slow pan over grey-looking rooftops	0060	**MUSIC IN:** 'Deep Dark Blue Centre' Graham Collyer Septet Deram SML 1005
MS JAMES CAMERON on Southwark Bridge – talks to cam.	0071	**CAMERON: (MUSIC FADES UNDER)** Oh God, not another programme about the racial problem, haven't there been enough of them already? I know what you mean. But out there somewhere are something like eight million Londoners and in every one of our heads is some sort of a prejudice. Well this is a programme about racial prejudice, if you like, but it's really about prejudice itself as it affects almost all of us, usually rather badly. But we're not

going to plug the injustices or rub in the guilt – if there is any. I doubt very much if we'll come to any conclusions even. We'll certainly find no solution. There's nothing definitive about this programme as you'll see. But by trying to find out about black people we're bound to find quite a lot out about ourselves.

CS man in street talking to cam.	0103	**VOX POP** In my view the island is already overcrowded and to say that some of these people have got the same rights as the ordinary resident in the country is probably morally just, but is it practical to do so in this tight little island.
CS oldish lady talking to cam.	0114	**VOX POP** Some people's against 'em, others are for 'em. And I say if they don't interfere with you why should you interfere with them. That's my idea of the thing. That's it, isn't it? **INTERVIEWER** But a lot of people feel there is a problem, why do you think that is? **VOX POP** Well, I think a lot of it's jealousy. **INTERVIEWER** Jealous of what? **VOX POP** Jealous of 'em because they seem to get by with everything.

SEQ. AT W. INDIAN DINNER/DANCE AT ALEXANDRA PALACE

Shot of the toastmaster	0130	**TOASTMASTER** My Lords, Ladies, and Gentlemen, please be upstanding to receive your Chairman. Give him a hand please.
H.A.S. hall and pan Chairman to his seat	0137	
		APPLAUSE
	0138	**COMMENTARY (CAMERON)** The West Indian citizens of North London meet for their reunion and

dinner at the Alexandra Palace. It is very correct and tranquil, indeed almost heavy with decorum; this is a society that treats its occasions with a formality that most of us have long forgotten.

Zoom in to Chairman	0147

General shots dinner being served	0150

MUSIC IN
Recorded live at dinner/dance.

0161

COMMENTARY (CAMERON)
OVER MUSIC)
These neighbours of ours are long established here, and for this evening they unite in London as it might be Kingston, Jamaica, or Port of Spain, with the stresses and tensions of a minority life left outside and forgotten. Tonight they revert to the manners and formal conventions of the strict society from which they came years ago when they left the Caribbean for our country looking for . . . what, I wonder?

Tracking shots along dinner tables	0180

There had been nothing for them in the islands, but everything was waiting here, or so it was said.

(MUSIC AND COMMENTARY OUT)

W. INDIAN STANDING CONF.

CS JEFF CRAWFORD   0181

CRAWFORD
We were made to believe that Britain was Utopia, Utopia on earth, and this wasn't the case. I came here with the impression that I was going to be welcomed with open arms – the most wonderful country in the world: everybody was honest, everybody was polite, everybody was sincere. People didn't swear at each other. Everybody went to church. I came here to be shattered.

WS group of West Indians including Jeff	0183

LIBRARY FILM OF IMMIGRANTS ARRIVING IN THE FIFTIES	0193
	0196

COMMENTARY (CAMERON)
In those days of the Immigration they did not, after all, intrude unasked. Britain was, everyone said, the Mother Country. Whatever is said now, in those days they came as guests.

CS JEFF CRAWFORD	0203	**CRAWFORD** When I used to go to school I can remember, sometimes I laugh at it so as not to become too angry, every Friday at the end of the school week one would have to turn to the East where there was a rather tattered Union Jack hanging on the wall: boys stood at attention and saluted, girls stood at attention, and we would have to sing the first verse of 'God Save the King' as it was at that time, subsequently 'God Save the Queen'.
ALEXANDRA PALACE Toastmaster	0218	**TOASTMASTER** Mr Chairman, my Lords, Ladies, and Gentlemen, please be upstanding for the Royal Toast by Miss Veronica Gerald.
Pull back – H.A.S. all people standing for toast		**VERONICA GERALD** Ladies and Gentlemen, the Queen.
LIBRARY FILM – QUEEN'S VISIT TO WEST INDIES (PATHÉ) Queen cutting tape and driving through cheering crowds in open car	0232	**FX CHEERS**
	0243	**CRAWFORD** (v/o) And I remember when Royalty came out to the West Indies we would be bussed three or four miles away and given little flags to wave. Of course the car would whip by before you'd started to wave your flag and out of sight.
CS JEFF CRAWFORD	0249	
PATHÉ FILM: QUEEN'S VISIT Queen getting off plane and being greeted – various shots	0251	**MUSIC IN** 'God Save the Queen'
	0263	**MUSIC OUT**
Track past waving crowds	0263	**COMMENTARY (CAMERON)** When they left home what a change it must have been of culture, of climate, of manner: it needed a huge adjustment.
B.B.C. LIBRARY FILM: Black man working on railway in snow	0264	
	0267	**(COMMENTARY OUT)**
Several shots black men in cold, grey, rainy streets etc.		**TRAIN FX ETC.**

		CRAWFORD: (Starts v/o) What still abhors me is the double standard, the hypocrisy of the Britisher. When he says 'yes' he means 'no'. When he says 'no' he means 'yes'. And I still find it difficult at times to accept the Britisher's word.
MS JEFF CRAWFORD	0290	
		VOX POP
Man in street talking to cam.	0294	I think on the whole that the relationship between coloured and white is very good in this particular district. I mean, there are districts that don't understand coloured people.
		INTERVIEWER Why is that?
		VOX POP Well it's because I don't think they understand them.
ALEXANDRA PALACE: DINNER/DANCE Shots of people dancing	0303	MUSIC IN Recorded live at Alexandra Palace Dinner/Dance.
	0308	COMMENTARY (CAMERON) The same Alexandra Palace; the same decorous black ties. But the night has developed; the starch has melted; the Caribbean comes irresistibly surging back.
General shots of people dancing	0315	MUSIC UP
James CAMERON dancing	0321	
	0331	MUSIC OUT
		COMMENTARY (CAMERON) But these are the older generation. What about their children who are growing up here?
		VOX POP
Man in street talking to cam.	0334	When the immigrant children get a good standard of education, to see a coloured child who talks with a broad cockney accent he's one of us. But you can never in a million years change the colour of his skin.

247

INTERVIEW BERNARD
COARD/CAMERON
3-s COARD L. wife on R. and   0342
James R. f/g with back to cam.

CAMERON
So many people say that everything will
be all right with this problem that we
face at the moment as soon as education
really takes a grip on the whole
community. Well, that's your
profession, Mr Coard; how far do you
think education is making out in that
direction?

COARD
Well it depends what you mean by that.

CAMERON
The elimination of prejudice and
particularly racial prejudice.

COARD
Yes, well I think in fact not only is
education not helping to eliminate
racial prejudice at the moment but
indeed it is helping to foster and
encourage it. Just a few weeks ago in

CS COARD   0369

my class I was reading a story written by
a woman psychologist in fact, she
lectures in psychology at a university, I
won't call any names but in fact she's
written numerous story books in
reading series for children used all over
the world. And in this story she talks
about two white boys who go out to this
island of the golden sands where they
visit this white rock – which is described
in favourable terms – where they meet
a white unicorn – the white unicorn is
very helpful to them in their project.
And finally they encounter black pirates
on the high seas. Pirates would have
been frightening enough a story for any
child but it had to be black pirates.

CS MRS COARD   0401

CAMERON
It could be that you read more into that
than actually was intended.

3-s COARD, wife, and   0404
CAMERON

COARD
Yes well in fact this is quite often you
know, said but indeed there is no other
explanation for the fact that the white
children turned and looked at the black
children and said, and, you know, just
looked at the black children. In fact I

Zoom in to COARD		have read storybooks in the last half hour of the day on several occasions and the children are usually so gripped by the stories that they have no time to look at anybody else or even fiddle around with pieces of paper or anything. Yet on this occasion the white children looked at the black children and the black children looked embarrassed.
H.A.S. pan down buildings to playground – children playing	0423	FX CHILDREN SHOUTING
INTERVIEW CAROL BERGMAN/CAMERON	0427	COMMENTARY (CAMERON) If the teaching materials are loaded – what about the teachers? A New York teacher came to work in an immigrant area of London; she is Carol Bergman.
CS CAROL BERGMAN	0429	
2-s CAROL BERGMAN and CAMERON	0431	BERGMAN As I began to work there I discovered a very strange sort of attitude towards the children, which disturbed me considerably. The first one was the attitude of the teachers towards the children. The fact that they were black more or less put them into the category of being backward, it was assumed that they were backward. Also because some of them spoke with a West Indian dialect it was assumed that therefore they were backward. In fact as an American coming over I found it much more easy to understand the West Indian children than the cockney children.
CS CAROL's notebook	0454 0456	COMMENTARY (CAMERON) Carol was interested enough to keep a notebook on what she learned.
CS CAROL BERGMAN	0458	BERGMAN And I noticed that when a New Zealander spoke about a Pakistani boy, he said 'He's a Pakistani boy of Muslim background.' Meaning he's different, he's culturally different, he comes from a different culture. Whereas the English teachers always refer to all their foreign

249

children, no matter what country they were from, as coloured. And in fact they brought in the race thing from the start.

BLACK ARTS THEATRE WORKSHOP SEQ.
WS members of the Workshop grouped round and CAMERON   0470

COMMENTARY (CAMERON)
In Kensington the Black Arts Theatre Workshop tries to correct these false attitudes and to redefine itself in black rather than white terms.

CS Girl   0477

GIRL
Kids relate to heroes and the heroes are always white, you know. Even in the simple thing of cowboys and indians: the hero who is always in the right, God is on his side, you know, praying, the big pioneer sweeping across the New World conquering those savages, you know, and they're the heroes. And the black kids relate to the heroes and the indians are anti-heroes and they're down there as savages and so forth. And it's important. It gets into the minds of these kids, into their mentality, it can warp their mentality.

CS Man   0500

MAN
What we're doing is turning our back to you and re-creating our own mirror, so we look at ourselves as we are. We criticise ourselves. We quarrel among ourselves but in the process of building up ourselves, not to tear ourselves down.

Pan L. to CAMERON   0512

CAMERON
Well one of the things that's particularly interesting me since I know what the effects of the situation are, how do you suppose it originated? What made this situation start in the very beginning?

MS Girl
and zoom in to CS   0521

GIRL
Historically it's a matter of economics. You know, in England in the 19th century and the rest of the European countries right at the flourish of imperialism and colonialisation, for pure greed, you know, they wanted money from the New World, they wanted to build up their riches in the

STILLS SEQ.
CS Poster 'Slave for sale'
(Mansell Collection)   0537

		New World. And slaves were brought in as the cheapest labour.
CS slave poster (Mansell)	0539	
Drawing of Africans being led out of Africa to slavery (Mansell)	0541	MUSIC IN: 'Deep Dark Blue Centre' Graham Collyer Septet Deram SML 1005
Pan along diag. of slave ship (Jackdaw)	0544	
	0547	COMMENTARY (CAMERON over MUSIC) The slave trade in Africans to the Colonies, when men were merchandise, brought shame to the 18th century, defacing the record of the white man.
Indolent looking white man (Mansell)	0552	
Black slave – woman (Mansell)	0555	MUSIC UP
Slave auction (Mansell)	0558	
Another slave auction (Mansell)	0561	
Slave being examined (Mansell)	0562	
Slaves left to die in Africa (Mansell)	0565	MUSIC OUT COMMENTARY (CAMERON)
BLACK ARTS WORKSHOP Various shots of members talking	0567	For the black man, the slave trade left an ancestral memory of bitterness that is indelible even today – and especially among the Londoners of the Black Arts Workshop, since history is the root from which they draw this sense of identity, which is understandably exclusive, and sceptical of strangers. To begin with I think our camera rather muted them, and they accepted the intrusion with courtesy and reserve. I tried to ask for candour, and frankness.
	0582	Perhaps I got a bit more than I expected.
		CAMERON Don't you possibly consider the very presence of us here, me asking you questions whom you've never seen in your bloody life before, is that not symbolic of the situation that you might argue is so wrong?

MAN
Yeh, well that's part of what we're saying. It's still the boss and the . . .

CAMERON
Well why did I have to tell you to say it then?

MAN
No, no, it's a question of getting to the right point, getting to the right place to say it. Right now, what are you doing here now?

CAMERON
Yeh.

MAN
Yeh, I'm asking you, what are you doing here?

Pan L. to CAMERON   0605

CAMERON
We're doing here now, as I told you originally, we're trying to find out something about the whole question of human prejudice and you are a very great expert on it, therefore I'm asking you to help define what . . .

Pan R. to man

MAN
Why am I an expert on it? Why is a Jew not? Why is a Jew not? He was killed in Germany, wasn't he?

CAMERON
Who?

MAN
Jew, Jews were killed in there by Hitler, weren't they? Why didn't you go to a Jew?

2nd GIRL   0622

GIRL
Look, Irish people and Jewish people do not make controversial television. Black people do. If you ask a black person a question that you would ask somebody else, it will naturally, you naturally, James Cameron is expecting a certain kind of response from us. He, he knows what our group, to a

certain extent he has ideas about what the Black Arts Workshop is like. He's expecting a militant, ranting, raving expression from the people here. And the very sort of physical set up of the thing: we are not television stars, we cannot appear sort of completely at ease on a television camera with some, you know, I can see four or five white guys standing in front of me with Camerons, with cameras, each shouting questions at me. And, you know, you expect this sort of immediate response. It is almost like going from one stereotype image of a black man to another.

Pull back to reveal sound recordist   0650

MAN
To another. Well that's what he wants. That's what Cameron wants because he thinks, these people they've got knives and guns and everything. And they are good – they're going to stand up and do a war dance or something and shout down . . .

CS Man and pan L. to Girl   0569

(SEVERAL TALKING AT ONCE)

That's what the white liberal wants always.

GIRL
Also on black tv the black man in the starring role is always a super nigger. He's always a very highly qualified Brazilian diplomat, you know, or some highly qualified artistic person. He can't just be an ordinary . . .
. . . walking into record shop in Brixton and buy a couple of reggae records. He can't be anything like that, he must be a super nigger.

ANOTHER GIRL
Super nignog.

MS ANSELL WONG   0685

ANSELL WONG
It's true and it's things like these that really needle black people, you see. And little things. We may laugh at these but they really hurt down, deep down. (GIRL: Yeh it does.)

And it's things like these, seemingly little things, that are going to cause the explosion.

VOX POP

Man in street	0692

I think the coloured people don't do enough to make themselves liked. They walk about with a chip on their . . . I tell them straight, I don't mince no words or anything because the majority of them walk about with a chip on their shoulder and they got a very – I'm not saying all of them – got a very aggressive attitude. I mean we Jewish people have always tried to assimilate and make themselves liked, you know, but the coloured don't. They come to this country, they say 'We're 'ere, what you gonna do about it!'

MS JACK (member of Workshop)	0711

JACK

We've been talking about things that are very, very tangible but the white liberals like you are the subtle weapon of racism, you know. You are a sort of evidence that this society, this white society might have a conscience. And they use you and you use yourself to sort of dampen our revolutionary attitude.

H.A.S. JACK	0718

CAMERON

You think that there's no possibility whatever of our word ever being heard? You think that we will always be a dampening down?

Pan L. to CAMERON	0732

JACK

The point is that, as has been proven in the United States, the white liberal so far has always in the final analysis let down the black man when it comes to the ultimate situation, when it comes to, say, taking up arms against the white power structure of which you are a part. And if you want to be a positive force within our struggle then you must stop playing with rhetoric and the white liberal will have to come to terms with himself.

Profile shot of JACK	0739

CS CAMERON	0750

CAMERON
You think I'm assuaging the conscience of my ancestors?

CS JACK   0763

JACK
Indirectly and . . . yes, I would say that's so. In effect that's what it boils down to, yes. That's what it boils down to, yes.

CAMERON
But then you spoke then about the solution for the American dilemma – the taking up of arms. Do you think that will be the solution?

LIBRARY FOOTAGE
Violence and rioting in   0772
Chicago

JACK
No, I didn't say that. I didn't say that, no, no.

CAMERON
You did.

JACK
No, no, I didn't say that, I didn't say that. No, no, what I said, what I said was if you are to help us, if you are to help us you have to go all the way with us. The ultimate situation might be the taking up of weapons, might be. Now, now, now if that is the situation the question is will *you*, the white liberal, take up arms with us?

MS JACK   0776

CS CAMERON   0785

Pan R. to girl

CAMERON
No, I would take up arms with nobody in any circumstances, for any purpose.

GIRL
I think the crunch, I think the crunch is, the ultimate is – as Fanon says and Sartre says in the introduction to Fanon's book – is, can a man condemn himself? Can the white man in the long run turn round and look inside himself and say, you know 'I am . . .'

CAMERON
Most certainly, I would have thought.

GIRL
Nobody can condemn . . . nobody can
do this.

CAMERON
History is full of men who did that.

GIRL
Nobody can condemn himself. You
can't condemn yourself as a white man.

CAMERON
Why not?

GIRL
And say, you know, I will take arms, if
necessary, and kill my own people, you
know. I heard some woman saying a
whole lot of shit about – she's going,
she's a white woman going with some
black man – and she says if the
revolution comes she's going to be the
first one to pick up a gun and shoot
down some white people.

CAMERON
Does that seem to you to be a solution?

LIBRARY footage:	0826
rioting and violence in Chicago	

SILENCE

	0830
MS GIRL	0831

GIRL
I didn't say that. I said 'if', in the
ultimate it may be to take up and shoot
your own people but in the long run
perhaps worse is turning round inside
yourself and say 'I am rotten'.

LIBRARY footage:	0838
Chicago riots	

SILENCE

CS CAMERON	0840

CAMERON
Do you really think it is impossible for a
man to look inside himself and say 'I am
rotten and I belong to a wrong society'?

GIRL
When the deeds, when the deeds that
are done have been nasty enough, you
can't do it, you know.

CAMERON
Really?

MS Man talking   0849

MAN
Why is, why is he, especially the white liberal, why is he afraid of violence?

ANOTHER GIRL
Because he's a liberal.

MAN
Why is he always afraid of violence?

LIBRARY footage: 0856   SILENCE
Chicago riots

     0859   CAMERON
I'm not afraid of violence, I've lived among it for most of my life in one form
CS CAMERON   0862   or another, but I reject it as a means of implementing a humane policy, that's all.

ANSELL WONG
There's no question about a humane problem. This is not a humane problem. It's a political problem. It's a political and a social problem. And it's not a matter of humanity involved at all because white man is not human.

LIBRARY footage: 0876   SILENCE
Chicago riots

ANSELL WONG
MS ANSELL WONG   0889   It's not human because – and up to now we are still in a state of oppression, we are still suffering violence. And it's not a problem of . . . it's not a humane problem because to say it's a humane problem is like to reflect like what Jack said, my brother over there said, is that, you know, your white liberalism is coming through loud and clear. I mean and this thing is coming useless now, you know. I think it has developed into a useless situation.

2ND GIRL
It is developing into a useless discussion. This has gone beyond the
MS Girl speaking   0907   point of the ridiculous, right? Because

James Cameron is sort of trying to manipulate us. He, he . . .

ANOTHER GIRL
We're supposed to say what you want us to say.

2ND GIRL
We're supposed to say things and when we ask questions that make you feel either uncomfortable or is not in the pattern of the either the new, according to your new black militancy or to fit into the way you want it. You know you want us to sit here as a group and to sort of, you know, make something like explosive television for you as long as we don't ask you any awkward questions or put you on any spot.

Girl speaking	0930	ANOTHER GIRL Mr Cameron, why are you trying to get us all het up? (UPROAR) Yes, and you're giving it to him.
2nd Girl speaking	0933	2ND GIRL We should have brought a few guns and sort of lean up on the side . . . and have a sort of beret sort of stuck to one side and say 'Look at me! I'm big and black and bad!' You know, and that would have been beautiful. And I could have kept shouting things like, you know 'Black and beautiful!' you know, every sort of two minutes instead of commercials 'cos they don't have commercials on the B.B.C. That is what you wanted, man, you don't fool anybody here.
Tracking shots through streets of Notting Hill	0955	COMMENTARY (CAMERON) We were not, truthfully, trying to fool anybody, though I can see how it may have seemed. It is their dilemma, it is also ours. However one tries not to be glib in looking at this mutual problem, that is what one inevitably is.
	0964	DARCUS OWUSU You have a society with a million and a
Interior MANGROVE	0965	half black people on the sidelines. That

258

restaurant – zoom in to
DARCUS OWUSU

is what you have. Everything goes on, Parliament goes on, the economy goes on, everything goes on and all they want black people for is to produce whenever they want them to produce. Apart from that we stand on the sidelines rotting, dying, festering, all kinds of processes of degeneration you're going through on the sidelines while this society continues.

And the question is whose responsibility it is to pull us off the sidelines and involve us into this society.

But what I believe is that to involve us would mean serious and fundamental changes in the society itself. I mean we don't want to get involved in what is going on here: arms to South Africa; arms to Rhodesia; supporting America in the Vietnam war; sending people to prison. That kind of society we don't want to get involved in. But we don't want to fester on the side, outside, so there's one solution: We're coming in, and we're coming in with full force, with our own definitions, in our time, and anything could happen when we come in.

WS Interior MANGROVE	0987	
Tracking shot through Notting Hill street	1005	

1008   COMMENTARY (CAMERON)
Their Member of Parliament is a solicitor, Bruce Douglas-Mann.

Back of CAMERON L. and on R. BRUCE DOUGLAS-MANN sitting behind desk in his office   1010

CAMERON
If a state of racial tension is felt to exist or thought to exist, then I suppose you could say by definition it does exist as a fact?

Zoom in to DOUGLAS-MANN   1019

DOUGLAS-MANN
Yes, the fact that people believe that or have beliefs about the police, have beliefs about white people, have beliefs about black people, is important even if those beliefs are wrong.

COMMANDER P. NIEVENS of Scotland Yard at his desk, CAMERON in F/g to R.   1024

COMMENTARY (CAMERON)
I asked exactly the same question at Scotland Yard.

1026

CAMERON
How seriously do the Police take this feeling of grievance, true or false, but it's nonetheless there or expressed to be there very violently. Does this trouble you?

NIEVERS
Well, trouble, that's our business. We know, we understand about trouble and the problems of the community. We've been – as I said before – in this particular police force we've been in business a hundred and fifty years and we've weathered quite a number of storms. We've had varieties of a theme of criticism of the way in which we've done our duty. But I think our record stands favourable comparison with any other organisation in the fair way in which we administer the law.

W.H.A.S. policemen in the street   1053

1058

DOUGLAS-MANN
Well you have to realise that the police have a great deal of discretion as to who they prosecute and for what offences, because there are far more offences being committed every day than the police can possibly prosecute. For example, in one town where in 1958 there were practically no prosecutions for male importuning but the following year a new Chief Constable was appointed. The following years, 1959, there were thirty, rose to a hundred and five the following year, hundred and thirty-five the year after and two hundred and sixteen the year after that; whereas previously there had been no prosecutions. Well obviously the homosexuals in that city felt that they were being picked on because in the past there had been no prosecutions. Now, you get a similar situation with black people if the police in a particular area decide they're going to concentrate on enforcing the law in a particular field for which black people are liable to be involved.

MS DOUGLAS-MANN in his office   1066

General shot interior MANGROVE   1095

Man speaking in MANGROVE   1096

MAN
We enjoy ourselves. You know, we drink, we dance, you know, everybody enjoy themselves. The Police got to come and bang on the door and they, you know, search the place 'who's got drugs?', you know. Whether you got drugs or not they plant you with it, you know things like that. And if you try to resist arrest . . .

CAMERON
And you know that that has happened from personal experience?

MAN
Personal experience, it happened ten, twenty times, thirty times – I can name it.

MS DOUGLAS-MANN in his   1111
office   1113

DOUGLAS-MANN
In general black people commit less crime than the average member of the white community but proportionately they are more involved in cannabis smoking as this grows wild in Jamaica and it is not regarded by the majority of black people as a moral offence.

CS COMMANDER NIEVENS   1124

CAMERON
Accepting that the man who feels that he's got a sense of injustice usually tends to attribute his misfortune to an act of policy on the part of them – whoever they may be – could it still be possible that there are differences of approach between division and division in the police according to the circumstances in which they have to work?

COMMANDER NIEVENS
Yes, that's a fair observation but we have always . . . you see, I, as I see the situation, there is a thing in this country which is called 'police discretion' and I think it is most important that this discretion is allowed to continue because only the police officers on the ground in a given situation will know what is the right course of action at a

particular time. And I think you would agree and most other people who are able to stand off and look at the scene coolly and have a long cool look, will agree that what is right and proper in possibly Birmingham will not necessarily pertain in Tower Hamlets.

MS DOUGLAS-MANN   1172

DOUGLAS-MANN
I also know from the practical experience of working as a solicitor that the police do, as a matter of routine, strengthen the evidence which is brought in criminal cases. Now, I say that that is something I know as a matter of experience, I cannot prove it in a single case. But I have been practising in criminal cases for sixteen years and I think that any lawyer with comparable experience would agree that they know this as a fact that the police regularly as a matter of routine strengthen the evidence in criminal cases where they believe that the defendant is guilty.

CS BASIL in MANGROVE   1205

BASIL
Yes, there's an old saying that says that the innocent suffers for the guilty. And we see this with our people in the area walking down the road, being planted wrongfully, not doing a thing and being imprisoned for a number of months. So I mean somebody has to carry the can and that's how I see it.

CS DOUGLAS-MANN   1218

DOUGLAS-MANN
Because the police, of course, don't know the black community as well as they know the white community, they are more likely to make mistakes, and having made the mistakes, to back them up with perjured evidence.

General shot MANGROVE   1226

MAN
They do not like to see black people enjoy themselves. They do not like to see black people, you know, try to communicate with each other. They try to break up that scene, you understand?

MS DOUGLAS-MANN   1233

DOUGLAS-MANN
I think that if you are an articulate black man it is likely that you're going to be labelled 'black power' by the police. And I know of one case where a restaurant which was certainly the club of the articulate members of the black community which appeared to be constantly persecuted by the police.

MS COMMANDER NIEVENS   1245

CAMERON
I would have thought that it was to the advantage of the police to have these people congregate in certain known spots, I mean, if only for administrative police convenience, quite apart from any social benefit it might accrue. Would you agree with that?

COMMANDER NIEVENS
Well I don't really like to see it because it breeds an air of separateness and we have always in this country absorbed the waves of immigrants that have come since way, way back and they have been, as it were, seen to conform to the pattern of behaviour in this country. But one must admit that over this last few years this, a word which was used quite frequently when – you use the word 'colour', I understand they like to be called 'black' – these black people started to arrive then they, we found in the first instance that the words 'assimilate' and 'integrate' were used quite frequently whereas now there is almost a situation developing where we, by tacit agreement, allow separate development. Now I wonder sometimes whether this in fact is a good thing for them and for us.

CS men in MANGROVE   1300

MAN
They're pressurising us so much. They're squeezing us, right? And yet we can still get together and enjoy ourselves. They hate that. They want to know, well, listen man, I'm doing everything to these flippin' black people, right? I'm doing everything I can and yet how the hell can they enjoy

themselves, you know, how can they carry on normally.

CS COMMANDER NIEVENS	1312	**COMMANDER NIEVENS** In some areas which is predominantly black you will find that they are under, the citizens are under the mistaken idea that the law operates somewhat differently for them than what it does if they were members of the indigenous population. And this is quite untrue.
WS interior MANGROVE	1324	**MAN** The police in uniform have this authority to harass the black man and get away with it.
MS COLIN BOBB-SEMPLE L. and CAMERON R. in office	1328	**BOBB SEMPLE** On many occasions I have been told that black youths have been aggravated by police officers. Many of them complain to me as a lawyer, an articled clerk in a firm of solicitors, they complain to me and they say that the police molest them because apparently it's a crime, as far as the police are concerned, it's a crime for black youths to congregate in the streets, you see. **CAMERON** Just that, no more? **BOBB-SEMPLE** Well, many of them seem to express the view that they're very much afraid of being planted by police officers – that is planted with drugs and so on – And also of being beaten up by police officers inside police stations after they've been arrested.
COMMANDER NIEVENS L. and CAMERON R.	1358	**COMMANDER NIEVENS** It is a regrettable feature of society today that in this permissive society – as it's been called – that unfortunately the first time a youngster meets somebody who says no and means it, it happens to be a police officer.
BOBB-SEMPLE L. and CAMERON R.	1369	**BOBB-SEMPLE** I would feel scared still if I were taken in by a police officer, yes, I would.

Because so many black people have told me this that I myself would be afraid in such a circumstance.

Mounted policeman passing by in street	1376	**COMMANDER NIEVENS** All walks of society need to be contained in our ranks if we are to understand the problems of the community then everybody's voice has
CS COMMANDER NIEVENS	1382	to be heard in order that the laws of this country can be seen to be fair to all.

1386   **COMMENTARY (CAMERON)**
We asked if the police had to have a prejudiced policeman in order to understand prejudice.

COMMANDER NIEVENS
1388   Not at all, not to exercise the prejudice. What he needs, what the policeman needs is, what most of us I think have got, which is an all-round balanced approach to the problem that exists in the street – and don't let's get away from the situation 'in the street' because this is where it's happening and this is where the hostile situation develops so easily.

Argument in the streets of Notting Hill between white van driver and black woman   1405   **ARGUMENT IN STREET** between white van driver and black girl driver.

MAN
. . . why didn't you fucking look when you came out the turning. Nearly killed me.

WOMAN
If you were such a good driver you'd follow me. If you was a good driver.

MAN
What! Let you go?

(ARGUMENT cont'd.)

MAN
Black or white I've never hit a woman.

WOMAN
You can't, you haven't got the strength.

Man in street talking to camera	1431	**VOX POP** If they come here then they've got to obviously accept the way of life and I think that's the success – but it takes a bit of time.
Interior MANGROVE – DARCUS L. and CAMERON R. Zoom in to DARCUS	1435	**DARCUS OWUSU** When we come here we do not come naked, we have brought something with us. We have spent four hundred years in the West Indies making experiences, accumulating experiences, going through all kinds of processes. And when we arrive here we bring that with us.
CS Young girl in street	1445	**VOX POP** If they come over 'ere to settle down in our country they should settle to our, you know, ways of life. And a lot of them are eversuch nice people. I've got coloured friends so . . .
DARCUS OWUSU L. and CAMERON R.	1451	**CAMERON** I'm still groping to know whether there is a prognosis, whether there is a conceivability of an alteration in this situation or do we live like this till we die?
CS CAMERON and pan L. to DARCUS	1460	**DARCUS** I am beginning to see something. We are in this society but not quite part of it. We are not emotionally tied to Parliament, we're not emotionally tied to the educational system, we are not emotionally tied to trade unions so our slate is clean, and our creativity is there to begin to be implemented. I think some people in this society recognise that. I think that those who rule and govern our lives recognise this tremendous and unique contribution that black people have to play. And as such we are beginning to see the seeds of repression, bitter repression that have been sown.
COMMANDER NIEVENS L. and CAMERON R.	1481	**COMMANDER NIEVENS** I would also submit that no other group of people, organisation, or whatever,

MS NIEVENS   1489

does as much to come to terms with the problem certainly as the Police Service. Because, let there be no mistake about this, if this thin blue line ever collapses then the structured society in this country will collapse also, and I submit that you make way for a system of anarchy.

DARCUS OWUSU L. and   1499
CAMERON R.

DARCUS
There is nobody in this country who could incite a riot among black people. There are conditions that could incite riots. So that in that sense we have no control over those means so it is purely academic to discuss what kinds of means we're going to use.

CAMERON
That's a good answer. It is impossible always to discuss means until the environment for those means . . .

Zoom in to DARCUS

DARCUS
The actual situation presents itself. If you were to present me with a situation and then I look into the possibilities then of course I, as a person, would give a personal opinion on what kind of means to be used – but that is subject to a democratic process – we can't get into that at all, what means.

CAMERON
You don't think, Darcus, that we are all living in dreams, do you? That one day this environment will suddenly manifest itself and then the means will suddenly become blindingly clear?

DARCUS
The means are becoming blindingly clear because if you speak to black people and you speak to the youths they are already saying what kinds of means should be employed – they are violent. You look at them walking the street, the way they speak, the way they handle their social relationships: there is a violence which expresses itself, even sometimes creativity. Look at these

267

Shots of paintings on walls of MANGROVE	1548

paintings. There is an underlying violence about them. Anybody who looks at them will be able to see that.

CAMERON
Do you welcome that?

DARCUS
That is as it is. That is as it is whether I welcome it or not is not going to make an ounce of value.

MS DARCUS	1558

CAMERON
I wasn't asking you to assume an attitude, I was just wondering what it was, that's all.

DARCUS
As a person I feel extremely violent, extremely violent. This is not part of a congenital or inborn trait. It is the conditions under which I live and I'm very conscious of that. You know, I want to fight, I want to fight. I need to fight to express something. I need to argue, I need to scream. That is the position that British society has placed me in, even in the West Indies because they control the major sources of revenue down there as well. They have placed me in that situation where I feel

H.A.S. fast zoom in to buildings	1584

the need to explode.

FX TRAFFIC

SOLIDARITY WITH BLACKS DEMO	1585

whites demonstrating in streets of Notting Hill – various shots (B.B.C. News film)

DEMONSTRATORS CHANTING
Hands off black people! Hands off black people!

	1588

COMMENTARY (CAMERON)
In Notting Hill a little demo in the streets makes its protest. A tiny minority, even smaller than the blacks they defend. It won't make much difference to something that goes deeper than misunderstanding. And nor will this programme. I said at the start

that we would almost certainly finish as we began, with the unanswered question. What is the common factor of it all? What is behind our deadlock?

1634

SOUTHWARK BRIDGE
Pan up from feet to reveal   1605
CAMERON – track back in
front of him as he talks

CAMERON
It seems to me that every one of us thinks of everybody else wholly in terms of how they measure up to us – like or unlike. He's like me in this way or that way and those are the things I approve of. The other things in which he isn't like me, that's what's wrong with him. Like is OK. Differences – inferior or sometimes, maybe, a threat. Some things, of course, can be changed but the colour of your skin can't. If there is a conflict there it's one in which nobody can change sides, ever.

CAMERON walks past   1631
camera to other end of bridge

MUSIC IN:
'Deep Dark Blue Centre' Deram SML 1005 Graham Collyer Septet.

S/I END TITLES:

'PHOTOGRAPHY
PETER CHAPMAN'

'SOUND
GEOFF TOOKEY
MIKE BILLING'

'FILM EDITOR
PAUL O'DELL'

'PRODUCED AND
DIRECTED BY:
MICHAEL RABIGER'

FADE VISION   1647   FADE MUSIC

B.B.C. T.V.,
27th February 1971

'CAMERON COUNTRY'

'WHY PATRIOTISM?'

VISION	FOOTAGE	SOUND
SERIES TITLE SEQUENCE: Passport stamps, stills, title 'CAMERON COUNTRY'	0000	MUSIC IN: 'Garden of Delights' John Dankworth
Man in the street	0054	MAN Well I think people still feel patriotic, yes. INTERVIEWER Do you? MAN Yes, I think so.
MS MCKEWAN on horseback	0064	MAJOR MCKEWAN I think it means that you put your country before everything else when there comes a point of crisis.
Man in street		MAN Funny thing to do a documentary on, patriotism, why patriotism?
Union Jack	0084	MUSIC IN: National Anthem
S/I Title: 'Why Patriotism?'	0088	
WS waves lapping on shore	0101	MUSIC FADES INTO SOUND OF WAVES
	0119	MUSIC IN 'The White Cliffs of Dover' Vera Lynn Decca F 8110
LS Cliffs of Dover – pan L.	0132	
Seagulls flying over cliffs	0143	

270

LS Cliffs and pan L. to reveal	0178	MUSIC OUT
CAMERON	0188	CAMERON

This is the very edge of England. That way lies the world in which I work and this way lies England where I live, a very strange and complicated place. For years and years I've wondered just what is a country, what is loyalty, and to what should a man be true. I've lived most of my life in other people's countries which I've loved or not loved, as the case may be. But this is where my own country actually begins. I know about frontiers and this is one of the oldest and strangest ones in the world. I wonder why?

Exterior Village Church	0251	MUSIC IN: 'I Vow to Thee My Country' Templars Octet HMV C 5781
Graveyard of a country church	0259	
Small stream	0266	
Outline of tree against sky	0274	
MS CAMERON sitting at	0281	
typewriter	0282	COMMENTARY (CAMERON)

It seemed to me that there was no total image of a Patriot, or of Patriotism, nor could be, since it must always be expressed in a variety of parts:

Freeze frame – Cattistock Hunt	0297	The patriotism of tradition, and continuing symbols.
Freeze frame – JOHN FOWLES	0302	The patriotism of the intellectual romantic imagination.
Freeze frame – members of the NATIONAL FRONT	0307	The patriotism of exclusion.
Freeze frame – HUGH MCDERMID	0313	The patriotism of defensive nationalism.
Freeze frame – COL. COLIN MITCHELL	0318	The patriotism of the soldier, with his special loyalties.
Freeze frame – ex-patriate Americans	0323	The patriotism that found itself only in exile.

271

Freeze frame – members of KRISHNAMURTI foundation	0330	The patriotism that transcended patriotism, and rejected the obsolete divisions of mankind.
	0337	
CS CAMERON and pan down to his fingers typing	0339	FX TYPING
IMPERIAL WAR MUSEUM FILM Several shots of men marching to war 1914–18	0353 0356	FX FEET MARCHING COMMENTARY (CAMERON) Looking back two generations ago, almost the whole world went to war, basically in the name of Patriotism.
	0367	
CHELSEA PENSIONERS SEQ. WS group of Chelsea Pensioners at the Royal Hospital	0381 0389	It cost many million lives, in the name of this or that fatherland; even so, many survived. Some did more than survive, but became institutionalised in a museum of a generation.
CS's of various of the pensioners	0395	The Chelsea Pensioners remain today, unquestioning survivors of a less complicated age.
	0408	

CAMERON L. and pan R. round assembled pensioners   0419

PENSIONER
. . . giving a concert party – I was one of the party – in the Conservative Club, Blackfriars Road, on the night of August 4th, 1914. Suddenly, as we were getting the next number ready there was quite a disturbance, a noise and people went walking round in half sections, in twos round the hall, singing, 'they can't

CS Pensioner   0437

beat the boys of . . .' umbrellas at the slope, rolled umbrellas at the slope,

Poster: 'Boys of the Bulldog Breed'   0459

Conservative Club '. . . of the Bulldog Breed.' We thought they'd gone mad.

MS Pensioner   0464

'What's up?' 'War's been declared!' Right! Sudden explosion – patriotism – which they'd never given a thought to since they'd left school. And off we marched, straight over the Thames to Buckingham Palace, where we found, well, masses of people – you couldn't get near the Palace. All shouting

Still: Crowds outside Buckingham Palace August 1914   0484

'We want the King'. And we stayed there all night – well, most of us did. We were young then, I was just turned twenty, and

Still: Crowds outside Army Recruiting Office 1914   0505

we stayed there until next morning until we went to the various recruiting stations

IMPERIAL WAR MUSEUM FILM Men waiting to join up outside recruiting office.   0513

and joined up. In the joining up it was quite as dangerous, as many got injured – I don't think many got killed. Getting in

Int. office – men being sworn in	0525	there we were trampling them underfoot. We were sworn in in hundreds in the great hall, in hundreds – hold the book up and we were given a shilling and we went home to join up next day at military depots. And off we went to war quite full of it. We forgot our families, everything, and off we went to war. Now that was patriotism.
Men putting on their new uniforms	0538	
Men marching off to war	0548	
I.W.M. Film OUT	0582	**CAMERON** Therefore, the loyalty you owe to your country is greater than that you owe to your family?
Group of pensioners at Royal Hospital	0582	
		PENSIONER Yes, oh yes.
Poster: 'Why Britain is at War'	0566	**FX DRUM ROLLS**
Poster: Lord Kitchener 'Your Country Needs You'	0573	
Poster: 'Single Men Show Your Appreciation by following their Noble Example'	0579	
Poster: 'Men of the Empire – to Arms'	0585	
Postcard: Soldier against b/g of Union Jack	0588	
IMPERIAL WAR MUSEUM FILM Men marching off to war 1914	0591	**MUSIC IN:** 'Take Me Back to Dear Old Blighty' British Legion Choir Col. 33SX 11740
Men digging trenches 1914	0597	
	0617	**MUSIC OUT**
	0617	**COMMENTARY (CAMERON)** In later years wars took other names
Still: Gas Blinded Soldiers 1914	0633	and other motivations, but the First

273

Still: George V decorating soldier	0633	World War took the simplicities of Patriotism, invoked and perhaps exploited them, and the word was King and Country. It was never again to be quite so simple.
Still: George V inspecting troops	0642	
	0644	CAMERON How much do you identify the country with the monarchy?
CAMERON and Pensioners	0651	PENSIONER It is a must. That is definitely a must.
Group of Pensioners	0660	ANOTHER PENSIONER No monarchy in this country, there – it would cease to be a country. CAMERON So the Monarchy will endure? PENSIONERS Oh yes, must do.
CAMERON and Pensioners	0671	PENSIONER After all, as a nation we do love the pomp and ceremony and we look forward to it whenever it comes . . .
PRINCE OF WALES INVESTITURE (PATHÉ) H.A. LS Caervarvon Castle	0681	and everybody goes – or as near as possible. And that is, in my opinion, part of patriotism.
Queen places crown on Charles's head	0687	VOICE Hear, hear.
Buglars on ramparts of Castle	0698	ANOTHER PENSIONER I think it all boils down to heritage. There's not many countries can say they've got a heritage like we have.
Queen and Charles come to balcony and wave	0703	
PATHÉ FILM OUT	0707	CAMERON A lot of it was bound up in the Empire, wasn't it, in your day? Do you feel a sense of regret that that has now shrunk?
CS Chelsea Pensioner	0708	PENSIONER I do, very much indeed, very much. And I've often pondered over this and I think it's one of the most sorrowful things that ever happened to this country.

Union Jack flapping in wind – pull out to reveal Royal Hosp. – gun and cannon balls in f/g	0742	BUGLE
Pan down Edith Cavell monument to inscription: 'For King and Country'	0758	
CS inscription 'Sacrifice'	0770	
CS inscription 'Fortitude'	0772	
CS inscription 'Devotion'	0774	
CS inscription 'Humanity'	0777	
LS Cenotaph	0781	
Inscription on Cenotaph: 'The Glorious Dead' – pan down to tiny bunch of flowers at foot	0785	BUGLE OUT
CS bunch of flowers	0798	
WS sea lapping breakwater – pan R. to beach and town of LYME REGIS	0805 0826 0830	FX WAVES and SEAGULLS COMMENTARY (CAMERON) What is it that gives a country an identity?
CS 'National Character' being typed	0832	FX TYPING
LS Beach and Lyme Regis	0840	
INTERVIEW JOHN FOWLES/ CAMERON	0843	COMMENTARY (CAMERON) Is there such a thing as a national character? Some people believe there is – Lyme Regis is the home of the author John Fowles.
MS FOWLES in his living room in house at Lyme	0854 0856	
	0857	FOWLES I mean I know, when you have to fill in these ridiculous passport things if I can I always put 'English' as opposed to 'British' – because that's where my blood, my national attachments lie. Britain, I'm really, the Union Jack, you know, Rule Britannia, God Save the Queen, really have no time for that.

275

CAMERON
The symbolism associated with
patriotism is offensive, very frequently.

FOWLES
Well, the symbolism, yes, is vulgar and
offensive, certainly, I think, when the
country's got old, you know. There's a
time in every country's history where of
course patriotic literature is great
literature – I think we're at least three
hundred years past that.

0920 COMMENTARY (CAMERON)
John Fowles sees a special English
meaning in the oldest of English
Still: Robin Hood   0925 legends, the myth of Robin Hood.

0930

Still: Robin Hood and Little   0931
John

0932 FOWLES
Now I think what's interesting about
Robin Hood is, first of all that he
retreats from injustice, and this is very
CS FOWLES   0940 English – th.s business of seeing
injustice and not standing there but
retreating from it. You go into the
trees. Then you may fight a guerilla
warfare against it, I suppose that's the
best kind of England, or you may
possibly just stand and watch, and that's
another very characteristic English
habit, I think – of simply standing and
watching the world from the trees. I
mean, that's why our conversation is
sometimes so lunatic. You know, we
never say what we mean and baffle the
foreigners and they think we're
CS CAMERON   0987 perfidious – quite rightly so. But if you
have been abroad a lot and you
suddenly meet an Englishman, it's
MS FOWLES   0994 wonderful to get into this, you know,
this marvellous English sub-dialogue
where you really understand that the
things that are said are not the
important things, it's the things you
don't say and the gaps.

CAMERON
Then you understand the code.

FOWLES
You understand the code, yes. I mean, being English in one way is having a marvellous private cypher, you know, psychologically and linguistically. And that in a way, you know, does go back to Robin Hood. It's this mysterious business of never liking to be in the open facing people, say, as the Americans delight to do. It's this mysterious business of . . .

CAMERON
. . . avoiding the confrontation.

FOWLES
. . . sort of getting behind the leaves and peeping through the leaves, you know.

Waves lapping against beach	1057
	1064
BRITISH TROOPS IN ADEN (B.B.C.)	1074
Troops jumping out of truck	1079
CS words 'Military Power' typed	1098
CS COL. COLIN MITCHELL	1104
	1105
2-s MITCHELL L. and CAMERON R.	1121
	1122
	1125

COMMENTARY (CAMERON)
Patriotism isn't often reflective or even philosophic. The simplest form takes its character from conflict, and its most articulate spokesman is the soldier.

MITCHELL
Well I think patriotism and militarism are inevitably very close together. Probably the finest expressions of patriotism have been in the military sense.

COMMENTARY (CAMERON)
Colonel Colin Mitchell, now an M.P., had his year of fame as Mad Mitch of the Argylls. I asked whether he agreed that patriotism could never again be expressed through international wars.

MITCHELL
I think we . . . well, this is a very large subject. I mean, I think we've reached

the end of war being, warfare being expressed as it has been in the twentieth century, in fact in most of the nineteenth century. But I don't think for one moment that we've passed the sort of low threshold sort of warfare that seems to be taking its place. I mean, the, you know, the urban guerilla, the . . .

CAMERON
Now an urban guerilla might conceivably be doing what he does do as a revolutionary because he might well argue that he loves his country so well that he wishes to change its society. Therefore he might argue that he was a patriot.

MITCHELL
Well I think all revolutionaries probably do. I mean, I think that anyone who is prepared to be violent in a cause must obviously give himself some higher belief and his emotions must be channelled into a belief that he's doing the right thing. So therefore there's really no difference between the actionary and the reactionary man over this.

Zoom in to CS	1187

BRITISH TROOPS IN ADEN (B.B.C.)	1215
Aerial shots over Aden	1216

COMMENTARY (CAMERON)
In Aden 'our boys' carried the flag of something that was in fact already gone. The inevitable thing about Imperial patriotism was that by definition it had to deny the patriotism of other people – sometimes with the best of motives, sometimes the worst.

1241

British troops in Aden searching natives	1243

MUSIC IN:
'With A Song in My Heart'
André Kostelanetz CBS GPG 66004-4

1271

COMMENTARY (CAMERON) OVER MUSIC)
All over the world it took many years to learn that patriots had to accept history; and that other people loved their countries too. In Aden the lesson had not yet been learned.

1288

| | 1310 | MUSIC OUT |

MS CAMERON | 1311 | **CAMERON**
As one who professes it very vigorously

2-s MITCHELL L. and | 1315 | how do you define patriotism?
CAMERON R.

MITCHELL
I think it's probably the highest expression of nationalism, if that's not a contradiction in terms.
But I think it's the . . . in a sense you might say that patriotism had a spiritual quality about it which . . . it was love of country taken beyond the sort of hurly-burly of nationalism into a much more, a much stronger emotion.

CHAPLAIN ADDRESSING | 1357 | **CHAPLAIN**
TROOPS (B.B.C.) | | So put pride in your step, Cameronians, for as you march out of the army list you are marching into history. And from your proud place there no man can remove your name. And no man snatch a rose from the chaplet of your honour.

MS MITCHELL | 1408 | **MITCHELL**
What is most interesting to me as a sort of an ex-military man is that I would have thought, and I remember writing on one occasion, that people didn't in fact die for their country; that they were much more interested, if they had to die, in dying for something like their regiment or their ship or something – a smaller group that they could understand.

BRITISH TROOPS IN ADEN | 1437 |
FILM (B.B.C.) | | **INTERVIEWER**
Murder – troops standing around | | How do you think your battalion is
MS MITCHELL in Aden | 1441 | going to handle patrolling Crater?

MITCHELL
We're going to be extremely firm and extremely mean. These chaps have gunned down British soldiers – three of my own were killed here – and I have no compunction in saying that if some chap now starts throwing grenades or using pistols, we shall kill him.

Patrolling soldier in Aden | 1480 | Who was it who said 'My country right or wrong'?

2-s MITCHELL L. and   1484
CAMERON R.

CAMERON
It was Stephen Decatur.

MITCHELL
And G. K. Chesterton said 'saying my
country right or wrong is like saying my
mother drunk or sober'.

CAMERON
Yes, my country right or left.
(LAUGHTER)

MITCHELL
My country right or left, yes.

CAMERON
Yes, 'My country, I pray that she be
right, but it is my country right or
wrong' but I don't think anybody in the
world would subscribe to that
nowadays, do you?

MITCHELL
Well, you see again, I would.
I mean, despite the fact that I can

Zoom in to CS MITCHELL   1533
analyse this whole emotion.

CAMERON
Not if you knew it was wrong.

MITCHELL
Oh, I'm sure that I would give an
absolutely straight answer to that and
the answer is yes. I mean if Britain was
in a situation which was utterly wrong
and it was required of me to do
something for Britain in this context, I
would do it without flinching.

CAMERON
That's a very . . .

MITCHELL
I know, it's a very revealing remark but
I'm sure there's an awful lot of people
like me. You know, this is . . . After all
when you consider that for generations
we have bred ourselves on this
patriotism.

CAMERON
It's not, you wouldn't say that it's just a reaction of military training?

MITCHELL
I'm sure it is, yes. I'm sure it must be. I mean, it would be a terrible reflection on military training if they'd had a chap for twenty-five years and couldn't give him some of the right ideas, wouldn't it? (LAUGHTER)

CAMERON
Yes indeed.

WS village of Cattistock – 2 horses ride through	1616

COMMENTARY (CAMERON)
A subtle thing like patriotism doesn't necessarily mean the killing of people; the substitute is the killing of animals. The motivation is different, but there seems to be a kinship.

	1636
CS words 'Tradition' being typed	1637

FX TYPING

WS CATTISTOCK HUNT meeting outside pub in Rampisham	1643
	1645

MAJOR MCKEWAN
I don't think tradition and patriotism are necessarily synonymous. To be patriotic isn't necessarily to carry on old traditions. I think tradition is carried on where it's part and parcel of the period of life it's in.

MS MCKEWAN on horseback	1652
WS hunt gathering	1669

DORSET MAN
I think patriotism, myself, is doing anything any good for the country. I think it's up to everybody now to stand up for the meaning of it and put down anybody who's trying to get it away.

2 Dorset men watching the Hunt	1682
Girl on horse	1697
CS Hunt Secretary	1702

HUNT SEC.
My first reaction is to think of the enemies of one's country from without but I'm equally jealous of the reputation of my country from within. And I hate the expression but I can't think of another one, it's the image of one's country. And I'm as jealous of the image of my country and think it needs protecting from influences, evil influences from within it as much as

WS Hunt gathering	1720

MS Hunt Sec.	1740

from without. I'm thinking in terms of strikes and the modern quest for material rewards out of all proportion to the work involved in obtaining them.

Woman on horseback	1772

DORSET MAN
We fought two wars to keep our country clean and it's up to us to see that we keep it like that.

2 Dorset men	1775

Shot of hounds milling about	1784

MAN
The traditional things should be kept going shouldn't they? If we all sat and watched telly all night and didn't do the things that our fathers had taught us what to do, we'd be in a sorry state, wouldn't we?

Man on Horseback talking to cam.	1792

LS hounds and Hunt coming up hill track in front of them	1802 1804

MUSIC IN:
'A-Hunting We Will Go'
Owen Brannigan HMV CLP 1789

CS Hounds	1831

LS Hunt coming up hill – track in front of them	1839

	1856

MUSIC OUT

MRS BOILEAU
I deplore this feeling that there is, and there is a feeling, the townspeople don't understand us. And the country people resent that, we're not bumpkins, we've just got as good brains as anybody else.

MS MRS BOILEAU	1860

Hounds – pull back to reveal huntsmen as they gallop into field	1877

MUSIC IN:
'A-Hunting We Will Go'

WS countryside as horses gallop off into mist	1904

MUSIC OUT:

FX GALLOPING

NATIONAL FRONT SEQ.

Mr LOBB, MISS MCDONALD Mr O'BRIEN sitting in room	1923

COMMENTARY (CAMERON)
Some have a rather different tradition. There is an aspect of Patriotism that defines itself in the basest value-judgement – ethnically, or racially. It has had several names in

MISS MCDONALD and O'BRIEN – zoom in to NF badge on his lapel	1932

	1944	several countries; here it is called the National Front.
CS wood 'race' being typed	1947	**FX TYPING**
CAMERON's back f/g and LOBB and MISS MCDONALD on R.	1951	**CAMERON** Well, is it something to do with the actual bloodstream of one? Is there an ethnic basis in patriotism?
Pan R. to O'BRIEN and zoom in		**O'BRIEN** Yes, I think there is insofar as one can identify more readily with the past through one's descent from a known stock.
CS MISS MCDONALD	1982	**CAMERON** Yes, but would you then argue that there is such a thing as racial purity?
CS O'BRIEN	1998	**O'BRIEN** Purity is a relative term, is it not. I think purity of race is a thing which certainly helps one to identify as a nation. Obviously if we have a heterogeneous collection of nondescript peoples it is very difficult to identify them as a nation: it is very difficult for them to identify as a nation.
CS LOBB	1015	
Pan R. to CS MISS MCDONALD		**MISS MCDONALD** I think that we're subjected to so much immigration of every kind – we have people coming from Europe, from Africa, from Asia, and then on top of that we're going to join the Common Market . . . I hope we shan't join it, and there'll be still more people coming across from Europe. There'll be no sort of hindrance against them coming. And I think we're bound to lose our national identity.
CS CAMERON	1056	
MS LOBB	1071	**LOBB** Basically all the peoples of Europe are of Caucasite stock, the Angles and Saxons. And all these people are subdivisions of the Caucasite race. We have this in common. We are of a common racial background. But within the last ten, fifteen years other people have been coming into this country – Afro-Asian and Caribbean

immigrants and we contend that differences are inherent in the individual and that these differences of race arise genetically and they're not something that just arises from the environment.

Pull back to reveal CAMERON   2124

CAMERON
Well then, to put it on the line, then, you would not mind a polyethnic society that included Poles and Dutch, shall we say, but you draw the line at West Indians and Indians.

LOBB
It would depend how many came in. If we had two million Dutch immigrants or two million Polish immigrants, they would tend to stay with their own communities.

CAMERON
No, they wouldn't. They would assimilate in two generations and you know it, simply because they're white.

LOBB
No, no, I disagree with this. If you have a large-scale immigration in a short period of time into any country, then you have the hostility that builds up in the host community and the process of self-identification in the immigrant community. I mean, even over here now we're having the development of black power groups, which is the process of the immigrants re-establishing and reasserting their own identity as people of African stock or people of Indian stock.

CAMERON
Yes, but Mr Lobb you're identifying them purely on an absolutely physical basis. You've got Rothschilds in the Government at this moment, they're immigrant stock are they not. I mean, would you have them, would you put your same strictures on them? Or is it only black people?

Zoom in to LOBB	2255	**LOBB** My attitude to the Rothschilds is something different again – this ties in with our issues on finance and . . . but as far as the Jewish communities that came over here after the diaspora when the Jews spread out all over the world: those that went into Europe, a very small number of them, as their community developed over hundreds of years they've drawn in people from their particular areas where they live, and the Ashkenazim Jews who came over here from Eastern Europe are basically physically similar to the rest of the people of Eastern Europe. You have blonde, blue-eyed people who are Jewish by religion. There isn't a Jewish ethnic group any more.
	2334	**CAMERON** Well, Mr Lobb, then you're drawing the line on fair skin and blue eyes, aren't you? Don't think you should do that, do you? For the sake of the validity of your cause.
Frozen Frame: Group of American Ex-Patriates	2349	**COMMENTARY (CAMERON)** Can there be such a thing as negative patriotism? These expatriate Americans found their homeland asked too much, too great a betrayal of a greater loyalty.
Zoom in to CS HEINZ NORDEN	2351	**NORDEN** Patriotism is defined as love of country. Presumably you are required or motivated to defend what you love or even to die for it. This may be true on a fairly primitive level but on the level of what we ordinarily call patriotism it's absolutely phoney because the threats to countries are concocted. They are not real in the sense that ordinary people can call them real. It reminds me somewhat of old-fashioned romances, you know, where if one person in the cast showed one ounce of sense there would never be any story. Well if one government showed any sense there would never be any war. For patriotism is not necessarily something that you
CS CAROLEE GERWIN	2371	
CS MARILYN STAFFORD	2377	
CS HEINZ NORDEN	2384	
CS DAVID KENNEDY	2410	
CS HEINZ NORDEN	2417	

have to fight or die for – at least
not in the physical sense – it's on
a different level. It's that you want
to see the unique characteristics –
if there are such things – of your
country to be realised and to be part
of it. And particularly this struggle
which is not national, you know,
for freedom, for justice, for
decency, against cruelty, against
stupidity.

CS profile CAMERON   2455

CS DAVID KENNEDY   2461

CS CLANCY SIGAL   2466

SIGAL
We are living in a country which
produced the writer E. M. Forster who
said that he'd much rather betray his
country than his friends. It seems to me
that that is a genuine patriotism. And
that I increasingly, as I get older, I
really cannot connect patriotism with a
particular country. I have certain kinds
of feeling for the United States. I am
indelibly an American, I always will be
an American, that's what my so-called
cultural identity is, but I no longer
really connect that kind of feeling with a
particular country. My own country,
I've been living outside the United
States for so long that my own country
is sort of spread out all over the place;
it's partly in Britain, it's partly in the
United States, it's partly in
anti-Vietnam War agitation, it's partly
wherever people really fight the
bastards, really, I mean that's real
patriotism. And I think it's extremely
dangerous when you become addicted
to a particular country and say you
cannot change your nationality like a
shirt. Why not change your nationality
just like a shirt? It doesn't mean you
have any less love for a particular
country or the friends in that country or
the issues that are really important in
that country. But I think it is so
dangerous to say that I will be this thing
and I am that thing and I will take
responsibility for everything that
happens as a result.

Pan R. to MARILYN   2591
STAFFORD

GERWIN
Like, that's my country right or wrong.

HEINZ
No, I haven't said that.

SIGAL
That's my country right or wrong
coming in the back door.

STAFFORD
What you're saying really is that you're
against nationalism also?

SIGAL
I'm for localism, whatever that is.

STAFFORD
Localism, yes, yes, cultural
development.

SIGAL

Pan L. to CLANCY SIGAL	2615	I think especially given the experiences of the mass suicide of the First World War, given the experiences of fascism in the Second World War, we ought to swear off completely all grand concepts, you know, including a sort of grand concept of internationalism. We have to start with what we feel, with what's close to us, with what's tangible, with our friends, with the things that move us – and not with the things that are supposed to move us from the outside.
Aerial tracking shot over Scottish countryside	2650	
	2655	COMMENTARY (CAMERON)
Pan R. from countryside to reveal MCDERMID's cottage	2662	Up in the emotional edges of the land are patriots of a more particular kind still, with a patriotism within patriotism, dedicated to the smallest unit: Scottish
H.A. WS interior cottage – MCDERMID L. and CAMERON R.	2682	nationalism. The most celebrated is the bard of the Lowlands: poet, Communist, and Scotsman, Hugh
	2692	McDermid
CS word 'Culture' being typed	2689	FX TYPING
	2691	MCDERMID
MS MCDERMID and CAMERON R. and zoom in to MCDERMID	2694	Above all, the true Scottish patriot must be able to say like the Czech poet, J. S. Macha (phon.) in his tractate of patriotism, and I'm substituting the words Scot and Scottish for Czech and

. . . 'I am a Scot, even as I might be a German, Turk, gypsy or negro if I'd been born elsewhere. My Scottishness is the portion of my life which I do feel, not as delight or bliss, but as a solemn and inborn fealty. My native land is within me alone.' Now that seems to me the Scottish position.

MS MCDERMID and CAMERON

2759

CAMERON
Well how does a man ever acquire a sense of purposeful national identity?

Zoom in to MCDERMID

MCDERMID
He can communicate that sense after he's acquired it himself but very few people, it seems to me, ever can acquire it. Poets should and have done in all the literatures of Europe. That's why poets have been in the forefront of nationalist movements in every country I know. And they can communicate it but people not endowed with creative, artistic gifts of one kind or another seem to me to be debarred constitutionally from acquiring that. They can adopt it when it's manifested by other people and make it their own in that sense and act accordingly but to develop it in themselves seems to me to be impossible.

CAMERON
Everybody needs a spokesman in fact.

MCDERMID
They need a spokesman.
James Harvey Robinson in a very dynamic book called 'Mind in the Making' said that all the arts and the sciences, right from the dawn of history in all countries, had been created by an infinitesimal proportion of the population. And that infinitesimal proportion was a constant in all ages and in all countries. And if that little proportion was eliminated then the whole of the rest of mankind wouldn't be able to reconstitute the arts and the sciences or anything that we call civilization. Now that's a profoundly

anti-democratic sentiment, and I believe it. I see not reason to doubt it at all.

(LAUGHTER)

CAMERON
I like that, yes, I like that.

COMMENTARY (CAMERON)
Perhaps the opposite to devoted regional nationalism is equally devoted anti-regional anti-nationalism – among those, and they are not many, who oppose all the synthetic identities of political division are the students of the Krishnamurti school in England.

FRANÇOIS
I mean, what does it mean 'to love one's country'? What do you love in your country? If it is the fields and the sky and the trees and so on – are they different from anywhere else? And why separate one part of the world and say 'This is the part I love' and not love the rest?

HOPPEN
Isn't patriotism becoming obsolete? Wasn't it a product of the city state where you had countries that were small and isolated from one another and that now, with the modern world, in which pollution affects the whole world, in which even the shipping lanes in the Channel can no longer be controlled by England, in a sense we are all involved with each other and if there's a disaster in Pakistan it affects the world. Perhaps, five hundred years ago, we never would have known of their disasters, so countries could be isolated and they could feel that they were special.

CAMERON
I believe that nobody could deny that it is completely obsolete in the political and technological sense; whether it is necessarily in an emotional sense obsolete, I don't know. If it is true that

Aerial tracking shot Scotland 2949
(B.B.C. Library) 2951

KRISHNAMURTI
FOUNDATION 2976
DISCUSSION
WS group of Krishnamurti 2979
students – zoom in to
CAMERON and FRANÇOIS

DONALD HOPPEN and students 2997

Group of students sitting round 3005

CS DONALD HOPPEN 3013

2 students 3063

CS HOPPEN and zoom back to 3069
include students and
CAMERON

Students – pan R. to CAMERON	3088	people must seek for a sense of group identity somehow their loyalty does not necessarily imply lack of criticism, that's what I really think patriotism or loyalty means. A revolutionary would argue that he is a true patriot because he loves his country well enough to see it must be changed for the better. You can be sufficient of a patriot that you want to blow up your country. It's not as paradoxical as it sounds.
and pan up to include FRANÇOIS	3132	FRANÇOIS But then you have to go further and see that what has to be blown up is not your country but that which in yourself makes you attached to a country, because that is really the problem. Unless I feel secure anywhere in the sense that I am free enough to live anywhere without having to belong to a religion, a group, a national . . . a patri . . . a nation, I can't live anywhere in peace because I am creating discordance, I am creating the wrong aspects of patriotism which is defence and attack.
CS word 'Homeland' being typed	3185	FX TYPING
Country stream rushing along – pan R. along it to reveal cottages at its banks	3188 3197	COMMENTARY (CAMERON) So far all is vanity, saith the prophet, all is theory, all is in the intellect and in the head. Somewhere it must be in the gut; somewhere something goes on with a daily meaning, and it isn't to be found among the thinkers or bigots or refugees or perfectionists. Perhaps it was to be found exactly where we began, in an English country village. The taproom of a Dorset pub can be sentimentalised, but it can also be real.
Static shot of country church	3217	
WS old cottages in Cattistock village	3225	
Exterior shot of Greyhound Pub Sydling St Nicholas	3232 3239	
CS sign outside Greyhound pub	3241	CAMERON What is there in the character of the British people that you think is worth preserving? Why is our character worth keeping?
Interior pub: CAMERON L. at bar	3249	

pan R. to JACK WATSON,
publican

WATSON
Well I think because we are what we
are.

CAMERON
That's no answer, Jack.

WATSON
Well I think so. I mean, for instance,
we're going decimal on account of
Europe: why didn't Europe change to
pounds, shillings, and pence?

CAMERON
Well, because there are more of them
than there are of us perhaps.

WATSON
Well it's hard luck on them, isn't it? I
mean, as far as I'm concerned, in all
fairness, with all due respects, without
being bigoted or nasty to anyone, we're
better than them. Why should we have
this man – he's gone now, he's dead,

Group of people in pub   3302

CS JACK WATSON   3307

isn't he, poor bastard – De Gaulle: no,
no, no. What right has that man got to
turn round and say whether we should
have gone into the Common Market or
whether we shouldn't have gone?

CAMERON
Dear Jack, it wasn't . . .

WATSON
After all, we pulled him out of the shit,
didn't we?

CAMERON
It wasn't he who suggested we went
decimal, for God's sake.

WATSON
No, but I mean, this all-embracing
thing, I feel it's all-embracing, decimal,
Common Market, and all that goes with
it.

MS CAMERON leaning on bar   3348

CAMERON
Would you argue that we, alone in the
whole world, should be the people who
are not decimal?

Pan R. to WATSON behind bar	

WATSON
Well we've done it for many, many, many years, I think eight, nine hundred years, haven't we? Shown them how to do it . . . all the rest of them.

Customer in pub	3370

MAN IN PUB
This is the thing, we've taught the rest of the world. This is the thing with the English people – they don't show pride or tell everybody what they've done all the time. But we did: we showed the rest of the world, in fact we educated half of it. We found half and we educated the other half, didn't we? Haven't we got something to be proud of?

WATSON
It's all very well to say it's taken by force of arms. I mean it's just an excuse to say that.

Pan to VIC, customer and local shopkeeper	3405

VIC
But tell me, why does the average Englishman never speak about patriotism and yet we hear so much of it from Wales and Scotland? This is something I just cannot understand.

MAN IN PUB
We don't go shouting our mouth off to everybody that comes along. We're very reserved people.

VIC
Because we're a very, very old establishment.

MAN IN PUB
Of course we are. We don't have to tell anybody, they already know.

TROOPING THE COLOUR (PATHÉ)

Queen on horseback, she salutes	3429
H.A.S. Guards slow marching	3434
CS people watching	3441
Guards trooping the colour	3445

WATSON
All you have to do is to go down to Buckingham Palace and see all the Americans standing there, and they'd give their eye teeth, their back teeth, and all the dollars they've got if they had the backing that we have.

Several V.L.S's trooping the colour	3453	**VIC** But you can't suddenly put on a show like this. This has been built up over years. (CHATTER) **WATSON** That's us. This is us. We are the show.
Queen on horseback saluting	3471	**VIC** I'll agree, but you can't establish a thing
LS trooping the colour	3475	like this overnight.
(PATHÉ FILM OUT)	3481	**CAMERON** What are you trying to prove? I mean,
Interior pub. CAMERON and others	3491	what does it mean? It's very pretty, I agree. **MAN IN PUB** It means we're still here. We're not just going to fall into Europe – not going to be wrapped up in them. We're us and that's it. It doesn't matter what they do. When you see the way they live in other countries – Egypt, India, Africa – it's a joy to come home, isn't it, to a lovely little island like ours. **CAMERON**
CS WATSON	3519	Supposing the Common Market did come about, what would you argue
WS interior bar – CAMERON and Others	3525	would be the things about this country that would be imperative to preserve and to keep. **VOICE** Certainly not the changing of the Guard! **CAMERON** No, of course not! **GIRL** The Royal Family!
CS Girl in pub	3553	**CAMERON** Let's follow that up a moment: you say the Royal Family would be a thing worth preserving, why?

GIRL
It's the apex of the triangle, in my opinion.

CAMERON
Of the triangle? Of which the other bases are what? I mean, what is the rest of the triangle?

GIRL
Well, everyone has their part in, you know, it's the social structure and the monarchy, it's the class system of Britain.

CAMERON
Well where do you feel yourself in this great triangle?

GIRL
Right on the bottom.

CAMERON and Woman in pub   3603

WOMAN
The family of the monarchy are trained from birth to do their job.

CAMERON
Yes, would you tell me what the job is?

WOMAN
Well anybody can be . . . it's the same as the feudal system really. The Lady of the Manor, I know it's old hat, but the Lady of the Manor did a lot of good in her village in her day.

JACK WATSON behind bar   3631

CAMERON
What good did she ever do?

CS Woman   3644

WOMAN
Well she did what the National Health Service does today, perhaps, doesn't she?

CAMERON
I don't know.

WOMAN
She was the forerunner of the Social Security. She was there to be the adviser and in a good sense, there were good and bad of course, but the lady in

a good manor was there to help the
social life of the village, she was
somebody that the village turned to for
help and advice.

CAMERON
In what way does the monarch at the
moment fulfil that function?

QUEEN DISTRIBUTING
MAUNDY MONEY (VISNEWS)
several shots   3711

WOMAN
Well I don't know whether she does in
that sort of way but the stability is the
same, it's gone through.

QUEEN UNVEILING PLAQUE 3723
(B.B.C. LIB.)

QUEEN VISITING HOSPITAL 3730
(B.B.C. LIB.)

And we've got an example of family
life, a mother and father and family all
living together, to all intents and
purposes, happy together, all doing
their own job.

Interior pub – CS Woman   3738

PRINCE OF WALES   3747
INVESTITURE (PATHÉ)
H.A.S. Royal Coach containing
Queen, Duke of Edinburgh,
Princess Anne

CAMERON
Yes but so do you and I, don't we?

WOMAN
Yes I know we do but so many families
don't. Family life is disintegrating in
certain places.

(PATHÉ FILM OUT)   3772
CS woman in pub   3773

CAMERON
Really?

WOMAN
Well yes.

CAMERON
Do you feel that?

WOMAN
Well I feel it, yes I feel it. You can't
help but feel it from the national press,
from television. We don't feel it so
much in the villages.

CS pub sign outside Greyhound 3788
pub

and pan down and L. to reveal 3802
CAMERON walking towards
cam. – track back in front of him

CAMERON
I've been trying to sort all that lot out
on paper and it's certainly not very
easy. It's probably necessary to come to
a village like this with its very special

295

Tracking shot of village from CAMERON's p.o.v.	3848	sort of values to realise what a completely changeless thing the English character is. In a West country community like this patriotism isn't a thing that has to be explained or articulated because all people are reluctant to define what they intuitively comprehend to be right. It's clearly under some sort of a threat here. People talk about the disintegration of the family, not because they personally have any experience of families disintegrating around them, but they're using it as a form of symbolism for the disintegration of the big family, the feudal society of which they approve, and the monarchy which is the apex of the triangle they describe. Well, the
MS CAMERON – track in front of him as he talks to cam.	3886	Common Market, for example, does offer a threat to that concept because it represents a shift from the cosy sort of paternalism to a form of democracy that I'm perfectly sure is foreign to the British character. Now, joining a European federation is a sort of a
Tracking shot of village from CAMERON's p.o.v.	3910	sacrifice in a way. The difference between the Commonwealth and the Common Market is that one we could dominate and the other we can't. In one *we* represented the apex of this triangle: in the other we would simply be a unit and we might be obliged to learn democracy the hard way. In a place like this I think that would be a very big lesson to learn.
MS CAMERON – track in front of him	3951	The lady wished to preserve the monarchy because it represents stability and that is the cardinal word – stability. If it ever came to a choice between stability and progress, I know which would win here.
LAST NIGHT OF PROMS (B.B.C. LIB.)		MUSIC IN: 'Land of Hope and Glory' L.S.O. conducted by Colin Davis
S/I Caption: 'WHY PATRIOTISM?'	4006	
S/I Caption: 'PHOTOGRAPHY PETER CHAPMAN'	4026	

S/I Caption: 4032
'SOUND
GEOFF TOOKEY
RON EDMUNDS'

S/I Caption: 4046
'FILM EDITOR
DAVID MARTIN'

S/I Caption: 4081
'PRODUCED AND
DIRECTED BY:
MICHAEL RABIGER'
B.B.C.tv

FADE VISION   4111   FADE SOUND

B.B.C. T.V.,
3rd April 1971

OBSERVER, 1978

The *Observer* article speaks for itself. I suspect that it was done for advertising-promotion. But I had spent my childhood in Brittany; I knew it before I knew England. I have always been a sucker for nostalgia.

*　　*　　*

BRITTANY REMEMBERED

My father invented Brittany for me. If we had made successes of our lives I might never have known the place. As things were, I started by knowing little else.

As a youngish and fairly penniless barrister my father stumbled on a talent for writing rather fanciful fiction, so he abandoned the Temple for the typewriter and sought his meat from God and the weekly magazines. Reckoning that you could write as well in one place as another he looked for where he could stretch the bread. In those days, just after the First World War, the economic paradox was that a pound went much further in Europe than at home, so off we went to France, where he reckoned that our income would work out at some £9 a week: riches.

As a Scotsman my father argued, reasonably, that the north of anywhere was better than the south, so he settled on Brittany. At least, he insisted, the folk there were Celts and not Latins, so we shall almost be kith and kin. He was to learn better later, but no matter. That was how we came to set up home in St Malo, at least to start with.

To begin with we lived in a succession of furnished rooms – furnished, that is to say, in the French provincial style, which leaves little room between the chair-legs. I must have been about seven or eight years old. My father needed peace to work, so I was chased out most of the day. Thus I came to know our little corner of north Brittany.

I remember St Malo as a city of enormous and over-whelming dimensions, the biggest place on earth. It was, and of course is, a seaport of modest size, on the right bank of the river Rance estuary; it did very little but send its fishermen out every year to the codbanks of Newfoundland. Their departure was the occasion of great ceremony by the Bishop, with blessings from God and everyone very drunk on cider. In those days most Bretons wore the local costume: lovely lace caps for the women and satin doublets for the men. We seemed to live in a permanent *fête folklorique*.

My memory is of the great sixteenth-century ramparts, with towers and gates and the causeway, the *sillon*, which linked the granite island with the mainland. To me, as a schoolboy, it was the centre of the world. I could imagine nothing grander. We rather despised Dinard, the resort across the river, because it got the tourists – neither hard up, as we were, nor picturesquely rich, like the people of Deauville. Dinard is for the bourgeoisie, said my father, himself an archetypal *bourgeois-manqué*. Nevertheless we would occasionally take the ferry over there, for the sake of the ice-cream.

That was long ago. Towards the end of the Second World War the German garrison of St Malo held out and was shelled into ruin by the Allied guns. The English had done it once before, in 1693, without success: the second time they blew it into surrender. We called it 'fruitless obstinacy': had the positions been reversed it would have been 'heroic resistance'. After the war the Bretons put St Malo together again very exactly, but it is not the same, any more than the scrupulous reproduction of obliterated Warsaw is the same. The shape and the stones are the same. but there is something lost.

By and by my father, as usual, grew restless, and we moved down the coast to a place called Paramé. I never heard that Paramé was distinguished for anything whatever. St Malo, after all, had Jacques Cartier and Chateau-briand; Paramé never had anyone but us. Later, I believe, it became popular with English schoolteachers of slender means, for the same reasons that took us there: it was accessible and cheap. It also had miles of flat and empty beaches, and inland elaborate and eerie rock-formations and peculiar megalithic remains and standing-stones. The Bretons were unashamedly pagan, accepting that witches and fairies abounded among these archaic mysteries. They lived on charms and sorcery. This much delighted my father, who approved of any sort of eccentricity, and had a strong Celtic affinity with the preposterous.

Inland there were great desolate tracts of moorland punctuated by these weird devices of what I took to be millions of years ago. It sounds like a morbid ambience but it was not: suddenly a romantic glen would appear lined with primroses, as though to say: 'This is what we can do when we want to.'

I was greatly more attracted to the rock-pools, little aquaria whose population changed every day. In those days we sometimes even found lobsters. I am told that the rapacious Bretons have now fished the lobsters to extinction, or nearly. In my days off from school I could reckon on a fifty-fifty chance of finding one, thrashing around in the unexpectedly shallow water.

First of all we took rooms on the top of a pub called the Café du Centre, of which I can remember little except that the daughter of the house, who must have been about ten, tried to seduce me from time to time. She would break into my room when I was in bed calling musically: 'Voici – Jeanne en chemise!' I never knew what to do about this. Nor, I believe, put to the point, would she have done. So I cowered under the blankets till she went giggling away.

I had a childish habit of walking in my sleep. My father and mother used occasionally to go out for the evening to the rather drab little Casino up the road to spend two or three francs on a calvados. One night I woke up in a panic to find myself there beside them in my nightshirt: I had unconsciously walked the two kilometres in search of them. The management was outraged and my parents disgraced.

Worst of all, however, was when I strayed down to the cellar of the café and opened all the traps on the huge storage barrels of cider before I returned contentedly to bed, leaving the cellar knee-deep in cider and the proprietors aghast with horror. Then we had to go.

We moved then to a terrible little house called the Villa Le Chesnot, of a tasteless ugliness that approached the sublime. My father used to say that he valued the essential purity of its vulgarity. It never bothered me. Anyway, it was from there I had to plod unwillingly to school.

The *externat*, or village elementary, was in the neighbouring parish of St Servan, in the department of Ile-et-Vilaine, an appalling establishment with the amenities and academic standards of Dotheboys Hall. A book could be written about the tribulations of that school. Could be? Has been, and by me. I flinch from repeating myself. It was the total non-education of that school that later drove me, a wholly unqualified bilingual semi-literate, into the only trade capable of absorbing such as me, that of journalism.

What I remember most keenly, is that it involved a four-kilometre walk every morning, to arrive for my penance at seven. That meant starting pretty early, since I had to call at the *boulanger* for my lunch tartine, five inches of bread with a lump of paté, and to pause awhile at a stagnant pond on the way that teemed with newts. I formed a good relationship with the newts, the basis of a lifelong affection for the reptile kingdom – lizards, tortoises, snakes and so on – that to this day I find few people share. Nevertheless for a long time the Breton newts of St Servan were my best friends. They neither offered nor asked for affection, only recognition and the occasional maggot.

On Sundays I was sent to the cinema. This was an important ritual occasion, because it happened only once a week, in a hall in the local village of Rotheneuf. As far as I recall I saw but one film, an interminable serial which in retrospect I, imagine, must have been Pearl White, or a local variant. Every episode ended with the heroine being about to be run over by a train or thrown over a cliff or devoured by a lion, which made it obligatory to return next week to see how she got out of this fix, which, somehow she always did. I paid three *sous* for this brief treat. Do they still charge three sous today?

We had no car – who did? – but sometimes when my father could afford it we took the bus here and there, to Cancale, the archetype of all fishing villages, to the Mont St-Michel, not then as now infested with postcard-vendors and mendicant priests, and even as far as Rennes, which was a big deal because my father knew a restaurant-owner who gave us cut-price *moules-marinières*, an ambrosial memory, on which we could live for several days.

So it went on. Then quite suddenly I had to return from Brittany to Britain, and it all disappeared.

Observer,
31 December 1978

GUARDIAN, 1974–

I had been a loyal reader of the *Guardian* ever since it was made in Manchester and run by C. P. Scott. It always had a nice eccentricity that appealed to me; in those old days it never seemed quite to know what it was up to, which was exactly the same case as myself.

One day long ago the *Guardian* sent the kind and friendly Geoffrey Moorhouse round to interview me, which was intriguing, a couple of old acrobats devising a mutual trick. When we had gone through the ritual and settled for a drink he asked me casually why, after all my trudgings round the newspaper scene, I had never worked for the *Guardian*.

I could think of nothing to say except; 'Well, you know, they never asked me.'

The next day they did. The archangel Linda Christmas, then Features Editor, came round and said: would I do a column for the *Guardian*. Nobody could contradict Linda Christmas, so I said: yes, please.

I have been doing one ever since, and shall continue to do so for as long as I am allowed to do so.

The following pieces have been selected out of hundreds, mainly I imagine to show that their theme is themelessness, that as far as the weekly column is concerned anything goes, so long as it seems to stand up for the twenty-four hours that is the measure of the journalist's immortality. Sometimes there is a hint of a journalistic after-life, as there is here. I am grateful; I hope it is deserved.

* * *

WARD PERFECT

Coming on five-thirty: cocktail hour in T Ward, drinks from the trolley on the house. I'll have the usual, love. It's a little thing of my own – digoxin and water, potassium to taste, and a dash of diuretic to keep the party flowing. After that those of us who can walk do the social calls round the beds of those who can't, or won't.

We are a right grotty lot in T Ward Surgical, with our drips and our slings and our plugs and plumbing, and the better we begin to feel the more troublesome we become. One of our guests, old Bert, has the illusion he is in some sort of ship and keeps climbing up things; he is no fuss except when he has the horrors in the night. It is my opinion that he has them only to cadge another cocktail from the night sister. I used to try it too, but I lack artistic courage and had the horrors pianissimo, which did no good at all.

It cannot be long now before I am in a position to print my handbook-to-hospitals – probably to be known as the Good Ward Guide. For some time now I have been conducting researches into these institutions, the number of which I can scarcely remember but whose qualities I surely do. Not one gastronomic knife-and-fork among the lot, to be sure, but that as it happens is of no consequence to me. There is something a little eccentric, even eerie, about having to be fed through one's *nose*; it would be hard to claim this as a social asset, but at least it abolishes the importance of cuisine.

I must declare interest: I am an almost irrational partisan and defender of the National Health. I feel about the N.H.S. as some people feel about Mozart, or Marx, or Manchester United: that sometimes there may be slip-ups, but basically the theme has angels' wings. I have even another dimension: I doubt if Mozart ever saved anyone's life: the N.H.S. has done that for me twice. I am not an impartial witness in the case of the old N.H.S., which is why my heart bleeds for it now – an unfortunate turn of phrase, doctor; I am not referring to your anti-coagulants.

A curious paradox haunts all our State medical services. The iller you are, of course, the better they work. Only too many rueful people can tell of the exasperating frustrations, the maddening delays and evasions that torment those in the queue who are not ostentatiously at death's door. On the other hand you do not find many customers who have really been steered through the tunnel by the N.H.S. who do not sing hosannahs to it, sometimes immoderately, even sentimentally, and who must now puzzle at the perversity of a Government that is allowing its party's one transcendental achievement to stifle and stumble into a bureaucratic labyrinth, bearing with it some of the most skilled and generous public servants alive.

I have by now gathered a pretty varied set of experiences in the old sawbones trade. (I spent three-score years of a fairly *mouvementé* life without illness or injury: if my share has been concentrated in a recent short space I would argue that is a straight bonus.) And all those of my acquaintance who know, from the high-priest consultants who sitteth on the right hand of God, to the porters who wheel you through the assembly-line, will agree – sadly, bitterly, angrily, patiently – that the whole deal is becoming so strapped and strangled that some aspects and departments are actually facing collapse.

The paradox is that the last person to be made aware of all this is the lucky bastard in the bed. Only a week or two ago a committee of medical gurus reported to the Prime Minister that the N.H.S. needs a swift transfusion of at least £900 millions. For all I know this may be correct and if the figure is true it is not very much. The thing is that the hospital people from top to bottom, unlike most misused and exploited groups of workers, do their damnedest to conceal their difficulties from the customers.

Today for the second time in a year the hospital service is balancing on the edge of an ugly industrial row, only this time the boat is being rocked not from the crews' quarters, where we are, but from the bridge. The barricades are being prepared no longer down here among the nurses and technicians and para-medics (last April's Government survey showed nurses as the lowest-paid skilled workers in Britain) but up at the top of the heap, the professional élite, the consultants, and as everyone now knows the trouble is over the Government's proposal to remove the fee-paying beds from the State hospitals.

This is the most preposterous industrial dispute ever heard of since the Poor Law of 1598 (which, by the way, with an amendment 140 years ago, was the base of all English health services right up to Nye Bevan's N.H.S. twenty-six years ago). It involves a very small section of well-to-do professional men who not only want jam on it, but someone to spread it for them. It is so blatantly self-seeking (or so it seems from T Ward here) that surely it could be supported only by people who approve the consolidation of privilege for its own sake, a social ordinance.

There is no question of 'abolishing private practice', at a stroke or otherwise; only of preventing public facilities being used for private gain. No union as far as I know demands that bus-conductors reserve special seats in the bus for which they charge personal fees. The miners are not encouraged to charge tourists for a trip down the pits. Yet a handful of prosperous medicine-men (and what a tiny minority of the doctors they are, albeit eminent, articulate, and loud) require to earmark little slabs of the N.H.S. facility for their own use, in their own time, and at their own price. You could knock me down with a catheter.

Yet who can these indignant and militant healers be? I never met one yet and I spend a hell of a lot of time among doctors of both renown and otherwise. I may be a rarity among State customers, but I never yet encountered a professional member of the N.H.S. of any grade or degree who was not almost sacrificially loyal to the National Health, or whoever for a moment puts his or her interests before mine. So who can these powerful people be, who have brought about the resignation of Lord Halsbury as chairman of their pay review body because they suspected him of being on our side? Can they all be exclusive to North-east England, as it would seem? Certainly never a one of them has had a go at me, thank God.

From the very start of course they had the toughest of lobbies. Aneurin Bevan could get the N.H.S. off the ground at all only by making profound concessions to the powerful B.M.A. and the royal colleges. He undertook that consultants would not be compelled to join the Service full-time, nor does Barbara Castle insist on it now. Private practice can carry on to its heart's content, though not subsidised by us. About half the nation's consultants, after all, already work full time for the N.H.S., and more do so every year. The idea is naturally to get the lot of them in one day, and this may well come to pass as the job becomes economically more attractive. But nobody is asking the part-timers to pack it in so long as they use their own resources, and give the 4,000-odd private beds in public hospitals back to the people. I would say that is not as onerous a deal as getting your lunch through your nostril.

There is however another nagging aspect of this whole dilemma, one much canvassed among the younger doctors and technicians who are already questioning a lot of assumptions, including their own, and that is that this whole spectacular confrontation is in fact a whacking great red herring, obfuscating the intrinsic confusion of the N.H.S. itself. Inevitably a system of this size and scope was driven, with the best of intentions, into a sort of elephantiasis: bureaucracy breeding compart-mentalisation, over-management, over-specialisation, rules fathering more rules, experts creating needs, a stimulated demand and an inadequate supply, technology chasing its own tail. And so on.

What did we expect? This still is the enduring democratic triumph of the '40s, the monument to Bevan and the envy of the world. I warned you I belong to the fan-club. Last year I was working at an American West Coast college where by a mad chance I met the surgeon who had, believe it or not, invented the plastic piece of ersatz cardiac machinery by which I live. He worked out that my previous year of surgery and aftercare would, in the U.S. have cost not a cent less than $30,000. This is an Alice in Wonderland calculation; the whole business cost me, of course, the price of my stamps. And here we are again. Everybody hanging on a shoestring but me.

The other day our department ran out of some sort of disposable needle – not very expensive, but the allocation had to wait, while the begetters of the N.H.S. mounted some vain and ridiculous naval pantomime in South Africa. I know of a hospital whose cardiac unit is gravely handicapped because the Treasury cannot sanction £11,000 worth of new equipment – probably a twentieth of the cost of sending Dad's Navy to strike fear into the Soviet fleet in the Indian Ocean.

But one does *not* judge the National Health by its aberrations; one does not judge one's surgeon or registrar or houseman by the B.M.A.; one does not judge a hospital by its environment; all of them transcend their institutions. Inescapably your simpleton of a patient judges the whole system by its nearest and most ubiquitous factor: the nurses.

Everyone knows there is something fairly supernatural about the good nature of hospital nurses; the thing is a truism; their industry and their humour, their limitless patience with disagreeable and dirty old men and tiresome and randy young ones, the filthy and sometimes frightening things they have to do for so long and for so little. Once in a blue moon they take their grievances to the press and the public as they did this year, and are glad to be raised to a marginally living wage. I have never in my life seen one take it out on a patient – never, and only a nurse knows what stinkers we patients be.

All regular customers of all hospitals are aware of the risk of going overboard for nurses, simply because they get us at our most vulnerable, and because there is a real need to propitiate them, and nothing propitiates a nurse more than adoration. That, of course, and obedience. There is as a rule no problem in this; it is just not easy to articulate it without mawkishness.

One nurse here, of a nature both kind and bright, quite startled me the other day by telling me that she had never read a newspaper. Not just that she didn't habitually read the papers; she had never in her life, which was twenty-three years long, read the words of any newspaper, anywhere, nor felt any need or curiosity to do so. And reading-time went to getting up exams. If the world blew up she would doubtless get to hear about it somehow. No printed comment or observation of any kind had any interest for her – but absolutely none; this must surely be unique.

I am not yet sure I quite believe this Arcadian story. Yet most critics who want to send up journalism say they ignore it for its falsity, triteness or whatever; this bland lassie neither knew nor cared: she had just never tried to judge. It was peculiarly humbling. When I get out of here I have one or two colleagues in mind to whom I must introduce this paragon girl.

And then at night when the pains arrive along comes what must surely have been Miss Somewhere of 1972 and needles in a little peace. She is doing a forty-five hour week on night duty for which she gets time and a quarter. (If a junior doctor is dragged out at two in the morning he will still have to do his normal shift next day. For his seventy-hour week he will be paid £40.)

So roll on six a.m., when the lights go on and the clatter starts and the day begins. At least for us.

Guardian,
18 November 1974

IT ISN'T ALLAHABAD

I have a very valuable picture – to me only, that is; it is worth about 5p. I suppose, or possibly a bob or two more since it is signed by one of the half-dozen great statesmen of the century – which was taken about twenty years ago in the garden of the Indian Prime Minister's house in New Delhi.

It shows the Prime Minister, Jawaharlal Nehru, with his daughter Indira and her small son Rajiv. The little boy is scratching his ear, his mother is smiling down at him; her father is looking broodingly at the ground, as though at the shadows that were soon to overwhelm him, his country – and now his daughter and inheritor of his enormous office: Mrs Indira Gandhi, that willowy young woman in my picture, Prime Minister now in her father's place, and now convicted of political malpractices and corruption to maintain that place. If it is possible to be shocked and not surprised, that is what I am.

For a Prime Minister to be indicted in a High Court of her own country for offences so grave would surely be a startling thing even if her nation were not, as it is, by far and away the biggest parliamentary democracy on earth. In twenty-eight years of independence nothing has been so damaging. The case against Mrs Gandhi is under appeal, and consequently, I suppose *sub-judice* still in some way, but in any case I did not propose to comment on the Allahabad court processes, which I do not wholly understand and which are not particularly meaningful. This is a time of bitter regret for India, with which I am so involved, and for the Nehru family, who are at least a partial cause of that involvement.

Mrs Indira Gandhi has been convicted on three charges of corrupt malpractices in connection with the elections in Uttar Pradesh four years ago. If these are upheld on appeal she must cease to be Prime Minister and will be debarred from holding public office for six years, which effectively means that she will be disgraced forever. In the meantime she proposes to stay in office, which suggests either a lot of courage or a lot of brass neck. It will be a very tense few months in the Indian Parliament, I should imagine. I am glad this is not going to be one of my Indian Summers. (And what a punctuation-mark for International Women's Year.).

A day or two ago I was asked by Thames television to discuss this matter with a charming Oxford student called Zareer Masani, who had the consummate bad luck to publish his biography of Mrs Gandhi on the very day of this catastrophe. It turned out to be a derisory two or three minutes, to accommodate an item about child motor-cyclists. It seemed an indifferent way to mark the twilight of the most important woman politician in the world, but again not surprising.

It would be an impertinence to claim to know Mrs Gandhi, but her father was I think incomparably the greatest man I ever met, and the Nehru family showed me much kindness and consideration in the days of their eminence. Pandit Nehru was a big influence in my life. The legend had already faded before last week's debacle to his daughter, and the last days of Nehru's rule were clouded with equivocations and futilities, but I remember the days during and after the torment of Independence when he was very kind to me. He was the most complex of men, afflicted as one could see even then with the strangely incompatible attributes of compassion and vanity, of which his daughter and successor inherited only one.

I recall the young Indira Gandhi of those days, her father's châtelaine and protector, herself compensating for a lost marriage by watchfully guarding her father's brief moments of privacy and rest. My old photograph in the Prime Minister's garden tells a lot about the Nehru dynasty. The fact that it became a dynasty is in itself a sad thing; Republican dynasties are to me intrinsically wrong whether they be Kennedys or Nehrus.

It was inescapable that this one should be undermined by the banal issue of corruption. Indian corruption is almost as leaden a cliché as Indian poverty. There is no way of assessing its extent. I can say this without contempt or patronage, since my own family roots are now shared equally between our countries.

I once wrote: 'In India corruption, public or private venality, is sanctified by the oldest of traditions; it is denied by nobody; indeed the totality and pervasiveness of Indian corruption is almost a matter of national pride: just as India's droughts are the driest, her famines the most cruel, the over-population the most uncontrollable, so are all aspects of India's corruption and bribery the most wholly widespread and spectacular.'

Many Indians resented this. 'It is unfair and unkind,' they said, 'to challenge us with what cannot be denied.'

Mrs Indira Gandhi, Prime Minister of 500 million people, has now been formally convicted of what is acceptably a way of life, of doing in high office what everybody does in low office. This is in no sense to excuse it – nor will it for a minute be excused by her enemies, who are legion, and who have prospered by malpractices infinitely worse than hers, but who endlessly denounce 'that woman' because she professes Socialist principles, and who have now caught her flat-footed in exactly the sort of fiddle that has always been their own way of life. It is as though a head of government should go to the block for a parking-ticket.

Throughout its entire twenty-eight years of independence India has been governed by one party, the Congress Party. It is now fragmented, but *plus ça change*, and so on. Congress has been sustained by corruption forever, by the black money from the wealthy business houses, who as quid pro quo have been tacitly allowed to run their own parallel economy for their personal enrichment, and the growing impoverishment of the people. This was the case even in Pandit Nehru's day; it was no secret that this honest man in his final weariness was well aware of the sycophancy and corruption that surrounded him, and remained silent while it flourished, because he was too vain to acknowledge it and too weak to fight it.

For years it has been a life-style, the acceptance that every official can be bribed, every commodity can be adulterated, every scarcity exploited, every privilege bought. The true irony is that the Prime Minister, Mrs Gandhi, has now been caught on a procedural point of order that is routine a dozen times a day to her detractors.

Mrs Gandhi is convicted of using the machinery of government to win her election in Raj Bareli in 1971. Every incumbent head of Government in every country uses that advantage. Mrs Gandhi was clumsy enough to let her opponent get a toe in the door, which was either excessively foolish of her or uncommonly smart of her opponent. It is interesting that he was not a representative of the moneybags groups, or of the extreme right-wing Hindu set, but allegedly a Socialist. This is where Mrs Gandhi now finds herself, in a quasi-Wilson situation, denounced by those she claims, with diminishing conviction, to represent.

The tragedy of the Nehrus has been on an almost classic pattern: they proclaimed and believed in the principles of social democracy and sustained and promoted their party through the nastiest aspects of unbridled and dishonest capitalism. Pandit Nehru was a sincere and skilful demagogue, too intelligent not to know of the crookery around him but too sensitive, or too vain, to admit it, and too busy or too weak to challenge it. His daughter, born and bred in the devious Congress tradition, doubtless believes in what her father believed, but she is too harsh and abrasive a personality to exercise charm, and arrogant enough to think that power was a permanent substitute for skill.

This is a strange misjudgment, in a woman who in her own person is both charming and skilful. For a politician with these attributes it was a stunning folly, for example, to provide her young son Sanjay with an official licence to build India's only mini-car – at such a time, when India cries for foodgrains not mini-cars. Or, for that matter, to indulge in the lunatic extravagance of a nuclear explosion in Rajasthan – a gesture that would have made her father flinch with horror.

This Allahabad court-case was no surprise to any literate Indian; it had after all been on the cards for four years. Yet let it be said for India that it did take place; it is doubtful whether any other Asian country would have thus arraigned its Prime Minister so publicly and humiliatingly. This is a very considerable plus for a country so haunted with minuses.

It is improbable that Mrs Gandhi will resign; the appeal may not be heard for a long time, almost certainly not before another general election. She is still very strong, and still carries immense resources of patronage. The Indian people are volatile and emotional, but they are not like the Irish: they have a limitless capacity for forgetfulness. Mrs Indira Gandhi will survive, a tarnished but durable decoration on a sad and eternal civilisation.

Guardian,
16 June 1975

OILY WATERS

Not everyone likes the Shah of Iran as much as does Mr James Callaghan. Or for that matter our Ambassador in Tehran, Sir Anthony Parsons, who has just dutifully echoed Mr Callaghan's enthusiastic support for the Shah's methods of dealing with his dissidents, which would seem to be by shooting them dead in public thoroughfares when they have the impertinence to demonstrate against what they, doubtless mistakenly, hold to be an oppressive and tyrannical regime.

After all, it is argued, they were at least allowed to demonstrate before they were shot. That mistake will presumably be corrected now that twelve Iranian cities are under martial law.

'My Government,' said the Ambassador (meaning of course your Government, and my Government), 'has been heartened by the determination which you have shown to maintain the stability and security of Iran along the lines of your present Monarchy. We wish your Government well in their tasks.'

It somehow seemed a fairly gratuitous piece of bootlicking from a diplomat who was supposed simply to be opening the British Pavilion at the Tehran Trade Fair. However, since Britain's trade with Iran is now worth around £2,000 millions, a little fawning is doubtless in order. One does not become an Ambassador by saying what one thinks. On the other hand for all I know His Excellency was saying what he thinks. You never can tell.

What I still like to call Persia but the Persians like, or are obliged, to call Kesh-var-e-Shahanshahi-ye-Iran, when they can spare the time, is still not especially familiar ground to those of us who are not in the business of oil or armaments. The general image is that of a very big sandy place with a landscape punctuated by petroleum installations, ruled by a vastly well-to-do despot of theatrically handsome demeanour with a penchant for elegant uniforms and the marrying, and subsequently divorcing, of a succession of very attractive wives.

Having visited the country from time to time I would say that is a not wholly inaccurate definition. There is, to be sure, a population of some twenty-odd million Iranians, but nobody hears much about them until they get shot, except for the occasional one who comes over here and puts in a bid for Buckingham Palace, or some such. Verily a nation of extremes.

It is natural that almost the sole symbol of this great nation to us should be its head man, the Shah, or more properly the Shananshah, HIM Mohammed Reza Pahlevi, since nobody else ever seems to get a look in. Those who have met him – as, for example, his strong disciple Lord Chalfont – describe him as a man of marked intelligence, and well intentioned. A benevolent despot is I believe the phrase, though it would seem that the benevolence has not been strikingly apparent of late.

The British, being themselves a kingdom, or perhaps a queendom, have this curious attachment to monarchy in all its manifestations, feeling that it represents some otherwise indefinable age-long continuity.

This attribute is also fostered by the Shah. A year or two back he threw a vast and lavish celebration to mark what, as far as I can remember, was presented as a thousand years of royal rule. This was a con-job of mammoth proportions, the implication being that the Shah was the current incarnation of a long, long line. This, of course, was total illusion. The dynasty of His Imperial Majesty is exactly fourteen years younger than I am.

In October 1925 the last of the ruling Qajar dynasty, Sultan Ahmed, was deposed after a rebellion led by one Reza Khan, a soldier in the Cossack Regiment. He had himself made first Prime Minister, then Shah – Reza Shah Pahlevi. He was the first of his line. He was the father of the present chap.

When the Second World War came about he made the serious miscalculation of going along with the Axis side. Then, when the Germans invaded the U.S.S.R. in 1941, Anglo-Soviet forces moved into Persia and booted him out. His successor, the present incumbent, ascended the throne, and very prudently switched sides.

The war ended, but the fuss did not. In 1951 the Persian Majlis, or Parliament, ordained the nationalisation of the oil industry, which largely consisted of what is now B.P., Purveyors in Ordinary to the Rhodesians. One Dr Musaddiq became Prime Minister (who remembers Musaddiq, the Weeping Warrior?) and another frightful row broke out, during which this new Shah, too, discreetly left the country. After the smoke died down he returned, and there he is. So much for the age-long lineage.

As I said, not everyone seems to share our Mr Callaghan's appreciation of the firm smack of Persian Government. The number of dead demonstrators is witness to that. And not only them: all over London Tube Stations are graffiti which say, to those who can read Persian: Down with the Shah. It seems an unlikely region for propaganda of that specialised kind. Yet all over the Paris Metro the same slogan appears. It is to be seen, in its incomprehensible bitterness, in Hamburg and Amsterdam and Rome. Not long ago I was in Bangalore in South India, and there it is again.

It is clear that there is some international orchestration of overseas Persians who do not like the Shah, and who presumably are overseas for that reason. What purpose these slogans fulfil I do not know. What can the Tube passengers on the Central Line or the buses of Bangalore do about the Shah? I suppose they could refuse to use public transport that is ultimately dependent on oil. They could refuse to buy any more petrol, or use any more plastics. It would suit me. I must say, but I don't see it catching on.

The security forces in Iran open fire on civilians in the street. The British Government is 'heartened by their determination'. I suppose it is understandable. Oil must be much on Mr Callaghan's mind just now.

DR NORMAN STANDS ACCUSED. . .

Dr Edward Norman, Dean of Peterhouse and God's oracle on the B.B.C., is most obviously a devout and presumably sincere believer, and his marathon Reith Lectures on the radio have left me with the vivid impression that in Mr Norman's view Jesus was evidently no Christian.

This is a troubling paradox from a gifted and articulate scholar, a young academic rooted in reaction. His argument (perhaps rather arbitrarily synthesised) is that the churches are wholly wrong in associating themselves with matters of social consequence and secular concern, that contemporary Christianity is horning in on worldly considerations better left to the politicians. This, Dr Norman implies, would not have happened in Christ's time.

To me this goes absolutely counter to history – or what passes for history in the very subjective reportages of the time. I think J.C. should have the right to reply.

Christ preached a heavenly destiny, true, but he did simultaneously concern himself deeply with man's sufferings and inequalities on earth; he was a social reformer; he fervently engaged himself in the Palestian politics of his time and therefore fell foul of the Establishment, both Roman and Sanhedrin, and was punished by death on the cross. If the confrontation of Jesus and Pilate was not political then I do not understand the word.

According to the gospel of Dr Norman – as I read him – Jesus Christ identified himself with the values of his mortal world and thereby betrayed his mission, as does his Church today.

Nobody has ever accused me of being a theologian, so the only charge I can bring against Dr Norman is of being a perilous pedant. Dr Norman is a religious man and I am not: it is therefore an impertinence for me to challenge him on his own ground. Nevertheless in any imperfect eye Dr Norman stands accused of black heresy, and the B.B.C. for providing a forum for didactic revisionism that would have made even the late Sir John Reith flinch.

This newspaper had a guarded editorial criticism the other day of Dr Norman's theme, that the Christian Church is in error in concerning itself with current affairs. In my opinion it was too guarded, as is necessary in *ex cathedra* pronouncements. Dr Norman's argument should not have been criticised; it should have been denounced.

Consider some of Dr Norman's theses in his final broadcast. 'The instinct which once prompted holy warfare, rather than diplomatic accommodation, is now rampant in a secularised form; it is let loose in crusades for human rights, or to extinguish what is judged to be racism or economic exploitation.' Implicitly that is *wrong*.

The Dean of Peterhouse implicitly condemns a Christian crusade for human rights and majority rule and against 'what is judged to be racism'. He objects to the modern Church's 'need for theology to be rooted in the day-to-day struggle of people to overcome the conditions that sentence them to poverty and oppression.'

In the name of Dr Norman's God, what the hell is wrong with that?

'Now there may be sound enough reasons for men to act in the hope of preventing the sufferings and lessening the injustices of human society. *But* . . .' Listen to that awful but, I will bet that Jesus Christ wouldn't have put in that smug self-satisfied 'but'. 'There are no sound reasons for identifying the accompanying politics as themselves true.'

What is this prig talking about? If sufferings and injustices are to be remedied how is that to be done other than politically? Will the new Jerusalem emerge from a pulpit in Peterhouse?

'Christ's teaching calls on the loyalty of men with a unique authority, originating outside historical circumstances, upon its deliberate evocation of timelessness. That should make us cautious of identifying the ultimate Purpose with the shifting values of society.'

If one can penetrate the pretentious opacity of the prose, one takes this to mean that Christians should not bother about the life today, only the life hereafter. Was this why Jesus had his hands nailed onto a piece of wood?

'There may be sound enough reasons for men to act in the hope of preventing the sufferings and lessening the injustices of human society.' Listen to the pious conceit of the man: there *may* be sound enough reasons. Presumably, according to this man's logic, there equally may not. There *may* be sound enough reasons for men to promote and encourage suffering and injustice; indeed we know that only too often they are. Dr Norman would judiciously evaluate these alternatives in the light of – of what?

I was happy to see that Val Arnold-Forster in her radio column in this paper had a bit of a go at this man too. She was writing about a prize-winning programme from Radio Forth, 'The Lanthorn', about an interdenominational centre in Livingstone used by a variety of congregations as a church, recreation hall, canteen, social circle – all the mundane purposes the Reith Lecturer condemned.

'Unlike Dr Norman, many of the Christians expressed themselves in the woolliest of sociological clichés. But, unlike Dr Norman, they sounded kindly, optimistic, and above all, humble.'

Might almost verge on the political too, if politics is, as I suspect, about people.

Guardian,
11 December 1978

EMPIRE GAINS

Days of dilemma. Days of brine and posies. The other day the Prime Minister was good enough, or rash enough, or absent-minded enough, to give me a C.B.E., and I was impulsive enough, or vain enough, to take it.

It caused much honourable dispute among my family, and mirth among my friends. I was told that by taking an Establishment gong, however mysterious its meaning, I had joined the Establishment and supinely surrendered all values of importance. This may well seem so, but it was not intended to be so. In any case they say, what say they, let them say.

I must admit that at the outset the situation seemed to have a most attractive irony. To be made a C.B.E., of all things – that is to say a Commander, no less, of an institution I had spent years of my time trying to diminish, or even abolish – seemed to me to argue an official whimsicality that I had never associated with our mirthless administration. I took it in that sense, assuming rather hastily that this inference, of a somewhat far-out joke, would be generally understood. Sometimes it was, sometimes it wasn't.

I was of course flattered. In all the years of my life I have received no official recognition for anything I have done (reasonably enough, since I did little enough for them) nor expected it, nor required it, nor asked for it, nor even wanted it. When it came, in my sixty-eighth year, it came in a form – a C.B.E. – so comically preposterous that I thought nobody could possibly take it seriously. Many did – with generosity, with reproach, with hilarity.

I was urged by my nearest and dearest to turn the thing down. It seemed to me that to do so would be a gesture of extraordinarily petty arrogance, inflating the obviously routine affair ('Well – anyone else would you say, P.M.?') to a piece of ludicrous pomposity. Downing

Street had offered it in goodwill, for reasons I know not; I am not big enough nor important enough to be convincingly churlish about something done with good intent. I am not even a Beatle.

It has always seemed to me that the Honours List is one of the dottier and more harmless eccentricities of our undefined Constitution. Former paid-up members of the Communist Party accept peerages without batting an eye. Happily married old gents become Knights Bachelor. Lifelong anti-colonialists become Members of the British Empire. Charming and gifted girls become Dames (that which we know there is nothing like). Middle-aged servants of the Royal households, join the Victorian Order, whatever that means.

I cannot imagine that my flinching from his nice C.B.E., would have brought a tear to the eye of Mr Callaghan or sent him sulking to his tent. The list of people in this order of the civil list took nearly forty-eight column-inches of microscopic type, squeezed into the page as tightly as the stonehand could ram it. I can't be bothered to count us but there must be hundreds and hundreds. Let me rationalise it once again; I am clearly part of a mass movement. C.B.E.s of the world unite; you have nothing to lose but your – what?

Clearly it won't get you tickets for Wimbledon, nor bows from head-waiters, nor free homes in tax-havens. It carries no title, thank God, and unthank God, no dough. What, no silk knee-breeches? No funny hat? Not even a little rosette for the buttonhole?

The State, which denies me the pension I have paid up for years because I obstinately insist on continuing to work for my living, now permits me to Command the British Empire. It is interesting, and nicely pointed, that it waited until I was entitled to command something that vanished years ago. Qui s'excuse, s'accuse. Woe unto them that draw iniquity with cords of vanity. (Solomon, that old prig.)

However, you may henceforth Call Me Madam.

One thing to start 1979. A few readers reprimanded me for my criticism of the Reith Lectures of Dr Norman, who argued that Christianity was not concerned with human affairs. Many times more wrote to console me, and kindly. I wish I could reply personally to them all but I simply can't. Let me please thank them here. And of course, love and peace for the year that is come.

Guardian,
8 January 1979

AFGHAN ROULETTE

Deplorable and arrogant and dangerous as the Russian invasion of Afghanistan is, let us not forget that it has all been done before. We tried it first. That is, after Alexander the Great, but that was long ago. The first major invasion of Afghanistan happened in 1839, and it was done by the British, who showed more or less exactly the same emotional anxiety of the Russian Bear as everyone is, understandably, showing now.

We went into Afghanistan to topple its ruler, Dost Mohammed, and replace him by a more amenable puppet called (as though it mattered now) Shah Shaja, following exactly the same pattern as Mr Brezhnev is using now, to swap an Amin for a Karmal and get in before the others do.

The difference is that the British forces were resoundingly defeated, leaving but one survivor to footslog it all the way home. However, in 1878 they had another go at Kabul, again with much the same excuse as Mr Brezhnev is using now: the alarming encroachment of the other Imperialist Power on the Afghan border.

Afghanistan had to be a 'buffer state' whether she liked it or not. It never was much fun being an Afghan in those days, for just the same reasons as now. The Tsar Alexander II was as big an expansionist as Queen Victoria, and Afghanistan was forever the nut between the crackers, as of course it is to this day.

The Afghans were in a fix. They are an excessively proud and independent people, but they were sandwiched, and needed protection from someone. They first tried the British, who snubbed them, so they turned to Russia, though all these eccentric folk wanted was to have their wild and savage country to themselves.

Not so, however: after the Second Afghan War came the British occupation of Kabul, Kandahar, and the Kurram valley, and the British control of Afghan affairs for an annual subsidy of £160,000 – the price of an English country house today.

I mention all this tedious history merely to suggest that Mrs Thatcher's indignant reaction to the admittedly crude and brutal Russian provocation is a bit of humbug, as is President Carter's. Our Lord Carrington protests that 'this is the first time that Soviet troops have been used outside Europe.' True. And how often have British troops been used outside Europe – in Africa, China, South East Asia, even America?

Has President Carter *already* forgotten Vietnam? And Cambodia? Have we forgotten Suez? Or, for that matter, Afghanistan?

My own simple view, of one who hasn't been to Afghanistan for years, and who didn't like it much even then, is that this is a conflict of hypocrisies. Or rather, perhaps, of twin naïvetés. Not the *geopolitik* of the thing, just the moral outrage. Increasingly I feel, as the Powers square up to each other in a childish and perilous confrontation that inevitably threatens us all, that one's life is dominated by two terribly strong infants, obsessed with a machismo that would be ridiculous if it were not so horribly dangerous.

And now Mr Harold Brown, U.S. Defence Secreary, is in Peking. It is suggested that 'this is the time to play the China card'. I do not know exactly what that means, but the implications are chilling. Anyone who 'plays the China card' at a moment like this risks taking the step before the last.

No war has ever been 'justified', but once upon a time they were thought to have some sort of moral purpose, like the Crusades, however far-fetched or fanatical. This coming one, if it comes, will be for sheer naked undisguised gain, which is the moral philosophy of our time.

The Soviets want access to the warm-water ports, which means edging ever southwards, and which will inevitably involve Iran.

The U.S. feels that Iran needs but one involvement at a time, namely hers. Britain, scampering eagerly at her heels, proclaims a sort of powerless devotion, and sends Lord Carrington off to Turkey and Pakistan on a wholly enigmatic errand.

America proposes to cut her grain exports to Russia, from which several million Communist cattle will mainly suffer. We threaten darkly to boycott the Olympic Games. A pettifogging gesture indeed, but if all international crises could be resolved by eliminating the world's most numbing public event then it would be only too welcome. But the Olympics won't save Afghanistan, because they can't, and everyone knows they can't.

Somebody wrote to the papers urging that Afghanistan must remain a buffer state 'as Nature intended her to be'. Nature had nothing to do with it, but never mind. It could be said that destiny ordained President Carter to be a buffer man, poor soul. Yet, if the situation has proved anything it is that Brezhnev can be as clumsy and cruel as Carter can be clumsy and well-intentioned. The Soviet Union has done itself the worst P.R. job since Hungary, and it will not be forgiven any more readily than will the Americans for Cambodia.

Everyone must denounce the cynical and in the end stupid Russian action in Afghanistan. Let us make our disapproval clear, even though we are disappointed parties in the power game. We are all in this for the ultimate lolly, as we always have been.

But for any sake let us not adopt this high moral attitude of being concerned for the integrity of a single non-aligned country, that we are defending the principles of the U.N., when we are in fact concerned solely (a) with pride, (b) with oil, (c) with Presidential politics, (d) with the imminent succession in Moscow, and somewhere (down in x, y, and z) the future of Afghanistan.

Guardian,
8 January 1980

I COULD DO NO LESS THAN GO ON STRIKE. . . BUT WHOM TO GO ON STRIKE AGAINST?

I awoke with a sudden spontaneous sensation of solidarity with the strikers, wherever they may be. I cannot account for this except that possibly remorse had come for some critical and even harsh words spoken the previous night. I felt a need immediately to express an identity of purpose with the gallant lads who are showing the flag, or perhaps the poster, outside works entrances in their hour of need and getting shoved around something rotten by the coppers outside the gates and the wives when they get home.

I decided that I could do no less than go on strike too.

I signalled this by not turning up for work that morning. This was somewhat complicated, since as soon as I get up I am already in a manner of speaking at work, because my shop floor, which in the trade we call 'desk', is just the breadth of a wastepaper-basket from my bed. Perhaps I should get the Factory Inspectors to look into this.

It was clearly necessary to distance myself from this symbol of slavery, so I went downstairs to consult my shop steward, who happens for the time being to be me, as to the proper course of action that would express our sympathy for the brave boys of the British Steel Corporation and the like.

The first problem was whom I was to go on strike against. I have no employer, except as the officials define it: myself. In one way that made it easier, in another more difficult. On the other hand, I would find no especial hostility or aggro from my employer; on the other hand, the gesture would have little meaning anywhere else since the refusal of a self-employed scribbler to work at the bench has few of the qualities of drama that inspire headlines.

I could, it is true, take up a position outside my factory door, with or without inflammatory placard, but since my factory door is that of my own house it would be assumed, by anyone who noticed, that I had merely lost my key and was waiting for my wife to return and let me in. It was most improbable that I would be joined by a surging crowd of fellow-evangelists sufficient to attract the riot squad, for although my neighbourhood abounds with self-employed geniuses they were unlikely to share my burning need to stop earning the odd bob and join the Movement.

I could of course constitute myself a legal picket since, as we all know, a trade unionist, which I am, has legal immunity when acting in furtherance of a trade dispute, and though the Employment Bill limits the right to picket to the work-place of the individual picket I was well within that limit since the premises in question were not only my work-place but my bedplace and my hearth and home, and in my new-found fervour I considered I had a proper right to question the legality of any old stray freelance to come in and type away at my bench and take the bread-and-dripping from my mouth.

The Tories' consultative document put out last week sets down that industrial action is lawful against the employer with whom the employee is in dispute or his 'first customers', whatever that means. The 'first customer' in my case being the *Guardian* newspaper, should I therefore move my protest line to Farringdon Road? But I am not in dispute with the *Guardian* newspaper; very far from it. I could not see how my solidarity with the plucky boys of the Bill Sirs gospel would be advantaged by my picketing the hand that feeds me, especially as it is such a long way away.

I was therefore left with one expedient: to picket myself. It could be argued that I, an employee, am technically in dispute with my employer, both of them being myself. But that is nothing new; I have been in dispute with myself since I was about six, for reasons quite unconnected with industrial confrontation, and I had never considered it a national issue. Nor, as the morning wore on and my shop steward grew restless, did I see it so now.

Nevertheless it was still imperative to stand up, as they say, and be counted. At the very best the count would be one. Would the indomitable steel men shower me with bouquets, or rivets, or whatever they use as an accolade? Doubts intruded. I have never liked the word 'workforce'. 'Workers' are plural, and have a meaning; 'workforce' is singular, and has not. Except in my case: I am a one-man workforce. Or at least from time to time.

By now it was evident that my personal industrial action could very soon bring my employer to his knees, as though the poor devil were not almost there anyhow. How this would advantage his alter ego, his employee, was what exercised me, during my soul-searching over the dauntless legions of Corby or Sheerness or whatever. My loyalties, always divided, began to disintegrate. What about the employer/employee's starving wives and families, doomed hereafter to sell their bodies on Hampstead Heath for what in the circumstances can only be called a pot of message?

Were this personal strike of mine to be a bid for increased income rather than a noble gesture both my employer and I would consider settling for a rise of around some 190 per cent, give or take a few quid for teabreaks. The trouble is, our wages are ineluctably bound to piecework, as indeed are those of our learned leaders, John le Carré, and Len Deighton, and the Blessed Barbara Cartland.

We called a committee meeting. The two of us returned, defeated. Employer and employee collaborated on this little column. Heroism is not always in vain.

Guardian,
26 February 1980

THE EDGE OF REASON

The theory of relativity has never been my especially strong point, if I have such a thing, which increasingly I doubt. My friend and fellow-toiler in the newsprint vineyard, Mr Bernard Levin, quoted me the other day (in *The Times* newspaper; how grand) as saying, or rather screaming, after some imbecile aeroplane ride across the Pacific, that I had been travelling for days and all I had been given to eat was five breakfasts.

Mr Levin said but the truth, as is his wont, and his concern was something that has troubled me for years. It is a consolation that my learned leader shares with me an ignorance of natural laws that everyone else takes for granted. Why is the time different in other parts of the world? Why if I travel to Asia must I always arrive at dawn when I know that it is in reality only dinner-time?

If I travel to New York why must I be obliged to be taken out to lunch again, which I have already had hours before? How, when I go by Concorde (that is to say *if*, since I have never been able to afford it) does it come about that I actually arrive an hour before I left?

I am sure there must be acceptable reasons for this folly, but I have had neither the wit nor the time to work them out, any more than I can understand why Australians should celebrate Christmas in midsummer other than because they are a perverse people who will go to any length to spite the Poms. Hanging for ever upside-down may have something to do with it.

What inspired Mr Levin to his lucubrations on the space-time continuum was the International Date Line. This is a thing – or a concept, or a theory – of which I have disapproved ever since I first heard of it, which is many years ago. If you are fool enough to go all the way round the world you find yourself, if you are travelling one way, with a week with two Thursdays. Going the other way you are stuck with a week with no Thursday at all.

Nobody, as far as I know, can remember which way is what, nor is it of the slightest importance except to those who live in Samoa or the so-called Friendly Islands, who are so close to the International Date Line that they have probably long ago abandoned days of the week altogether.

This preposterous International Date Line once had a certain significance for me, because I once accidentally crossed it on my birthday. This meant that it vanished; the day was eliminated from the calendar. I reflected somewhat on this phenomenon. If I could arrange to do the same thing every year, would I never grow any older? It seemed logical. I would have discussed the matter with Dr Albert Einstein, had he not been dead.

Are those people immortal who live exactly on this arbitrary division between today and tomorrow? (They must be extremely few, because this famous Date Line is drawn to wiggle through the Pacific, avoiding almost all inhabited places.) All one knows when crossing this strange frontier in an aeroplane is that the captain sends one a glass of champagne, which seems a curious way of celebrating the mysteries of time.

I have been told that physicists argue that anyone who spent a century in an outer-space vehicle would return to earth to find everything in the world that much older, while he himself had remained exactly the same age as when he had left. I have never been to outer space, so my mortal experience has always seemed the precise reverse.

We are verging on the metaphysical, which must be checked. Part of the source of our dilemma, my friend's and mine, is having been so long conditioned in the conventional mythology that the world is a sphere. It is of course, as everyone of experience knows, nothing of the kind: it is a disc. (Not to be confused with a disco, though that is unhappily possible.)

The world or, to be more pedantic, the Earth, is of the nature of a very large circular bit of matter, analogous to a huge coin.

Many people have argued in denial of the flat-earth theory, but I remain unmoved. They show me a satellite picture of the Earth, and they show a sphere only inferentially; in fact they represent a disc. They insist that people like Francis Drake and Pan-Am pilots have gone *round* the world, to which I can only reply that they have gone round the edge of it, and the reason they have not slipped off the edge is that they have taken very good care not to do so.

They cite the phenomenon of ships vanishing over the ocean's horizon, concealed by the earth's curvature. To this again I can but reply: how many hundreds of cases are on record of ships vanishing over the horizon, never to be seen again? They demand why, if the earth is flat, does the sun daily rise in the east and set in the west? Answer: because that is what it does: what the sun does with itself between dusk and dawn is its own business.

Then why, they cry, is there eight hours' difference between the time in England and that of Hongkong? This, I say, is where we came in, and the answer is: because you make it so. My daughter who lives in Hongkong rings me up and says it's a lovely evening, while I know perfectly well it is a rather disagreeable morning. She too has been conditioned by the spherical illusion.

The fact is we live on a great flat thing that goes round and round like somebody spinning a tenpenny piece, and if every so often it spins a few hundred Australians off the edge into limbo, who will miss them?

This is still no explanation of why at roughly 180 degrees of longitude, give or take a few aberrations, Wednesday should turn into Thursday, and vice versa. You may take it or leave it, but don't, I pray, blame me. And don't go too near the edge.

Guardian,
1 April 1980

HEAVEN RAISER

Until a few days ago I had an uncommonly good friend, just about a quarter my age. He was called Nicky, and we got on remarkably well, considering he was only sixteen when he died last week, and I am a bit older.

Whenever we met, we argued on wholly equal terms about the affairs of the world, about which he cared at his age perhaps more than I do at mine. The world for Nicky was something that needed to be put right, as soon as he got the hang of how.

I mention this just because these days it is the done thing to shoot down the teenagers for their selfish and careless frivolity. Maybe I have done that myself in my time; I shall no longer.

Several years ago they diagnosed a cerebral condition that was terminal, or so they said. Nicky would have none of that stuff. He not only survived but also vanquished it. You would have thought he almost scorned it, because from then on he engaged himself most cheerfully in learning and reading and studying the antics of the society he was to inhabit for such a short time. Proper young junior wrangler was Nicky.

All the things our lot, the journalists, wrote about as though everything were to be measured in column inches – as everything is – he took seriously, or at least carefully. Even as a small vivacious boy, he took politics to heart. That is unfair: not politics; he just in his merry way felt part of the human condition, which contains much to enjoy, but also a hell of a lot to question.

When there was time from his schoolwork, or indeed his games, he got down to considerations like confrontation, refugees, nationalism, deprivation, injustices – all the things we think teenagers reject. Probably most do.

He sometimes exasperated his thoughtless grown-ups by talking far too much about things of which children are not supposed to care – like apartheid and racism and disarmament. He argued even then that if he, young Nicky, did not care, nobody else would.

Nobody listened enough, except sometimes I did. As far as I was able, I egged him on. That was how I got to know him then, and why I sorrow for him now.

As a schoolboy he was sufficiently curious about something – I have forgotten what – to write to the President of the United States requesting some sort of explanation of whatever it was. The President was discourteous enough not to reply, but it was hard to discourage Nicky. He wrote, at intervals to Mrs Thatcher, to Secretaries of State. He wrote to Field Marshal Auchinleck, who was and is a family friend, albeit just eight decades older.

Some came off and some didn't; the determined young inquisitor realised that you can't win them all. So he would sit down and write some more.

'What do you think,' said Nicky to me quite recently, 'can anyone ever change anything?'

I said: 'I've been trying for a damn long time, and I never brought anything off, but you may.'

'Why?' said he. 'Because I'm younger?'

'Yes. And I dare say brighter. Anyone's brighter than me.'

'Not anyone,' said Nicky. 'Probably quite a few.'

In retrospect I think his parents know that he felt he had so much to say because he had so little time in which to say it. We may be thinking in hindsight, but I do not believe Nicky thought that way. Strange that a sixteen-year-old should leave concerned not about his future but about ours.

He brought more verve and care into his sixteen years than most of us do in thrice that time. I shall never again sell teenagers short, anyhow.

This little boy – as I first knew him, and young man as he came to be – was full of zest and love of life, and he enjoyed the things kids enjoy, and he wrote to Washington because he had something to say to the President of the United States.

Sometimes he telephoned me to ask what on earth I meant by something I had written, and really wanted to know. Unless you are in this crazy business, you cannot imagine what sort of reward that is.

That is why I am writing this total irrelevancy today, forgetful of a hundred things of greater importance, because one vigorous and questioning life has been untimely quenched, and no one will ever know why.

Now you are in heaven, Nicky, give 'em hell.

Save a place for me.

Guardian,
29 July 1980

BERTIE'S BOOSTER

Now that most of the clotted cream and treacle has dripped off the eulogies to the Queen Mother for her eightieth birthday, I feel able to at last reveal the story of my brief association with the gracious lady many years ago. The indiscretion is unlikely to figure greatly in the official royal biographies, so it might as well figure momentarily in mine.

At the time the lady was on the throne, and I was in Sussex. Very late at night, I got a phone call from the foreign desk of a newspaper, which was not the *Guardian*. It was to this effect: would I go to India, and there was a plane booked at six next morning. Reasonable enough, it seemed to me. I asked why. The man on the phone said he had no idea; the foreign editor had gone home, leaving this urgent requirement.

Had it occurred to the foreign editor, I asked, that I had only that very morning got *back* from India, and I knew damn well there was no story? The hireling replied: 'All I know is it says here, "Get the six a.m. tomorrow."'

So, obedient to a fault, as I always am, I got it. In those days there was no question of 747s and soft seats; you travelled on horrible converted Yorks or Lancaster bombers; it was hell, and it took forever. A lifetime later I decanted at Karachi and found a feeder to Delhi. I cabled back asking, with respect, what the hell I was supposed to do?

To which, in the fulness of time, my master gave reply. (He is still a friend of mine, or I would tell you his name.) 'Most sorriest,' he said. 'Didn't mean India, meant South Africa stop proceed Capetown soonest accompany royal tour.'

Anyhow, that is how I came for the first and last time to be part of a Royal Party. Never having been what you might call an over-enthusiastic monarchist, such a thing had not occurred to me. In the event, it turned out to be rather fun.

We travelled in what was called the White Train, and in a style to which I have always vainly hoped to become accustomed. We went all over the place. South Africa is, mostly unfairly, a vividly beautiful country, and we were fed and watered profusely. There was practically nothing to do.

No two personalities could have been more different than those of the King and the Queen. She was, then as now, composed, eager, on top of every situation; he was tense, unbearably nervous, alternating diffidence with bursts of temper. At the time there was a frightful cold spell in Britain; the papers were full of snowdrifts and power failures and freeze-ups; he kept saying he should be at home and not lolling about in the summer sun; never was a man so jumpy. The Queen kept smiling through.

Three or four times a day the White Train stopped at some wayside halt, where everyone was formally lined up. The King would stand shaking at the door of the train, dreading the inevitable encounters. The Queen would appear beside him, looking (the word is inescapable) radiant, or at any rate full of beans.

'Oh, Bertie, do you see, this is Hicksdorp! You know we've always so wanted to see Hicksdorp! Those people there with the bouquets – they must be the local councillors. *How* kind! And those people at the far, far end of the platform, behind that little fence – I expect they are the Bantu choir. How kind! We must wave, Bertie.'

And with a little nudge, the King found himself on terra firma, clearly wishing he were anywhere else on earth, with his wife just as clearly having waited all her life to see Hicksdorp.

One evening he called some of us press people along to his dining-car, ostensibly because he had a communication to make, but more probably to relieve the deadly boredom of the Hicksdorps and the Bantu choirs. I believe it to have been the only Royal Press Conference ever. We found him behind a table covered with bottles of all sorts of things, with which it would seem he had been experimenting, with some dedication.

'We must not f-forget the purpose of this t-tour,' he said, bravely, because his stammer was troublesome for him, 'trade and so on. Empire cooperation. For example. South African b-brandy. I have been trying it. It is of course m-magnificent, except that it is not very nice.' (It was in those days quite dreadful.) 'But,' he said triumphantly, 'there is this South African liqueur called V-Van der Humm. Perhaps a little sweet for most. But, now, if you mix half of brandy with half of Van der Humm . . . Please try.'

The South African journalists were ecstatic. They, and their fathers before them, had used this Brandy-Humm mix for generations; nevertheless they applauded the King for having stumbled on something as familiar to them as gin-and-tonic. Their stories could have done the South African liquor trade no harm.

We arrived one day at a place called Outshoorn. This was a centre of the ostrich-feather trade, and ostrich-feathers had suffered a sad decline since, I imagine, the days of Queen Alexandra. Our passage through this empty place was I supposed to stimulate it – to which end the King was detailed to nip a tail-feather off a sacrificial ostrich for the cameras, presumably to create a renaissance of feather-boas.

The King was understandably more nervous than usual – the ostrich even more so, its head and neck buried in a long stocking-like thing, as if it were for an execution. The King fumbled the operation, and his tweezers nicked a quarter-inch off the ostrich's backside, at which the unlucky bird made a fearsome screeching hullabaloo, from which we all retreated in terror.

Enter the queen, stage right, as usual in total smiling command. She took the clippers from her husband, and there and then did an absolutely expert featherectomy – snip. She spoke to the nearest bystander, who happened by chance to be me.

'We do a lot of gardening at home, in the Palace,' said the Queen. 'The King is good at the digging and the weeding. It is I who concentrate on the secateurs.'

Here endeth the first and last of my Monarchical Memoirs. Let me be the last to wish the old lady a happy birthday. The ostrich can look after itself.

Guardian,
5 August 1980

RIOTOUS GENTILES

If policemen were universally good and wise, which they are not, and if Asians were all reasonable and temperate, which they are not, and if all skinheads would jump in the lake, which they will not, places like Southall and Brixton would be tolerable to inhabit. As it is they are not, and there is little sign of reason creeping in.

This is the most futile of social dilemmas. It has no rhyme or reason or rationality. It derives from the most arbitrary and absurd of nature's aberrations – that of slicing up human kind into racially distinguishable groups – and the Almighty, or whatever, compounded this error by allowing society to identify these groups economically and isolate them geographically. It doesn't say much for divine purpose, and even less for human sense.

Clearly in these communal rows blame cannot be allocated exclusively to one side or another since, once the shindig is under way, it is a free-for-all. Nevertheless the Southall rampage was clearly a skinhead provocation, since the skinheads do not live in Southall and have no stake in the community; and furthermore, being skinheads, were obviously up to no good.

There can be no point in being a benign and friendly skinhead. They did not travel all the way to Southall to distribute alms or read texts; they were out for mayhem, and naturally in what amounts to an almost self-contained ghetto they got it, as they knew they would.

I frankly admit to being prejudiced about skinheads, whom I find visually unattractive and behaviourally repulsive. It was no special surprise to learn that the coaches in which this lot travelled to Southall, carried National Front banners and, while I agree that skinheads and the National Front were made for each other, neither was made for me, nor indeed for Southall.

The yobbos had bused in for a pub gig by some sort of skinhead group called the Four Skins, presumably so named to emphasise in the crudest way its uncircumcised 'gentile-ness'. Why these East-enders thought it a good idea to travel miles across London to do their gig in a Southall pub is not, I would have thought, a matter for much speculation. It could not possibly have been for anything other than provocation.

Thereafter, naturally, everyone has a different version of what started the riot. A friend of mine, Darshan Kalhan, who runs the Maharajah Stores in the Uxbridge Road, tells me that some of the skins invaded his shop, abused his wife, Nirmal, and smashed his windows, apparently for no reason at all.

Of course the Asians reacted, and doubtless over-reacted. Who can ever define how these follies precisely begin? This was a situation waiting for a detonator. When it came it turned the neighbourhood into a disaster area. The poor old Hambrough pub is now burned out. It should of course have known better than to have taken a booking for a mob like the Four Skins in a place like Southall. And the Asians should have known better than to play into the skinheads' hands.

But why, in what we insist on calling this day and age, should these dotty considerations still be so important? Southall has been virtually an Asian town for nearly twenty years. Its cinemas show Asian films; its people go to Hindu temples and Sikh *gurdwaras*. I am personally far from sure whether this sort of urban segregation is for the good but, without any question, it is inevitable.

Whether or not one believes in the possibility that a multiracial community was a good idea in the first place, somehow or other society has just got to come to terms with it now. You cannot de-racialise a body of people as big as ours, and it is useless to try to do so. The Empire-builders should have thought of that two centuries ago. We, after all, colonised the coloureds; they did not colonise us. Not until now. And, indeed, why not?

The eccentric fact in all this is that Southall, unlike Brixton or Bradford, is not an especially deprived or oppressed area. Within their own terms the Asians of Southall are fairly prosperous, provident, running their own businesses, minding their own concerns with almost alarmingly dedicated industry. They do not fight among each other. They do not challenge the National Front until obliged to do so.

The one celebrated casualty of disturbance in Southall was the New Zealand schoolmaster Blair Peach in 1979, and still no one knows just how he died.

I have lived happily in bi-coloured societies most of my life. Whatever the Four Skins may say, I do so still.

Guardian,

SUNDAY TIMES

The *Sunday Times* piece here was not done by me at all, but about me. To be reported about is a great boost for a reporter's ego. Whether Susan Raven did an accurate job on me only time will tell, but she was terribly sweet.

*   *   *

A LIFE IN THE DAY OF

In the old days I used to get up very early, half-past six. I reckoned to get a whole day's work done by eleven o'clock. It was because of having worked so long in India and Africa, where it was the only effective time.

My life took a great big hiccup in 1971 however, when I had this awful car accident in India, which damaged my heart among other things so that I now have a pacemaker.

Now I get up usually about four o'clock and have my breakfast. It's always the same thing. Marmite mixed with peanut butter on wholemeal bread with an onion on top. I hate eating. I had a super time once, being fed through the nose. No mastication, no effort.

Then back to bed for two or three hours. I don't read in bed, you can't if you share a bedroom. My wife Moni and I both get up about eight. I always wear the same clothes.

I have to take a lot of drugs – anti-coagulants and heart stimulants. I take three pills as soon as I wake up, and I have to go every few weeks to have the dosage checked. The pacemaker is replaced every two years. It's in my groin. The surgeon would have put it in what they call 'pectoral development', but I've got as much pectoral development as a herring. Taking pills is just a chore. I don't have any emergency treatments. I notice no difference, except that I run out of steam earlier than I used to.

Annie – who used to be Moni's nurse – makes breakfast. I have a cup of coffee and fruit. We only listen to the headlines on the radio. We take *The Times*, the *Guardian*, the *Hampstead and Highgate Gazette* and the weekly magazines. I turn to the letters page first –

after the obituaries; that was a habit inculcated by my father, who said if he wasn't in them he was alive, and could get up.

I had thirty-five years of incessant travelling as a foreign correspondent so only in the last few have I had a home of my own. It's the greatest conceivable luxury to me, staying at home. The great beauty of my life now is that I know that no-one will ring me at eleven p.m. and tell me to go to Rhodesia in the morning. Though I'd hate to think I'd never see the world again, if I do go abroad I do it at my own pace.

I do a little walking, up to the shops and so on, but I'm very slow. I've decided to do my best to stop gadding about. Moni's very itchy-footed – she was the first woman to drive from India to London, in the days when you had to drive by compass.

Quite often I have to go down to the B.B.C. at Shepherd's Bush and spend hours going through films. I usually go by tube. But T.V. needs a lot of preparation and basically my idea is to stay at home all day and work. I sit down and work pretty solidly until four p.m. I work upstairs in a little self-contained joint I've got.

At lunchtime my regime is normally a glass of sherry or gin and tonic because although I adore whisky I don't like it during the day. Cheese and biscuits, and fruit. Just now it's a peach and mango. (Moni: 'Soon it will be something else. Recently it was always a banana, but he's gone off bananas. He's like an expectant mother – he has real fads.')

Around four o'clock I go back to the papers, especially on Saturdays and Sundays. My regime is exactly the same as on weekdays, except if I get terribly tired I tend to spend the whole of Sunday morning in bed.

When Moni gets back from her job at Air India we look at the news on T.V. and we have a drink – oh yes, we're on to whisky by seven o'clock. In the evening I drink it *copiously*, as much as anyone will let me.

Then hopefully someone will ring up and invite themselves round. Our various children are round almost continually, and Moni's son Kiron lives with us. In the summer the television is banned to another room because of this bloody cricket. I've never been to a cricket match. I'm a Scotsman born, and I was brought up in France.

Dinner varies from eight to ten or eleven o'clock, perhaps depending on television. It's almost always Indian food, which all our English children like too. It's very informal. We watch television, but very selectively. Only the news in the evening. And always *It Ain't Half Hot Mum*, with great avidness. And we used to watch *Match of the Day*, because of the opening tune which is the only music in the world I can recognise.

One of the great dimensions in life that I miss is that I do not understand music. And if you're scratching away trying to make words all day long you find you can't bear print in the evenings. I'm sorry to say I haven't read a novel for years. I occasionally get books to review – one a fortnight for the *New Statesman*.

Round about ten p.m. I go back to another one-and-a-half hours' work because it's a sedative. I always throw it away next day because it's useless – but I've broken the back of it. I have my bath in the evenings, I find it wonderfully soporific. I have nightcaps, of course I do. I'm thinking of having one now [five p.m.]. I go to bed very late, about midnight. I wear a lunghi in bed, I was inducted into that some thirty years ago in India. Moni wears one too, but with a top.

We lead a very quiet life. (Moni: 'Oh, James, you do tell whoppers. We go out all the time and people come round quite a lot. Sunday is the only day we're quiet.')

Sunday Times,
19 February 1978

SUNDAY TELEGRAPH MAGAZINE

The Royal Wedding! Hosannah in the highest! I am not a monarchist, but I cannot personally see much about these two youngsters to resent, except that they cost too much. The only point about this article is that I had to telephone the copy into the paper while the ceremony was still going on. It took me back to the old days. When it was all over I went back to bed, as I imagine so did they.

*   *   *

THE ROYAL WEDDING: 29 JULY 1981

It remains a unique mystery how an occasion like this, which in reality affects the lives of but two people, should command the rapt attention of the biggest audience ever assembled for any event, at any time anywhere.

I was but one among 750 million people watching the marriage of this young man and woman. If the wholly illusory fairy tale can virtually bring the world to a stop it must have meaning. It demands superlatives. The most lukewarm loyalist must concede that it cannot be happening by chance. The British may be accused of being bankrupt, but this is the thing they do better than anyone else on earth. The British – or perhaps the English – rise to royal occasions as of unquestioned right. It cannot be rationalised, it is illogical and wholly romantic – and, in the dire economy of today, even a little arrogant – but on a day like this you would argue that at your peril. It is, naturally, magnificently stage-managed. Punctuality is the prerogative of monarchs. Everything happens dead on cue. The procession of lovely carriages is timed to leave at 10.20, it leaves at 10.20. The bride is timed for 10.55, she leaves her coach at 10.55. The Strand is jammed with an immovable mass of cars, somehow it evaporates as it could never do in real life. Everyone moves into St Paul's as though timed by stopwatch. The bride was, as programmed, beautiful. Everybody had apparently been speculating about her wedding dress: it looked lovely.

She is, to most people's surprise, as tall as the Prince. The official portraits are obviously silly; he would need to be seven foot tall to tower over her as he does on the postage stamps.

St Paul's, the cathedral church of the City of London, is the biggest Protestant establishment in England. By a quaint chance it seems to have occurred to nobody that traditionally it is ascribed 'to the site of the Temple of Diana'. The now and living Diana will make a good Princess. Watching, I should not wish to plight my troth in such pitiless publicity. One's heart goes out to her. One trip, one stumble over that enormous train, one unprepared expression would have been graven on film. But this twenty-year-old has already become a professional. And she is clearly enjoying it.

As ever, the Queen Mother stole the show. This splendid lady cannot miss. The Queen when unobserved rarely smiles; the Queen Mum never stops. The cameras, rightly, cannot leave her alone. May she live for ever. May they all, for that matter.

It was, and is, a national celebration of clearly sincere and generous affection.

Why otherwise should these thousands of people subject themselves to this long ordeal of audience? We are a curious people. This immensely rich and privileged pair occasion no resentment – indeed, most elegantly, on the contrary. It can never be explained, but it can be understood.

Sunday Telegraph,
2 August 1981

JOURNALIST

THE FOREIGN BEAT

Barring nerves, alarums, fatigue, boredom, coronaries, broken homes, falling hair and the recurrent palsy, the Foreign Correspondent's job is probably the easiest in the trade. I have been doing it for some twenty-odd years; I wouldn't do otherwise, or so I say.

At the routine moments of total despair I think: well, my God, if this was the only way out from the late sub's cell, then I can take it. The foreign beat was the rope over the wall; after being what responsible opinion holds to have been by several lengths the most outstandingly lousy deputy-chief-sub in the recorded history of Fleet Street *anything* was a happy release, both for them and for me.

This is what is known as the jauntily cynical approach, generally considered suitable for the calling, like a first-name acquaintanceship with at least five Foreign Ministers, and a capacity to write trenchant short pars while drunk in fashionable foreign bars. Like these attributes, it too is almost wholly legendary.

The great majority of Foreign Corrs I know, and I used to know them all, have been fretful, dutiful men, vaguely and permanently ill at ease, covering the insecurity with much unconvincing bonhomie, obsessed with time-differentials, shifting deadlines, cable-rates, hotel bills, perverse copy-takers, and endless nagging anxieties about the activities of their competitors.

The myth that foreign correspondents do all their work in pubs, milking each other's rumours, arose because of this compulsive need for everyone to be at all times where he can keep an eye on everyone else. At critical moments of a difficult running story you can throw a whole bar into a condition of neurotic doubt merely by strolling away, with the kind of studied furtiveness so easily recognised, leaving the company to chafe and brood and speculate until you return, ostentatiously buttoning up your flies. This is known as the deep and loyal camaraderie of the profession.

I have been a travelling reporter so long I have the greatest difficulty remembering where it all began; my children think I covered the Crimean War. (This is untrue; to the best of my knowledge it was Alan Moorehead.)

It is the case, however, that by now there is practically no country in the world, and certainly no continent, that I haven't been to and usually worked in. Not long ago that was a kind of small distinction; today there are dozens of newspapermen who travel far farther and faster than I, and with much greater efficiency and ease.

But I was lucky. I do not know how else I could have lived the life I have, and seen what I have, and learned what I have; the going was good. It was hard, and disenchanting, and sometimes a bit tormenting, and in doing it you lose many things that bless and console the lives of other men. But you continue to do it, because somehow you can do no other.

A few weeks ago the B.B.C. had me do a steam show on the psychological business of the foreign correspondent trade, a sort of What Makes Jimmy Run. I tried to explain that, while it takes everyone differently, the effect on me was a kind of disembodiment.

When things were really moving, and one seemed to spend one's life being projected about the place in a cylindrical sardine-tin, the terrible moments between sleep and awakening were sometimes a nightmare of doubt as to where the hell one was – sometimes even *who* one was. It was not always very nice.

The corollary to this has always been that one tends almost passionately to identify places with people – to consider some faraway job not geographically, but in terms of who one knows there, whom one can call up on arrival to have a drink and fill one in, who runs the communications, has one any special drag with the hotel, whom one can talk with, fight with, sleep with, debate with. One can be lonely. But less and less, as the world closes in; one has always been there before.

Of course the feeling grows that you are always seeing the world at its worst; that unless such-and-such a joint were in some sort of mess you wouldn't be there. The compensation for that is that you tend to operate in shoals; it is quite extraordinary how certain accepted bars in Bangkok, Singapore, New York, Nicosia, Paris, Berlin, Beirut seem at certain moments to be populated by precisely the same cast of characters.

And most of them are good. It is easy, and rather silly, to romanticise the trade, to attribute some special values to colleagues because you encounter them in peculiar places, and because you are mutually necessary. Nevertheless I am endlessly grateful for the huge advantages I have had in knowing and working with some of the most stimulating, rewarding and generous people in the business, and in their friendship, as in so much else, I have been very lucky.

One now verges on the serious. What does a chap have to have, or be, to make a go of this branch of the trade? I am damned if I know. Nothing technical, that I have ever been able to spot. I have the luck to be more or less okay with a couple of languages, since I was reared in a wild succession of French village schools; the price for that was formal ignorance; I am about the most under-educated man I know. I never even learned to count, and to this day I employ someone to do my expenses.

What else? A certain resilience, I suppose, an acceptance of all manner of administrative chores quite unconnected with the business of writing, since the getting of the story is a very small part of the job of getting it back to the office. Mostly, I would say, an awful and continuing curiosity, and a kind of obsession with the notion that everything that goes on everywhere, anywhere, is part of a recognisable human pattern.

I have a feeling, probably a bit absurd, that you really can't consider a story anywhere on earth in total isolation; even if only subconsciously you must be aware of what a bloody small world it is; and it is the inter-action of things that makes the job absorbing. At least I feel that, which is probably why I have often fallen down so badly on important detail.

A few strong prejudices help. If you want to be solemn about it you can call them values, or beliefs, or what you will; something, anyway, that permits one occasionally to get pretty angry, or even the reverse.

I have never been too good at the basic principle of reporting, which is total objectivity. I imagine I have been a bit subjective about everything I've ever done; I get no pleasure out of facts I dislike, and a great deal from those I do, and I am told it creeps into the copy. Somehow I feel it's a little late in the day for regrets. One survives.

I can't really be objective even about this. I am loaded with memories, of good times and rotten times, of strokes of good fortune, and some terrible flops. I wouldn't have had it otherwise. All I know is that, however long you have been at it, one never sits down at the typewriter, in the dreary hotel bedroom or the Press Room or the rooftop or the dugout or the office desk, staring at that ghastly blank paper, but what one says: brother, this is it; this time they will find you out.

And if you feel it with enough doubt and worry and misery and fear – somehow, they don't.

Journalist,
2 December 1963

INDEX

Adelaide, 52, 54
Aden, 277, 278, 279
Adler, Sebastian, 214–15
Afghanistan, 318–20
Ahmed, Sultan, 312–13
Aitken, Max, Lord Beaverbrook
　see: Beaverbrook, Lord
Akrotiri, 233
Albania, 77–8, 86–9, 114, 115
Aldermaston, 100, 105
Alexander II, Tsar, 318
Alexander the Great, 318
Algeria, 77, 84–6
Allahabad, 308, 311
Allerton, Mark, 187–9
Amin, Idi, 318
Anders, Bill, 205, 206, 207
Anderson, Alf, 181–3
Ankara, 106, 107, 108, 234
Anne, Princess, 295
Argentina, 19–22, 177
Armege, 2, 5
Arnold-Forster, Val, 315
Asquith, Herbert, 112, 126
Athens, 106, 107, 234
Attenborough, David, 167
Auchinleck, Field-Marshal Sir
　Claude, 35, 326
Auschwitz, 16, 90, 177
Australia, 50–54, 97, 323, 324
Avon, Anthony Eden, Earl of
　see: Eden, Anthony, Earl of Avon

BBC, 1, 22, 77, 149, 167–8, 314,
　334, 340
Baldwin, Stanley, 112
Banda, Dr Hastings, 165
Bangladesh, 131, 132, 152–4
Barcelona, 49, 54–6, 57
Beaverbrook, Lord, xiv, 11, 27, 101,
　124–6, 150

Belsen, 16
Bengal, 36, 131, 152–4
Bergman, Carol, 249–50
Berlin, 15–19, 89–91, 112, 223
Bevan, Aneurin, 49–50, 61–4, 113,
　305, 306
Bhutan, 35, 36, 92, 93
Bikini, 22–5, 51, 53, 54, 197
Billing, Mike, 269
Billingham, Howard, 197
Birla, G. D., 12, 14, 64, 66
Blundell, Michael, 59
Bobb-Semple, Colin, 264–5
Borman, Colonel Frank, 198, 199,
　205, 206, 207
Bormann, Martin, 176–7
Botha, Louis, 72
Bradford, 331
Brezhnev, Leonid, 318, 319
Brighton, 63
Brittany, 299–302
Brixton, 329, 331
Bron, Eleanor, 167
Brown, George (Lord
　George-Brown), 105
Brown, Harold, 319
Bucharest, 115
Buchenwald, 18, 90
Budapest, 60
Buenos Aires, 19, 20
Burma, 83, 93

Cairo, 172
Calcutta, 132, 153
Callaghan, James, 311, 313, 317
Cambodia (Kampuchea), 141, 319
Cameron, Moni, 333–5
Campbell, James, 63–4
Canada, 172
Cancale, 302
Cap d'Ail, 150

Cape Canaveral (Cape Kennedy), 81, 216
Carnoustie, 184
Carr, Gene, 220
Carrington, Lord, 318, 319
Carter, Jimmy, 318, 319
Carter, Paul, 220
Cartier, Jacques, 300
Castle, Barbara, 306
Cattistock, 281, 290
Cattistock Hunt, 271, 281–2
Chalfont, Lord, 312
Chamberlain, Neville, 155
Chapman, Peter, 269, 296
Charles, Prince of Wales, 274, 338
Chateaubriand, François-Rene de, 300
Chesterman, Arthur, 242
Chesterton, G. K., 280
Chicago, 255, 256, 257
China, 132–6, 174, 175; and Albania, 86, 88; and India, 27, 32, 33, 65–6, 91–3, 115; and Laos, 71; and Tibet, 35, 36, 37, 38, 39, 65–6, 83; and U.S.A., 148; and U.S.S.R., 113–15
Chou En-lai, 92, 93
Christmas, Linda, 303
Churchill, Randolph, 230
Churchill, Sir Winston Spencer, 149–50
Clark, Dr Kenneth, 118
Clerides, Glafcos, 225–8
Coard, Bernard, 248–9
Cocoa Beach, Florida, 216
Colombia, 176, 177
Congo, 165
Connolly, Cyril, 165
Cook, Chris, 220
Cousins, Frank, 62, 64
Crankshaw, Edward, 115
Crawford, Jeff, 245, 246, 247
Crossman, Richard, 64
Cuba, 103, 115, 121, 123
Curzon, Lord, 165
Cyprus, 67, 101, 106–8, 221–41
Czechoslovakia, 16, 97

Dalai Lama, 35, 37, 38, 64–6, 92
Dallas, 101, 119, 121, 122
Dandi, 13
Dar-es-Salaam, 159
Davies, Harold, 64, 140
De Valera, Eamon, 120
Deauville, 300
Decatur, Stephen, 280
Deedes, William Francis, 104
Delhi, 33, 93
Denktash, Rauf, 225–7
Derbyshire, Delia, 220
Dhekelia, 228, 231
Diana, Princess of Wales, 337–8
Diem Ngo Dinh, 67, 68, 141
Dien Bien Phu, 70, 71, 137, 155
Dinard, 300
Doenitz, Karl, 18
Douglas-Mann, Bruce, 259, 260, 261, 262, 263
Dover, 270–1
Dubocq, Marcel, 2, 3, 4
Dundee, 6, 7, 157, 178–9, 183–4, 187, 190, 191, 192–4, 195
Dykes, Alan, 220

Eban, Abba, 152, 171
Eden, Anthony, Earl of Avon, 155, 163
Edmonds, Ron, 242, 297
Efthyvoulou, Alex, 222, 232, 233, 235, 240, 241
Egypt, 151, 171, 172
Eichmann, Adolf, 177
Elizabeth, Queen, the Queen Mother, 45, 72, 327–9, 338
Elizabeth II, Queen, 45, 274, 292–3, 295, 338
Episkopi, 228, 231
Ethiopia, 159
Everett, Kenny, 167

Fairservice, Don, 220
Famagusta, 236
Fanon, Frantz, 255
Farmer, James, 118
Feisal, King of Saudi Arabia, 152

Finland, 234
Foot, Sir Hugh, 123
Foot, Michael, 63, 131
Forster, E. M., 286
Fowles, John, 271, 275–7
France, 84–6, 137, 141, 155, 169
Franco, Francisco, 49, 55, 56, 57
Friendly Isles, 323
Fulbright, Senator J. William, 147
Fullerton, Romey, xiv

Gagarin, Yuri, 81
Gaitskell, Hugh, 63
Gandhi, Indira, 152, 154, 165, 308–11
Gandhi, Kasturba, 13
Gandhi, Mohandas Karamchand,
    xiv, 11, 12–14, 33, 50, 118, 196
Gaulle, Charles de, 15, 84, 86, 97,
    120, 291
Gerald, Veronica, 246
George V, King, 274
George VI, King, 41–7, 72, 327–9
George-Brown, Lord
    see: Brown, George
Gerwin, Carolee, 285, 286
Germany, 73, 77, 88, 89–91, 235, 313
Ghana, 165
Gheorgiadis, Polycarpos, 237
Gibraltar, 56
Glasgow, 9, 182, 190–91
Glenn, Lieutenant-Colonel John,
    80–82
Gluckman, Professor Max, 57, 58
Goebbels, Joseph, 15
Goldwater, Barry, 129–30
Gomulka, Wladyslaw, 59, 60, 61
Gould, Donald, 166
Gray, Jesse, 127
Greece, 107–8, 222, 224–5, 226, 232,
    236, 239
Grimond, Joseph, 103, 105

Hailsham, Lord, 109–10
Haiphong, 71
Halsbury, Lord, 306
Hanoi, 70–71, 133, 136, 137, 139, 140,
    141, 147, 148, 168, 169

Hardcastle, William, 77
Hardie, Keir, 64, 101
Hardy, Bert, 27
Harlem, 126–30
Held, Al, 215
Hertzog, James B. M., 72
Hess, Rudolf, 176
Hitler, Adolf, 4, 9, 72, 176, 177, 181,
    252
Ho Chi Minh, 71, 141, 150, 168–70
Hogg, Quintin
    see: Hailsham, Lord
Holloway, Marshall, 22, 24
Holmes, Justice Oliver Wendell, 105
Home, Lord, 120
Hong Kong, 71, 173, 324
Honolulu, 54, 147
Hood, Robin, 276, 277
Hopkinson, Tom, 27
Hoppen, Donald, 289
Houston, 198, 199, 200, 204, 205,
    206–7, 209, 211, 212, 213, 214,
    215
Hoxha, General Enver, 115
Humphrey, Hubert, 147
Hungary, 59–61, 319
Hyannis, 121

Illingworth, 155
Inchon, 27, 28–32
India, 167, 308–11, 333, 334,
    335; and China, 27, 32, 33,
    65–6, 91–3, 115; and
    Independence, xiv, 11, 13, 196;
    and Korean War, 32–5; and
    Pakistan, 131, 152–4; and Tibet,
    36, 37; and U.S.S.R., 93
Iran, 311–13, 318
Iran, Shah of (Mohammed Reza
    Pahlevi), 311–13
Israel, 139, 151–2, 170–72
Italy, 123

Jamaica, 261
Japan, 169
Joan of Arc, 4–5, 158
Johannesburg, 72

Johnson, Lyndon B., 121, 143–4, 147, 148–9
Jordan, 171
Jugoslavia, 114

Kabul, 318
Kaganovich, Lazar, 59
Kalhan, Darshan, 330
Kalhan, Nirmal, 330
Kalimpong, 36–7, 38, 65
Kampuchea
    see: Cambodia
Kandahar, 318
Keeler, Christine, 112
Kennedy, David, 285, 286
Kennedy, Jacqueline, 119, 121–2
Kennedy, John Fitzgerald, 114; and
    arms race, 103; and civil rights,
    117; death of, 101, 119–22; and
    space programme, 82, 200, 218
Kennedy, Joseph, Snr, 121
Kenya, 57–9
Khan, Ghaffar, 13
Khedda, Ben Youssef Ben, 86
King, Dr Martin Luther, 118, 122
Klosiewicz, Wiktor, 59, 61
Komar, Waclaw, 60
Korea, 27, 28–32, 33, 67, 74, 75, 76
Kosygin, Alexei, 140
Kraft, Christopher Columbus, 202–4
Krishnamurti Foundation, 272,
    289–90
Krushchev, Nikita: and Albania, 86,
    88; and arms race, 78–80, 103;
    and Berlin, 90; and China, 114,
    115, 134, 135; and Poland, 59, 61
Kutchuk, Dr Fadil, 106, 107
Ky, General Nguyen Cao, 147
Kyprianou, Spyros, 225, 241
Kyrenia, 222

Lacouture, Jean, 148
Ladakh, 92
Laos, 69–71, 141
Lee, Jennie, 64
Lee Kuan Yew, 173
Lenin, Vladimir Ilyitch, 79

Levin, Bernard, 322, 323
Lhasa, 37, 65, 83
Livingstone, 315
Lloyd George, David, 126
Lovell, James, 199, 205, 206, 207
Luang Prabang, 69–71
Lyme Regis, 275

MacArthur, General Douglas, 28
McDermid, Hugh, 271, 287–9
Macha, J. S., 287–8
McKewan, Major, 270, 281
Macmillan, Harold, 103, 111–13
McNamara, Robert, 142, 143–4, 148
Makarios III, Archbishop, 101, 106,
    107, 108, 237–40
Malan, Daniel Francois, 72
Malaysia, 173
Malcolm X, 127
Mandela, Nelson, 122, 124
Mansfield, Senator Mike, 147, 148
Mao Tse-Tung, 133, 150, 169, 175;
    and Nehru, 33; and Tibet, 39; and
    U.S.S.R., 114, 115
Marples, Ernest, 83
Marquand, Richard, 178, 197, 220
Martin, David, 297
Mary, Queen, 45
Masani, Zareer, 309
Mau Mau, 57–9
Medus, Derek, 220
Melbourne, 54
Mengele, Josef, 177
Mesta, Perle, 121
Mikoyan, Anastas, 120
Miranda, Miguel, 21
Mitchell, Colonel Colin, 271, 277–81
Mitchell, Sir Philip, 58
Mohammed, Dost, 318
Molina, General Sosa, 21–2
Molotov, V. M., 79
Moorhouse, Geoffrey, 303
Moran, Lord, 149–50
Morphou, 236
Moscow, 113, 114, 115, 134, 168, 169,
    320
Mountbatten, Lord, xiv, 11, 13

Muggeridge, Malcolm, 155, 163–6
Mussadiq, Dr Mohammed, 313
Mussolini, Benito, 9
Mussoorie, 64, 65, 66

Nan-ning, 133, 135, 136
Nasser, Gamal Abdel, 171, 172
Nehru, Jawaharlal, 11, 12, 13, 27; and
    China, 91, 92, 93; and Indira
    Gandhi, 308, 309, 310; and
    Korea, 32–5; and Mao Tse-Tung,
    33
Nepal, 35, 36, 93
New Delhi, 308
New York, 127, 128, 129, 214
New Zealand, 97
Nhu, Madam Ngo Dinh, 141
Nicosia, 67, 222, 223, 225, 229, 230,
    236, 240
Nievens, Commander P., 259, 260,
    261–2, 263, 264, 265, 266–7
Nixon, Richard, 174–6
Nkrumah, Kwame, 165
Norden, Heinz, 285–6, 287
Norman, Dr Edward, 314–16, 317
Notting Hill, 242, 258, 259, 265, 268
Nu, U, 83

O'Dell, Paul, 269
Ohanga, Benaiah, 59
Onassis, Aristotle, 150
Onassis, Jacqueline
    see: Kennedy, Jacqueline
Orr-Ewing, Lord, 104
Oswald, Lee Harvey, 119, 121
Outshoorn, 328
Owusu, Darcus, 242, 243, 258–9, 266,
    267, 268

Pakistan, 93, 131, 152–4, 319
Paphos, 228
Paraguay, 177
Paramé, 300
Paris, 84–6, 168
Parsons, Sir Anthony, 311
Patel, Vallabhbhai, 13

Peach, Blair, 331
Peking, 132–3, 134, 135, 174, 175;
    and Afghanistan, 319; and
    Albania, 88; and Moscow, 114,
    115; and Tibet, 39; and Vietnam,
    147
Penney, Sir William, 51, 53, 54
Peron, Juan Domingo, 19–22
Peron, Maria Eva Duarte de, 19,
    21–2
Peter, Prince of Greece, 37
Pham Van Dong, 168
Phari, 65
Philip, Prince, Duke of Edinburgh,
    120, 295
Poland, 49, 59–61
Porbandar, 13
Portugal, 124
Poznan, 60
Pretoria, 122, 124
Profumo, John, 111, 112
Pusan, 28, 74

Rabiger, Michael, 269, 297
Raeder, Erich, 18
Raj Bareli, 310
Rajagopalachari, Chakravarti, 13
Rajasthan, 311
Rajk, Laszlo, 61
Rampisham, 281
Raven, Susan, 333
Reith, Lord, 314
Rennes, 302
Rhee, Synghman, 33, 74–6
Rhodes, 172
Robinson, James Harvey, 288
Robinson, John
    see: Woolwich, Bishop of
Robson, Michael, 242
Rokossovski, Konstantin, 59, 60, 61
Rotheneuf, 302
Ruby, Jack, 119, 121
Rundstedt, General Gerd von, 15
Rushton, William, 167
Rusk, Dean, 147, 148
Russell, Bertrand, 165
Rustin, Bayard, 127

Saigon, 67, 69, 96, 137, 144, 147
St Malo, 299–300
St Servan, 301, 302
Salamis, 221, 228
Samoa, 323
Sartre, Jean-Paul, 255
Saudi Arabia, 152
Scott, C. P., 303
Scott, Simon, xiv
Seoul, 31, 32
Sewell, Frederick, 177
Seychelles Islands, 101, 237
Shaja, Shah, 318
Shinwell, Emanuel, 63
Sigal, Clancy, 286, 287
Sikkim, 36, 93
Singapore, 68, 69, 173
Sirkapur, 153
Sirs, Bill, 321
Skouriotissa, 235
Smuts, Jan, 72
South Africa, 13, 41, 46, 72, 73, 74, 118, 122–4, 327–9
Southall, 329–31
Spain, 49, 54–7
Spandau Jail, 18, 176
Speer, Albert, 18
Stafford, Marilyn, 285, 286, 287
Stalin, Joseph Vissarionovitch, 72, 78–80, 88, 150
Strachey, John, 11
Strong, James, 207–8, 213
Strydom, Johannes, 72, 73
Suez, 319
Suslov, Mikhail, 112
Swigart, John L., 218–19
Sydling St Nicholas, 290

Tanganyika (Tanzania), 159
Tehran, 311, 312
Tel Aviv, 151
Ten Hsaio-ping, 113
Texas, 200, 211
Thatcher, Margaret, 318, 326
Thomas, David, 242
Tibet, 35–9, 65, 66, 83
Tiran Strait, 151

Tirana, 86–9
Tito, Marshal, 115
Tookey, Geoff, 269, 297
Trevelyan, John, 99
Turkey, 107–8, 222, 224, 225, 227, 232, 234, 319

U.K.: and Afghanistan, 318, 319; archaism of, 95–100; and Argentina, 20; and atomic bomb, 102–3, 135; and Berlin, 18; and Cyprus, 221, 222, 228, 231, 233, 236, 239, 245; and Iran, 311, 312, 313; and National Health Service, 305–8; and security, 103–5; and South Africa, 123–4; and Spain, 56; and state control, 6–9; and Vietnam, 141
U.S.A., 173, 254, 286; and Argentina, 20; and Australia, 97; and Cambodia, 319; and China, 148; and civil rights, 116–19; and Cuba, 103, 115, 121, 123; and Cyprus, 233, 235; and health care, 306; and Korea, 75, 76; and nuclear tests, 135; and security, 104; and South Africa, 123, 124; and space race, 81–2, 203; and Spain, 55; and U.S.S.R., 134, 319; and Vietnam, 139, 140, 141–4, 146–9, 169, 319
U.S.S.R., and Afghanistan, 318–20; and Albania, 87, 88; and China, 113–15, 133–4, 135; and Egypt, 172; and Germany, 313; and India, 93; and Poland, 59–61; and security, 104, 105; and space race, 81, 82, 218; and U.S.A., 134, 319
Ustinov, Peter, 192
Uttar Pradesh, 66, 308

Verwoerd, Dr Hendrik Frensch, 71–3, 122
Vicky (Victor Weisz), 49–50, 131, 145–6
Victoria, Queen, 318

Vietnam, 132, 133, 134, 135, 136–44;
    and boat people, 172–4; and
    France, 155; and U.K., 141; and
    U.S.A., 139, 140, 141–4, 146–9,
    169, 319
Vladivostock, 33
Vong, King Sisavong, 70
Vouni, 228

Waddell, Matt, 188–9
Walker, Edwin, 121
Warsaw, 59, 60, 61, 300
Washington, 116, 117, 118, 119, 120,
    148
Watson, Jack, 291–4
Weisz, Victor
    see: Vicky

Wells, John, 167
West Indies, 246, 266, 268
White, Edward, 205
Wiesenthal, Dr Simon, 177
Willicombe, Ken, 242
Wilson, Dr Charles
    see: Moran, Lord
Wilson, Sir Harold, 149, 161, 310
Wintour, Charles, 131
Wong, Ansell, 253–4, 257
Woolwich, Bishop of (John
    Robinson), 99
Wu-han, 133

Yahya Khan, 154
Yatung, 35, 38
Yuang Chung-Hsien, 33

Book Tokens

**Give them
the pleasure of choosing**

Book Tokens can be bought
and exchanged at most
bookshops in Great Britain
and Ireland.

NEL BESTSELLERS

T51277	'THE NUMBER OF THE BEAST'	*Robert Heinlein*	£2.25
T50777	STRANGER IN A STRANGE LAND	*Robert Heinlein*	£1.75
T51382	FAIR WARNING	*Simpson & Burger*	£1.75
T52478	CAPTAIN BLOOD	*Michael Blodgett*	£1.75
T50246	THE TOP OF THE HILL	*Irwin Shaw*	£1.95
T49620	RICH MAN, POOR MAN	*Irwin Shaw*	£1.60
T51609	MAYDAY	*Thomas H. Block*	£1.75
T54071	MATCHING PAIR	*George G. Gilman*	£1.50
T45773	CLAIRE RAYNER'S LIFEGUIDE		£2.50
T53709	PUBLIC MURDERS	*Bill Granger*	£1.75
T53679	THE PREGNANT WOMAN'S		
	BEAUTY BOOK	*Gloria Natale*	£1.25
T49817	MEMORIES OF ANOTHER DAY	*Harold Robbins*	£1.95
T50807	79 PARK AVENUE	*Harold Robbins*	£1.75
T50149	THE INHERITORS	*Harold Robbins*	£1.75
T53231	THE DARK	*James Herbert*	£1.50
T43245	THE FOG	*James Herbert*	£1.50
T53296	THE RATS	*James Herbert*	£1.50
T45528	THE STAND	*Stephen King*	£1.75
T50874	CARRIE	*Stephen King*	£1.50
T51722	DUNE	*Frank Herbert*	£1.75
T51552	DEVIL'S GUARD	*Robert Elford*	£1.50
T52575	THE MIXED BLESSING	*Helen Van Slyke*	£1.75
T38602	THE APOCALYPSE	*Jeffrey Konvitz*	95p

NEL P.O. BOX 11, FALMOUTH TR10 9EN, CORNWALL

Postage Charge:
U.K. Customers 45p for the first book plus 20p for the second book and 14p for each additional book ordered to a maximum charge of £1.63.
B.F.P.O. & EIRE Customers 45p for the first book plus 20p for the second book and 14p for the next 7 books; thereafter 8p per book.
Overseas Customers 75p for the first book and 21p per copy for each additional book.

Please send cheque or postal order (no currency).

Name ....

Address ....

....

Title ....

While every effort is made to keep prices steady, it is sometimes necessary to increase prices at short notice. New English Library reserve the right to show on covers and charge new retail prices which may differ from those advertised in the text or elsewhere.(7)